GERMAN NOVELLAS
OF REALISM II

The German Library: Volume 38

Volkmar Sander, General Editor

GERMAN NOVELLAS
OF REALISM II

Edited by Jeffrey L. Sammons

CONTINUUM · NEW YORK

1989

The Continuum Publishing Company
370 Lexington Avenue, New York, NY 10017

The German Library
is published in cooperation with Deutsches Haus,
New York University.
This volume has been supported by a grant
from Stiftungsfonds Deutsche Bank
at Stifterverband for the Deutsche Wissenschaft.

Printed in the United States of America

Library of Congress Cataloging-in-Publication Data

German novellas of realism II / edited by Jeffrey L. Sammons.
    p.   cm.—(The German library; v. 38)
Contents: Krambambuli / Marie von Ebner-Eschenbach—L'Arrabbiata
/ Paul Heyse—St. Thomas—Celtic Bones / Wilhelm Raabe—
Aquis submersus—The white horse rider / Theodor Storm—Plautus in the
convent / Conrad Ferdinand Meyer—Flagman Thiel / Gerhart
Hauptmann.
    ISBN 0-8264-0320-4 (pbk.) ISBN 0-8264-0319-0
    1. German fiction—19th century—Translations into English.
    2. Short stories, German—Translations into English.   3. English
fiction—Translations from German.   4. Short stories, English—
Translations from German.   I. Sammons, Jeffrey L.   II. Series.
                    PT1327.G386   1989
833'.01'0812—dc19   87-30608
                                                             CIP

Acknowledgments will be found on page 331,
which constitutes an extension of this page.

Contents

CONRAD FERDINAND MEYER

GERHART HAUPTMANN

Introduction

The remarks on German realism in the introduction to the preceding volume in The German Library apply in general also to this one and will not be repeated here. We are now moving gradually toward the end of the century. This is, of course, an artificial boundary; the advent of a recognizably modern literature in Germany is more adequately located in the 1890s. Some changes may be detectable, however, in this volume. We seem to be leaving behind us the string of shy, maladroit neurotics; the writers grow more competent and secure, perhaps reflecting a society that, despite its immense strains, was becoming more consolidated and confident. Even the mentally disturbed Paul Heyse and Conrad Ferdinand Meyer seem to have had a firmer grip on the conduct of their lives than Adalbert Stifter, Franz Grillparzer, or Eduard Mörike. The "poetic," i.e., idealized aspect, begins gradually to yield to a realism that is first more mimetic and then more critical. At the end of the volume, with Gerhart Hauptmann, we capture an early phase of one of the writers who straddle the boundary to the literature of our own century; with them we can see how the modern was not always an abrupt break, but also could be rooted in the fertile soil of nineteenth-century literature.

Marie, Baroness von Ebner-Eschenbach, was born in 1830 as Countess Dubský in Zdislavic, Moravia. At the age of eighteen she entered upon an uneventful marriage with an army officer and scholarly scientist, Moritz von Ebner-Eschenbach, who through their fifty years together cordially supported her literary aspirations. Czech and French were her mother tongues rather than German, which she began to learn rather late in her childhood. At first she expended, with Grillparzer's encouragement, a good many years in pursuit of the drama before becoming persuaded that it was not her true calling. Only in the 1870s did she turn to fiction and earn a measure of recognition for her reservedly critical, dryly observant social novellas and novels, centered primarily in the aristocratic, patriarchal, agricultural milieu she knew best. After her death in Vienna in 1916 she began gradually to be somewhat forgotten, but more recently she has become a beneficiary of a renewed interest in women writers. Annette von Droste-Hülshoff was the only post-Romantic woman writer to obtain a firm position in the traditional German canon, but there were others of importance in their time, some of whom are now undergoing a reassessment. However, even before interest in Ebner-Eschenbach revived, her little story *Krambambuli* (1883) enjoyed a wide and enduring readership. On first acquaintance the reader may find it a little slight, but it needs to be read thoughtfully. It may appear that Droste-Hülshoff's vision has been shifted into a more conservative direction, to identification with the forester and condemnation of the poacher. But the instincts of the dog make no such distinction, and his little soul is pulled apart in a conflict of loyalties he cannot solve, perhaps as a reproach to the unnatural divisions among men. The story, incidentally, is drawn from an experience of Ebner-Eschenbach's brother; she had completed it before the course of real-life events turned out just as she had imagined them.

Paul Heyse, who was born in Berlin of a Protestant father and a Jewish mother in 1830, is included in this selection less on his own literary merits than owing to the fact that in 1910 he became the first German imaginative writer to win the Nobel Prize for Literature (the first ever was the historian Theodor Mommsen in 1902). He died, also in Berlin, in 1914, though he spent much of his literary career in Munich. Modern readers may find it difficult to reconstruct the reasons for Heyse's vast national and international reputation in the second half of the nineteenth century. He attained a considerable reputation as a poet, especially as a translator from Italian and Spanish, but he was best known for his novellas, of which he wrote more than a hundred. These works are little read today, and modern readers who come to them afresh may find them unchallenging and routine, even slick. But, before the advent of Naturalism submerged Heyse's reputation, they were very popular, and he played a rather large role in literary life. He maintained a consistently liberal and progressive outlook, and, although a severe depressive who was intermittently forbidden by his physician to write at all, he was blessed with a winsome personality that earned him the affection of many in the literary and intellectual world. He became the director of the Schiller Foundation, established to aid needy writers, a post that no doubt made him seem even more amiable to some. *L'Arrabbiata* (1855), a youthful, both characteristic and average Heysean novella, has remained his most widely read prose work; Americans of the older generation who learned German in school may remember it as an intermediate text. It belongs to a group called *Italian Novellas,* an appellation that refers not only to their setting but also to their form, for Heyse's theory of the novella was oriented on Boccaccio. In content the story is utterly conventional; the reader will know how it must turn out virtually from the beginning. The artistic effort is expended on the form, on exact pacing and rhythm and on the economical disposition of narrative resources. It would not be unjust to designate Heyse a formalist, within his own compass an idealistic devotee of art for art's sake.

Wilhelm Raabe, who was born in 1831 in the Lower Saxon town of Eschershausen and lived an externally uneventful life in Wolfenbüttel, Stuttgart, and Braunschweig until his death in 1910, has already been introduced to English-speaking readers in volume 45 of The German Library. His case is the opposite of Heyse's; his reputation, once entangled in damaging misapprehensions, is now spectacularly on the rise. Although modern critics are likely to look upon his late novels as his finest achievements, he wrote a large number of novellas and stories. Almost a third of his total life's work consists of historical fiction. These narrations are often placed in settings of war and marauding. His attitude toward such things was not military or heroic, but one of grieving at atrocity and human waste. *St. Thomas,* first published in 1866, may be the most grueling of these texts. One of three works set around 1599 and drawn from a continuation of Schiller's unfinished *History of the Rebellion of the Netherlands,* it describes a scene of slaughter and pestilence so historically pointless and wasteful of humane values that it drives the one character with a relatively balanced and ethical perspective, the preacher Leflerus, to the edge of madness. But Raabe was not only one of the most tragic writers of mid-nineteenth-century Germany; he was also one of the most comic, and it seems evident that these two modes were related in his imagination, for he sometimes accompanied his most bitter and pessimistic works with his most farcical and ludicrous ones. For example, not long after completing *St. Thomas,* he began work on *Gedelöcke* (1866), an absurd story drawn from a real event, which tells how a Danish freethinker whipsawed the bigotry and obscurantism of his contemporaries with his own corpse. We have opted to include here a somewhat earlier farce, *Keltische Knochen* (1864–65, "Celtic Bones"), also based loosely on a personal experience, as is explained in the notes. It, too, was nearly contemporaneous with one of Raabe's most somber stories, *Else von der Tanne* (1865, "Elsa of the Fir"). In *Celtic Bones* we see the strong satirical bent that lay at the root of most of Raabe's humor and comedy.

Theodor Storm was born in Husum in Schleswig in 1817 and trained for the civil service, in which he worked as a judicial official. His personal life was often stressful—he was disappointed in love, then married a woman to whom he was bound more in friendship than passion, then fell in love with another woman whom he married after his first wife's death, and he was to have sorrowful experiences with his sons—but some of his troubles were owing to external circumstances. He refused on principle to serve the Danish administration that occupied Schleswig and Holstein in the 1850s and was obliged to seek refuge in Prussia, where he was far from happy. Immediately after Bismarck's victory over Denmark in 1864 he returned to his post in Husum, where he remained until his retirement in 1880. Storm was a poet of some accomplishment (examples in volume 39 of The German Library, *Poetry 1750–1900*), but he is best known as a specialist in the novella. Of some fifty novellas, perhaps a half dozen have come to occupy a firm place in the canon, and the most highly regarded is the last of them, *Der Schimmelreiter* (1888, "The White Horse Rider"). Storm defined the novella as "the sister of the drama," and many of his works have the shape of tragedy. Often set in the grey, relatively featureless landscape of Germany's north coast, they tell stories of missed connections between human beings, of too-lateness, and of failures of character and courage that damage and sometimes destroy lives. *Aquis submersus* (1876) is a well-known example of this type. But *The White Horse Rider* reaches out to larger and more modern issues. Hauke Haien, a naturally gifted, self-taught mathematician and engineer, becomes dike reeve, a post of immense responsibility in these coastal flatlands. But his unavoidable sense of his own superiority generates an arrogance that brings him into conflict with his stolid, prescientifically superstitious fellow citizens, and their self-interested hostility wears down his spirit until he makes an error of omission with disastrous consequences. The famous triple frame of the story distances narrator, author, and reader from its supernatural elements while retaining them in suspension as symbolic correlatives of the ambiguity of Haien's enduring achievement and its tragic cost. The novella is also one of the great love stories in German literature, austere and unsentimental, but no less moving for that. Storm was deathly ill while writing this work. To keep his spirits up, his family, friends, and physician engaged in a conspiracy to persuade him that he did not have cancer, and he appeared to believe them, but an allusion in the text, flagged in this volume by a footnote, suggests that he knew the truth. In the summer of 1888, a few months after completing the novella, he died in Hademarschen in Holstein.

Conrad Ferdinand Meyer was born in Zurich in 1825. He had a considerable independent income, upon which he lived a modest and, for the most part, rather withdrawn life, first under the repressive care of his mother, then with his sister, and finally marrying, not very happily, at the age of fifty. All his life he was beset by the threat of mental illness, which he had reason to believe was inherited in his family. But he struggled bravely against it, several times seeking psychiatric help and striving to lead a normal and productive life. He did finally succumb in his late years, spent some time in a mental institution, and died in Kilchberg in 1898. Very erudite in European culture, nearly bilingual in German and French, he became one of the most interesting German-language poets of the nineteenth century. He began with unpromising, derivative forms, but then labored over a relatively small number of poems for some twenty years, rewriting, rearranging, borrowing images from one to another, until he came up with a corpus of verse that lies on the threshold of modern symbolism and makes of Meyer a significant precursor of Rilke (examples in volume 39 of The German Library, *Poetry 1750–1900*). His well-crafted novellas, on the other hand, exhibit his introverted aestheticism and his turn away from his times toward a more congenially imagined past, characteristics that set him at the opposite pole from the vigorous, earthy realism of his Swiss contemporary, Gottfried Keller (for whom see volume 44 of

The German Library). The relativizing perspectives and ambiguities of the novellas have preoccupied recent critics, who see in them harbingers of modernism. Several are set in the Renaissance, the period in which he seems to have felt most at home. *Plautus im Nonnenkloster* (1881, "Plautus in the Convent") has been selected here not because it is his best—Meyer himself did not hold it in high regard—but partly because it is his shortest and partly because it is one of his wittiest, a characteristic not common in a writer of such high seriousness. The hero of the story is clearly not the central figure, Poggio, but the "barbarian" Swiss girl who exhibits high moral integrity and courageous self-discipline against her perfectly normal instincts; a touch of Swiss-German nationalism is not to be missed. Meyer was anxious that we should sense the dubious aspect of Poggio's character. But other considerations work a little bit across the grain of Meyer's overt intention. After all, it is Poggio's wit and cultivated intelligence that rescue the "barbarian" girl from her dilemma for her true, earthly vocation. Furthermore, despite the undercurrent of licentiousness in Poggio and in the Renaissance setting generally, there is also a sense of utopian longing for an age in which a man of culture could be on easy terms with a man of power, and religion could be acknowledged but worn lightly and in unstressful alliance with an immersion in the culture of pagan antiquity.

Gerhart Hauptmann was born in Obersalzbrunn, Silesia, in 1862. He began as a sculptor, but, after a marriage brought him independent wealth, he launched upon an ultimately triumphant literary career. He won the Nobel Prize for Literature in 1912 and at his death on his Silesian estate at Agnetendorf in 1946 he was one of the most prestigious of all German authors and one of the most renowned of European playwrights. He began his career among the Naturalists, achieving major fame with such plays as the Ibsenian *Vor Sonnenaufgang* (1889, "Before Sunrise") and the great social drama *Die Weber* (1892, "The Weavers"), but he soon began to develop a mystical tendency, indigenous to his native Silesia, and for the rest of his career he oscillated between Naturalist and mystical, Neo-Romantic modes, though in later years he was to write dramas on Classical Greek themes as well. His early novella, *Bahnwärter Thiel* (1888, "Flagman Thiel") is associated with the Naturalist movement and also attracted a great deal of attention. With its subproletarian, inarticulate central figure, it owes much to Georg Büchner's *Woyzeck* (originally written 1835–37), which had been recently rediscovered and exerted a significant influence on the Naturalists in general and Hauptmann in particular. But it also shows clear indications of the mystical strain that remained curiously intertwined with Hauptmann's social realism. Both features, the earthy Naturalism and the search for a new transcendence, point to developments in the literature of our own century and make of the novella an appropriate conclusion to our selections from nineteenth-century realism.

J. L. S.

GERMAN NOVELLAS
OF REALISM II

Krambambuli

Marie von Ebner-Eschenbach

O ne takes a fancy to all sorts of things; but genuine, imperishable love comes to a person, if at all, only once in a lifetime. So, at least, thought Gamekeeper Hopp. How many dogs had he had and been fond of! But only one of them had been really dear to his heart, unforgettably dear—Krambambuli.*

Hopp had bought him at the Lion's Inn in Wischau from an unemployed deputy forester—or rather he had bartered for him. At the first sight of the dog he had been seized with the affection that was to endure to his last breath. The eyes of the beautiful animal's owner bespoke the rascal. He sat at a table in front of an empty brandy glass and railed at the innkeeper for not giving him a second drink for nothing. A small fellow, still young, though frayed as a dead tree, with auburn hair and a sparse beard. His hunting jacket, probably left him when he quit his last position—the remains of past glory—bore traces of a night passed in a wet ditch.

Although Hopp was not eager to mix with such doubtful company, he took a seat beside the fellow and started a conversation with him. He soon found out that the good-for-nothing had already delivered his rifle and gamebag to the innkeeper as pledges, and that he now wanted to pawn the dog; the innkeeper, however, the dirty usurer, wouldn't hear of a pledge that had to be fed. At first Mr. Hopp made no mention of his interest in the dog. He orderd a bottle of Danzig cherry brandy and began to pour drinks.

Well, in an hour's time it was settled. The gamekeeper bought twelve bottles of the brandy and turned them over to the fellow; and the vagabond handed over his dog—not easily, it must be said to his

---

*Danzig cherry brandy, and by extension student slang for any form of cheap brandy. A popular student drinking song bears the title "Krambambuli."

honor. When he fastened the leash around the animal's neck, his hands trembled, and it seemed as if he'd never finish.

Hopp waited patiently, and quietly admired the wonderful dog. At most he was two years old. In color of hair, he was only a few shades darker than the scoundrel who was giving him away. On his forehead he had a mark, a white stripe that ran right and left in small lines like needles on a fir twig. His eyes were great, black, and gleaming, bordered with small light yellow streaks, clear as dew; his ears were long and faultless. And faultless, in fact, was everything about the dog, from the claws to the fine sensitive nose, the powerful, supple figure, and the stance, which indeed was beyond praise: four living pillars that might have borne the weight of a stag, yet weren't much thicker than the legs of a hare! By Saint Hubert, this creature must have had a pedigree as old and pure as the family tree of a knight of the Teutonic Order! The gamekeeper's heart leapt with joy over the bargain he'd got. He rose, took the leash, and asked: "And what's his name?"

"The same as the brandy for which you got him—Krambambuli," came the reply.

"Fine, fine, Krambambuli! Let's go! Come on, come on! Forward!"

Yes, long might he call, whistle, tug at the leash—Krambambuli didn't seem to hear him. The dog turned his head toward the man he still considered his master, sidled up to him, and only howled when the latter shouted at him: "Beat it!" and gave him a kick. Only after a fierce struggle did Mr. Hopp succeed in getting possession of the dog—who, bound and gagged, finally had to be stowed into a sack. For the several hours it took Hopp to hike to his home, he had to carry the sack with Krambambuli over his shoulder.

It was two full months before Krambambuli, beaten half to death—and chained to a sharp spiked collar every time he tried to run away—finally realized to whom he belonged. But when his subjugation had been completed, what a dog he was then! No tongue could describe, nor word measure, the height of perfection that he achieved—not only in the practice of his calling, but also in daily life as a zealous servant, a good comrade, and a true guardian and friend. "He lacks only speech," it is said about other intelligent dogs, but Krambambuli didn't lack it: his master, at any rate, carried on long conversations with him.

The wife of the gamekeeper became downright jealous of "Buli," as she disdainfully called him. "Have you nothing to say to me, only to Buli?" she said one night. "For all your talk with that animal, you are forgetting how to talk to humans."

The gamekeeper admitted to himself that there was some truth in what his wife said, but he didn't know how to help matters. What should he talk about with his wife? They'd never had children, they were not allowed to keep a cow, and domestic fowl do not interest a huntsman at all in a living state, and not very much when roasted. And in tree farming and hunting stories, again, his wife took no interest. Hopp finally found a way out of his dilemma: instead of talking to Krambambuli, he would talk about him, about his triumphs everywhere and the general envy his possession excited, about the "ridiculous sums" offered him for the dog, which he of course had refused.

Two years had thus gone by when one day the Countess, the wife of Hopp's employer, appeared at the gamekeeper's home. He knew at once what the visit meant, and when the good and beautiful lady began: "Tomorrow, Hopp, is the count's birthday—" he softly broke in with a little grin:

"And Your Grace would like to make a gift to his lordship and are convinced that Krambambuli would be appreciated more than any other present."

"Yes, yes, dear Hopp." The Countess blushed with pleasure at this obliging attitude, and said how grateful she felt, and asked him just to name the price to be paid for the dog.

The old fox of a gamekeeper chuckled, looked very humble, and then came out with his proposition: "Your Grace, if the dog remains in the castle, does not bite through his every leash or break his every chain, or, if he can't, does not strangle himself in the attempt, then Your Grace may have him gratis, for then he'd no longer be of value to me."

The experiment was made, but it didn't come to anything like a strangulation. The Count had lost his joy in the obstinate animal before things came to this pass. In vain had they tried first to win him by love, and then to tame him through coercion. He bit everyone who came near him, more often than not left his food untouched, and—though a hunting dog doesn't have much weight to lose—wasted away. After a few weeks Hopp received the message that he should come and fetch his hound. He didn't hestitate; and when he went to the kennel to get the dog, there was a reunion of boundless rejoicing. Krambambuli let out a wild howl, sprang up on his master, propped his forepaws on the gamekeeper's chest, and licked away the tears running down the old man's cheeks.

In the evening of this happy day, they walked together to the inn. There Hopp played cards with the doctor and the Count's overseer, and Krambambuli lay in the corner behind his master. From time to time Hopp looked around at him, and then the dog, though apparently deeply asleep, would immediately beat the floor with his tail, as if he wanted to announce: "Present!" And when Hopp, forgetting himself, would triumphantly hum the little tune "How Goes my Krambambuli?" the dog would sit up in dignified respect, and answer with his light eyes: "All goes well with him."

In those weeks a band of poachers were carrying on their activities, in a really reckless and brazen fashion, not only in the count's forest, but in the whole district as well. Their leader was supposed to be a dissolute fellow. He was called "Red" by the woodsmen who'd seen him in saloons of evil repute, by the foresters' helpers, who, though already on his track here and there, had never succeeded in catching him red-handed, and finally by his own informers, of whom he had several among the riffraff in every village.

Damage to the game and woods reached a record high, and the aroused forest employees grew increasingly irritable. Thus it occurred only too often that little people, caught at some insignificant woodland offense, suffered harsher treatment than they would have at other times, and harsher than was properly justified. This caused great bitterness in all the villages. The hatred first turned against the head forester. He received many warnings: the outlaw gunman, it was said, had sworn he'd take vengeance on him.

The head forester, an audacious man and also a rash one, brushed aside the talk. Undaunted, he let it be known far and wide that he had asked for the most uncompromising ruthlessness from his subordinates, and that, in the case of dire consequences, he himself would assume the responsibility. He repeatedly exhorted Hopp to the strict performance of his duties, and sometimes reproached him with lack of "pluck"—at which, of course, the old man only smiled. He would wink down at Krambambuli on such occasions, and the dog then would yawn loudly and with obvious disdain. Neither he nor his master took offense at the head forester.

The head forester was the son of the unforgettable man who had taught Hopp the noble art of hunting, and whose own son as a small boy had, in turn, been initiated by Hopp into the rudiments of the profession. The vexations the boy had caused him, Hopp considered, even to this day, a joy. He was proud of his former pupil and loved the head forester despite the rough treatment that he, like anybody else, experienced from him.

One June morning Hopp was with him once again, this time at one of his police actions. It occurred in a stand of linden trees at the edge of the manorial park that bordered the Count's forest, and in the neighborhood of the tree farm—which the head forester, had it been up to him, would have surrounded with land mines! The lindens stood in their most beautiful bloom, and a dozen small boys were crawling around on the branches of the magnificent trees like squirrels, breaking all the twigs they could reach and throwing them down. Two women were promptly picking up the twigs and stuffing them into baskets already more than half-filled with the fragrant loot. The head forester fell into an immense fury. He had his assistants shake the boys from the trees, unconcerned about the height they fell from; and while they crawled around his feet, whimpering and crying, one with a battered face, another with a dislocated arm, a third with a broken leg, he soundly beat the two women with his own hands. In one of them Hopp recognized, with an eerie feeling, the wench rumor had marked as the sweetheart of Red. And when the baskets and kerchiefs of the women and the hats of the boys had been confiscated, and Hopp had been ordered to take the stuff to the courthouse, he couldn't ward off a sinister premonition.

The order that the head forester shouted at him, wild as a devil in hell—and, very much like the Devil himself, surrounded by tormented, lamenting sinners—that command was to be the last he ever gave to Gamekeeper Hopp.

A week later Hopp met his superior again in the linden forest— dead. From the condition of the body, it could be seen that it had been dragged through marsh and scree in order to lie in state at this place. The head forester lay on cut boughs, his forehad adorned with a large wreath of linden blossoms, and a linden-blossom garland was wound around his breast as a bandoleer. His hat lay near him, upside down, filled with wildflowers. His gamebag had been left him by the murderer, only the cartridges had been taken out and linden blooms stuffed into the bag instead. The beautiful breechloader of the head forester was missing and had been replaced by a miserable shooting iron, whose strap had been slung, in mockery, across his shoulder. (Later the bullet taken from the chest of the murdered man proved to fit exactly the barrel of this shooting iron.)

At the sight of the disfigured body, Hopp had grown stony with horror. He could not have moved a finger, and his brain was as if numbed. He stared and stared, and at first thought nothing. Only after a while did he manage to look beyond the corpse and at once asked himself: "What is the matter with the dog?"

Krambambuli was sniffing the dead man, running around him with his nose to the ground as though he'd gone crazy. He'd whimper, and then again let out a shrill yelp of joy, or make a few leaps, or yowl—and it was as though a memory, long dormant, had been awakened in him.

"Here!" called Hopp. "Come here!"

And Krambambuli obeyed, but looked at his master in the greatest excitement and, to put in the gamekeeper's parlance, "said" to him: "I entreat you, above everything in the world, don't you see it? Don't you smell it? Oh, dear master, look! Use your nose! Oh, master, come! Come over here!" And with his nose he nudged the gamekeeper's knee, and then slunk back to the body, looking over his shoulder repeatedly as if to ask: "Are you following me?" Then he'd begin to lift the heavy gun and push it, and finally tried to seize it in his teeth.

A shudder ran down the gamekeeper's spine, and all kinds of suppositions began to dawn upon him. But speculations were not his business, and, too, it was not up to him to enlighten the authorities with guesses; rather, it was his duty to leave things as he had discovered them and go straightway to the courthouse. So he did simply what was his duty.

Before all the forms prescribed by the law in the case of such catastrophes were complied with, the whole day and also a part of the night had elapsed; and only then did Hopp, before he went to sleep, turn to his dog.

"My dog," he said, "now the police are on the move and now there will be raids without end. Shall we leave it to others to cleanse the world of the renegade who shot to death our head forester? My dog knows the dirty tramp, knows him, yes indeed. But nobody needs to know that, and I've told no one about it. I, haha!—I would bring my dog into this affair! No, sir—not me!" He bent over Krambambuli, who sat between his knees, and pressed his cheek to the animal's head and accepted the dog's grateful nuzzling in return. And he was just beginning to hum: "How Goes My Krambambuli?" when sleep overtook him.

Psychologists have tried to explain the mysterious urge that frequently draws a criminal back to the scene of his crime. Hopp knew nothing about these learned theories, but nevertheless he kept wandering with his dog, without peace or respite, through the linden forest. On the tenth day after the head forester's death he thought for the first time of something else besides revenge, and occupied himself for a few hours in the Count's forest marking trees to be taken out in the next cutting.

His work finished, he hung his gun over his shoulder and took the shortcut through the woods toward the tree farm near the linden forest. When he turned into the path that ran along the beech-tree fence, he seemed to hear something rustle in the leaves. But deep silence reigned again in the following moment—deep, prolonged silence.

He might have thought it had been nothing out of the ordinary if it had not been for the dog, who stood with bristled hair, his neck stretched forward, his tail straight out, and stared transfixed at a place in the fence. "Oho!" thought Hopp. "Just wait, you killer, if it's you!" He stepped behind a tree and cocked his gun. His heart beat frantically—and his already short breath almost failed him completely when all of a sudden Red stepped onto the footpath. Two young hares hung from his gamebag, and over his shoulder he carried the breechloader of the head forester. What a temptation to fell the ruffian from the safe ambush!

But never would Gamekeeper Hopp have shot at even the most vicious enemy without warning him first. With a leap he sprang from behind the tree, out on the path, and shouted: "Surrender, curse you!" And when the poacher ripped the breechloader from his shoulder, the gamekeeper fired, the gun gave a click but—oh, all of you saints!—no report. It had leaned too long against a tree in the damp forest with its bullet inside—it refused!

"Good night, so this is what death looks like!" it ran in the old man's head—and at the same time his hat flew into the grass. The outlaw had had no luck, either! Moreover, he'd wasted the one shot that he'd had in his gun. And no sooner had he pulled another cartridge out of his gamebag than Hopp shouted:

"Sic him, Krambambuli, sic him!"

"Here, to me! Come here, Krambambuli!" beguiled a tender, loving, and, alas, so familiar voice from the other side. "Come here. . . ."

But the dog—

What now occurred happened much faster than can be told.

Krambambuli had recognized his first master and ran toward him—halfway. Then Hopp whistled and the dog turned; Red whistled, and the dog turned again; and then, stunned and overpowered, he writhed in desperation on a spot midway between the gamekeeper and the poacher.

Finally the poor animal gave up the struggle and made an end of his doubt, though not of his agony. Barking, howling, belly to the ground, body taut as a tendon, head raised as though he were calling heaven to witness his anguish, he crawled to his first master.

Seized with a thirst for blood, Hopp took out a new cartridge with trembling fingers; but he inserted it in his gun with quiet assurance. Red again had his barrel aimed at him. This was it! And both men knew it as they looked at each other through their sights. But whatever their thoughts, they pulled the triggers as calmly as a couple of marksmen in a painting.

Two bullets flew: that of the gamekeeper to its mark, that of the outlaw into the air. For the latter had lurched: in the very split second he pulled the trigger, the dog had jumped up at him in a tempestuous greeting. "Beast!" the outlaw managed to hiss. Then he fell, backwards, and never moved again.

Hopp walked slowly up to him. "You have had enough," he thought; "it would be a shame to waste another shot on you." Yet he put his gun on the ground and inserted a bullet. The dog sat erect before him, his tongue hanging out, panting in short, loud gasps, and looked at him. And when the gamekeeper had loaded his gun and took it in hand again, they held a conversation, of which a living witness could have heard just as little as the dead Red.

"Do you know for whom this piece of lead is meant?"

"I can imagine."

"Deserter! Traitor! Perfidious, wayward cur!"

"Yes, master, yes."

"You were my joy. Now that's over. I can take no more joy in you."

"Understandable, master"—and Krambambuli lay down, put his head on his outstretched forepaws, and looked at the gamekeeper.

Yes, if only the accursed brute had not looked at him that way! Then he would have brought matters to a quick conclusion—and would have spared himself and the dog, too, a great deal of pain. . . . But you don't shoot a creature that looks at you that way! Hopp murmured half a dozen oaths between his teeth, each more blasphemous than the preceeding, shouldered his gun, took the young hares from the outlaw, and went away.

The dog followed Hopp with his eyes until he disappeared between the trees. Then he stood up, and his spine-chilling howl of woe rang through the forest. He turned around in a circle a few times and then once again seated himself bolt upright near the dead man.

And thus he was found by the investigating officers who, guided by Hopp, appeared at nightfall to inspect the body of the outlaw and to have it removed. Krambambuli yielded a few feet when the gentlemen appeared.

One of them said to the gamekeeper: "Why, that's your dog."

"I left him here as a guard," answered Hopp, ashamed to confess the truth.

What was the use? It came out anyway, for when the body was loaded on the wagon and moved away, Krambambuli trotted behind with his head lowered and his tail between his legs.

The next day the bailiff saw him roaming around not far from the room where Red lay. He gave him a kick and called to him: "Go home!" Krambambuli flashed his teeth at him and ran away—according to the man, in the direction of the gamekeeper's home.

Yet he never arrived there, but instead took up the miserable life of a vagabond.

One day Krambambuli, gone wild and lean as a skeleton, came

skulking about the shacks of the cottagers at the end of the village. All at once he fell upon a child who stood in front of the last hut, and greedily tore from him the piece of bread he was eating. The child stood rigid with terror, but a small spitz came running out of the hut and barked at the thief, who then let go of his loot and fled.

The same evening, before going to sleep, Hopp stood at his window and looked out at the gleaming summer night. It seemed to him as if he saw the dog sitting on the far side of the meadow at the edge of the forest, steadfastly and longingly looking toward the abode of his former happiness—the truest of the true without a master!

The gamekeeper closed the shutter and went to bed. But after a while he got up and walked again to the window. The dog was no longer there. And again he tried to sleep. And again he could not.

He could stand it no longer. He could stand it no longer without the dog. So be it. "I'll bring him home," he decided, and upon this resolve he felt as if reborn.

He was dressed by the first gray of dawn. He asked his wife not to wait for him with the midday meal, and hurried off.

As he opened the door of the house, he found Krambambuli. The dog lay dead before him, his head pressed against the sill that he had never more dared to cross.

The gamekeeper never got over his loss. Sometimes he forgot that he'd lost the dog, and at such happy moments, engrossed in thoughts, he would intone his familiar "How Goes my Krambam—" But in the middle of the word he'd stop, shake his head, and utter, with a deep sigh: "A pity about the dog!"

Translated by Paul Pratt

L'Arrabbiata

Paul Heyse

The sun had not yet risen. Over Vesuvius lay a broad belt of grey mist, stretching towards Naples and casting the little towns on that part of the coast into shadow. The sea was calm and silent. But, by the marina that lies in a narrow inlet beneath the tall rocky cliffs of Sorrento, fishermen and their wives were already stirring, about to haul ashore on stout ropes the skiffs with their nets that had lain out all night fishing. Others were making their craft ready, preparing their sails, dragging out oars and yards from the great vaults with their iron-grilled gates carved deep into the rock to store the sailors' gear overnight. There were no idle hands to be seen; for the old men too, who would be going out themselves no more, took their place in the long chain of fishermen hauling at the nets, and here and there an old woman stood with her spindle on one of the flat roofs or busied herself with her grandchildren, while her daughter was helping her husband. "Look, Rachela, there's our *padre curato*,"* said one grandmother to a little creature ten years old, who stood beside her with her own little spindle. "He's just getting aboard. Antonino is taking him across to Capri. *Maria santissima,*† doesn't his reverence still look sleepy!"—and with that she waved her hand to a short, friendly priest who was just making himself comfortable in the bark below, after carefully picking up his black skirts and spreading them out on to the wooden bench. The others on the shore paused in their work to watch the departure of their parish priest, who nodded friendly greetings to right and left of him.

"Why does he have to go to Capri, then, Grandmama?" asked the

* "Father curate."
† "Most holy Mary."

child. "Haven't the people there got a priest of their own, so they have to borrow ours?"

"Don't be silly," said the old woman. "Enough and to spare, and the finest churches and even a hermit, that's something we haven't got. But there is a lady there, a *signora,* who lived here in Sorrento for a long time and was very ill, so that the *padre* often had to go to her with the Sacrament, when they thought she wouldn't live another night. Well, the blessed Virgin was with her in her need, so that she grew fit and well again and could bathe in the sea every day. When she left here and went over to Capri, she gave the church and the poor people a great pile of ducats, and she wouldn't go, they say, until the *padre* promised to go and see her over there, so that she can confess to him. It's wonderful, what a lot she thinks of him. And we can count ourselves blessed that we have a man like that for our parish priest, a man as clever as an archbishop, that the gentry ask for. The Madonna be with him!" And she waved to the little boat below them, that was just about to cast off.

"Shall we have clear weather, son?" the little priest was asking, as he looked over towards Naples with a doubtful gaze.

"The sun's not out yet," the youth replied. "It'll soon clear this bit of mist."

"Let's be on our way, then, so that we are there before it gets too hot."

Antonino was reaching for the long oar, to drive the boat into open water, when he suddenly paused and looked up to where the steep path leads down from the little town of Sorrento to the waterfront.

The slim figure of a girl came into sight above them, hurrying down over the stony steps and waving a handkerchief. She carried a bundle under her arm, and was dressed shabbily enough; but she had an almost lordly way, only a little wild, of throwing her head back, and her long black hair braided round her head stood upon her brow like a diadem.

"Why are we waiting?" asked the priest.

"There's someone else coming for the boat, I expect they want to go to Capri too. If you don't mind, *padre*—she won't slow us down, it's only a slip of a girl, hardly eighteen."

At this moment the girl appeared from behind the wall that

encloses the twisting path. "Laurella?" said the priest. "What would she be doing in Capri?"

Antonino shrugged his shoulders.

The girl came towards them with quick steps, looking at the ground before her.

"Good morning, *l'Arrabbiata!** called out some of the young sailors. They would have had more to say if the presence of the *curato* had not restrained them; for the defiant silence with which the girl received their greetings seemed to provoke the spirited lads.

"Good morning, Laurella," the priest now called too. "How are you? Do you want to come to Capri with us?"

"If you don't mind, *padre!*"

"Ask Antonino, he is the *padrone* aboard this ship. Every one of us is lord and master in his own place, and the good Lord God over us all."

"Here's half a *carlino*," said Laurella, without looking at the young sailor, "if I can come for that."

"You need it more than I do," muttered the lad, and pushed aside some baskets of oranges to make room for her. He was going to sell them in Capri, for the rocky island does not bear enough fruit for the needs of all the visitors.

"I don't want to go for nothing," answered the girl, and her black eyebrows quivered.

"Come along, my child," said the priest. "He is a good lad, and doesn't want to grow rich on the little you have. Here, climb in"— and he stretched out his hand to her—"and sit down beside me. Look, he has laid his jacket there for you, to give you a softer seat. He didn't treat me so well. But that's always the way with young people. More trouble for one of the fair sex than for ten of the cloth. Now, now, no need to make excuses, Tonino, it's the way our Lord has made us; birds of a feather flock together."

Meanwhile Laurella had come aboard and, after pushing the jacket aside without saying a word, had sat down. The young sailor let it lie where it was and mutterd something between his teeth. Then he gave a powerful shove against the wall of the quayside, and the little boat sped out into the gulf.

* "The furious one."

"What have you got in your bundle?" asked the priest, as they glided across the sea lightening with the sun's first rays.

"Silk, thread, and a loaf of bread, *padre*. I have to sell the silk to a woman in Capri who makes ribbons, and the thread to another."

"Have you spun it yourself?"

"Yes, sir."

"If I remember rightly, you have learned to make ribbons too."

"Yes, sir. But mother is worse again, so I can't leave home, and we can't afford to pay for a loom of our own."

"Worse? Really? When I called on you at Easter she was sitting up."

"Spring is always the worst time for her. Since we have had the big storms and the earthquakes, she has had to stay lying down because of the pain."

"Keep on praying, my child, and ask the Holy Virgin to pray for you. And be good and hardworking, so that your prayer may be heard." After a pause: "As you came down to the shore, they called out 'Good morning, *l'Arrabbiata!*' Why do they call you that? It's not a pleasant name for a Christian girl, who should be gentle and humble."

The girl's sunburned face glowed all over, and her eyes flashed.

"They make fun of me because I won't dance and sing and stand about gossiping like the others. They ought to leave me alone; I'm not hurting them."

"But you could be friendly to people. Leave dancing and singing for others who have an easier time of it. But even one whose life is hard can spare a kind word for his neighbor."

She cast her eyes down and knitted her brows tighter, as if to hide her coal black eyes beneath them. For a while they sailed on in silence. The sun now stood above the mountains in splendor, the peak of Vesuvius thrust through the clouds that still gathered about its foot, and the houses on the plateau of Sorrento could be seen, sparkling white amidst the green orange groves.

"Have you never heard anything more of that painter, Laurella, that Neapolitan, who wanted to marry you?" asked the priest.

She shook her head.

"He came that time and wanted to paint you. Why wouldn't you let him?"

"Why should he want to? There are others prettier than I am.

And then, who knows what he might have done with it. He could have used it to cast a spell on me and done something to my soul, or even killed me, so mother said."

"Don't believe such wicked things," said the priest, seriously. "Are you not always in God's hands, and can a hair of your head be harmed against His will? How could a man with a picture in his hand like that be stronger than the Lord Himself?—And in any case, you could see that he was fond of you. Why else would he have wanted to marry you?"

She said nothing.

"And why did you refuse him? They say he was a fine man and quite handsome, and he could have kept you and your mother better than you can yourself now, with your bit of spinning and silk making."

"We are poor folk," she said, fiercely, "and mother has been ill for a long time now. We should only have been a burden to him. And I am not fit to marry a *signore*. If his friends had come to see him, he would have been ashamed of me."

"What a thing to say!—I tell you he was a gentleman. And what's more, he wanted to move to Sorrento as well. It will be a long time before another one like that turns up, that might have been sent from Heaven itself to help you out."

"I'm not going to marry, never!" she said, obstinately, and as if to no one but herself.

"Have you made a vow, or do you want to enter a convent?"

She shook her head.

"People are right to hold your willfulness against you, even if that name isn't a pretty one. Haven't you considered that you're not alone in this world, and that your stubbornness only makes your sick mother's life and her sickness the harder to bear? What sound reasons can you have for refusing every honest hand that offers you and your mother support? Answer me, Laurella!"

"I do have a reason," she said softly and hesitantly. "But I can't tell you what it is."

"Can't tell? Can't tell me? Your confessor? I thought you knew that he was there to help you. Didn't you know that?"

She nodded.

"Then unburden your heart to me, my child. If you are right to do as you do, I will be the first to say so. But you are young and have seen very little of the world, and one day later you might be sorry, if you find you have thrown away your happiness for the sake of some childish notion."

She cast a fleeting, nervous glance at the lad sitting towards the stern of the boat, rowing busily away, with his woollen cap pulled down over his forehead. He was staring sideways into the sea and seemed to be lost in his own thoughts. The priest saw her look and leaned his ear closer to her.

"You didn't know my father," she whispered, and her eyes darkened.

"Your father? He died, didn't he, when you were scarcely ten years old. What has your father—may his soul rest in paradise!— what has he to do with your willful ways?"

"You didn't know him, *padre*. You wouldn't know it, but mother's illness was all his fault."

"Why was it?"

"Because he ill-treated her and beat her and kicked her. I can still remember the nights when he came home in a rage. She would never say a word, and would do everything he wanted. I used to pull the blanket over my head and pretend to be asleep, but I would cry all night long. And then when he saw her lying on the floor he used to change all of a sudden and lift her up and kiss her so that she would cry out that he was stifling her. Mother told me I was never to say a word about it; but she took it badly, she has never got over it, all these years that he's been dead. And if she should die before her time, Heaven preserve us, then I know who it was who killed her."

The little priest shook his head and seemed uncertain, after her confession, whether to approve or blame. Finally he said, "Forgive him, as your mother forgave him. Do not keep thinking about those sad scenes, Laurella. Better days will make you forget all that."

"I shall never forget it," she said and shuddered. "And let me tell you, *padre,* that's why I shall stay a maid, so I shan't have to obey anyone who ill-treated me and then made love to me. If anyone now tries to hit me or kiss me, I can defend myself. But my mother couldn't defend herself, couldn't fight the blows or the kisses, because she loved him. And I'm not going to love anyone if it's going to make me sick and wretched."

"Now aren't you behaving like a child and talking as if you knew nothing of life on this earth? Are all men like your poor father, to give way to every whim and passion and treat their wives badly? Haven't you come across enough honest people hereabouts, and women who live in peace and harmony with their husbands?"

"Nobody knew how my father treated my mother either, for she would rather have died a thousand times over than go complaining to anyone. And all that was because she loved him. If that's what love is like, making you shut your mouth when you ought to be crying out for help, and leaving you defenseless against worse than your worst enemy could do to you, then I'll not throw my heart away to any man."

"I tell you, you are a child and don't know what you are saying. A lot your heart will ask you about it, whether you want to love or not, when the time has come for it; then it won't be any use, any of the notions you're getting into your head now."

After another pause: "And that painter, did you think he was the kind of man that would ill-treat you?"

"He sometimes had the kind of look that I used to see in my father's face when he was asking my mother's forgiveness and taking her in his arms to say sweet things to her again. I know that look. A man can give you that look and find it in his heart to beat his wife when she'd never done anything against him. I was frightened when I saw that look again."

With that she said no more, and remained silent. The priest too was silent. He thought of all kinds of fine things, to be sure, that he could have said to the girl. But the presence of the young sailor, who had seemed more agitated towards the end of her confession, sealed his lips for him.

When, after two hours' journey, they arrived in the little harbor of Capri, Antonino carried the clergyman from the boat over the last shallow waves and set him respectfully down. But Laurella hadn't wanted to wait for him to wade back again and fetch her. She tucked up her skirt, took her wooden clogs in her right hand and her bundle in her left, and paddled quickly ashore.

"I expect I shall be a long time on Capri today," said the *padre*, "and you don't need to wait for me. It may even be tomorrow before I come home. And you, Laurella, when you get home again, give your mother my regards. I shall be in to see you some time this week. You'll be returning before night?"

"If there's a chance," said the girl, busying herself with her skirt.

"You know I have to go back too," said Antonino very casually, or so he thought. "I'll wait for you until Ave Maria. If you're not there then, I shan't mind."

"You must be there, Laurella," the little man spoke up. "You must not leave your mother alone all night. Have you far to go?"

"To Anacapri, to one of the vineyards."

"And I have to go to Capri. God bless you, child, and you, my son!"

Laurella kissed his hand and let fall a good-bye that seemed meant for the *padre* and Antonino to share, but Antonino for his part took no notice. He touched his cap to the *padre* and didn't look at Laurella.

But when they had both turned their backs on him, it was only for a short time that his eye followed the cleric, making his way with effort over the deep shingle of the beach; then he turned to look at the girl climbing the hillside to the right, shielding her eyes with her hand against the sun's glare. Before the path disappeared behind stone walls, she stopped for a moment as if to take breath, and looked around her. The seafront lay at her feet, all around the steep cliffs rose, and the sea was azure beyond compare—it was indeed a prospect worth stopping still to view. As chance would have it, her glance skimming Antonino's boat met the glance he had cast in her direction. They made a movement, each of them, like people excusing themselves for something that they did not mean to do; then, tight-lipped, the girl continued on her way.

It was only an hour after noon, and Antonino had already been sitting for two hours on the bench in front of the fishermen's tavern. Surely there was something on his mind, for every five minutes he would jump up, go out into the sunshine, and carefully scan the paths that lead to left and right towards the island's two townships. He didn't like the look of the weather, he told the landlady of the *osteria*.* Yes, it was clear now, but he knew that tinge about the sky and the sea. It had been just like that before the last great storm, when he had only just managed to get the English family ashore. Didn't she remember?

* "Inn."

No, the woman said.

Well, she was to think of him, if it were to change before nightfall.

"Are there many ladies and gentlemen over there?" the landlady asked, after a while.

"It's just starting. It's been bad up to now. The ones who come to bathe haven't shown up yet."

"Spring was late. You'll have earned more than we have on Capri."

"There wouldn't have been enough for macaroni twice a week, if the boat was all I had. Just a letter to take to Naples now and then or a *signore* to take out fishing—that's all. But you know my uncle has the big orange groves and he's a rich man. Tonino, he says, as long as I'm alive, you'll be all right, and I'll see you're taken care of when I'm gone. So I got through the winter, with God's help."

"Has he any children, your uncle?"

"No. He was never married. He was abroad for a long time, and made a tidy penny. Now he wants to set up a big fishing business and put me in charge of it to look after it properly."

The young boatman shrugged his shoulders. "Everyone has his bundle to carry," he said. Then he jumped up and looked at the weather again to left and right, although he surely knew that it only comes from one direction at a time.

"I'll bring you another bottle. Your uncle can pay for it," said the landlady.

"Only another glass. This wine of yours is fiery stuff. I can feel it going to my head already."

"It won't get into your blood. You can drink as much as you like. Here's my husband just coming, you'll have to stay and talk to him for a while."

And indeed, his net hanging over his shoulder, his red cap set on his curly hair, the *padrone* of the inn came striding down grandly from the hill. He had been taking fish to town; that fine lady had ordered it, to serve to the little priest from Sorrento. As he saw the young boatman there, he waved his hand in cordial welcome, then sat down beside him on the bench and began to talk and ask questions. His wife was just bringing another bottle of real, unadulterated Capri, when the sand rustled on the beach to their left and Laurella came along the path from Anacapri. She nodded a curt greeting and stood there, hesitant.

Antonino jumped up. "I must go," he said. "It's a girl from Sorrento that came over this morning with the *signor curato* and wants to get back home to her sick mother by nightfall."

"Well, it's a long time till nightfall," said the fisherman. "She'll have time for a glass of wine with us. Here, wife, bring another glass."

"Thank you, I won't," said Laurella and stayed at a distance.

"Pour it out, wife, pour it out! She'll change her mind."

"Let her be," said the lad. "She's an obstinate one; if she doesn't want to do something, then the saints couldn't persuade her." And with that he bade a hasty farewell, ran down to the boat, untied the painter, and stood there waiting for the girl. She turned and nodded once more to the landlord and his wife, and then walked with uncertain steps towards the boat. She looked round first in all directions, as if she expected other passengers to be coming. But the seashore was deserted. The fishermen were asleep or were at sea with rods and nets; a few women and children were sitting in the door-ways, asleep or spinning, and the visitors who had come across in the morning were waiting for a cooler time of day for their return. She was not able to look round for too long, for before she could stop him Antonino had taken her up in his arms and was carrying her like a child to the skiff. Then he jumped aboard after her, and with a few strokes of the oars they were on the open sea.

She had sat down towards the bows and half turned her back to him, so that he could only see her from the side. Her features were even graver now than usual. Her hair hung low over her forehead, a willful expression played about her finely chiseled nostrils, her full lips were tightly pursed. When they had been traveling thus in silence across the sea for a while, she began to feel the sun, took her loaf of bread out of her kerchief and bound the cloth over her braided hair. Then she began to eat from the loaf, which was her midday meal; for she had had nothing to eat while she had been on Capri.

Antonino did not simply watch for long. From one of the baskets which that morning had been full of oranges he produced two, saying, "There's something to eat with your bread, Laurella. Don't think I've been keeping them for you. They had rolled out of the basket into the boat, and I found them when I was stowing the empty baskets on board again."

"You eat them. My loaf is enough for me."

"They're refreshing in the heat, and you have had a long way to walk."

"They gave me a glass of water up there, that refreshed me."

"As you like," he said, and let them drop back into the basket.

Silence again. The sea was as smooth as glass, and made scarcely a ripple against the keel. And the white seabirds too, that rest in the caves ashore, hunted their prey in soundless flight.

"You could take those two oranges to your mother," Antonino began again.

"We have enough of them at home, and when they are all gone I can go and buy some more."

"Go on, take them, and my compliments to her."

"She doesn't know you."

"Then you could tell her about me."

"I don't know you either."

It was not the first time that she had denied knowing him like that. A year ago, just after the painter had come to Sorrento, it happened one Sunday that Antonino and some of the other young village lads were playing *boccia** in an open space beside the high road. It was there that the painter had first seen Laurella, as she went by bearing a water-pitcher on her head, taking no notice of him. The Neapolitan, struck by the sight of her, stood gazing after her, although he was standing in the middle of their bowling alley and with two paces could have left it clear. A ball struck his ankle, as a sharp reminder that this was not the place to lose himself in contemplation. He looked round as if expecting an apology. The young boatman whose throw it had been stood defiantly silent amid the group of his friends, and the stranger found it prudent to avoid a quarrel and withdraw. But people had talked about the little scene and began to talk about it again when the painter paid open suit to Laurella. I don't know who he is, she said crossly, when the painter asked her if it was for the sake of that rude youth that she was refusing him. And yet some of that talk had come to her ears. Later, when she had met Antonino, she had recognized him, after all.

And now there they sat in the boat like the bitterest of enemies, and both their hearts were beating like death. Antonino's usually

*Usually the plural *boccie,* an Italian game of bowls.

cheerful face was flushed with anger; he dug his oars into the waves so that the spray flew over him, and his lips quivered from time to time as if he were speaking words of malice. She pretended not to notice and wore her most unconcerned expression, leaned over the gunwale of the skiff, and let the waves run through her fingers. Then she untied her kerchief again and tidied her hair as if she were by herself in the boat. Only her eyebrows puckered still, and in vain she held her wet hands to her burning cheeks to cool them.

Now they were out on the open sea, and far and wide not a sail was to be seen. The island was left behind them, the coast lay far off in the haze, not even a seagull was there to break the solitude. Antonino looked about him. A thought seemed to come to his mind. Suddenly the color drained from his cheeks, and he let fall the oars. Involuntarily Laurella looked round to see what he was doing, tense but without fear.

"I must be done with it," the lad burst out. "It's gone on far too long and it's a wonder to me that it hasn't been the death of me. You say you don't know me? Haven't you stood there watching often enough when I went by you like a madman, with my heart filled to overflowing with what I wanted to tell you? Then you would pout like that and turn your back on me."

"What did I have to talk to you about?" she said curtly. "I could see you wanted to start something with me. But I didn't want people gossiping about me when there was nothing in it, nothing! For I don't want you for a husband, not you nor any other man."

"Nor any other? You won't always talk like that. Because you sent that painter packing? Pah! You were only a child then. One day you'll start feeling lonely, and then, mad as you are, you'll take the first that comes along."

"No one knows what the future may bring. Perhaps I'll change my mind. What business is it of yours?"

"What business of mine?" he cried out, and started up from the thwart so that the whole boat rocked. "What business of mine? And you can ask that, when you know very well how I feel? A miserable end to any man you treat better than you've treated me!"

"Did I ever make any promises to you? Can I help it if you are out of your mind? What right have you got to me?"

"Oh," he shouted, "it's not in writing, I admit, I haven't had a lawyer draw it up in Latin and seal it; but let me tell you this, I've as much right to you as I have to go to heaven if I've lived a good life. Do you think I am going to stand by and watch you going to church with another man, and the girls shrugging their shoulders as they pass me by? Am I going to stand for a disgrace like that?"

She drew back a little and flashed her eyes at him.

"Kill me if you dare," she said slowly.

"No job should be left half done," he said, and his voice was hoarse. "There's room for us both in the sea. I can't help you, child,"—and he spoke almost with pity, as if he were dreaming—"but we must both go under, both of us, at once, and now!"—he screamed, and seized her suddenly with both hands. But in the same moment he drew back his right hand, the blood was flowing, she had bitten him savagely.

"Must I do what you want?" she cried, and pushed him away with a quick movement. "We shall see if I am in your power!" And with that she leapt overboard from the boat and disappeared for a moment in the depths of the water. Straight away she came up again; her skirt was clinging tightly to her, the waves had loosened her hair and it hung heavy about her throat; with vigorous strokes of her arms she swam powerfully away from the boat towards the shore, not uttering a sound. The sudden fright seemed to have robbed him of his senses. He stood in the boat bending forward, staring fixedly in her direction as if a miracle were taking place before his eyes. Then he shook himself, rushed to seize the oars, and made after her with all the strength he could muster, while the bottom of the boat turned red with the blood that flowed freely over it.

In a trice he was beside her, quickly as she swam. "In the name of the Blessed Virgin," he cried, "come aboard! I must have gone mad; God knows what clouded my mind. It was like a flash of lightning from heaven in my brain, that made me blaze up so I didn't know what I was doing or saying. I'm not asking you to forgive me, Laurella, only to save your life and come aboard again."

She swam as if she had heard nothing.

"You will never get to land, it is still two *miglie*.* Think of your mother! If anything should happen to you I should die of horror."

She measured with her glance the distance to the shore. Then, without replying, she swam up to the boat and took hold of the

* "Miles."

gunwale with her hands. He stood up to help her; his jacket, that had been lying on the seat, slid into the water as the girl's weight tilted the skiff to one side. Deftly she hoisted herself up and climbed into her former place. When he saw that she was safely aboard, he took up the oars again. She meanwhile twisted out her dripping skirt and wrung the water from her plaits. As she did so her gaze fell upon the floor of the boat and she saw the blood. She looked quickly at his hand, pulling at its oar as if unhurt. "Here!" she said, and held out her kerchief to him. He shook his head and rowed on. At last she stood up, went over to him and bound the cloth tightly about the deep wound. Then, despite all his resistance, she took one of the oars from his hand, sat down on the other seat, but without looking at him, fixed her eyes on the oar, stained with blood, and drove the boat on with powerful strokes. They were both pale and silent. As they came closer to the shore, they were met by fishermen, coming out to drop their nets for the night. They called out to Antonino and teased Laurella. Neither looked up or answered a word.

The sun was still fairly high over Procida when they reached the marina. Laurella shook out her skirt, that had almost completely dried in crossing the sea, and leapt ashore. There again, spinning on the roof, was the old woman who had watched them set out that morning. "What have you done to your hand, Tonino?" she called down to them. "Christ Jesus, your boat's awash with blood!"

"It's nothing, *commare*,"* answered the lad. "I cut myself on a nail that was sticking out too far. It'll be gone tomorrow. The blood comes so quickly, curse it, it makes it look worse than it is."

"I'll come and dress it with herbs for you, *comparello*.† Wait, I'm coming."

"Don't bother, *commare*. It's all done, and tomorrow it'll be gone and forgotten. I've a sound hide, it grows quickly and heals any wounds."

"*Addio!*" said Laurella and turned to the path that climbs the hill.

"Good night!" the lad called after her, without looking up at her. Then he carried the things out of the boat and the baskets too and climbed the few stone steps that led to his cottage.

---

*Correctly *comare*, "gossip, crony."
†"Little crony, pal."

There was no one except him in the two little rooms where he was now pacing up and down. At the small window openings, which only had wooden shutters to cover them, the air came in with a breeze, more refreshing than out on the calm sea, and he felt better in the solitude. He stood for a long time before the little image of the Mother of God too and gazed reverently at the starry halo she wore, made of silver paper stuck on. But it did not occur to him to pray. What should he have asked for, now that he had lost all hope?

And the day seemed to stand still. He longed for it to be dark, for he was tired, and the loss of blood had affected him more than he liked to admit. He felt a violent pain in his hand, sat down on a stool, and untied the bandage. The blood that had been stanched came spurting again, and his hand was badly swollen around the wound. He washed it carefully and cooled it for a long time. When he took it out again, he could clearly see the marks of Laurella's teeth. "She was right," he said. "I was like a wild beast and I don't deserve any better. I'll give Giuseppe the kerchief to take back to her tomorrow, because she won't be seeing me again." And so he washed the kerchief carefully and spread it out in the sun, after he had bandaged up his hand again as best he could with his left hand and his teeth. Then he threw himself down on his bed and closed his eyes.

The bright moonlight woke him from a half-sleep, the pain in his hand at the same time. He was just jumping up again to calm the throbbing of his blood in some water when he heard a noise outside. "Who is there?" he called and opened the door. Laurella stood before him.

Without stopping to ask, she came in. She threw off the kerchief that she had tied over her head, and put a little basket down on the table. Then she drew a deep breath.

"You've come for your kerchief," he said; "you could have saved yourself the trouble, for I would have asked Giuseppe first thing tomorrow to bring it back to you."

"It's not about the kerchief," she answered quickly. "I have been on the mountain fetching herbs for you, to stop the bleeding. Here!" And she lifted the lid from the basket.

"You shouldn't bother," he said, without any trace of bitterness, "you shouldn't bother. It's better already, much better; and even if it was worse, it would be what I deserved. What are you doing here at this hour? Suppose someone came and found you here? You know how they gossip, even though they don't know what they are talking about."

"I don't care about anyone," she said fiercely. "But I want to look at your hand, and put these herbs on it, for you won't be able to manage with your left."

"I tell you it isn't necessary."

"Let me see then, and I'll believe you."

She seized his hand without further ado, as he could not stop her, and untied the strips of rag. As she saw how it had swollen, she started and cried out: "Jesus Maria!"

"It's gathered a bit," he said. "That'll be gone in a day and a night."

She shook her head: "You won't be able to go to sea for a week like that."

"The day after tomorrow, I hope. What does it matter, anyhow?"

Meanwhile she had fetched a basin and washed the wound anew; he endured it like a child. Then she put the healing leaves of her herbs on it, that eased the burning straight away, and bandaged his hand with strips of linen she had brought with her.

When it was done he said, "I'm very grateful. And listen, if you want to do me another kindness, forgive me for going mad like that today, and forget all that I said and did. I don't know how it happened myself. You have never given me any cause to behave like that, you really haven't. And I'll never say anything more to offend you."

"It's my place to ask you to forgive me," she broke in. "I ought to have explained everything differently and better and not made you angry, being dumb like that. And as for that wound—"

"It was self-defense, and high time I was brought to my senses again. And as I said, there's nothing to it. Don't talk about forgiving. You've been kind to me and I'm grateful. And now go home to bed, and here—is your kerchief, so you can take it with you straight away."

He held it out to her, but she was still standing there and seemed to be struggling with herself. At last she said, "You've lost your jacket on my account too, and I know the money for the oranges was in it. I only thought of it on the way. But I can't make it up to you, because we haven't got it, and if we had it would be mother's. But

I've got this silver cross that the painter put on the table for me, the last time he was with us. I haven't looked at it since and I don't want it in my box any longer. If you can sell it—that must be worth a few piasters, mother said at the time—then it would make up for what you've lost, and what's left I'll try to earn spinning, at night when mother's gone to sleep."

"I'm not taking anything," he said curtly and pushed back the little shining cross that she had taken out of her pocket.

"You must take it," she said. "Who knows how long it will be before you can earn anything with your hand like that? There it is, and I don't ever want to set eyes on it again."

"Then throw it into the sea."

"It's not a present I'm giving you; it's nothing more than your right and what belongs to you."

"Right? I've no right to anything that's yours. If you should ever meet me again, do me a kindness and don't look at me, so I shan't think you're reminding me of what I owe you. And now, good night, and let that be all between us."

He put her kerchief in the basket and the cross with it, and shut the lid on them. But when he looked up and saw her face he was startled. Big, heavy drops were pouring down her cheeks. She let them flow.

"*Maria santissima!*" he cried, "are you ill? You are trembling from head to toe."

"It's nothing," she said. "I must go home," and she tottered towards the door. Her tears overwhelmed her, and she pressed her forehead against the doorpost and sobbed loud and violently. But before he could reach her to hold her back, she suddenly turned and fell about his neck.

"I can't bear it," she cried and pressed him to her as a dying man clutches at life, "I can't bear to hear you saying kind things to me and sending me away from you with all my guilty conscience. Beat me, kick me, curse me!—or if it's true that you are fond of me, even after all the harm I have done to you, then take me and keep me and do what you want with me. But don't send me away like that!" Violent sobs interrupted her once more.

He held her for a while in his arms, speechless. "I still love you?" he cried at last. "Holy Mother of God! did you think I had lost all my heart's blood with that one little wound? Don't you feel it beating there in my breast, as if it wanted to leap out to you? If you are only saying it to tempt me, or because you are sorry for me, then go, and I will forget that too. You shan't think you owe me anything, because you know what I suffer for you."

"No," she said firmly and looked up from his shoulder and straight into his face with her tear-filled eyes, "I love you, and I'll have to confess it, I've been afraid of it for a long time and fought against it. And now I will behave differently, for I can't bear it any longer, not to look at you when you pass me by in the street. And now I am going to kiss you," she said, "so you can tell yourself, if you should be in doubt again: she kissed me, and Laurella will kiss no man but the man she is going to marry."

She kissed him three times, and then she freed herself from his embrace and said, "Good night, darling! Go to sleep now and let your hand get better, and don't come with me because I'm not afraid, not of anyone, only of you."

And she slipped through the door and vanished in the shadow of the wall. But he stood a long time looking through the window, out at the sea over which all the stars seemed to be wheeling.

The next time the little *padre curato* left the confessional where Laurella had been kneeling so long, it was with a quiet, private smile. Who would have thought, he said to himself, that God would so soon take pity on this strange heart? And there was I reproaching myself for not having warned her more severely against the demon obduracy. But our eyes are too shortsighted for the ways of Heaven. Well then, may the Lord bless her and let me live to be ferried over the sea by Laurella's eldest, in his father's place! Well, well, well, *l'Arrabbiata!*

Translated by F. J. Lamport

St. Thomas

Wilhelm Raabe

1

Don Francisco Meneses

In the great Bay of Guinea, betwen fifteen and fifty nautical miles from the coast of the African continent, lies the Guinea Island group, named individually as follows: Fernao do Po, Isola do Principe, Annobon, and São Tomé.* Though presumably recorded long ago in the logbooks of the Carthaginians and Phoenicians, they were rediscovered by the Portuguese anno Domini 1472, and the flag of this once-intrepid seagoing nation still waves above Saint Thomas and Prince Island, whereas Fernao do Po and Annobon have fallen into Spanish hands; yet neither the Portuguese nor the Spanish have a very good notion about what to do with their portion.

Awakening a time long since past, we shall tell a tale from the year 1599, when Francisco Meneses was governor of Saint Thomas and paid for the honor with his life.

But it was not only the viceroy who perished on that occasion.—

In the year 1599, it was not the flag of Portugal, but that of Spain that fluttered above the castle of Pavaosa,† and Don Francisco held watch for Don Philip III**—for which the battle of Alcassar†† was to

---

*Fernando Po, now called Bioko, and Annobón are today provinces of the Republic of Equatorial Guinea. Principe and St. Thomas are joined as the independent nation of São Tomé and Príncipe.

†In Raabe's sources spelled Pavoasa, today town of São Tomé.

**(1578–1621), king of Spain from 1598.

††Alcazarquivir in Morocco, where King Sebastian of Portugal was killed in battle

blame. In regard to this battle, a German chronicler* of the period writes:

"Three kings did wage war one with the other for a kingdom, and yet no one of them did obtain that kingdom, but rather he, of whom no man had thought it, became king. For it was the battle in Africa wherein the three kings did perish, namely Sebastian, the King of Portugal, Abdelmelech and Mahometh, two Barbarian kings of Mauritania, and upon the side of the King of Portugal there lay dead the Duke of Avero, the bishops Conimbricensis and Portuensis, likewise the Papal Legate, the Margrave from Ireland, Christopher of Tavora and many other lords, brave knights and noblemen all. Abdelmelech, the Barbarian king, was buried in the city of Fess, interred with the selfsame habit, garb, and excellent ornament of gems and pearls wherein he did depart this life. Many of the captured noblemen made bold to ransom the dead body of the Portuguese king, and proffered the new Barbarian King Hameto ten thousand ducats therefor, but the Barbarian King gave them answer that ransom of a dead body for gold were unseemly, and had them bear that body unto Alcazara and there bury it in a pilgrim hostel."

Our honest German historian knew exactly where the young, brave King Sebastian lay buried; but poor Portugal did not know it and did not want to believe the man's grave to be in the pilgrim hostel at Alcassar. With unshakable certainty, it hoped for his return, and the harder the times, the heavier and more intolerable the yoke of their new ruler became, the more this longing and hope took root in the hearts of a people who had not forgotten its days of grandeur and glory.

The new ruler called himself Don Philip II of Spain, and—after a brief interregnum by Cardinal Henry† and the dreamlike reign of King Antonio, the Prior of Crato* *—his wicked general, Ferdinand

---

in 1578, so that Portugal was inherited by his uncle, Philip II of Spain. Sebastian became a mythic figure of nationalism in Portugal, where the hope of his return long endured. Adventurers claiming to be Sebastian recurrently appeared.

*Heinrich Bünting, *Braunschweig and Lüneburg Chronicles*, ed. M. H. Meybaum, 1620.

†Uncle of King Sebastian, ruled Portugal from 1578 to 1580.

**Antonio, Prior of Crato, an illegitimate offspring of the royal family, briefly styled King Antonio I, was promptly defeated by Alba's forces in 1580.

Alvarez of Toledo and Duke of Alba,* subdued that unfortunate nation for him.

Thus, from 1581 on, Portugal was a poorly governed, oppressed province of Spain and was drawn inevitably into all the misfortune and misery of that declining realm, and the English and Dutch treated its coasts and colonies no differently than they treated all other Spanish property they could lay their hands on. And so it came about the Portuguese island of Saint Thomas was also a Spanish possession, and its viceroy, as noted, was the Spanish colonel Don Francisco Meneses, a brave, but poor man, who had taken this obscure post in the Bight of Biafra because no one else had wanted to take it, and who, governing from his residence, the castle of Pavaosa, maintained the respect of the natives, a strong, handsome tribe of Negroes, and with the help of his Spanish and Portuguese colonists and troops of occupation, did everything within his power both to cause the sugarcane planted there to flourish as desired and to hold high the banner of Don Philip III, defying every false Sebastian and every challenge of the English and Dutch.

* * *

A hammock was hung between two palm trees in the garden of the castle. Broad-leaved tropical vegetation of the sort engendered by the equatorial sun shaded the swaying bed; a mountain stream rushed past the lovely resting place and—here covered by bushes and blossoms, there free to leap glistening stones—hastened toward the sea. Fragrant was the garden of the castle of Pavaosa, and shimmering with many bright colors; but the air vibrated above it; the rushing, murmuring, clear, dancing water was a malicious mockery, the shade did not cool.

The men cursed the dreadful sun, the women fainted away beneath it; to anyone not born in this place, life was a torment; and dreaming feverishly, a young woman lay asleep in the hammock between the two palm trees in the garden of Don Francisco Meneses, governor of the island of Saint Thomas beneath the equator.

Doña Camilla Drago was dreaming of snow falling along the

---

*(1507–82), general and statesman in the service of Philip II, well-known to German readers as a character in Goethe's *Egmont* and Schiller's *Don Carlos*.

banks of the Schelde and the Waal, of a piercing north wind from the sea, of ice flowers in the round windowpanes set in heavy lead, of ice on the Dutch canals, of a rowdy storm wind setting the roof tiles rattling in the night and rowdily tossing the weather vanes about on the high-peaked gables, and her uncle, the governor, jaundiced and withered, bloodless and goateed, black-eyed and crook-nosed like the good knight Don Quixote of La Mancha, sat at the head of her swaying couch, held her hot hands, shook his head, and said to himself:

"With all due respect for the Supreme Council of War in Madrid and for my liege, Don Philip III, this is indeed no place for a young lady to reside, not to mention that there may well be better retreats for an old disabled gentleman, who from his sixteenth to his sixtieth birthday has done his arduous yet happy duty, on foot and on horseback, and even on board many a ship. There really are quite a few spots, be they in Spain, in Portugal, or even in the West Indies, where an old knight could rest his bones more comfortably, not to mention that the reason one sits here is so that one may be forgotten—oh Holy Virgin, not to speak of this young lady, my niece, as well!"

The old man pulled the tips of his well-waxed moustache through his fingers, tweaked his goatee, and amid much shaking of his head, lost himself in deepest reflection on the vanity and injustice of this world, the waste of spear tips, sword blades, gunpowder and gallant Hispanic soldiers and knights wherever flags adorned with the lions and towers* waved and, naturally, came into conflict with its neighbor. He reflected deeply on all the good, average, and bad viceroyships on the near and far sides of the Atlantic Ocean, and most deeply on the frivolity of his noble Gothic ancestors, who had been unable to take good care of their own and thus of his own, but most deeply of all he reflected on his niece, Doña Camilla Drago.

This was the unending course of his thought: he, Francisco Meneses, had no personal objection to the island of Saint Thomas in the great Gulf of Guinea, directly beneath the terrible black line called the equator, and sitting in the castle of Pavaosa was a thousand times better than standing and creeping in the antechambers of the great

---

*Arms of the kingdom of Spain.

lords in Madrid; but this little, hot hand did not belong in such a viceroyalty—damned if it did!

Damned is a very nasty word, especially when it's intended to be shoved like a bolt behind such a row of thoughts, keeping out fearful images and imaginings that want to arise and portend the future!

The little hand, hanging so limp and feeble from its floating couch, had its own story, its own tempestuous, adventurous history—about which one may read in what follows.

2

Doña Camilla Drago

The broad plains of Flanders expanded in the freshest drenching green, and the rainbow stood like a bridge above the land; the riders and their mounts shook the gleaming drops from them, and like the steeds of Neptune just arisen from the sea, the heavy Frisian draft horses steamed and snorted before their great clumsy coach, which had just been halted by Prince Moritz's* scouting party. In the distance, behind the green hedges, along the ditches, pistol shots were still being exchanged between the Spanish coach's fleeing escort and the provincial riders in hot pursuit; inside the coach itself, however, clear, female cries of lamentation and help were followed by the silence of the grave, and the wind-tousled and powder-blackened ruffian who had made this catch and was now carefully opening its door, had no idea at all what he was to do with this heap of fainting ladies. Neither he nor any of his horsemen carried smelling salts about with them in their pockets or saddlebags.

With a most discourteous locution, he shoved his hat from his right ear to his left and grabbed at his disheveled hair; but he was really not an evil fellow; for as his comrades were about to lay hold with rougher hands and inspect their booty at close range, he

---

*Prince Maurice of Orange (1567–1625), stadtholder of the Netherlands, commander in the Dutch war of independence from Spain.

protested with a coarse but honest "Hold it!" And when a young maid, all but a child, unwound herself out of the convulsively tangled embrace of her duenna's and her two chambermaids' arms and began violently addressing him in the Spanish tongue, he grumbled somewhat gruffly that he didn't understand her gibberish and, beating back the greedily thrusting hands of his horsemen yet a second time and slamming the coach door shut, climbed back on his steed with a groan and gave the command: "Forward march—to headquarters!"

By "headquarters" he meant those of the famous Dutch colonel Heraugière, the conqueror of Breda,* who, having withdrawn from the town of Huy on the Maas—likewise conquered but then surrendered again to La Motte, the master of the Spanish campaign—was at the moment holding a council of war with his officers in a dilapidated and plundered mill; and he, along with several of his officers, understood not only Spanish but French as well. But although they were certainly just as brave, as hardened as Signior Petruchio of Verona and just as often as he had seen the sea rage like an angry boar chafed with sweat, just as often as he had heard in pitched battle loud 'larums, neighing steeds, and trumpets' clang, unlike him they did not consider a woman's tongue to give ". . . not half so great a blow to hear / As will a chestnut in a farmer's fire";† on the contrary, they were mightily dismayed by Señora Rosamunda Bracamonte y Mugadas Criades, who, gradually recovering from her faint, had now awakened and was lamenting her imprisonment among heathens with extraordinary volubility. The Dutch gentlemen shrugged their shoulders as one and held their hands to their ears, and Heraugière began to show his teeth, which was always a bad sign, when the equally imprisoned little girl broke into the circle of grim Beggar Knights, and calmly, coolly took the floor. Once a lance corporal had led the howling duenna out of the miller's parlor, they learned from the child that she was the daughter of the Spanish colonel Don Alonso Drago, that until now she had been living in a nunnery in Liège and had just been on her way to Bruges, where her father was training a regiment of German auxiliaries for Count Fuentes.

"I'm really quite sorry, Doña Camilla, that fate has led you into

---

*Colonel Charles de Heraugière (1556–1601) captured Breda in 1590.
† *The Taming of the Shrew*, act 1, scene 2 (1.4 in some texts).

the path of my scouting party," Heraugière said more politely than
was his custom. "We are headed for Hertogenbosch, and we shall
have to take you and your ladies along with us. Heaven does not
often grant us such a lovely hostage; but please have no worry, I shall
ride next to your coach, and should Mynheer von La Motte persist
in not bothering us, you shall experience no further inconvenience
other than the rough heavens and having to travel by night on a few
occasions. Forward, gentlemen, fresh to the saddle, so that we may
escape from the death sentence of these Liègians and their pious
bishop!"

And Heraugière was as good as his word. He kept order among
his men this time—just as he had once done in the hold of that
world-renowned peat-boat, which deed had so amazed Paul Antonio Lansavechia* and his Italians at Breda. Not the least harm
came to Señora Rosamunda Bracamonte y Mugadas Criades. Not
one of the Dutch horsemen had been so hardened by war that he
would have dared violate that good lady's charms and virtue, and
the two young chambermaids kept no travel diaries. It was a chilly
May in that year of 1595, but the dreamer in the hammock on Saint
Thomas recalled her involuntary journey through the bishopric of
Liège and the province of Brabant much as someone dying of thirst
in the desert recalls a cooling spring.—

The brave Heraugière's march ended, for the time being, in Hertogenbosch; he took a polite farewell from the daughter of Colonel
Drago, who served Count Fuentes far too zealously for them to give
him back his child in return for the customary ransom. In The
Hague, beside one of its slowly flowing canals, was the house of
Mynheer van der Does, and Prince Moritz's young Spanish hostage
was entrusted to his, or better, to his wife's care and supervision.
There ducks swam in the canals in summer, there crows hopped
about the ice in winter, there storks went strolling in the meadows
in frog season, and there in the meadows of southern Holland,
Mefrouw van der Does took the *niña*† by the hand, making her days
of captivity as pleasant as possible and mothering her as if she were
her own child. Mefrouw did have a child of her own, but one that
could no longer be led by the hand as could her Spanish "chick-

---

*Paolo Antonio Lansavechia, commander of the fortress of Breda. Heraugière had
hidden his troops in a ship carrying peat.
†"Girl."

adee." Georg van der Does, a wild lad, came home only when his ship was being caulked in dry dock at Vlissingen or Scheveningen or lay trapped in the ice somewhere. The youth of Holland had no time for sitting still and learning manners and decorum, and Georg the seaman was no better than his fellows. In the winter of '95, however, he was home on leave, sat at the family fireside and treated them to a hundred grisly tales of on-board battles, of boardings and sinkings of the enemy, of pirates hanged, and was very bashful in the presence of their pretty Spanish guest. In the summer of '96 he was home with a head-wound and—once Señora Rosamunda Bracamonte had taken him by the ear several times, given him a good shaking, and warned him to behave himself—would take quite decorous, though somewhat lachrymose walks with her on his arm, across the green meadows, among the storks and white and yellow flowers. He would listen, petulant and fretful, to his mother's stories about Margaret,* the regent during the good old days before the arrival of the Duke of Alba, about William of Orange,† the Counts Egmont** and Hoorn,†† and poor prince Don Juan of Austria;§ he even found the Spanish miss rather a bother on account of her duenna, the lady Rosamunda—Doña Camilla Drago in her hammock beneath the equator smiled as she thought of him.– – – – –
– – – – – – – – – –

Two gaudy birds came through the dark blue air and playfully chased one another around the two palm trees in the garden of the castle of Pavaosa. Through half-closed lids Doña Camilla watched their splendid tropical plumage shimmer in the sun; their harsh voices hurt her ears. They fluttered and chattered in the high tree-tops, they climbed about the trunks, and suddenly they shot away again, toward the Guinean sea, which shone here and there through

*Margaret of Austria (1480–1530), daughter of Emperor Maximilian I, regent of the Netherlands 1507–15 and 1518–30, highly regarded for her wisdom and intellectual qualities.
†(1533–84), stadtholder of the Netherlands from 1555, led the rebellion against Spain and was murdered.
**Egmont, Count of Lamoral (1522–68), moderate supporter of William of Orange, executed on Alba's orders; well-known to German readers from Goethe's drama.
††Philip, Count of Hoorn (1518–68), executed with Egmont.
§(1547–78), natural son of Emperor Charles V, stadtholder of the Netherlands from 1576, fought against William of Orange but with insufficient support from Philip II.

the foliage. Doña Camilla Drago watched them disappear and laid her hand to her eyes, smarting from all the brilliance and play of color: she thought of January 24, 1597—of the battle at Turnhout,* of her father's grave in the deep snows of the north.

Under the command of Count Varax, the troops of Archduke Albert of Austria left their Brabantine winter quarters: Neapolitans of the Trevigo regiment, Germans of Sulz regiment, Albanians under Niccolo Basta, Spaniards under Don Juan de Gusman, Don Juan Cordua and Don Alonso Drago, Walloon infantry under Barlotte and Cozuel, Walloon cavalry under Grobbendonck. Near Gertruideberg, Prince Moritz assembled his forces, eight thousand infantry and eight hundred horse, and against them Robert Sidney led five hundred English from the forces occupying Vlissingen and Briel. At about midnight between the 23rd and 24th of January, the Dutch army arrived at Ravels, and at the break of day came upon the enemy, which having held a council of war, was already in retreat toward Herentals. The grimmest of encounters then took place. With savage violence, the Scots under Murray and Zeelanders under De la Corde hurled themselves at the enemy, followed boldly, though prudently, by the English under Sidney and Lord Vere. The cavalry under Counts Hohenlohe and Solms did a marvelous piece of work on the moor of Thieltsch, and along with Count Varax, Don Alonso Drago was shot dead at the very start of the battle. By eleven o'clock, the might of Spain lay fallen in the snow. The Dutch sent thirty-eight infantry flags and the standards of Drago's cavalry back to The Hague; bells rang out in all the free provinces at the news of victory; Prince Moritz of Orange was received in great triumph at The Hague;—it was through his intervention that the daughter of Alonso Drago was given her freedom by the puissant States General. The trumpets blown in all the streets of The Hague in celebration of the glorious victory at Turnhout did not, we may assume, echo like just any sound in Camilla's ear and soul. They blasted over land and sea, they had not yet died away, years later, and their sounds quavered above the palm trees in the garden of the castle of Pavaosa.—

In the spring of 1597, Camilla Drago said her farewell to Mynheer and Mefrouw van der Does, and this time Georg made a point

---

*Near Antwerp, where the Spanish were defeated by Prince Maurice. Raabe drew what follows from Carl Curths's continuation of Schiller's *History of the Rebellion of the Netherlands*, 1823.

of coming over from Scheveningen for the occasion. He was more bashful than ever and had less to say than ever, and once the litter bearing the Spanish miss had disappeared around the corner, he too disappeared, without so much as saying his customary good-bye to his downcast mother. Until evening cannons called him back on board ship, he sat on the dunes at the shore and drew pictures in the sand with his dagger.—

It was a long way from green Hague to the forlorn island of Saint Thomas in the Bay of Guinea. The escort rode beside Camilla's litter as far as Bergen op Zoom, and there, to the great delight of Señora Rosamunda, were relieved by Spanish cavalry. Under the guard of imperial and Italian troops, Don Francisco Meneses's niece traveled from Brussels to Italy, by way of the Rhine and Tyrol. From Genoa, a Spanish ship brought her to Barcelona;—in the fall of '98, Captain Giralto anchored in the harbor of Saint Thomas, and Philip III's viceroy had a volley fired from every rampart in honor of his niece and solemnly led the weary child over the blazing-hot soil that would be her home from now on. On Captain Giralto's arm, Señora Rosamunda Bracamonte likewise stepped ashore; her appearance made a great impression on the garrison, the colonists, and the naked black natives, the last of whom, seeing her imposing form, pressed their brows to the hot sand on both sides of the path.

3

Captain José Giralto

A shot of cannon-royal from Abreojos Tower shook the air—a signal that a ship was in sight. At the sound, many bright-hued birds flew up out of bushes and trees, and the governor, torn from his brown study, rose up quickly and, with one final worried glance at his niece, strode toward the castle; Doña Camilla Drago, however, did not stir. She had closed her eyes; she seemed to be fast asleep now; waving a colorful fan of feathers, a black woman took her uncle's place. A green snake uncoiled itself from the curious roots of a candelabrum tree, saw the sleeping girl and the smiling black slave, wriggled across the fine sand and vanished among broad leaves beside the brook; the whydah birds still warbled in the underbrush, but the sun was sinking into the sea. As the fiery ball touched the water, a resounding tumult arose along the shore and in the town—shot after shot fell from Abreojos Tower; the alarm bell of the castle began to swing; the black woman dropped her fan in alarm, Camilla Drago sat up terrified, a swam of serving girls rushed by, and were followed by Señora Rosamunda Bracamonte, moving at a faster pace than seemed appropriate to her dignity and clapping her hands above her head.

"By all the saints, what has happened? what is going on? what's the meaning of this noise?" the governor's niece cried.

"There's no rest from them anywhere!" the señora said, in great exasperation. "It's enough to make the Holy Inquisition itself doubt the justice of God—may He forgive me my sins! It's absolutely unbearable!"

"The heretics! the Netherlanders! the Dutch rebels!" the Spanish servants wailed. "They've come with a hundred ships. They've chased Captain Giralto across the sea and into the bay! May the Holy Virgin protect us, they've counted a thousand of their sails from our towers!"

"It's a fairy tale, a foolish horror story," Camilla said; but the duenna shook her head, the noise from the town of Pavaosa was growing with every moment, the signal drums of the garrison rattled along the castle ramparts, and Doña Camilla Drago hurried down the garden paths to find her uncle—the tropical night fell quickly.

Captain José Giralto and his brigantine *Corona de Aragon* had indeed entered the harbor of Pavaosa in a sorry state; he had had forty Dutch sailing ships breathing down his neck all the way from Gran Canaria and had escaped capture or sinking only by the multiple wonders of his cleverness and sailor's luck. The silence in the town and the palace had yielded to the wildest tumult; confusion reigned everywhere and grew as darkness grew; people ran in disorder with torches and links, artillery was set at the ready along the bastions, those colonists able to bear arms found their way, sword and spear and musket in hand, to the assembly points, horsemen galloped down the coast and into the interior to warn isolated inhabitants; murmurs and stifled laughter ran through the native blacks, who had likewise sent their messengers into the mountains, to their free brothers. From the sea to the highest mountain peaks, black warriors brandished their clubs, filled their quivers with arrows and tested the strings of their bows;—on Abreojos Tower, Don Francisco Meneses took his niece by the hand and sighed:

"My child, my child, how I wish you were sitting in some cloister in Madrid!"

"Well, I don't wish it, señor," said Doña Camilla Drago. "I am the daughter of a fine gentleman, I am your flesh and blood; if I were to tremble before every little cloud, I would bring dreadful shame upon two noble houses. By Blessed Michael the Archangel, dear uncle, we should thank God for these clouds of whose approach Captain Giralto has brought us news: it had really grown quite hot here on Saint Thomas. Forward, by land and sea and—close ranks, Spain!"

"You are a good child, Camilla!" the governor said; "I've always said so, but a man always blames himself too, especially when such a pretty young lady must be made to pay and suffer for his whims. Captain Giralto won't have miscounted—forty sails—truly, the next days will see a right lively bustle on the roads and upon the ramparts of Pavaosa!"

"All the better," said Doña Camilla. "And there they are, by the way!"

She pointed out into the night, in the far distance a few red dots flickered, the lanterns on the masts of the approaching Dutch fleet.

With the same solemnity with which Don Francisco had led his niece to shore a year before, he now led her down the steep stairs of Abreojos Tower and entrusted her to her women. He himself strode out to the bastion on the shore, where with great calm and prudence, he set himself anew to preparing the defenses of his viceroyalty.—

"I beg you, Señor Giralto, who is this archscoundrel who has sent these Dutch rascals down upon our necks once again?" Señora Rosamunda Bracamonte inquired of the captain of the *Corona de Aragon* beneath the gates of the palace.

"It is my pleasure to be of service to you, señora," the captain answered. "Admiral van der Does has hoisted his yellow flag on his ship, the *Orange*. A brave man, señora; an experienced man with a fine knowledge of the sea, except a bit too portly, too heavy for the deck of a ship. I've met him many a time northeast of Cape Finisterre, señora,—a portly gentleman, to be sure!"

"Why, I know him too!" cried the lady, not all that pleased. "I've met him several times myself, though on more solid ground. During our imprisonment by the heathens, he came now and again to his brother's house in The Hague. My God, my God, what a strange world we do live in!"

"I take the liberty of asking to be excused, señora," the captain said. "It is always a pleasure to rediscover an old acquaintance, and I would be very pleased indeed if I might put all my energies to giving the good admiral the reception he is due when he knocks upon my door tomorrow."

"And I shall take the liberty of including you in my prayers, señor. Who is your patron saint?"

"Don Joseph of Arimathaea,"* said the captain with a slight raise of his hat.

"I shall urgently commend you to his attention and care, captain. I wish you a most restful night!"

With two deep bows, the two took leave of one another. The señora pattered through the corridors more swiftly than usual in order to inform her young mistress who it was commanded the Dutch fleet; the captain, however, did not go to bed, but was very busy all night, both on shore and on board his vessel, with preparations for greeting the Dutch admiral; but before the gray of dawn, the governor chased him and his brigantine back out of the harbor.

"You have no right to let one of the king's ships be burned or scuttled, my good captain. Head for the Gabon River."

Doña Camilla Drago did not sleep either. Her pernicious lethargy had given way to the most feverish excitement; Doña Camilla was also watching from her window while the lights of the republican fleet floated upon the sea, as the long waves of the Atlantic Ocean swept and struck with a thud against the rocks and walls at her feet. To the great annoyance of Señora Rosamunda, all night long Doña Camilla Drago paced back and forth in her chamber or sat or leaned

---

*Saw to the burial of Jesus' body, Mark 15:43–46.

restlessly in the bay of the window and listened to the waves and the hubbub of the townspeople and residents of the castle of Pavaosa as they awaited the enemy, the archenemy.

4

A Dutch Expedition

In the crypt of the Escorial, next to his father, the Emperor Charles, Don Philip II slept his final sleep. The heavy gates had closed behind him, the sound of their boom had echoed away in the vaults; nothing at all could disturb the king's rest, not even the wild, triumphant shout that passed through the populace—from the Schelde to the Ems along the coast of the North Sea and far into the interior—as bells of the border towns, still in their shackles, announced the great news. Already by April 2, 1599, these free provinces had flung their latest letter of renunciation in the face of the new man who still called himself their ruler. They published a manifesto to all the nations and governments of Europe, in which they *forbade* all commerce by sea or land with the crown of Spain, Archduke Albert* and his consort and coregent Clara Isabella Eugenia, and by water and by land only the brave king of Denmark, Christian IV,† dared pay it no mind. What high-and-mighty gentlemen the beggars of 1566 had indeed become.

They hammered and banged in their shipyards day and night, and the living King Philip III heard the noise that his predecessor could no longer hear. They plaited ropes and cast cannons, they forged anchors and grappling irons, they devised a new tax and mustered troops, and on May 25, 1599, they sailed from the mouth of the Maas on their way to offer the new King of Spain their

---

*(1559–1622), called Albert VII, son of Emperor Maximilian II, stadtholder of the Netherlands from 1595; in 1599 he married Clara Isabella Eugenia, daughter of Philip II, who had transferred the Netherlands to her. In 1609 Albert negotiated the independence of the Netherlands.

†(1577–1648), king of Denmark and Norway.

personal congratulations on his enthronement. Seventy-five large ships with eight thousand sailors and marines took part in this congratulatory visit; the admiral was indeed, as Captain José Giralto had correctly reported, Mynheer van der Does, and he had been given two gentlemen, Jan Gerbrant and Cornelius Lensen, to serve as his rear admirals or *schouts-bij-nacht*. But when on June 11 they came knocking at Coruña, they found the door locked and the Spanish fleet nicely sheltered at anchor beneath the cannon of the fortress. After a heated attack and a violent, yet equally futile bombardment, a council of war was held, at which it was decided not to repeat the effort at Lisbon, but rather to attempt a raid of the Fortunate Islands. With a favorable wind, they arrived at the latitude of Gran Canaria on June 26 and cast anchor as close as possible to the city of Palma and its fortress Gratiosa.

"Now make your mother really happy for once and catch yourself a monkey with your bare hands, Georg, my boy," the admiral said to his nephew as he placed his foot on the *Orange's* companion ladder, ready to lead the landing troops.

The ladder swayed and creaked beneath the weight of this giant of a man, but it bore him. With a loud cry of exultation Georg van der Does jumped after him into the jolly boat, and with similar savage cries, the sailors and marines followed. Beneath the thunder of cannon and from every ship, boats were launched for the shore; but Gran Canaria likewise opened fire at the approaching enemy. The shallowness of the water soon prevented them from advancing further, the jolly boats ran aground, and many a good Dutchman fell to a Spanish musketball.

"Show them that the frogs of Zeeland and the water-rats of Friesland haven't forgotten their craft!" the admiral shouted. "Out of these washtubs; if you can't swim, wriggle! Long live the gentlemen of the States General!"

He was the first to leap from board and waded, gasping and snorting, toward the shore; a bullet scratched his shoulder, but he simply shook himself and said: "Pah!" First to gain solid ground were Georg van der Does and Heinrich Leflerus, pastor of Ysselmünde and chaplain of the fleet, the former with a sailor's knife in his hand, the latter with the Bible under his arm. "To hell with 'em!" said the first;—"Oh Lord, give victory unto Thy people!" cried the other.

And "wriggling" onto land behind them, came: admiral and *schout-bij-nacht,* captains, mates, seasoned sailors, able-bodied seamen, halberdiers and musketeers from Nord-Holland and Zuid-Holland, from Friesland and Gelderland, from Utrecht, Groningen and Zeeland. With great force they drove the islanders before them and chased them behind their ramparts. They stormed the citadel of Gratiosa on the first try and that evening were quite satisfied with their day's work. On the third morning, just as Mynheer van der Does was setting his foot on the companion ladder, the city of Palma thought better of it, sent a trumpeter and officer with a flag of truce to the rampart, and after brief negotiations, opened its gates. The entering Dutch forces found the streets rather empty, to be sure, for the majority of the populace had fled into the mountains with bag and baggage; but nonetheless they found plenty of booty, and at timberyards, shipyards, and in the prisons, they had the pleasure of removing the chains from a large number of their countrymen. Mynheer van der Does knew how to make a clean sweep of things; he thought even the bells of the churches and convents worth taking along, and he made no scruple about loading them aboard ship. On July 1, Henricus Leflerus preached before the assembled troops a sermon of thanksgiving for all the good things both found and enjoyed, whereupon, to crown their work, they set the city of Palma afire from one end to the other and amid thundering jubilation blew every fortification sky-high. Afterwards, they sailed with merriment and easy consciences for Gomera, where the *opperkerkvoogd** and pastor of Ysselmünde, Mynheer Henricus Leflerus, had occasion to repeat his sermon and where their sacks were crammed so full, that in order to secure the spoils, the admiral had to send Jan Gerbrant, the *schout-bij-nacht,* back to Texel with thirty-five heavily laden ships. From the stern of his brigantine, Captain José Giralto gazed across the water and saw the smoke from the burning colonies and the division of the Dutch fleet; but he also saw how the *Orange,* its yellow admiral's flag flying, turned its bow again to the southwest, and as we already know, he hardly took his eye off the Dutch armada until he had come abreast of Saint Thomas, having all the while, as we likewise already know, frequent opportunity to exchange fire with it.

*High church official.

The pastor of Ysselmünde, Mynheer Heinrich Leflerus, did not return to Holland with the *schout-bij-nacht*. Besides his being able to preach such wonderful sermons of thanksgiving and victory, he also kept a diary in which he noted many things that the admiral did not think worth incorporating in his log.

"Oh that men would praise the Lord for his goodness, and for his wonderful works to the children of men, that go down to the sea in ships, that do business in great waters!" he spoke with the psalmist,* and with amazement and shaking of his head passed the "dark sea," that cloud of dust by which the winds of the Sahara can enshroud the sea about the green headlands of the islands. This reverend gentleman also marveled greatly at the flying fish, and the remarks he brought to paper were of the most curious sort. To his great delight, Mynheer van der Does had them catch a shark for him, which gave him occasion to use the ravenous monster as a suitable text for his sermon the next Sunday and to attach to it all manner of pious meditations on the Antichrist, the unsuspecting Pope Innocent IX,† the good Sultan Murad III,** and King Philip III. He attempted to engage the admiral's nephew as an attentive partner in his nautical, geographical, natural-historical, philosophical, and theological observations, but as far as eagerness and cooperation went, Georg van der Does proved a most awful disappointment to that excellent gentleman's hopes. Georg van der Does had considerably greater interest in Captain José Giralto's brigantine, constantly evading Dutch grappling hooks and cannons-royal, than in the profound hypotheses and ever so subtle expositions of Henricus Leflerus, the pastor of Ysselmünde. Besides which, from the mouths of the prisoners from Gran Canaria and Gomera he had learned who was governor of Saint Thomas, the expedition's present objective, and reflected more often than one would have expected of him on the possibility of striking up an old acquaintance again.—

They sailed past the Cape Verde Islands, neither casting anchor nor repeating their sport at the Canaries; what mattered now was that they reach the coast of Brazil with all possible speed, intending to stop at the Guinea Islands only to take on fresh water, and neither

*Psalms 107:21, 23.
†Giovanni Antonio Fachinetti (1519–91), pope for two months in 1591.
**(1546–95), Ottoman sultan from 1574, who after his succession ignored the business of government.

the admiral nor the rear admiral had any presentiment of what fate might have otherwise disposed.

"Land, land! Land ho!"

A moment later, the distant blue cloudlet, the mountains of Saint Thomas, sank into tropical night.

5

The Landing

At the rising sun's return, they approached in a wide, sweeping semicircle: on the left, the admiral; on the right, Mynheer Cornelius Lensen of Vlissingen; in the middle, Mynheer Gerhard Storms van Wena. The Atlantic waves seemed to exult as they parted before the bows of their men-of-war; with a thousand-voiced, jubilant cry the fleet greeted the castle of Pavaosa as it rose from the water and fired a cannon shot to signal the town and the weak fortifications along the shore to ready themselves for defense.

Upon Abreojos Tower, beneath the banner of Spain, wafting gently and breathing in the morning breeze, stood Doña Camilla Drago. She saw the *Orange* wrap itself in a dangerous white cloud of smoke, a dull booming thud followed, a hissing and whistling passed by her, then the ground beneath her feet seemed to move: the castle and the town of Pavaosa answered the Dutch greeting with all the cannon on its seaward side.

In her chambers below, Señora Bracamonte moaned and held her ears, the Spanish maidservants lay loudly lamenting before the image of the Holy Virgin, and the black women lay on the ground and uttered inarticulate sounds of dread. Doña Camilla Drago held fast to the flagpole on Abreojos Tower. As the fumes and smoke broke here and there below her, she saw the sea covered with enemy jolly boats; the shouts and calls from the shore grew ever wilder, the crack of musket fire began to blend with the thunder of cannon; the equatorial sun reheated the paving stones and the ramparts of the tower, but at that moment Camilla was not as conscious of it as were the men from the north who were gaining the shore.—

"Good God Almighty, the sweat is pouring off me!" cried the admiral of the puissant States General as he flung his giant form onto the sand. "Forward, if you can still catch a breath! Chase the dons, who will; I'm finished for this morning!"

"Long live my noble uncle! Forward! Forward!" shouted Georg van der Does, leaping over his breathless relative and hurrying ahead with the gasping Dutch troops.

"Take the matter in hand and make the best of it, Mynheer van Wena!" the admiral called to that commander, who had just reached the shore. "Reverend Henricus, take your time, come here and take a little breather; we're not in such a great hurry to play at this child's sport."

The pastor of Ysselmünde removed his broad-brimmed hat and dried the sweat dripping from his brow.

"Mynheer van der Does," he said, "this is a hot country. How long do you intend to sojourn here?"

"Well," the admiral laughed, "we've got the shore, and Cornelius Lensen seems to be doing a good job with the castle and town from the sea; he's dealing out some gallant broadsides and will, we can hope, soon knock down those Spanish walls. I have hopes that it won't prove necessary for us to be singed till we're Moors."

"That's quite agreeable with me," the preacher sighed. "This is indeed a remarkable sun."

In a steady stream, new troops were leaping from the boats and hurrying toward the town in somewhat disordered haste, but the crack of musket fire gradually fell silent, the entrenchments along the shore had been taken by the Dutch, the ground between the sea and the walls of the town was strewn with dead and wounded; Dutch, Spanish, blacks, and mulattoes in a jumble; a messenger arrived from Captain Gerhard Storms to ask the admiral if it might not be proper and perhaps more convenient to demand the surrender of the governor of the island.

"It would be in vain, Mynheer Pieter Klundert," the admiral said to the midshipman who had delivered the question,—"I know the old fellow in there by reputation; but—you're welcome to try; it will give our men time to puff off this heat and to have a look at the lay of the land. Pipe the tune for the señor, mynheer; I'll follow you on foot."

Fifteen minutes later, the Dutch commander and Don Francisco Meneses held the friendliest of conversations at the town walls.

"I'll not leave one stone atop the other when I enter, señor," the admiral said, hat in hand.

"We have heard of your behavior on the Canaries in that regard," the governor replied with studied courtesy. "We shall, however, do our best to keep you outside as long as possible, señor."

"I have no doubts as to your courage and your resources, señor; but I shall nevertheless ask you once again if this is your final word?"

"The king permits no other."

"Well, then, I wish you a fine lunch and a pleasant siesta, Don Francisco. With your permission, I shall settle in before your walls, and I hope to see you again very soon."

"Farewell, Señor Almirante, and please accept my apologies for not inviting you to join me at lunch."

With two deep bows, of the Señora Bracamonte and Captain Giralto sort, the two leaders went their separate ways. Mynheer van der Does returned slowly to his fellows along the blazing-hot shore, and just as slowly, Don Francisco Meneses strode about the walls, to speak a cheering word here, give an order there, and everywhere revive the courage and hopes of his troops and of the colonists by his presence. The fire of the enemy troops had, of course, fallen silent during the negotiations; the sun entered its zenith, the powerful ships lay motionless in their half-moon around the outer harbor; but the troops that had landed lay motionless as well, wherever they could find even the scantiest of shade. They had cast off their cuirasses, their helmets, their wool and tarred jackets; the blades of their swords and daggers, the barrels of their guns, lying exposed to the sun, burned in their hands as if they had just emerged from the forge of the swordsmith. The siesta, which the governor of Saint Thomas did not take, the admiral of the Dutch expeditionary fleet did. He lay on his belly beneath a cloth stretched between trees and spread his gigantic limbs out as far as possible; beneath another roof-tent Heinrich Leflerus dreamed of his cool parsonage in Ysselmünde; Georg van der Does, however, sat alert and lively beneath a palm tree by the guard-post set furthest toward the castle of Pavaosa, and here, too he drew pictures in the sand as once he had on the dunes of the beach near Scheveningen; that now and again he could not suppress a yawn ought not be held against him.—

At four that afternoon, Don Francisco ventured a sortie against the Dutch, who held far too light an opinion of his ability to defend himself. He cast back several of their advance guards, still drowsy with sleep, and caused no little damage before being driven back by their superior force. The plantations lying nearest the town and castle went up in flames, some having been set afire by the owners themselves, some by pillaging enemy scouting parties. Late in the afternoon, artillery from the fleet was brought ashore; Mynheer van der Does and his officers walked clear around the town to determine an appropriate place of attack; except for the occupation of the beach, however, the only real gain that day came in the negotiations that were opened with the free black chiefs, deadly enemies of the Spaniards, who had descended from the mountains. They could provide him people who were a better match for the sun than his own men, and it was with a very grave countenance that Don Francisco Meneses watched from the walls as these dark figures appeared among the troops of the invaders. He knew better than anyone else that this did not bode well; he pressed his lips together and glanced apprehensively over his shoulder to the tops of the palms and tamarinds in his garden; his hand trembled for a moment as it played at the haft of his dagger; but then he removed his hat from his worried and fear-ridden brow and said:

"God's will be done as always; but I do wish she were sitting in a cloister in Madrid embroidering vestments or painting St. Agneses on parchment."

6

Galatea by Miguel Cervantes*

In the garden of the castle of Pavaosa, between the two high palm trees, Camilla Drago lay once again in her hammock; it was now the

---

*Cervantes's pastoral novel *Galatea* appeared in 1585, twenty years before *Don Quixote,* of which the characters in the story naturally cannot have heard.

third week after the landing of the Dutch. As always, the brook purled through the blooming thicket, as always, it danced around and past the shimmering stones intentionally laid in its path and knew nothing of how very much the world outside the protecting walls had changed. All the birds had been chased off by the Dutch and Spanish master marksmen, and the resplendent peacocks, the guinea fowls, the tropical herons that could not fly with their clipped wings, sat frightened and nervous on the ground under the overhanging bushes. Señora Rosamunda Bracamonte was also sitting on the ground, on a low cushion next to the spot where her young mistress rested, letting the beads of her rosary glide through her fingers, and had pulled her gown about her as tightly as the cringing peacock had tucked in its glorious plumage.

"Oh Tower of David,* how the heathen rage!" she moaned with each new explosion. "Oh Bearer of Joy, oh Rose of the Soul, Tower of Ivory, protect us, pray for us! Oh Maria, Queen of Angels, of patriarchs, apostles, martyrs, prophets, virgins, hear us! It must be true, my girl, that heaven has granted you the precious gift of serenity—how else could you lie there and not stir a muscle at such noises and horrors? I believe that if the world were to perish, you would not bat an eyelash. Truly, I believe you'll fall asleep on me despite this uproar—if I do say so!"

"I'm not sleeping," Camilla said in a gentle voice. "I simply don't quite rightly know what I should do. It is so strange, indeed I hear the battle, but I hover here with no body in the blue air. I lift my hand only with effort, and yet I am so light, so light! For a long while, I had a nasty fever—that was due to the sun; now I have recovered, and the glowing iron ring has been lifted from my brow. The heaviness has been devoured by the fire—I am so happy!"

"Dear Jesus, Doña Camilla, how you talk! Oh St. Barbara, our best warriors have fallen on the walls or on the rampart or lie tormented by their wounds;—fever reigns in Pavaosa, and your worthy uncle glowers more darkly from day to day: how can you speak of happiness, Doña Camilla Drago? At any moment the enemy may burst in, and they will come, those heathens, just as they came upon the people of Palma and Gomera. Captain Giralto told me about it before he returned to sea prior to the landing of the

*The series of epithets is taken from the Lauretanian Litany, a fifteenth or sixteenth-century encomium on the Virgin Mary from Loreto in Italy.

Dutch. One has no one to comfort or advise one since the captain crept off to his elephants and elephant hunters on the river Gabon; ah, Doña Camilla, I am an old spinster and have served you to the best of my ability from your swaddling days till now, bathed you, and instructed you in all good things, now repay me in kind and speak with me! Don't stare so into the heavens, into the empty air;—do you truly take delight in magnifying the terror in my heart? Anastasia died yesterday, Emerenciana has been hit by an Indian arrow, Thomasiana is sitting in the cellar bent over in cramps; consider that you have only me now, and be kind and rouse yourself, sit up and speak a word that one can lay hold of!"

"What's become of my memory?" Camilla asked. "What did you say, my dear, is the name of the commander before the town?"

The señora clapped her hands together. "Child, child," she cried, "What a pitiful thing you are! Holofernes—no, no, van der Does is the name of this Holofernes. We know him only too well, sad to say, from the days of our Babylonian captivity; he tortured us half to death back then with his tobacco pipe and his beer mug and his horrible laughter—"

"Right, right . . . if only I could separate my dreams from reality, Rosamund. There was also a lad, the son of the good lady in whose house we lived;—Georg was his name, Georg van der Does—"

"You saw him, you know, from Oriente Tower, the young scamp! He was a bad apple even in those days; but now the fruit is ripe and ready to fall. When I think of what jokes the *pillo,* the *bribon** played on me; how he dolled up the scarecrow on the road behind the garden in my best flared skirt and my pointed bonnet, it could even make me forget this miserable day. Yesterday he struck down our poor Lieutenant Lamma; oh, if only I could have him within grasp of my fingernails just once more!"

Camilla smiled and shook her head.

"How long ago it was since we walked those green meadows. Señor Miguel Cervantes probably couldn't turn our tale into a pastoral romance, but perhaps into a splendid comedy of marvels."

"Dear Jesus, how can you joke in such an hour and speak of the sinful foolishness of poets. Hark, hark, how they burst our ears with shouts."

"Poor Galatea, to be sure the island of St. Thomas is no resting

---

*"Rascal; good-for-nothing."

place for you with your shepherd's crook and sweet laments of love; the brave Ximena Gomes, the wife of the *campeador*,* would know better how to adapt herself to these times. I love the shepherdess and reed pipe."

"And yet your worthy uncle practically had to force you down from the walls?!"

"He should have left me there. There I lived as the others and with the others; there blood flowed in my veins; there was pain and horror; but also hope and triumph. There was the intoxication of being alive; but here—here, here is nothing but sun and dreams. There is no pain, no agony left in the fire that pours down from the heavens, but—"

She broke off and let her hand sink down on the shoulder of her old, loyal nurse.

"Dearest heart," the señora sobbed, "you'll break my heart; you are much crueler than the enemy out there at the gates. But just wait, only let us get rid of these ghastly Dutch heretics and of these islands that glow like embers, and I will have a word to speak to your worthy uncle. Captain Giralto cannot have vanished from the earth with his brigantine either; we'll pack your worthy uncle aboard with or without his consent and embark with every crate and carton. Let whoever will, be the king's viceroy here; but the best thing would be to leave the place to the black demons with their monkeys and snakes and sugarcane and elephant tusks. We shall sail away, and we know where we're going; oh, dearest heart, I was born in Alcala de Henares,† and as a young thing, I knew Señor Rodrigues Cervantes and his wife Leonor de Cortina quite well; I'll grant that this *Doña Galatea* her son Miguel has written is not so dear to me as my rosary and the Hail Mary; but since it pleases you, my dear, we shall live as they, beside some cool water, in cool groves, and sing and laugh and be happy."

"What a wild lad he was there in Holland," Camilla Drago said. "At first I was afraid of him as well; but we finally got along together quite well really. Georg van der Does—who would have thought that I would ever see him again? He was a merry fellow; he made me laugh despite myself. Oh, we did laugh a lot, before the battle at

---

*The Warrior, i.e., El Cid, in the Spanish national epic of that name; Ximena Gomes was his wife.
†Birthplace of Cervantes.

Turnhout, did we not, Rosamund?"

"It was quite pleasant," Señora Bracamonte said with a sigh and added silently to herself: "The good Lord knows."

"He has grown a great deal; he's become a man. Now he and his countrymen are standing before the town of Pavaosa; he ought to have brought me greetings from his good mother, from the old house, the shady garden, the people across the street, the fat baker with all those children, who knows, who knows—instead he had to kill poor Lieutenant Lamma; ah, it is so sad to be young as we are and yet to have seen so many, many things."

"Do not think of it, think of your homeland, and how content and happy we shall be there, once these wretched days lie behind us," the señora cried. "You dream too much, as you say yourself; yet, who knows, perhaps you will awaken in a moment in your Doña Galatea's cottage along the golden Tajo!"*

"It is truly not impossible," Camilla murmured: "who knows, if I shall not suddenly awaken, but not on the Tajo, but among the Ursulines in Liège; I do so much like being with those pious nuns— Sister Angelica always awakens me with a kiss—I wish she would come—I wish I were sitting up in my little bed now, listening to the morning song of the birds in the cloister garden and watching the grape leaves trembling at my window."

The noise of battle had gradually diminished and at last fell quite silent. The attackers must have retreated once again after long and fruitless labor. The sound of approaching steps crunched over sand in the garden; Don Francisco Meneses, too, was returning from the day's awful work.

The old cavalier looked quite savage; his face and hands were blackened with dust and smoke, his sleeves ripped at the elbows, his cuirass badly scraped and dented. He carried his long dagger in its leather sheath under his arm; he had both ends of his long moustache between his teeth and was grimly chewing away at them; he almost banged his nose on the bast rope of his niece's hammock and with a deep sigh, brought the long train of his gloomy thoughts to a conclusion.

As a man of little imagination and still fewer words, he at once said what he had to say:

"Camilla, the town can't be held any longer. What we could do,

*Tagus, river in Spain and Portugal, site of Cervantes's *Galatea*.

we have done; but we cannot go on. We have now received news from Captain Giralto in the Bay of Three Angels, brought to us by a fast galley from Santiago in Cape Verde: the armada of Coruña is on its way to attack the divided Dutch fleet. It is already proceeding southward from Gomera, and it is our duty to hold the enemy here until it arrives. This evening we shall set fire to the town of Pavaosa and pull back into the castle; it's a nasty game; but, Señora Bracamonte, if one has no choice, one is spared a great deal of headache, and that is the one consolation that I have brought with me, for you in particular."

"May God have mercy upon us; you are very kind, Señor Gobernador, and I thank you with all my heart," said the señora plaintively; Camilla Drago, however, took her uncle's hand and pressed it mutely to her lips. The old warrior turned quickly away and in the depths of his soul said as had Señora Bracamonte: "May God have mercy upon us!"

7

A New Sermon by the Rev. Heinrich Leflerus, Pastor of Ysselmünde

Mynheer van der Does, the admiral of the puissant States General, had a heavy gait. Wherever he emphatically set his foot, the impression was visible for a long time;—he had left a deep print in the sand on the shore of Saint Thomas as he leaped from the jolly boat. Since that moment the region about the town of Pavaosa was dreadfully changed. Axe, spade, fire and artillery had toppled, gouged, scorched and smashed; charred tree stumps and beams, heaped ashes and dried puddles of blood covered the ground in all directions, and the closer one came to the town walls, the more awful the devastation looked. Tents of all sorts had been pitched rather hastily beyond the range of the Spanish cannons; in everything the besieging troops had done, one could see unmistakably the fury of the equatorial sun, beneath whose rays they labored.

Every piece of iron or steel armor—cuirasses, helmets, casques, gauntlets—lay heaped in piles beyond the rows of tents or hung from posts and trees: like their black allies from the mountains, the Dutch army went into combat half-naked, and returned from the ditches and ramparts of Pavaosa in the same condition today.

They returned, and once again they did not bear the banner of Don Philip III with them; they returned in savage, fantastic, terrible waves, and Pastor Henricus Leflerus turned away shuddering, horrified at the sight. Between the marching ranks of the Dutch, the Guinean natives danced and leaped, brandishing their strange weapons or flinging them into the air with an ear-shattering cry and catching them again;—reeling and gasping, with fixed, vacant or dreadfully feverish eyes, the whites dragged themselves forward and every moment someone in their ranks stumbled to the ground, unable to wrest this short distance to the tents from the blazing air. They had left their wounded and dead behind where they had fallen, or had had to entrust them to the mercy and care of their savage allies; they listened neither to the trumpets nor the commands of their officers; and without the fresher reserves who had rushed in between them and the town, Don Francisco Meneses would hardly have had to yearn so greatly for the fleet of Coruña.

Even the officers had cast aside all their heavy martial ornaments; they wore their sashes across their naked chests; they had even left the belts for their swords and sheaths for their daggers behind, and now they thrust the bare swords into the ground and held a council of war in the shade of a tamarind, on a hill chosen for deliberations.

Leaning on the shoulder of his nephew, the admiral stood in the middle of his officers, a quite different man, sad to say, from when he proudly sailed from the river Maas, a quite different man from when he made the first leap of the conqueror onto the shore of Saint Thomas. His giant form was perhaps the worst suited for bearing the tropical sun; he had lost a lot of flesh, he snapped for air as a swordfish on the dunes snaps for water, his gaze was like that of his warriors, now fixed and drowsy, now eerily excited and wandering in confusion. He looked behind him now, back toward the town, and raised a clenched fist against it.

"Retreat, retreat, for the seventh time, retreat! Hell and damnation, if I had not felt the lash myself, I would not have believed it!" he shouted. "Gentlemen, gentlemen, what is this? are we bewitched?

have we been cast under a spell? What old woman has woven her net for us that we must ignominiously bang our heads against these earthen ramparts and palisades, and all in vain? Seven times! seven times! Mynheer Storms van Wena, you almost made it to the top; what brought you back so swiftly to the ground again?"

Mynheer Storms gave a fretful shrug of his shoulders and said:

"Ask one of the others, Admiral, sir; I believe, by the way, as you do that we have been hexed. They'll have a lovely song to sing about us back home, and have every right to do it."

"How true! How true!" the cry, along with a muffled growl, went through the circle of deeply offended bulldogs, and every single officer, marine and naval, turned aside, as had their admiral, to cast an angry glance at the poor town of Pavaosa.

"Without this sun, we would have taken it long ago!" cried a sweating Frisian from Hollum. "Give me a December morning in Ameland, and we'd have them for lunch."

"I thank you most respectfully for your words, Mynheer van Wendenkeerk," said the admiral peevishly. "Perhaps you could trouble yourself, however, to inquire of Cornelius Lensen in the fleet whether he did not by chance pack an extra snowstorm in the hold. How many men did we leave lying before that wretched hole this time?"

Each officer made a rough count of his band, and they added it up.

"That's another pretty sum!" Mynheer van der Does sighed. "If you add the fever, the palm wine, and those cursed Indian females, you'll find that in fourteen days the barrel will be emptied down to the dregs. The gentlemen in The Hague and Amsterdam will have a grim face to show whoever gives them the tally."

"How true, how true," Heinrich Leflerus, the pastor of Ysselmünde, said, foisting himself on the council. "Truly, gentlemen, give truth its due respect, and confess and take each upon himself his portion of blame for this misery, that the Lord may turn his wrath from you. Truly, the Lord gave you victory and glory and great booty in the Canaries, but pride has sprung up in your breasts as a man clad in armor. 'Who can oppose us?' you cheered lustily and leaped from your ships as if to a wedding feast. But look round you, whether Christian men and children and soldiers of the true faith walk before the throne of the Most High? Upon the graves of your brothers and countrymen you perform your bestial dance with black and wanton heathen women, as if no Dutch mother had suckled you, as if no pious wife, maid, or sister awaits you at home in tears and with a fearful heart. I walk among the tents while you press upon the walls of Edom with spear and bow, and my soul trembles with horror; for it is as in the camp of King Sennacherib of Assyria, of whom it is written: 'And when they arose in the morning, behold, they were all dead corpses.' *—I walk among the tents, and my bones do shake—my brothers are dying, they twist in the cramp of pain and depart with curses; they have foam at their mouths and die as do the blasphemers. Behold, behold, what cloud hangs over your tabernacles! The angel that blew over Sennacherib is in that cloud; you see him not, for the Lord has blinded your eyes and sent you stumbling; but I see it and I say unto you: in your shame you have soiled the ground upon which you walk, your good fortune has turned away from you, your banners are in retreat. Fall with your brows to the ground and strew ashes upon your heads, do penance in the dust. God's own sun as discomfited you; behold, it moves low toward its setting once again, yet but an hour and it will be night, the Lord does not desire your victory; so depart, depart, depart, wind up your anchor and cleave your ropes in two, turn back, turn back before the will of the Lord, or they will say of you in the morning: 'Behold, they were all dead corpses!' "

With a violent shout the Dutch commanders and their warriors, who had gradually crowded forward, interrupted this preacher of disaster. The admiral and Gerhard Storm went after him with clenched fists; a drunken sailor chased him with a club. Had not Georg van der Does and the good Frisian intervened, it is highly probable that the Rev. Henricus would have wandered through the camp no more.

"Muzzle him!" someone shouted. "Give up the island? Never! never! Toss that bird of ill omen in a jolly boat and send him back on board; his yowling and croaking and psalm singing have disturbed our camp long enough and spoiled our fun."

"Away with him," the admiral called. "When we shoot the victory cannons, he may creep out again. What do you say, gentlemen, shall we spite the padre and try again at midnight? shall we once more

*2 Kings 19:26; Isaiah 37:36.

show the dons how the Dutch can bite? There's an old proverb that says one should not wish the hunter well as he departs, and I would say that Mynheer Leflerus has not done that, and on his account then, we can try our fortune with all the more confidence. Who goes with me at midnight against Pavaosa?"

Those who lay dying sat up in their beds when they heard the lunatic shouts that followed this speech, and they thought the town was taken, and joined in the jubilation with their weak voices. Darkness fell again, and Georg van der Does led the preacher, now bent low, out of the raging army and to safety.

8

On Behalf of Lieutenant Pedro Tellez, Camilla Drago Declines a Request

The southern stars shone most peacefully down upon this arena of so many unleashed passions, of so much fear, want, pain, and anger, but the preacher and the young warrior did not look up till they had left behind them the camp and the last line of sentries. They strode silently arm in arm up the hill, until the mad tumult had died away to a hollow murmur, and then they stood there and turned around, and below them lay the besieged Spanish town, the noisy Dutch camp, and the sea with its illumined fleet. They both grabbed hold of their brows, the old man and the young one alike, and labored to wrest themselves from the stupor that held them fast: the young man's pulse was still hammering violently from the dreadful rigors of the last futile attack, and the preacher had likewise fought his battle and lost.

The more agitated, however, was Georg van der Does. By rights he ought to have screamed the loudest at the reverend gentleman and assaulted him, for his young, impetuous nature would have made him the last man to turn away from those obstinate, defiant Spanish walls; but now painfully laboring to catch his breath, he stood here beside the old man, and gazed down into the wild, chaotic depths of darkness and firelight and did not know why he had sided with this stern admonisher and preacher of misfortune.

Like the others, Georg felt the effects of this strange, disastrous climate; the merciless star had imprinted its stamp on him as well; he too felt enervation creep through his veins and bones, and the last few weeks had accomplished what fifty northern winters could not have—they had exhausted him. He had been overcome by a weariness that was at the same time a great uneasiness that could find neither bed nor lodging and ate away at him like the most fatal disease.

"You've sat yourself down on a formidable nest of ants, Reverend Sir!" he said to his companion. "Whew, you went off like a Gianibelli fire ship,* but you've not saved Antwerp for all that. Whatever were you thinking? We'd set our teeth to gnawing the ground before we'd abandon this heap of Spanish stones."

"My son, I understand quite well that it was not wise to speak at that moment as I did. You had come home to your tents, exasperated and angry, and I only increased your exasperation, but—it is indeed as I said. I know! I know! a shudder has come over me and a strange spirit is in me—I spoke the truth—the Lord wants to humble our pride, throw us down in our arrogance; but it is as it always is: they have eyes to see and see not, ears to hear and hear not. Triumphant conquerors have become gluttons, blasphemers, and children of Satan; I would give my own life a hundred times over if I could but sweep them up with a broom this very night and drive them onto their ships—"

"There you go again!" Georg cried. "But perhaps you'll have your way soon enough. Let us take Pavaosa, and you will see how quickly we turn our backs on this oven. But how can you think that I could go without having wished good day to my playmate there inside? That would indeed be something! I recently saw her white gown upon the walls, and it was as if I had been struck between the eyes. It may not matter much to you, Reverend Sir, whether we take Pavaosa or not, but I must enter, over trenches and ramparts, through the breach or through the gate, and it shall happen, believe you me!"

*Exploding fire ships to defend the port of Antwerp from an attack by the Duke of Parma in 1585, designed by the military engineer Federigo Gianibelli. The ships were partially effective but failed in their purpose. Raabe had this from Schiller's history and its continuation by Curths.

Dismayed and shocked, the Reverend Heinrich Leflerus lifted his hands to heaven.

"Oh God most good," he called; "what has this war done to your world? What terrors you speak through the mouths of babes, and they know it not! The living heart has become as stone; those who ought approach one another with flowers in their hands, extend instead the most dreadful suffering, even death itself with laughing mouths—"

"I don't wish to do any harm to the Lady Camilla," said Georg doggedly. But the preacher cried out:

"And for years she sat at the feet of his mother; she dwelt in the house of his father, and in his breast there is not one spark of mercy for her—no compassion for her in her need. He has seen it with his own eyes, how the bodies of women and children lay in the streets of Palma and the burning beams crashed down upon them; he knows that he can behold that same sight this very night, tomorrow, the day after tomorrow down below in Pavaosa; but it matters not to him; he thinks not, he feels not; he knows naught but his savage cry: Forward! Forward! Attack! Attack! Where he cannot assault the world with sword and pistol, it has no meaning for him!"

Georg van der Does stood there with clenched fists; now he shouted:

"What do you know about it? I certainly have thought of her; I have rejoiced to see her again, but we Dutch lads on the high seas have not been taught to make fine speeches. And I grant I've not had time always to be thinking of her either; but I have always wished her the best and every joy in life. What can I do about this war? Ask her countrymen, they know more than I what to say. How can evil befall her if I am at her side at the right moment? I shall find her in all the tumult, and no one shall touch her nor say so much as a wicked word to her. The only awful thing would have been for my uncle to have sent me home with Mynheer Jan Gerbrants."

"There is no use in speaking to this generation," the pastor muttered. "The Lord wished to make them of iron, he has laid them and their nation between hammer and anvil. The Lord alone can take their armor from them."

He turned away from the town and the camp and gazed with a sigh at the dark mountains and up at the stars; whereas the young man's attention seemed all at once to be riveted exclusively on the town and castle of Pavaosa; he had flung himself in a wild gesture onto the scorched grass, he lay there motionless and stared across the steep slope to the Spanish lights in the valley. And so both men remained for a considerable time, until Georg's astonished cry caused the pastor to turn his eyes back to look down.

Georg van der Does had leaped to his feet:

"What is that? There! there! Mynheer Leflerus, look, look!"

A red light was coming from the town of Pavaosa; Don Francisco Meneses had carried out his plan, and the insubstantial cottages and houses of the colony were in flames. With indescribable swiftness, the glow flew along the shore, across the sea and the Dutch fleet, and both camp and fleet answered this Spanish act of desperation with a cry of rage that knew no end, for they saw the largest and best part of the riches they hoped to gain perishing before their eyes.

"Ho there, that's nasty trick!" Georg van der Does shouted and without looking around for his companion, he bounded in great leaps down the mountainside's rocky rubble and underbrush and toward the camp. More slowly, yet likewise as fast as his legs would carry him, the pastor of Ysselmünde followed, and soon they were both borne away again on the wave of anger within the besieging camp.

But while the Dutch ran about in confusion or stood there dumbfounded and openmouthed, their black allies were already on the ramparts of the town of Pavaosa, dancing a fantastic shadow dance against the fiery glow that rose from it. With a howl of triumph they had thrown themselves on the ladders, like tigers they had climbed the palisades and walls, they were the masters of the spaces spared by the flames; their missiles whizzed among the populace as they withdrew to the castle, and one arrow from one of those quivers struck the governor, Don Francisco Meneses, on the drawbridge to the Del Oriente Tower. The governor grabbed the bright-feathered shaft, it broke off in his twitching hand and left its barb in his hip. One woman, dragging a howling eight-year-old boy behind her, was still stumbling across the bridge; then the chains and pulleys creaked and groaned, the heavy planks lifted, and the Indian arrows, still in search of their retreating oppressors, drove into the wood or bounced off the iron and stone.

At the edge of the trench that separated the burning town from the castle, the first whites appeared in the swarm of black warriors.

Georg van der Does swung himself up onto a pile of stones and called out:

"Mynheer van Meneses, surrender your castle! You can hold it no longer! The admiral offers you your life and freedom, with all the honors of war; Your Excellency, for your own sake and that of your people, surrender the castle!"

Along the walls of the castle, amid Spanish swords, halberds and muskets, the figure of a woman rose up:

"Don Francisco Meneses is with God!—The commander is Pedro Tellez! Remember Palma and Gomera; we shall not surrender Pavaosa!"

"Camilla! Camilla Drago!" Georg van der Does shouted; but from the far side of the trench the only answer he received was musket fire.

9

Spain, Close Ranks!

Inside the castle of Pavaosa, they had no time left to bury corpses in the earth with Christian rites, and had they found the time, there would have been no room: they sprinkled their dead with holy water, said a brief prayer over them and hurled them from the walls into the sea, which played with them for a while and then cast them onto the shore, to the Dutch. The only person buried in the court-yard of the castle with all military ceremony was the brave old viceroy, Don Francisco Meneses;—Mynheer van der Does had established his headquarters in an undamaged house at the furthest end of the ruins of the burned-out town.

Of all the subjects, male and female, of King Philip III still remaining in the castle of Pavaosa, Señora Rosamunda Bracamonte was the only one who proved equal to every turn of circumstance. She did not stride about in ecstasy through the heroic calamity, as did Doña Camilla Drago; she did not allow herself to be pushed forward like a machine, as did Señor Pedro Tellez, only then to flail away in desperation: she had not forgotten how to speak and told the wicked world her opinion, just as she had told it once to Colonel Heraugière. She wore her skirts tucked up, her sleeves rolled back and carried her nose very high—thus did she await the fleet from Coruña, keep discipline among the women and children of the colonists and follow her mistress wherever the lady led her: onto the walls in the face of the attacking foe, to the beds of the wounded and those ill with fever, to the seaward walls for the dreadful funeral rites.—

Don Francisco Meneses had in his last moments taken hold of his niece's hand with an iron grip:

"My poor child, my poor girl!. . . Call Pedro Tellez . . . let him lower the banner . . . our rule of Saint Thomas is at an end!" he had groaned, and without releasing her hand from the painful pressure of the stiffening fingers, Doña Camilla Drago had turned to those standing about:

"Señores, señores, oh tell him that Pavaosa is not yet lost, that the flag of Spain has not yet been cast beneath the feet of the Dutch, that we desire no other fate than that of Gratiosa and Palma!"

"Long live the king!" cried those in the tightly crowded circle, but an old soldier, named Juan Lodoiro, bent down to the dying man and said:

"Señor Gobernador, if it cannot be otherwise, then go your way in peace; the fleet will come soon enough to find us at our posts, if not, then take this comfort as a farewell, that those in the camp yonder have the *madorca**and that, even if we must follow after them, we shall drag them behind us on a gruesome chain. Remember, your grace, what a solemn escort we gave Prince Don Juan d'Austria in Namur† in '78; may it be a consolation to you that we shall march down these stairs in a still mightier throng."

Don Francisco did not remember. He took no further consolation from the events of '78. He died, and Camilla Drago stumbled away from his corpse and onto the walls of the castle:

"Spain! Spain! Spain forever!"

This was no longer the Camilla who had swung in the hammock,

---

*An infectious pestilence, called *la madorca* in Portuguese.
†Don Juan was buried with much pomp in the cathedral of Namur, now in Belgium; later his body was moved to Spain by order of Philip II.

nor even she who from Abreojos Tower had watched the Dutch squadrons upon the sea. She looked now like the lovely, yet deadly genius of this blazing island; it was as if the pernicious power of the tropical sun had found its body in hers; not Pedro Tellez, but Camilla Drago in league with the fire of heaven defended the castle of Pavaosa!

"And here you are at the watch again, my dear!" said Señora Bracamonte. "Oh Lord Jesus, it's getting to be of no importance what becomes of one. The scoundrels! the scoundrels! I am an old woman and have a good heart, but nothing gives me greater pleasure now than to pour a pot of boiling water on their heads. It's a miracle what all one can forget and what all one can bear, if one has one's job to do. And now those heretics and rebels have the *madorca* around their necks, thank God;—mine is truly a gentle and peaceable nature, but I wish them this misfortune, and I wish it above all for that portly rascal, Admiral van der Does; he has earned it a thousand times over for our and our good uncle's sake!"

10

The *Madorca*

Back now to the Dutch! They had Pavaosa, the town, and the *madorca* had them. The word of the preacher had come true, the angel of death had blown across Assyria, and if the fever chastised them with whips, the *madorca* now chastised them with scorpions:* the *madorca* was the true plague of this land, before which even the natives shrank back in terror when it appeared among these strange, blond-haired warriors. It melted the muscles and fat from the body, it knew no pity, and only flight from beneath the vertical rays of the sun could have still saved this wreck of an army. But their intoxication still held, they still did not have the castle of Pavaosa; they had found seventy heavy cannon on the ramparts of the burned-

*1 Kings 12:11.

out town and they directed them along with their own cannon at the castle; they knew that endless riches, the spoils of many years from the Gold and Ivory Coasts, lay piled behind those defiant walls: except for the pastor of Ysselmünde, there was no one who could utter the words "Holland, retreat!"

"Attack, Holland, attack!" echoed over and reechoed about the Spanish fortress.

And the *madorca* attacked the strongest, the mightiest first; it broke out among the Frisians, and the third day after the burning of the town, it grabbed Admiral van der Does, who towered a head above his entire army, by the hair and broke his sword arm. Death needed both arms, however, to embrace this giant and had to set both knees on his chest before mynheer yielded. He fought desperately, and like his warriors around the castle of Pavaosa, he battled for his life. But the *madorca* accomplished its task more quickly than the Dutch force on Saint Thomas accomplished theirs; by the second day after the onset of illness, the admiral grew quieter, and Mynheer Henricus Leflerus had easier sport with the *madorca* as he took his seat, Bible in hand, beside the admiral's pillow.

Now and then, officers of all ranks would crowd around the house serving as headquarters; Cornelius Lensen came ashore from the fleet to hear the last will of the dying man; Gerhard Storms van Wena reported that the castle would hold at most until the following night.

Georg van der Does sat at the foot of his uncle's bed, and whenever the pastor's gaze would glide from the Bible to that young man, it held fast, in great affliction, to the dull countenance and sunken figure. Every hour was numbered as a year by this unhappy Nordic army on the terrible island of Saint Thomas; the same restless exhaustion, the same feverish weariness shown from every face that shoved its way in at the windows or door of the cottage.

"Then take the wretched place and don't worry about me!" the admiral cried. "Get to work, gentlemen, and don't waste useless courtesies on a doomed man. Attack and cast it down;—get to your ships as soon as possible, and speak a good word for me back home. Take the place as lustily as you can, it's how I did things;—fate has shoved us into this blazing oven, grab hold and take whatever you can get, and be gone before the hatch is closed for good. Good gentlemen and brave comrades, go to it once again with all your broadsides, Cornelius! go to it once again with sword and dagger, Mynheer Storms! Be gone, Georg, my lad; the beast in my brain and guts has evil tentacles; Mynheer Heinrich Leflerus will attend me like a governess; he's promised the gentlemen of the States General he would. Forward, by land and sea for old Holland!"

"We'll take the place and use it to build a proud monument over your body, depend on it," said Cornelius Lensen.

"Bones and stones helter-skelter!" shouted Mynheer van Wena. "Hold fast to your bedposts till midnight; those within have lost their game, despite their sun. Hold on until midnight, and you shall hear the States cry 'victoria' once more at least, and if you don't want to stay on any longer then, why you can laugh and reserve quarters for the rest of us."

"So shall it be!" said the admiral, and each and every officer shook his hand and then stepped outside the cottage. Only the dying man's nephew and the old preacher stayed behind.

"There they go, with bronze and steel," said the pastor of Ysselmünde. "No earthly breath can melt their hard souls. Behold, oh hero, oh iron warrior, oh mighty commander of a hundred sails, behold, Mynheer van der Does, twilight falls, yet a little hour and it will be darkest night; you will not see again the daylight you have cursed. You are girded about with hundreds and thousands, but hearken how their shouts and clanging swords die away, it grows silent in your camp. Their words ring in your ear like the blaring of trumpets: Wait but until midnight, and your soul will depart hence with jubilation and triumph. But I, the servant of the Lord, say unto you, who advanced here over waves and over land with your thousands: You shall depart at midnight alone—alone, and though with the thunder of heaven they cry victory from the walls of the foe and their voices bear your name upward to the God's own miraculous flaming cross that illuminates night in this place, it will be as the ripple of the last wave ebbing from the sands of north Holland and no man shall hear it. Admiral, another cry shall ascend to heaven with that cry of victory and shall not fade away in your ear. They strike the weak with the strong, the women and children with the men, and you have had not one small word of mercy for them. 'Strike hard, cast them over, bring them down!' has been your word throughout your life; oh great admiral, you have shouted in the face of your foes on every sea, will you now cast that cry like a grappling hook on board of heaven as well? Mynheer van der Does, on every sea you have been answered by a like cry from your foe armed for battle; but behold now, it has grown dark; no one answers you now, your voice fades in this desolate world: fold, then, your hands for prayer and speak: Mercy, Lord, bestow your grace upon me and upon the wretched castle of Pavaosa;—have mercy, Lord, on *all* the dying, save the innocent from the hands loosed upon them, and—"

Georg van der Does took the old man's hand:

"He hears you not, Reverend Sir. Gaze upon his face."

"Then you shall hear me, lad!" cried the preacher, rising from his chair. "Go out for him and say: the lives I spare this night shall fall in the balance for him before the chair of the Almighty; the virgin whom I snatch from the hands of the savage black, the poor child that I bear from the flames, shall belong unto him; and when at midnight his officers of war shall cry out the words of Dutch victory in his name, your silence shall be of more value to him than all the thunder of their cannon and of more worth than all the triumphant shouts of this world."

Georg van der Does silently drew his pistols from his belt, he removed his sword from his side and laid his weapons at the foot of his uncle's bed. Mynheer Heinrich Leflerus laid his hand upon the young head:

"Go and spare them;—it is the most beautiful night of your life."

11

The Last Grain of Sand

For the last time Camilla Drago climbed down from Abreojos Tower as darkness again removed the sea from her gaze. The tower was near collapse; every wall of the castle lay in ruin, toward both land and sea; the deep trench that separated the castle from the burned-out town was half-filled with rubble and brickwork, and Mynheer van Wena was grimly correct in his claim that the last hour had come for the fortress of Pavaosa. The fleet from Coruña had not come today either; no further message from Captain Giralto had reached those under siege.

"We are lost!" Camilla said as she descended the half-demolished stairs of the tower. "There will be no rescue."

In the courtyard of the castle a large fire was burning, and it cast its flickering glow on the walls, on the vaulted ceilings and arched passages, on the faces and figures of the people crowded there. The sultry stench of pestilence could find no way out of the besieged quarters; clouds of virulent insects hung about the flames, and no matter how many of them perished in the fire, an equal number swarmed anew from out of the night. The Spanish and Portuguese soldiers and colonists, what was left of them and their wives and children, sat and stood, squatted and lay in a circle, and they all, except for infants and suckling babes, likewise knew that the fleet from Coruña could not arrive in time, that there was no help left for them in this world. The marrow of their bones had been eaten away, their powder had run out, the well was almost dry. Some of them prayed, the others wrung their hands in mute despair, the bravest and strongest gnashed their teeth; they had all climbed down from the walls into this ring of misery, and only Señora Bracamonte alongside Señor Pedro Tellez and the other officers were still leaning here and there against the shattered ramparts—the last watch of Pavaosa.

Doña Camilla Drago slowly strode into the glare of the fire, and the bearded men, the women overwhelmed by terror, the poor children, looked up at her as if they expected a miracle from her, a word, a smile, that like the nod from some wonder-working icon would transform their horror into the exultation of rescue and redemption.

But Camilla lowered her gaze and said:

"We must die, the king cannot help us; there is nothing but the desolate sea, the night and the enemy all around us;—above us is God; let us die as Catholic Christians! It is the will of God, who led us to this island and has decreed this hour of doom for us."

They did not scream aloud, they did not tear at their hair nor beat their breasts; they simply hung their heads lower, the sick pulled their blankets better over them, and the mothers hugged their children more tightly.

"Where is Señora Bracamonte, Señor Lodoiro?" Camilla asked.

"She is with the commandant, on watch upon the Moor Bastion," was his answer, and following these directions, the woman went looking for her old friend and sentry. She found her alone; Pedro Tellez had found himself another, remoter spot where he could write his report before the Dutch storm would make a muddle of his numbers.

Camilla kissed the loyal, courageous old woman.

"Soon, for the very first time we shall have a true homeland from which no one can ever banish us," she said, and the señora placed her hand over her lips:

"Be still! not a word more!"

"There is nothing more to say," said Doña Camilla Drago. "We have had time enough to prepare ourselves,—we can be silent now."

They stood upon the wall from nine until eleven; then they sat down on a heap of stones, and Camilla laid her head in the señora's lap. The night itself was very silent too; the camp of the enemy was hushed; all that stirred was an abundance of animal life. Large shining beetles and butterflies whirred about, and the voice of the Atlantic Ocean was louder by night than by day.

Everything was quiet in the castle of Pavaosa as well; but just short of midnight, a baby awoke at its mother's breast and began to cry, and the mother sang it a lullaby, as though it were still necessary.

At one o'clock it was all over. For the last time Admiral van der Does heard the thunder of battle; he raised himself up and then sank back, never to rise up again. Leaning in the frame of the door of the house, stood the Reverend Heinrich Leflerus. He watched the red glow of flames play about the ramparts of the castle and the tumult of the fighting throng on the wall. The shrill war cries of the blacks all but drowned out the shouts of battle from his countrymen and the death screams of the Spaniards, and the pastor of Ysselmünde knelt on the threshold and tried to pray; but he could only wring his hands.

The unarmed lad, whose soul he had won, had thrown himself at the forefront of the massed troops assaulting the breech of the doomed castle of Pavaosa.

"We came to take on water, and have been given blood to drink!" the pastor groaned, and his brow almost touched the earth.

At one o'clock it was all over, but Heinrich Leflerus waited in vain beside the body of the admiral for a message from the victors. No one came; Mynheer van der Does's soul had passed over into the great mystery, and no one gave it a thought. The pastor got up and strode on uncertain legs through the rubble of the town as far as the gates of the castle, now flung wide. He fell in with the throng on the lowered drawbridge; he barely escaped the dangers of being thrown down into the trench or crushed underfoot by the frenzied mob. In the arch of the gateway he met Mynheer Gerhard Storms, who clapped him on the shoulder and shouted:

"There you are, Reverend Sir. Well, we've done good work, and I do hope you'll have praise for us in your sermon tomorrow. Hey there, Moors, Frisians, and Dutchmen, make way for the Reverend! Ah yes, Mynheer Leflerus, it was a nasty piece of business, my men had to wait too long at the gates and grew impatient."

The old man stood in the courtyard of the castle of Pavaosa, he lifted his arms to heaven and simply cried: "Lord! Oh Lord, Lord!"

12

The Voices of Victory

They dragged on board of their men-of-war more than a hundred cannons, elephants tusks, cotton, great quantities of sugar, gold dust and gold coins, booty from the ladies' chambers, costly armor and weapons from the men's, hides of tigers and lions and last of all—the *madorca*. As if in flight, the Dutch force left the rubble of the town and castle of Pavaosa, the island of Saint Thomas, and one thousand two hundred corpses were tipped from board into the sea during the first fourteen days of the voyage. The fleet was divided a second time. Mynheer Gerhard Storms was to sail for Brazil with seven ships and the rest with the booty be brought home by Cornelius Lensen, the *schout-bij-nacht*. But Mynheer van Wena also died of the plague, and there was no one who could assume his place; his ships returned to the *schout-bij-nacht*, and after a mournful, stormy voyage the fleet returned to the mouth of the Maas at the beginning of the year 1600. "On many a man-of-war not six healthy men were found, and only two officers and Mynheer Henricus Leflerus, the chaplain, returned in full vigor," lament the reports from The Hague and Amsterdam.

The fleet from Coruña did not engage the Dutch, to the advantage of both. It had come as far as Gomera and had put to sea again to protect the islands of the West Indies, when it too, scattered by the storm and badly battered, had to seek renewed protection in Spanish harbors.

Three days after the departure of the enemy from Saint Thomas, Captain José Giralto once more anchored the *Corona de Aragon* under the demolished walls of Pavaosa, but no salute thundered from Abreojos Tower, and no one came to greet him as he strode down the plank onto land. He was not a soft man, this Captain Giralto, and he had seen many awful and dreadful things in his life with never a dampness about the eye;—as he stood now among these blood-spattered ruins, he wept.

He and his people attempted to cover the bodies of their countrymen with earth; but they buried but a few children's corpses and then desisted, for the equatorial sun still beat down upon Pavaosa, and the briefest sojourn was certain death. And so Captain Giralto only raised the banner of Spain again over the rubble and, beside it, in order at least to lighten his heart somewhat and "to honor the memory of Señora Bracamonte y Mugadas Criades," had seven blacks hanged whom he had found in the streets of the burned-out town. Then he raised anchor again and steered for Santiago in the Cape Verdes, to give them the news of how he had found Pavaosa and then departed from it—so that perhaps in due course, if conditions were favorable, a faint rumor of it might arrive at Madrid or the Escorial and elicit from Don Philip III the shrug of kings.—

How pale, how irrelevant, how insignificant all this has grown in the course of centuries! Two or three lines in a Spanish or Dutch chronicle, a page or a half of one in a scholarly German history of the United Netherlands, two voices for the poet!

A black girl sat on a outcropping rock under the palms of Saint Thomas. She wore a crown of feathers, and with it the tattered, stained, singed dress of a Spanish lady, and about her wrist a golden ring, the masterpiece of a goldsmith of Cordova. With a wild, laughing gaze she looked out over the sea and sang:

"Smoke rises from the shore, and my eye sees the great ships no more, they have grown small in the distance, the water has swallowed them up. The chains have fallen from the necks of my people, the hands of the warriors are red and the hearts of the maidens joyful. My people saw the great ships come from over the sea, they stood upon the mountains in great terror, but their terror has become exultation; the people of the sea gave their hand to my father and my brothers, and the hands of the warriors in the mountains are red and filled with riches. I hear no more the thunder of the white sorcerers; the vulture flies above the place of their tents, and the vulture's wife flies above the city of the those who attacked;—my brothers have thrown the torch into the fortress of the master; with my sisters I have danced about the slain, and the beautiful, white mistress had to give up this golden ring from her cold, stiff arm. The black people of the mountains have danced about the flaming grave of the prince of the sea people. They set fire to the house that held his corpse that no one might make a mockery of his bones. The great battle is over;—silent—silent—silent; the black ships have spread their wings; I see them no more. My father walks with bow and club along the shore of the sea and waits for what the waves will bring;—the vulture and the eagle know and laugh, and my heart is like their flight on high. We lay hidden in the caves and ravines of the mountains, for the ruler's arm was mighty in the fortress beside the water; he beat my brothers with the whip, and my sisters had to serve his maidens; but as the arrow flies from the bush, Abambu, the god of death, came upon him. The people of the sea have triumphed, but departed into the sun; Onarika, the snake, wound round them with a thousand coils and crushed their hearts. I see the magic ships no more: the staff of the king lies again in the hand of my father; the waves dance in the sunlight about my land; the gods of my people have saved us: I bear the ring of the young white princess; I am the king's daughter, and my brothers and playmates are building me my hut of green branches where the proud house of the white girl lies in ruin over her and her people!"——

Through a gray winter fog, an old man, clad in a black clerical coat, walks up and down along the shore by Scheveningen—the pastor of Ysselmünde, Mynheer Henricus Leflerus.

He had sat all that long morning in the house of Mynheer van der Does, between Georg's father and mother, and had had to tell the mourning parents over and over again about the calamitous expedition to the equator undertaken by the gentlemen of the mighty States General, about the brave admiral, about Georg and Camilla Drago. He was a good preacher, but a poor storyteller, and had had to keep the greatest horror within in his own heart: the parents could only wail and weep.

In the afternoon, around three o'clock, he could stand it no longer in the house. He walked through the garden and over the snow-covered meadow, where once the young Spanish prisoner had picked flowers and chased after butterflies with the wild Dutch lad. Slowly he wandered along the canal, ever further toward the sea. Now he stood on the dunes and watched the waves of the North Sea roll onto the beach; now he strode back and forth in the fog, shaken with cold, full of the terrors of remembering—it brought him close to madness to have to think of the sun of Saint Thomas here, on such a day as this.

"What shall I do from now on, now that I have returned home from such a journey?" he said. "Where shall I fly before the ghosts that pursue me? There is no peace anywhere; the dead reach out their hands to me on every side. On Pavaosa, Pavaosa, there is no prayer, no cry, no pleading, no labor, and no effort to protect me from the sound of your name. Oh Pavaosa, your walls lie fallen and yet they shall hold me prisoner until the grave; there is no rescue from those ramparts. Oh Pavaosa, the flames that crashed above you have long since died, but not in my breast. I see them lying there, your children, oh Pavaosa, and my soul is buried with them, like the lad whom I sent to you without armor or sword, spreading his arms wide to you. I saw your youth, your loveliness, your beauty torn and dismembered—woe is me! I saw the smoke of your ruins float away over the waters and the peaks of your mountains sink into the waves: your name, oh Saint Thomas, chased the ships of my people across the ocean; it cast us up again, like men lost, onto the shores of our homeland. We went forth, men and warriors, we left our manhood and our strength with you, oh Saint Thomas. Those of us who have returned home creep about like shades and fear the sight of the sea; for, behold, the waves snap and leap like dogs and bay your name, Pavaosa, Pavaosa!"

Translated by John E. Woods

Celtic Bones

Wilhelm Raabe

Trapped in the rain! . . . Who, at the mention of those words, does not feel the phantom of memory rise within the soul, the memory of an hour—two hours—a day—two, three, four—eight days, when he or she was also trapped in the rain on a street corner, under an archway, with a friend, male or female, in a village tavern, up on the Brocken, the Inselberg, the Rigi, or the Schafberg?*

It is a dismal picture—trapped in the rain! It comes creeping toward you, gray, grim and grouchy, sends out a hundred chilling, damp tentacles to wrap about your heart and is as difficult to shake off as any other unpleasant, uncomfortable, and untimely happenstance of this world.

As we drove out of Ischl, the lovely ladies were promenading along the esplanade in the brilliant sunshine, and not a single sufferer of hemorrhoids, scrofula, or glandular ailments but what had borne his or her complaint out into the fresh air; even their Royal and Imperial Highnesses† had gone out for a ride.

In the vicinity of Laufen,** with its shrine to the most lovely and gracious Mary in the Shade, that other very beautiful—though indeed very willful—lady, Mother Nature, pulled a veil of fog over her face, and as our boat pulled out into the lake, the veil and our hopes for a beautiful day were all turned to water. It seems that rain most delights in falling on the most pleasant regions; but perhaps it was also the fault of the gentle poet traveling with us, who, you see, had been born in the sign of Aquarius.

---

*The Brocken is a mountain in the Harz, where the Witches' Sabbath was supposed to take place; the Inselberg a mountain in Thuringia; the Rigi a mountain range in Switzerland, and the Schafberg a mountain on St. Wolfgang Lake near Ischl.
†Kaiser Franz Joseph and his family spent summers in Ischl.
**A town near Ischl.

There were three of us, and the poet was, say what you will, the noblest among us; unfortunately his name was Krautworst and he came from Hanover; he did not, of course, admit gladly to either, but rather usually chose to present and represent himself as the author of "Life's Blossoms"—or on occasion, following the shining example of others equally oppressed by prosaic names and places of birth, Roderich von der Leine.* He had latched onto us at the Archduke Karl Inn in Linz and had kept a tenacious hold on me at least, raving about Linz and routinely letting drop mysterious hints that he had had quite some experiences there. His frequent day-dreamings and moonings gave rise to the assumption that he was on the verge of turning those experiences to poetic account; his lyric labor-pains often alarmed me somewhat, though they had less effect on the third of our number. This third person was, without representing himself as such, a mystery and as closed a man as the poet was openhearted and effusive. He signed hotel registers with a terse Zuckriegel; I had my doubts, however, whether this was his real name, until at the Three Ravens in Vienna, he got himself involved in a perfectly pointless argument, which brought him and me before the Royal and Imperial police, who required him to show his passport. He was indeed named Zuckriegel, of which fact he was not ashamed, and was assistant professor of anatomy at a small university in northern Germany, although both outwardly and inwardly he had much of the hangman about him. Only a person of his ill-tempered nature could have found it in his heart to pluck and tickle every nerve ending of such a good fellow as the poet by unrelenting mention of the hated name Krautworst.

Zuckriegel had undertaken this journey in order to visit the bones of the unidentified tribe at the Rudolf Tower above Hallstatt,† and if possible to steal a skull or some other superfluous skeletal remains for his osteological collection or, as he preferred to express it euphemistically, to appropriate them.

---

*Gottfried Keller satirized the fad of second-rate writers taking pretentious noms de plume in one of his Seldwyla novellas, *The Misused Love Letters,* written in the 1850s in Berlin but still unpublished at the time Raabe wrote this work.

†A town in Upper Austria where beginning in 1846 a prehistoric site was excavated that gave its name to the Hallstatt Culture. A dispute developed as to whether the bones were Celtic or Germanic. Raabe visited the site in 1859. The Rudolf Tower was built in 1299 by Emperor Albrecht to protect the local salt mines. All the place names in the story are authentic.

He loved to appropriate things for himself, as for instance the best seat in the coach, the best morsels from the tavern board, all the newspapers after dinner, and so on. On our "canoe" trip across Lake Hallstatt, he had appropriated the bench just behind the broad back and skirts of the charming boatwoman and sat there protected from the rain, while the wind blew it in our faces.

Despite the splendid summer weather, our trio had fared poorly in Ischl: the gentle poet being afflicted by the ravishingly dressed ladies, Zuckriegel by himself and by an American clergyman and his family, which, only a thin wall away, had exasperated him with their endless nightly prayers and adenoidal hymns; I had let myself be induced by the inscription on the spa-hotel (*"In sale et in sole omnia consistunt"*)* to try the nauseating salty brew and test its effect on my own constitution—a sound one, thank God—, and had subjected myself to its dangers, not without success.

The inscription on the statue of Hygeia†

> Earth's luckiest gift, 'tis said
> Is having your health today—
> To that I reply, ah nay!
> Far better, regain it instead,

gave me only a modicum of comfort; "regaining" my health after such an infernal pint was in no way as pleasant as my comfy condition prior to taking a rash sip from Hecate's cup.** We rented a fly, set Roderich von der Leine up on the box beside the driver, and, as already noted, drove out to the ever-gracious Virgin Mary in the Shade, and then, the rain over, on through Goisern and Sankt Agatha to Gosaumühle, where we climbed damply down and where Zuckriegel got entangled in a war of words with the driver, which we other two stayed out of, because we knew the charioteer was right and that he knew how to hold up his end.

We rented the canoe, which is to say a punt with a fat young lady and a boy, and were rowed across the lake by said boatwoman, whom the poet of "Life's Blossoms" "had imagined more picturesque," while I, for my poor part, had no regrets at that moment

---

* "Everything becomes firm in salt and sun."
† Bronze statue of the Greek goddess of health in Ischl.
** Hecate was the Greek goddess of ghosts and magic.

that the day had grown dark, for it matched the landscape. Had it not been for my two companions, the boy, and the boatwoman, most likely Virgil's shade would have risen up out of the black waters to offer his services as a guide on the further shores at his customary fee.

Yes, the water of the lake was black; black the precipitous cliffs lost in black clouds; none of us three tourists could be sure if, just behind that gloomy curtain of clouds, there did not begin an enlarged hell that encompassed *all* the major and minor malefactors added since September 14, 1321,* and was awaiting Roderich von der Leine to describe it anew. The man's name, Krautworst, would be no hindrance, inasmuch as Dante, when translated, means nothing more than "buckskin"; but Krautworst himself was a hindrance, since the eerily imposing scenery made not the least impression on him; he was freezing; he talked about changing his stockings, about his rheumatic toothache, and whined for a cup of tea.

Zuckriegel was already a different man: the proximity of the Celtic or whatever bones and his seat behind the walruslike back of our female Charon had put him in a easier frame of mind; at that moment he resembled less a hangman than a vagabond butcher; whether his seat also put him in an erotic frame of mind, I of course cannot say, but now and again it did seem so.

After a journey of some two hours, we became convinced first, that behind the curtain of fog and rain lay not the beginning of and entrance to the Inferno, but Hallstatt itself—or better, Hallstatt did not lie but rather, clung—, and second, that the fee for our journey was not going to be cheap. The canoe thrust onto land at the Seeauer;† and however erotic the frame of mind into which our solid boatwoman had put Zuckriegel, this did not in any way hinder him from getting into a squabble when it came to paying her.

Led by a waitress, we drippingly stalked across the dripping garden and into the guest house, and with teeth chattering Roderich ordered a cup of their hottest bouillon. Behind him the sea murmured, though without demanding him as its victim; on the contrary, it seemed sincerely glad to be rid of him. I drank coffee; Zuckriegel, however, decided to have a potent grog, the preparation

*Date of Dante's death.
†A hotel on the lakeshore.

of which he personally supervised in the kitchen, since he believed, and not unreasonably, that this remote nook of the world might not be up to preparing this pleasant drink correctly. He did not change his suit; *he* stayed as he was, and in the heated atmosphere of the taproom began softly to give off steam. The poet appeared after a short time, during which he had not been missed, but as if replaced by a substitute. He had driven out of Ischl in brilliant white from head to foot, now he presented himself in checked plaid from head to foot, and if it was his intention to cause a stir in Hallstatt, this getup was indeed suitable for achieving that end; it would have seemed the most natural thing in the world to see it moving along a tightrope strung from the top of the church steeple. All eyes present in the taproom virtually leapt from their sockets, and the waitress leapt into the kitchen with a quite uncivilized screech, whereupon a moment later a curious throng of noses appeared pressed flat against the panes of the dark sliding window next to the stove. The poet could be content with the impression he had elicited. And that he was, and filled the taproom with amazement a second time by drinking his bouillon like any other normal, nonchecked gentleman; they all appeared to have expected the opposite.

The heavens now revealed that their intentions toward us had been good; for if during our journey they had only dripped softly, now that we were safely housed at last, they showed no further constraint and opened the reserve gates. It was two o'clock, and it was raining cats and dogs; the innkeeper rejoiced at our presence in his establishment, and from his distant cranny an autochthon assured us that we were not the first people to have arrived in Hallstatt in such weather, nor would we most probably be the last to leave by weather just as foul. This aborigine was unfamiliar with *Faust* and was filled with amazement yet a third time as the checkered poet recited with hollow eyes and hollow voice:

"How wretched! wretched! not a soul will ever comprehend that more than *one* creature has sunk into the abyss of this misery, that the first did not settle the debt of all!"*

The anatomy professor brazenly took up the burden and asked in the words of Mephistopheles:

---

*This and the following two quotes are from the prose scene, "Gloomy Day; Field," in the first part of Goethe's *Faust*.

"Why do you do business with us, if you cannot follow through? . . . Have we forced ourselves on you or you on us? Go on, Herr Krautworst, go on, and don't look so cross! Surely I haven't *checked* your progress?"

Herr Krautworst did not go on, he was greatly annoyed by Zuckriegel's quotation, but could do nothing to counter it, and only some five minutes later, as the anatomist demanded the kitchen bulletin from the landlord, did he recall Faust's outraged cry: "Don't bare those ravenous teeth of yours at me that way! It disgusts me!"

It was too late to insert this additional quotation:—we ate our midday meal, I succeeded in establishing peace, though one armed with knife and fork, between the man of science and the man of poesy. But when, after the meal, the anatomist remarked: "Upon my word! this is truly a rain worthy of the *Muses' Almanac*; this is poet's weather, Herr Krautworst. If only it doesn't wash away my bones!" the poet shoved back his chair, grabbed for his umbrella, hung his plaid cape over his shoulders, and strode out the door with one devastating glance at the scoffer. It was as if with titanic contempt Prometheus had turned his back on the vulture. "For God's sake, go grab him!" Zuckriegel called to me. "Now I've gone and put him in just the mood to return in half an hour with all his experiences of Linz rhymed and metered. Just see if he doesn't have his revenge; hold onto him, bring him back, I'll apologize!"

"*You're* what I'd call a wonderful traveling companion," I said and followed after the good Roderich. In such weather, the anatomist was not to be borne *solus cum solo;** that burden was too heavy for the shoulders of any one man. From the door I could see how he placidly stretched himself out over three chairs and pulled out the book he'd brought along to read on the trip, a volume from Avé-Lallemant's history of German crooks and swindlers,† through the study of which he was eagerly preparing himself for his grand enterprise;—through a dark, low passage, I found my way into the open air, or into what can be termed the open air in Hallstatt, and at the entrance met my host, of whom I inquired what you could "see along Lake Hallstatt" in such weather.

---

*"Alone with one alone," from a saying that it is not to be presumed that the Lord's Prayer is being said when one person is alone with another.

†F. C. B. Avé-Lallemant's *German Crooks* appeared in four volumes from 1854 to 1862.

"Hallstatt!" said the innkeeper, and he was right, three times over; Hallstatt is a remarkable sight by any weather. Nowhere in the world perhaps are there so many flights of steps in such small space as this. You have the impression that some giant hand has taken the town and vigorously jiggled and joggled it, flung it against the boulders rising perpendicularly from the lake—and that it stuck there. It's said the sun never reaches it two months out of the year, and I can believe it. Where the roofs stop, the streets begin; in no city on earth must it be as dangerous to drink a drop too much as here. You get dizzy climbing up, and dizzy climbing down;—even if you're not in your cups, you're hardly sure on your feet, and the delight you feel whenever you peek out between two gray house walls or through whatever hole you find in the masonry and rocks, and behold the surface of the lake and the Steier Alps on the far shore, is always accompanied by a certain uneasiness, a close cousin of the nightmare. In Hallstatt, the houses have the right to get drunk; Providence watches over them and keeps them out of harm's way in the most impossible places; if however, one of these houses should ever fall—something the aforementioned Providence is sure to prevent—, it would undoubtedly take all its companions with it into the abyss, and the whole place would collapse like a house of cards, though with more of a boom. Baedeker remarks quite correctly that you can find neither horse nor wagon in Hallstatt, and you can only marvel that that great tourist looked for either in the place. I didn't even see a single jackass. Since, however, my host had called it to my attention, I sought out the town's millstream and, once set gently on the proper path, I arrived at the romantic brook to find Roderich von der Leine standing—notebook in hand and a silver pen to his melodic lips—in a dark archway beside the spray and splash and surrounded by an attentive, though amazed circle of older and younger Hallstatters of both sexes. Not wishing to ruin either his mood nor mine, I postponed my visit to this famous millstream for another time and for now yielded uncontested possession of its courses to the poet—one ought not disturb Diana at her bath, nor the poet, however enticing the opportunity.

I bashfully withdrew and ended up via a circuitous path at the newly erected Protestant church, which fulfilled its purpose nicely and which after such a long struggle to get it built ought to have given me great satisfaction; but as it was locked, I left it unvisited and turned my way instead toward the Catholic church.

Catholic churches are always open, and you can always find your way to them, if you search diligently, concerning which fact Roderich von der Leine, or, as I may call him here, Krautworst of Hanover, could offer remarkable evidence from his own store of experience.

Stairs, stairs, stairs! Up, down, up! Wet walls covered with luxuriant, very healthy wall vegetation, overhanging bushes of all sorts dripping away—a cemetery of splendid beaded green, old and new gravestones and crosses, natural and artificial flowers drenched with rain, golden spangles and ribbons, a cemetery with a view across a low wall, a cemetery with a view across the most marvelous lake to the "Dead Mountains"—and I rejoiced that I need not write a poem and had no reputation to uphold like the author of "Life's Blossoms," but instead, once I had drunk my eyes full of this beauty chastely veiled in rain, could quietly retract my umbrella and my aesthetic antennae, and visit the interior of the exquisite old chapel. I do not know in what year and by what artist the altar shrine was carved, nor does it matter to me in the least, just as it didn't matter at all to the old woman kneeling before it. I sat down in a dimly lit pew and listened to the murmurs of the old woman and the chink of the drops falling from the Gothic-arched windows outside and to the sough of the rain in the trees, and offered no resistance as Zuckriegel and Krautworst gradually faded to mythic personages within my soul and I myself became something with no meaning for real life, for the world of business and offices. I vanished before my own eyes during those magical minutes—and earnestly protest any thought that I might have fallen asleep; I knew quite clearly and without being in the least bit startled what was happening as the old woman ended her prayers, hobbled over to me, and held her open, bony hand under my nose. Nor did I dream that her name was Dominika Schönrammer and her son's Seppel Schönrammer, and that with many an anxious tear she told me the reason for her appeal to my good heart and my purse, which was that said Seppel was at present not at home, but yonder—behind the mountains— down below—in Italy, defending his country for his emperor.*

And all at once I recalled that we were dating letters with 1859

---

*In the war between Austria and France in Northern Italy in 1859, which prevented Raabe from traveling to Italy. He was annoyed at the poor performance of the Austrians.

and that I had left Vienna and fled to the mountains only because I
wanted to rid my soul of this calamity for a few hours at least. Ah,
dissolute Vienna—in all its misery it could still amuse, as it tried to
find comfort amid accumulating disaster. While young, robust Italia
leapt out of its diapers and tossed its bottle away, hitting its old
grouchy nursemaid Austria on the nose, Vienna—not, as is well-
known, the most moral of the world's cities—busied itself with the
study of statistical tables on the morals of France, finding its comfort
in the loosening of all bonds of morality in that Gallic nation and
awaiting its salvation in the decreased population that inevitably
resulted from such abominable depravity. Unfortunately I cannot say
what sort of medal the clever young man received who first provided
the great minds of Austria with this splendidly plausible theory. He
certainly deserved one.

But Seppel? Seppel Schönrammer?! Can we let this Joseph
Schönrammer elude us? A cemetery with a view of Lake Hallstatt, a
poor, old mother beneath the weeping heavens—a pale, charming
rustic lass who now climbs the steps to the church to bring a
consecrated candle to the Virgin Mary and assist the old mother in
her pleas for the life of her son,—three pages of manuscript, which,
quite apart from any pecuniary advantage, would cause the value of
our auctorial stock to soar in every gentle female breast,—oh,
Roderich von der Leine, oh Rodrigo, Rodrigo!

Sad to say—sad, not only for the ladies, but for me as well: such
literary pathos cannot be executed at this point. The melting emotions of love appear to have been quite foreign to Seppel's breast to
date; upon *this* "unplayed piano" those "first consecrating silver
tones"* had not yet sounded. Seppel Schönrammer had left behind
no young bride perishing with worry and pain; but he had cursed
like hell as he had been forced to march off with knapsack, shooting
iron, and mess tin to defend what others had married together. And
in his usually quite unsuspecting breast had arisen some nasty
suspicions about that mess tin; ah, and they proved true, the mess
tin was to remain as empty as Seppel's heart and skull, and only its
hollow rattle against his knapsack proved its indispensability for a
brave and properly outfitted Austrian *miles impeditus*† whether on
the march or in battle.

---

*Cited from Schiller's *Cabals and Love*, act 4, scene 7.
†"Soldier hindered by his burden."

And though I may now entertain no hope of moving my readers, male and female, by this episode of my sojourn in Hallstatt, the old woman's tale moved me quite deeply nonetheless, and I gave her one of those gulden notes that the government has had printed in quantities which, while not exceeding the need, do exceed arrangements agreed upon.*

With best wishes for one another and for Joseph off in Lombardy, we said our farewells; with a last glance over the wall, I left the cemetery and descended again to the Seeauer, driven by a need to inquire how Zuckriegel had borne the burdens of his existence during my absence. Needless to say, the rain still fell steadily.

My excellent sense of direction—which never came in handier than in Hallstatt on Lake Hallstatt—led me back to the hotel with few detours, and passing through the aforementioned back gate and dark passage, I arrived safe and sound at the door to the taproom. But there I stood stock-still, listening—Zuckriegel had his voice turned up to its highest register, and another voice was simultaneously singing the antistrophe with him, with extraordinarily disharmonic effect. The kitchen crew pressed into the hallway, intimidated but excited; knowing, however, that our traveling companion only too gladly and too often got himself involved in altercations, I opened the door to the taproom and entered. I stood there, full of doubts and glued to the threshold, my mouth open wide—and the door wasn't closed either.

I've seen a conjurer in the Prater† in Vienna take a live rabbit by the hind legs, rip it apart in the middle, and then present a gaily struggling animal in each hand to his amazed and enthusiastic audience. A similar experiment appeared to have been performed on Zuckriegel the anatomist—he was present twice over in the Seeauer's taproom and was now engaging in the most violent argument with his doppelgänger. The book on German crookdom had been thrown disdainfully to the floor, ditto two of the chairs on which the large, and likewise tall, man had been taking his midday rest. Each of the fellows—gaunt and dyed a leathery gray on gray—was gesticulating with a notebook in his hand while arguing with

---

*A coinage treaty worked out in Vienna in 1857 regulated the value of the gulden throughout the German states, but in the following year Austria introduced a new, devalued gulden of its own. Raabe as always is touchy about policies that sabotage steps toward German unity.

†Amusement park in Vienna.

the other at the top of their respective voices. The stranger was steaming just as Zuckriegel had steamed before—proof that he could not have entered so very long ago.

"For God's sake, my good anatomist! gentlemen! gentlemen!" I implored loudly as I leapt in between the two overheated combatants. "Control yourself, Herr Zuckriegel, please! What is going on? what has happened?"

"And I tell you you are wrong from start to finish!" Zuckriegel shouted. "I shall refute your statement point by point;—will you please calm down and hear me through?"

"No!" croaked the adversary who so resembled him. "Why should I calm down and listen, since you won't let me finish what I have to say? Go ahead and stick to your opinion;—I shall oppose you in writing; I shall lay your hypotheses before the world and place them in their proper light."

Zuckriegel popped up and down like a long-necked jack-in-the-box. His neck developed an elasticity that gave you the shudders; it must have been made of even more stretchable stuff than a rubber band. "Write, scribble! I shall write you off the face of the earth, write you flat as a bedbug. I will thump away at your crass ignorance until the moths come flying out of it; I shall—"

I grabbed my outraged traveling companion around the neck and pushed him back; I also pushed the gray stranger away as he moved closer and held the two fighting cocks apart with my dripping umbrella.

"My good anatomist," I said, "I beg you to introduce me to this gentleman,—my good anatomist, I ask you please to calm yourself,—dear sir, let me play the mediator, allow me to open the peace conference—"

"I am Professor Steinbüchse from Berlin," the stranger said. "Professor of antiquities, and have set out on a scientific expedition to the newly discovered graveyard on Lake Hallstatt in the Salzkammergut."

"Ah!" said I, but Zuckriegel shouted:

"He claims they are Celtic bones; when any child can see—"

"This child here sees them as Teutonic skeletal remains," shouted Steinbüchse, "when any unre—"

"Wait, wait, wait, gentlemen!" I likewise shouted with all the power in my lungs. "No new breach of the peace! no unnecessary aspersions! no learned turns of phrase! Please, my dear professor, have you just now returned from visiting the bones in question?"

"I am on my way to them."

"You have not yet seen these bones then?"

"Only through the intermediary of publications."

"And you have not yet been up to the Rudolf Tower either, correct, Herr Zuckriegel?"

"In this weather? I'd have to be a fool! The bones aren't going to get washed away, and I can wait. Was peacefully lying here on my back, reading my Avé-Lallemant, when I was attacked by this—"

The rest of his speech was lost in unintelligible mutterings, in which I think I heard something about "Boeotian swindler"; in the hoarse voice of the neutral ambassador mediating at a peace conference I cried:

"Shake hands, my good sirs. Without further incident—as you are colleagues, so be brothers. Science is best advanced through the serene alliance of all forces. Let us peaceably eat our dinner together and tomorrow morning, manly, meek, and merry, let us ascend to these mysterious bones and settle this argument on the spot."

For several ominous moments the two scholars gazed grimly at one another; but then Steinbüchse revealed that his resemblance to the anatomist was not quite so great; he declared himself prepared to hold his peace and his tongue until tomorrow morning, adding, however, that he would climb up to the Rudolf Tower tomorrow morning no matter *what* the weather.

With a growl Zuckriegel retrieved his book of villains from the floor, but did not condescend to any further concession in the matter of this painfully achieved *treuga Dei.** The fact that the gentle poet came skipping into the room at just that moment contributed more than anything else to bring tempers under control; the soothing magic of poesy was quite clearly made manifest once again.

Roderich von der Leine was very wet, so wet that it would have been best had he hung himself up to dry on a wash-Leine. But he gave that no thought whatever. His organs of vision were in their well-known fine frenzy rolling;† he too was holding a notebook in

*"Peace of God"; refers to days on which the Church in the middle ages forbade all quarrels.

†Shakespeare, *Midsummer Night's Dream,* act 5, scene 1.

his hand, a dripping one. The birth was accomplished; under the influence of the refreshing spray from the Hallstatt millstream, the author of "Life's Blossoms" had transmuted his experiences in Linz into rhyme; Zuckriegel gave a mighty groan.

I introduced Professor Steinbüchse and the poet, and the professor revealed yet another dissimilarity to the anatomist; he was polite, he was patient, he was in fact attentive toward the poet and cordially begged him not to let his own presence deter him from reciting his poem. Perhaps he was all this, said all this, only because he noticed and understood all of Zuckriegel's grimaces, snorts, shrugs, and contortions.

"Yes, read on, recite for us!" I said, treading as it were in the professor's footsteps.

"Would it not be better if you first changed your clothes?" Zuckriegel sighed. "You could easily catch a nasty cold, Herr Krautworst. It would indeed be a shame if in your youthful recklessness you were to deprive yourself of your life and the world of your as yet unborn and yet undying works."

Since his white outfit was still hanging wet by the kitchen fire, Rodrigo could only have thrown himself into his Adam's costume had he wished to follow Zuckriegel's tender, solicitous suggestion. His inner agitation, however, caused him to soar above all rheumatic or bronchial worries:

> Belonging now to gods on high,
> No earthly thing dared him approach.*

"Won't you at least change your stockings? I would strongly urge you to do so. Young poets are indeed so given to cerebral congestions," Zuckriegel said in veritably piping tones.

The poet only shook his head distractedly; he leafed violently through his notebook.

"Well then, in the name of Satan's minions, let it rip!" Zuckriegel snorted, at the end of his tether now, having spent himself fully in demonstrations of courtesy and mildness.

Roderich von der Leine turned to us:

"Have you seen the millstream yet, gentlemen?"

---

*Cited from Schiller's poem, "The Power of Song."

"No," I said, nor had Steinbüchse thus far had the pleasure.

"You must see it," the poet cried with emphasis. "Unique!—romantic in the highest degree. There is an old dark archway with a niche and within it a picture, a picture of Saint—if I am not mistaken—Saint Sebastian; there I stood for over two hours."

"I did not see the millstream; but I did see you, dear friend, but did not wish to disturb you."

Roderich nodded his head toward me gratefully, but then jerked his notebook to his nose and began, at first shyly, but then with increasing courage and with those well-known sidelong glances to his listeners:

> Veiled in gray, the mountains glower
> Down upon the foreign town,
> Ceaseless falls the heavy drizzle,
> While I sadly yawn and frown.*

"Just like me," Zuckriegel grumbled, having testily stuck his nose back into his Avé-Lallemant.

> God, oh God, things must turn better,
> God, have mercy on me here!
> In my misery do but send me
> One of Thy sweet angels dear!

"Me too! 'Tis my urgent plea!" sighed Zuckriegel.

> Golden-locked, with eyes of azure,
> Slender, trim, and fair of brow
> Let him be my comforter—with
> Wings Thou needst not him endow.

"I could use them however!" sighed Zuckriegel.

> From the steeple, bells are humming;
> Through the muddy, murky city
> Pious Christians wend to worship;
> God, oh God, show us Thy pity!

---

*In Krautworst's verses Raabe parodies his own. Several years earlier he had begun to write poetry, but then came to take an ironic view of his achievements.

"What demands these fellows have! But know no pity themselves," groused Zuckriegel.

> Send an angel down from heaven,
> From the sun, a radiant beam;
> Do not let me perish, weeping
> In this vale where sorrows teem!

"Nor me, I implore!" said Zuckriegel; but the poet called our
attention to the fact that his poem was delicately segmented and that
now a new series of images was commencing. He continued:

> Coiling blue and gently wafting
> Fades the odor of cigar;
> Ceaseless falls the heavy drizzle,
> And I gasp as with catarrh.

Zuckriegel groaned: "I no less so."

> Hanging halfway out the window,
> Now I listen to the drops
> Down below in narrow alleys
> Banging on umbrella tops.

Zuckriegel knew precisely what *he* would love to bang on.

> And my eye, so drowsy, weary,
> Spies the house across the way,
> Creeps from cellar up to gables,
> Wanders down again to stay.

Zuckriegel's eye, portending disaster, crept upwards on the poet
and only wandered down again as the latter went on:

> At the butcher's door the carcass
> Of a disemboweled ram.
> Ah, how dreadf'lly it resembles
> My poor soul—how sad I am!

Zuckriegel growled: "A ghastly verse, but nonetheless the only
one that has my complete approbation." Aloud he called: "Herr
Krautworst, my compliments to you on your knowledge of the inner
man. Please, recite that last rhyme once more;—what did your poor
soul's condition resemble at that remarkable moment?"

"Part the third!" said Roderich von der Leine, disdaining the anatomist.

> High behind reflecting windows,
> In its polished cage of brass,
> Squawks a parrot, and its squawking
> Wakes within me fear en masse.

"But it appears to have attended a good school!" Zuckriegel chimed in.

> There a lady in red velvet
> Feeds him candies, soft and sweet.
> He then squawks *merci!* and flutters
> As my pulse now skips a beat;

> For he represents an image
> Of my wild and mad career,
> Since with flutterings and *merci*'s I've
> Braved the world, its smile and sneer.

Zuckriegel's disdain waxed to the point that during the verses that followed he was able to express himself solely in gestures bordering on dislocations.

> And a lady in red velvet
> Once did offer me such sweets;
> And *merci! merci!* I rage now,
> When I think back on those treats.

> Oh thou green and yellow parrot
> In thy shining silver bands,
> Hang thyself upon they fetters:
> Sweets are sour from such hands.

"Very!" sighed Zuckriegel and added with a glance much like an incision: "Yes, but if only he would hang himself!"
"Part the fourth!" said the poet.

> And once more, so drowsy, yawning,
> I my eyelids lift on high;
> While my gaze sweeps ever upward—
> Near the roof it stops to lie.

Near the roof—what do I spy there?
God, oh God, can this be true?
Through the dreary splashing rainfall
Comes a sun-bolt into view!

Near the roof an open window
All entwined with flowery ranks!
God, oh God, you've come to rescue!
Thank you, god of poets, thanks!

"My compliments to him," grunted Zuckriegel, "but he could have had better things to do."

Near the roof an open window
And an angel's face within,
Eyes the bluest, arms the fairest,
Braids of gold, pink mouth, sweet chin!

Near the roof lies all of heaven;
Far is every earthly stain!
Near the roof lies bliss eternal!
Lovely saint, oh I would fain

Plead for your dear guardian mercies—
Not with wink, nor eyes at play;
Lovely saint, oh lovely goddess,
Won't you nod your head my way?

"It would be pure lunacy for her to do the fool the favor!" grunted Zuckriegel, putting himself totally in her situation.

Ah, she rises from her love seat;
Elfinlike, in wreath of white,
Round her mouth a smile of angels,
Chaste she stands in pure sunlight.

Devil take it! Oaths and curses!
God, oh God, what does this mean?
Lovely angel, sweetest goddess!
She has closed the shade between.

"Brava! Brava!" shouted Zuckriegel, grinning as he clapped his hands; but with a triumphant glance his way, Roderich von der Leine said:

"Part the fifth!" and the anatomist sank down again behind his world of German knavery.

> Ceaseless comes the rainfall's patter,
> And I add my sighs and frown;
> Veiled in gray the mountains glower
> Down upon the foreign town.
>
> Now I spy my red-bound guidebook,
> Pick it up, while back I sink,
> Heavy yet with limbs so limber,
> In my armchair, and I think
>
> Of the passage where 'tis written:
> "Linz is such a lovely town,
> Badly paved and overcrowded,
> But with theater renowned!"
>
> Linz, oh Linz along the Danube,
> Ever, Linz, I'll think of thee:
> To thy fame, to thy theater,
> I devote this poetry!
>
> Linz, oh Linz along the Danube,
> Linz in Upper Austria,
> At the thought, my eye doth moisten
> And my heart goes oom-pah-pah.
>
> Ah that little white lace curtain
> At the window near the roof—
> Ah, the thoughts it now awakens
> Of my foolish heart give proof!
>
> All the gods, both male and female,
> Stand now at the poet's side,
> Though he go through flame and carnage,
> Or through rain, they are his guide.
>
> Ah that little white lace curtain,
> Dearest, dearest, ope' it not!
> In the sweet God-given twilight,
> You're the dearest God has wrought!

The poet portentously clapped his damp notebook together, and what then occurred approached a miracle. Zuckriegel threw his volume on German swindlers to the floor a second time, though this time not in anger. He stood up, strode over to the poet, took his hand with suspicious tenderness and said to him once again in those piping tones:

"Herr Krautworst, is this poem really your own? Did you really write it yourself, my youthful Heinrich Heine, or whatever that fellow's name is?!* If indeed your 'Tavern's Blossoms'—no, 'Life's Blossoms'—, unfortunately all quite unknown to me as yet, are cut and sewn from the same stuff, then I implore you send me a free copy. Here is my exact address—postpaid if I may be so bold to ask it of you. And should on some distant day, spinal consumption—"†

"Sir," Roderich shouted, beside himself with anger, "Sir, I am so bold as to beg you to leave me alone; your effrontery begins to exceed all bounds!"

"Calm yourself, calm yourself, my young friend," Zuckriegel said with a smile, "You have indeed produced a capital poem. Brilliant. A sparkling little masterpiece! Our praise must be quite flattering; but please do not gaze down at us haughtily from the heights to which our admiration has lifted you. I know that the *furor poeticus*** can account for some of this; in our ward for the mentally distracted we had—'

Professor Steinbüchse and I both realized at the same moment that it was high time to intervene. We lavished the poet with our most earnest praises, spoken in tones of high seriousness. I likewise called his attention to the fact that, out of cold yet beautiful egoism, the poet must regard people as no more than clay made for him to knead and shape. I convinced him that the anatomist could have meaning and substance for him only as "material," never as a creature "capable of insult";—Roderich von der Leine took the measure of his worth on Zuckriegel's unworthiness, and as if our personalities had been created for one another, we four took our evening meal together in tolerable harmony; but after supper a monstrous difficulty arose.

When we inquired about our sleeping quarters, our host announced that he could only provide us with two chambers and that the gentlemen would have to make do with sleeping two to a room;

*Zuckriegel means this as an insult, as Heine was widely disliked at this time; Raabe, however, admired him.
†Heine died in 1856 after long years of suffering from a paralytic disease.
**"Poetic madness."

the beds were excellent, however, and would meet our every wish; both chambers were also separated by a single wall and both had a view to the lake.

"I don't give a damn about that!" said Zuckriegel. "Herr Kraut-worst, we two shall sleep together—and can conspire beneath a common blanket. We have not said all we have to say to one another yet, and now shall have the pleasantest opportunity to do so; I customarily do not fall asleep until the wee hours."

Roderich looked at the anatomist the way the wicked stepmother looked at the barrel full of nails and adders in which she was to be placed. Terror, loathing, disgust and fear passed over his gentle features.

"Of course we shall sleep the night together," I whispered to him. "You shall have a revenge beyond your fondest wishes; Steinbüchse and Zuckriegel shall be tucked in together."

Deeply touched, the poet shook my hand under the table and then abandoned it—the table that is—as quickly as possible and, with the innkeeper lighting his way, went off to take possession of a bedroom for himself and me.

"Well, Professor, my nose tells me that the two of us are going to have to crawl in together," Zuckriegel said, casting an amused, mocking glance my way. "Let us, however, frustrate the sweet expectations of these two young men; let us not break the armistice we have concluded; let us snore."

"Goes without saying," Steinbüchse said, totally convinced of the firmness of his character and his will. "I intend to sleep a good sleep,"[*] he added with the faith of a Wallenstein in his stars, and I admit that with deep regret I began to believe in the determination of the two scholars.

We three wished one another a pleasant rest, and when I reached my bedroom I found the author of "Life's Blossoms" already cozily cocooned in his feather comforter. Only his immortal head, wrapped in a red silk scarf, poked up out of the pillows.

"What are they up to? Have they gone to bed?" he asked.

"They've each ordered another glass of punch. I fear the night will pass more peacefully than we had hoped."

---

[*]Cited from Schiller's *Wallenstein's Death*, act 5, scene 5.

"I believe just the opposite;—sleep well, dear friend; I shall wake you when it's time."

"My best thanks to you in advance. Good night!"

In the first doze of slumber I faintly heard the poet reciting:

> Quam iuvat immites ventos audire cubantem
> Et dominam tenero detinuisse sinu—*

but, "rustled to sleep by the babbling," I was resting too soundly to follow any more sumptuous Latin reminiscences from Roderich's school days; the lake and the rain had the same soothing influence on me as the latter had had on the elegiac poet Albius Tibullus.

I do not know how long I slept; but for some time I had been dreaming that, like the knight Don Quixote, I was in Agramante's camp and had just been called by King Sobrino to undo the confusion that had broken out,† when suddenly I was awakened by the whispers of Roderich von der Leine:

"Dear friend, best friend! They're at it! they've locked horns! Listen, do you hear them?! Ah!"

I had just been listening to Signore Ludovico Ariosto laugh while writing his *Orlando Furioso* and watching as he stroked his thin beard; now here I was again, lying in my warm bed in the Seeauer on Lake Hallstatt, one hour after midnight, listening to the rain at the window, watching by the dull shimmer of the night-light the Hanoverian poet as he sat up in bed, and hearing from just behind the thin plank wall between chambers the tumult of a battle that could only have its origin in the intellectual collision of Steinbüchse and Zuckriegel.

How many glasses of punch those two excellent fellows had drunk could only be proved by the bill come morning; at any rate they had had enough and were banging each other over the head with the bones of the Celts and Teutons in a fashion that would have amused any disinterested eavesdropper, but had to be a perfect delight for a prejudiced party like Roderich von der Leine.

Whether the two heroes had entered their chamber quarreling or had only first begun to pick a learned bone with one another when

---

*"What a pleasure to lie listening to the howling storm and clasp one's beloved to one's breast," Tibullus, *Elegies*, 1.1.

†An allusion to *Don Quixote*, part 1, chapter 45.

once in bed, I do not know; Rodrigo claimed it was the former; I cannot, however, quite believe that; for Zuckriegel was not a man to recline serenely on his back without having first stretched his opponent across it, and Steinbüchse, though somewhat softer, milder, more humane in other things, was almost or perhaps the veritable equal of the anatomical whittler when it came to stubbornly championing his opinions on the field of scientific battle.

I now no longer felt myself called to play the mediator, but instead, enjoyed myself royally; and the face of the author of "Life's Blossoms" was also worth observing in the soft illumination of the night-light.

We two eavesdroppers did not have to worry about hearing evil of ourselves on this occasion; the two punch-drunk members of the *universitas literarum** called each other the most dreadfully crude names with a truly classical naïveté. The more difficult it became for each to outtrump the other, the more ingenious their pronouncements, and no word was so elevated but what the other could cap it with one still more so. They spat in each other's face, morally speaking, and I am convinced that several times Zuckriegel missed only by a hair's-breadth having ballads sung about him to the accompaniment of a barrel organ and grisly illustrations at some county fair.

"He's bit the bedpost! Sure as I live, dear friend, he's biting the bedposts for pure rage!" the gentle poet said with exultant, though restrained jubilation.

"And the other one has stuffed the blanket in his mouth. Truly, dear friend, if we don't bang on the wall with the bootjack, by tomorrow morning they'll both be lying ill with a bilious fever."

"Not for anything in the world!" the poet begged. "Do not disturb their circles!† Bilious fever! Bah, you only need to look it up in the philosophical yearbooks, in their medical magazines. They can handle a great deal without any impairment of their health. Just listen, that's the one from Berlin going at it great guns again. That's it! Grab hold of him, Professor—go at it, go at it! Hurrah, a very palpable hit! That's telling him!"

A loud thump behind the wall followed, interrupting the poet's

*"The totality of learning," i.e., the university.
†An allusion to the last words of Archimedes before he was killed by soldiers.

cheers; after the thump came the hollow echoing rumble of a fall; Roderich and I leapt out of bed and onto our feet, though still on this side of the wall—for it now seemed to be our duty as honorable men and Christians to prevent the spilling of blood. But a higher power had already intervened.

True, Professor Steinbüchse of Berlin was singing *"Io triumphe!";* But Zuckriegel the anatomist did not set his fine set of teeth into that throat. True, anatomist Zuckriegel had jumped out of bed to collar his opponent; but spirits had conquered spirit, for the doughty anatomist had drunk far too much punch; he was now measuring the floor with the length of his body and snoring like a baby at its mother's breast, though somewhat more loudly.

The professor gurgled in triumph for another five minutes, then he too dozed off, pulling every stop on the register of nose, larynx, head, and glottis. Now the two worthy gentlemen were keeping the promise they had made to themselves and to me: they snored, but only after the battle was done.

On this side of the wall we listened for a while yet, but then the sawings, trumpetings, and raspings grew steadily more regular, if not more melodic, so that we too gave ourselves over to balsamic sleep. Roderich fell asleep with an "ah" of unutterable contentment. And thus was Zeus's will accomplished for today; how things would work out on the morrow likewise lay in the lap of the Gatherer of Clouds.—Why had he trapped us in the rain on Lake Hallstatt?—

I had intended to awaken early and be present at the first appearance of Zuckriegel and Steinbüchse and, as I was their junior, politely and dutifully to inquire how the two gentlemen had rested. But when I opened my eyes, I noticed that, like the two scholars, I had overestimated my moral energies somewhat, and as I hastened half-clad to the window to convince myself with my own eyes that the rain had not yet ended, to my great astonishment I spied beneath two umbrellas four gray legs wandering back and forth in opposite directions in front of the garden pavilion. And when at that same moment the wind turned the two umbrellas into two tulips, I saw to my skeptical amazement that it was—they—Zuckriegel and Professor Steinbüchse.

Deep in his morning slumbers, the poet was most probably

---

*"Hurrah, triumph," cry of Roman soldiers in the victory procession.

searching for a word to rhyme with "depth," for he was making awful groans while fearfully and convulsively grabbing at the blanket with his hands. I did not feel called to help him out of his dilemma; with winged haste I washed and dressed so that I could join the two gray perambulators in the garden and inquire of the peripatetics what spirit it was that caused them, after such a stormy night, to walk like this—back and forth, now beside, now opposing one another—along the fog-shrouded shore of Lake Hallstatt.

I hurried down the stairs, called for my morning coffee, then, likewise beneath a raised umbrella, entered the garden, and putting on my most ingenuous face, joined the two savants to offer them something that I indeed could not give—which was a good morning.

They looked distraught, haggard from lack of sleep, and peevish enough, but any thoughtful person would have had to admire them; and I—who have a good and open eye for anyone clever and deft enough to reconcile himself or herself to the moment and its attending circumstances—I suddenly felt for them a respect of which until then I had had no notion.

How Roderich von der Leine's petty yet implacable petulance dwindled to its true size in comparison to the truly grand display of character shown by these two men of science! Zuckriegel and Steinbüchse had provoked one another, had called each other by pretty names; but what were their personages compared to their high purpose for being here at Lake Hallstatt! The scholarly passions that had so fearfully enflamed the souls of the two martial heroes during the night, now lay cringing on the ground, to the extent that was possible. The alcoholic cloud that had filled the combatants' brains had dispersed into a light, hazy mist; Zuckriegel was too big a man to avenge his bruised brow on the professor, and Steinbüchse of Berlin was too high-minded to remember that at midnight he had been called a "silly ass." Of the memories from yesterday and last night, only the shared confidences of those cozy evening hours, before the punch had taken effect, lingered on: Steinbüchse had whispered into Zuckriegel's ear that he too had come "to look around for something useful" in the graveyard of that unidentified folk at the Rudolf Tower, and, in case it wasn't handed over voluntarily, for little money or for a few good words, he would avail himself of "his rights as a scholar." Since the professor's eye was directed more to bronze fibulae, needles, sword hilts, and arrowheads, whereas the anatomist had use for nothing but bones, bones, and more bones for his collection, the two greedy souls were not poaching on each other's territory in any way. They had extended their hands across their steaming glasses for a most fervent handshake, and, in order not to spoil each other's hunt, had sworn to go marauding only as a team and, whatever the dangers of the enterprise, to come to one another's assistance with eloquence, cunning, and if need be with force. The events of the night could in no way alter their expeditionary plans, and so, having drunk their coffee, the two learned conspirators were wandering up and down in the garden overlooking the lake and each time they passed, they gazed at one another with dark and sullen looks, but without murder in their eyes.

They wanted to embark on their new argonaut's quest at nine o'clock, to capture their Helen, to plunder and be done with it. It had just struck eight, so that I had more than enough time to drink my own coffee in comfort and to await the awakening of the poet.

Around eight-thirty, Roderich von der Leine appeared, this time in his white outfit again. The plaid outfit was now hanging on a line beside the kitchen fire, the object of the admiring stares, strokes, and grins of a great many inhabitants of these mountains, who otherwise had no reason for being in said kitchen.

The greetings exchanged by the poet and the other two gentlemen had their fascination for the attentive observer; but Zuckriegel had poured out his bile and spite in such quantity during the night that he was relatively insipid in the early morning hours; his mood was something like that of a cobra after a pious but wily Hindu has thrown a flannel cloth between its fangs into which it voids its venom. But now I informed that excellent young man from Hanover of my intention to accompany the two scholars on their dangerous but glorious expedition. Alarmed and trusting not at all in Zuckriegel's moderation, he jumped up from his chair, toppling it and a milk can, and pulled me into a corner to whisper:

"I beg you, I implore you! What are you doing? Stay here with me, do not go with those two soulless monsters! I have thought it all out, and one cannot leave Hallstatt without having first seen the Veil Falls, the Spurtle Falls, the Woodbrook's Beard and having cast a glance at the Dachstein and the Karl Glacier. People would laugh in our faces were we to return home without those memories;—I beseech you not to rush to your ruin, but to come with me; I have so much to say to you yet, we are so wonderfully compatible. It will be raining just as hard on the path to the Rudolf Tower as it will in the Echer Valley, oh do come with me!"

If anything could have moved me to follow in the divine minstrel's radiant footsteps, it would have been that last true, ah indescribably true, observation. But my mind was made up; I chose to be washed and rinsed along the path toward those unidentified bones rather than down the Woodbrook's Beard. I generally prefer the beauties of a human soul to the beauties of nature, and to enjoy the company of Zuckriegel and Steinbüchse, I would have most joyfully missed all the splendors of the Salzkammergut landscape, along with the most heavenly sunshine—and all its songbirds and gentle beasts of the wood thrown into the bargain.

With a deliberate shake of my head, I withdrew myself from the entwining arms of the author of "Life's Blossoms" and said:

"Dearest friend, I cannot force you to follow us, but would if I could. When will better material for a comedy ever be flung directly before your feet?"

Roderich von der Leine started, looked up, looked at me, looked at the two scholars who were busy packing their satchels with grim resolution—though leaving room for their plunder; for an instant I thought I had bound his fate with ours, but in the next moment he sank back and sighed:

"I can't do it! I haven't the strength! I can bear *that* man no longer. As I awoke this morning, after the triumph of last night, I firmly believed that it would be possible; but I was mistaken; I am the bird, and he is the serpent that charms me with its baleful eye. I cannot even look at the fellow from the rear any more."

And seeing that all further attempts at persuasion would be in vain, I abandoned the high-strung poet to his lonely path and turned back to my two scientific adventurers; their genuinely classical serenity filled me anew with admiration.

Never had two more determined highwaymen had their host fill their wicker-bottles with rum than these two academic brigands. Leonidas at Thermopylae,* Curtius as he gazed into the chasm

*Leonidas, King of Sparta, defended the pass at Thermopylae to the last man against the Persians in 480 B.C.

before he leapt,* and, in more modern times, Blücher as he declared on his way from Ligny to Waterloo: "It really can't work, but it's going to have to work!"†—they may all have gazed before them as did Zuckriegel and Steinbüchse at this solemn moment. I too handed the innkeeper my flask, and then—then, defying death itself, we set out into the ominous gray of morning fog and drenching, unyielding rain, while Roderich von der Leine—shivering and with grudging, involuntary admiration—watched us go. Perhaps, for one weak moment, he was even envious of his hated traveling companion, the steel-hearted anatomist.

Since these were now the first steps that Zuckriegel and Steinbüchse had taken in the quaint streets of Hallstatt (until now they had not considered it worth their trouble to stick their noses out of the inn), they also expressed considerable amazement at the flights of stairs, and Steinbüchse assured us that, thank God, such things were unknown in Berlin. But the stairs led in a steep zigzag past the last houses and further up the mountain, until after a quarter of an hour they became a heavily shaded path that continued to zigzag. The way to the Rudolf Tower is hard to miss, even for two scholars whose thoughts are racing far beyond their immediate path.

Vigorously, yet mutely, Steinbüchse and Zuckriegel stalked ahead; their company had thus far provided no entertainment. Both had pulled their hats down over their noses as far as possible, both had pulled their umbrellas down over their felt hats as close as possible, and neither made a single misstep, although the path was very muddy and slippery from the rain.—Nor did either of them notice anything of what could be seen through the gaps and cuttings in the dripping forest: the most splendid portion of the lake's caldron with all its boiling, roiling fogs and vapors. Their thoughts were with those bones, and each of them was reviewing for himself the various strategies employed by great field marshals who had set out "to appropriate" something or "to avail themselves of their rights."

And so from time to time, I hurried on ahead of the two queer fellows so that I could exercise my rights of standing at some

---

*According to legend, Curtius saved the city of Rome by leaping into a chasm that had opened on the Forum.

†Gebhard Leberecht von Blücher (1742–1819), Prussian commander at Waterloo, was famous for his bluntness.

appropriate spot and enjoying the ever-expanding view. When the two umbrellas had gradually worked their way up even with me, I would climb further as well. Suddenly, in the middle of the road—not of our life,* but of the mule track—my gaze fell on a very wet bench, which demanded, so it seemed, that I read and ponder an inscription of no recent date;—the two umbrellas were once again quite close at hand, and I stood and read:

"Here did rest His most illustrious Majesty, Maximilian, King of the Romans, on his way to visit the Salzperg, on the 5th of January anno 1504."

"Who sat here? where did whoever he was sit? when did whoever it was sit?" shouted Professor Steinbüchse of Berlin at the very same moment, bounding forward like a tiger and flinging me to one side without further ado, before I could answer:

"The first Emperor Maximilian, also known as the Last Knight of one Anastasius Grün of Vienna."†

Professor Steinbüchse satisfied himself of the reality of this fact, jotted down the inscription in his notebook, and sat down on the wet bench in order to absorb that experience as well. Zuckriegel, however, strode disdainfully on past without so much as a glance at this historic, eternally memorable spot.

"It's all the same to me who sat there, you, good colleague, or King Maximilian; if only I get my skull," he said.

This remark gave fresh forward impetus to the professor as well, and after another half hour of climbing we arrived at the Rudolf Tower and with it the arena of our greatest adventure.

The manly heart did beat against the ribs** as we stood before these walls erected by Emperor Albrecht and then pulled at the bell of the Royal and Imperial Inspector of Salt who now resided there, so that we might be allowed entry into the little museum housing finds of antiquities, ammonites, and other curiosities. A maiden supervised our visit, and I was terribly interested in this collection of Celtic or Teutonic punch bowls, crafted with much skill and taste, though unfortunately quite rusty. We did not yet attempt our theft

*An allusion to the opening line of Dante's *Inferno*.

†Anastasius Grün, pen name of Count Anton Alexander von Auersperg (1806–76), published a series of ballads about Emperor Maximilian in 1830 entitled "The Last Knight."

**Cited from Schiller's youthful poem, "In a Battle."

here, for that would have been too risky; but Zuckriegel used a moment, during which the mountain maid's attention was totally engaged in watching Steinbüchse's delighted raptures over a priapic monster tarnished a dark green, to grab hold of me by a button and to hiss in my ear:

"My good fellow, it all depends on you now whether I achieve my journey's purpose or not. This female will lead us to the grave sites in any case;—you're a good-looking, urbane fellow—pay attention— you're my friend, you're—she's looking this way!—in short, lure her away—get her undivided attention for just one brief moment—and I shall be eternally grateful;—the girl's not all that bad; just steal a kiss, just one single kiss as we're standing there beside our fore- fathers' bones. You can't mind just one kiss, not when it's a matter of such noble purpose as osteology."

"I can see that you've learned some things from the book you brought along on your travels; but do you really wish, without the least bite of conscience, to sacrifice me to your scientific urges, to your base desires?" I asked reproachfully.

"Not in the least, my good man! What risk is it for you? I'll take off with my skull; Steinbüchse can watch out for himself, and no harm would come to either you or me if they should collar him. You yourself, dear fellow, can follow after, slowly, innocently, coolly, like a disinterested, harmless tourist. We shall then meet again at the lakeshore, at the Seeauer, and celebrate our victory, and best of all, after I've returned home, I shall send you my treatise on skull formation among the prehistoric ancient, modern, and contempo- rary races of mankind. What do you say to *that?* Can you resist that?"

"No!" I said. "Here is my hand; it shall be no fault of mine if you don't obtain your heart's desire. Now, let's go."

"Well, my charming child," Zuckriegel prattled on sweetly while slipping quietly as a blindworm to the side of the alpine beauty, "well, my angel, we've had sufficient time to observe these pleasant trifles; how would it be if we were to head for the graves now, my sweet rose of the graveyard."

He tried playing up to her further still by patting the sweet thing's cheek, but she angrily evaded his anatomist's hand and pulled a rusty key out of a leather pouch that hung under her apron, while inviting us, with glances demanding gratuities, to follow her.

"Truly, she's a most charming guard at the portals of the under-world, good colleague!" said Zuckriegel quite loudly to the scholar from Berlin; but Steinbüchse only whispered:

"This is it! Don't let the propitious moment slip by! Can you run?"

"With skull in hand, like a telegraphic dispatch."

"So can I! All else lies in the hands of the gods," Steinbüchse said with self-assurance, and we hiked on toward the graveyard, through bog and moss, dripping brambleberry bushes, and other en-cumbrances.

Someone had rigged a curious mechanism by which to preserve the newly discovered graves and their skeletons and so present them to a curious or inquisitive public at an extra charge. A wooden box had been lowered into the earth—a coffinlike box with a hinged door and a large padlock—over the skeleton lying in unaltered position, exactly as it had been carefully dug up. The public assem-bles around the box, the alpine maid tries for a considerable time and without success to force the rusty key into the lock; finally the lid springs open, the public rubbernecks, stands tiptoe and man-ifests its satisfaction, its interest, its horror and rarely its sympathy in word and gesture. The female public squeals of course, because it cannot bear to see any skeletons.

These poor dead warriors and women, these youths and maidens! It is not pleasant, after so many centuries of peaceful, undisturbed sleep to be awakened by such a deformed, stunted, foolish race of men and have yourself gaped at. How would it be if such a thou-sand-year-old set of decomposed bones would pull itself together with a clatter, stand up, rub the sleep from its hollow eye sockets, and angrily reach for its bronze sword to lay into the hemor-rhoidally afflicted, the crinoline wearers, the professors and the yawning, idle tourists?

What a jolly dashing and leaping down the mountain that would be; what all would the nineteenth century lose on its way down the serpentine path to Hallstatt! What all would the old Celt or Teuton be able to gather up in the way of spectacles, chignons, snuffboxes, parasols and umbrellas, rubber shoes, lap rugs, lorgnettes! Huzzah, what a memento of your trip, ladies and gentlemen, once you're sitting safe again in the railroad car or at home and can think back to that primeval spook!

But I digress; in fact I still have to tell about a dashing and leaping down the mountain, during which several objects were lost along the way that were declared to be rightful booty by the pursuing avengers of the dead.—

The maid from the Rudolf Tower knelt down beside her box and with growing vexation worked away at the stubborn lock.

Zuckriegel reached for Steinbüchse's hand, pressed it meaningfully and encouragingly, let go of it and whispered:

"Brother! Colleague! this is it! Courage, courage! Each of us will have to grab what he can get his hands on,—irrespective of his specialty! Brother, we'll sort it out at the bottom of the mountain and divide it fraternally!"

To me he called aloud:

"Memento! cedo tibi puellam!" which being translated is: "Stand by, my good man! Distract the young lady!"—

The lock now opened with a bang; the maid flung back the lid of the box, the two scholars shot forward, their eyes flaming with greed—there the Celt or primal Teuton lay on his left side, well preserved, peaceful, and comfy, his sword beside him, at his breast a green clasp, which looked terribly like a sat-to-death sofa spring. It seemed as if a sly smile were playing across the skeleton's bared teeth, with an expression that said: "Come, kiss me!", and Zuckriegel would have done just that with pleasure.

But what happened now proves once again that a well-thought-out, nicely laid plan of attack can be wrecked by the haste and violence of the moment. The greed of the two scientific body snatchers did not permit me to fulfill my promise to charm and fetter the attention of the maiden.

With a cry that seemed to have a zoological basis, Zuckriegel and Steinbüchse fell upon the Celt and helped themselves. But the maid of the Rudolf Tower likewise let out a cry:

"Help! Robbers! Thieves! Holy Virgin! Mary and Joseph! Max! Inspector! Franz! For God and Jesus' sake, help! They's gettin' away with the bones!"

And up out of the hole leapt Steinbüchse and Zuckriegel, the former as fate would have it with the Celt's skull in one hand and with two giant arm bones and a piece of rib in the other, the latter had the bronze sword, the breast clasp, and various other antiquarian bagatelles. Over moss, stone, and underbrush, they fled, leaving umbrellas behind, losing their hats. Half-faint with delight, I sank down onto the nearest tree stump.

But things were stirring all about. From all sides the doughty descendants of the problematical Celt or Teuton streamed in, responding to the maiden's cry, some with axes, others with mighty cudgels. A few breathless words by the maid sufficed to send them on the track of the robbers, whose fluttering coattails were just vanishing into the depths of the forest. The noise of flight and pursuit echoed in the distance, and as the suspected accomplice of the bone rustlers, I allowed myself to be led off through the rain to an astounded Inspector of Salt.

It was not easy for me to prove my innocence in this incredible affair. They spoke of wanting to have me transported to Salzburg in irons; they spoke in voices that grew ever rougher, ever shriller; but I behaved well, kept cool and collected, and directed their attention to my papers, which showed me to be a respectable gentleman and a harmless tourist and in no way a scholar or body snatcher. It would have indeed been most remarkable if the high moral dudgeon I exhibited at this shameful event had not stilled the waves of anger emanating from the sensible, gentlemanly official who interrogated me. There was solace as well in the abandoned umbrellas and hats, and in Steinbüchse's silken handkerchief, which had been arrested by a loyal thornbush. "My good sir," I said, "your antediluvian graveyard appears to be quite extensive; have them lay another primal Teuton bare and set your box with its lid, lock and bolt atop it. What do you care about a *single* Celt? Simply by looking calmly in the other direction, you may do an immense service for science, for osteology and archaeology, and that alone ought to give you some satisfaction."

"We'll see what our people bring back," the official said. "I'll not release you till then, sir. . . ."

A hoarse victory cry from the gate of the Rudolf Tower interrupted him—the pursuers brought back *everything*, skulls and arm bones, ribs, sword and clasp, and in addition Zuckriegel's toupee and Steinbüchse's spectacles. Steinbüchse and Zuckriegel, however, they had let get away.

"They jist tossed it all behind 'em, 'nd lost the rug 'nd spectacles!" the fiends crowed.

"So," the official said, with a merry smile and much satisfaction, "now we shall restore to the departed what is rightfully his, and I shall ask you, good sir, to give my compliments to your learned friends. The objects they left behind shall of course remain with these folks as payment for their troubles. The warmest of good-byes and I beg you, do me the honor some other time."

With that the inspector took his leave and went off to patch his Celt back together. I left as well and slowly climbed down to Hallstatt, but had to stop every five minutes, giving vent to my inner glee and letting my imagination range freely as it pictured our imminent reunion at the Seeauer.—

Beneath the back entrance to the inn stood Roderich von der Leine, peering, so it seemed, with some excitement out into the rain. Following his expedition to the Woodbrook's Beard, he had had to throw on his plaid outfit again and was awaiting me with itchy impatience. Once he caught sight of me, he began, waving both upraised hands violently, a dance of delight.

"There you are! there you are at last! Oh friend, what a story! Splendid, marvelous, oh, I can't stand it!" he shouted to me.

"Where are the other two gentlemen?" I asked as calmly as possible, but the poet was too excited to be able to provide a clear report; except I did make out, to my great regret, that Professor Steinbüchse of Berlin, "wet as a tomcat and wearing one of the landlord's old caps," had rented a fly and driven off, beside himself with rage, to Gosaumühle.

"Oh, the way they went for each other! oh, the things they said to each other! oh, the way they looked!" Roderich cried, and with him following, I strode into the taproom.

There sat Zuckriegel! The picture of utter human wrath and impotent outrage. He had not changed his clothes and had simply wrapped a few bright handkerchiefs around his bald head. When he caught sight of me, he let out a hissing howl and grabbed the aforementioned head with both hands; gnashing his teeth, whimpering with rage, he spat his questions, so to speak, in my face:

"Do you know? have you heard? do you know what happened?"

"Only in rough outline, my good Professor."

"Oh the scoundrel, the scoundrel, that vile Berlin scoundrel! I tell you, we would have made it out; I tell you, we would have gotten away with the goods, if it hadn't been for that wretch! What did he do in his abject terror as those *pecus** chasing us moved in a little closer? My skull, my skull, he tossed it at our pursuers, most probably to get them to stop for it, all the better to save that rusty piece of tin I had kept safely till that moment. In my rage and with equal right, I of course hurled that silly old cheese-knife to the devil, and even as I ran, in my despair and fury, I called him a muttonhead or whatever. So then the beast flung away my arm bones and ribs as well and screamed: 'Muttonhead? There! there! it can all go to the devil!' Naturally I threw the rest of his scrap iron at his head, while behind us the dolts were bellowing like Satan himself; since they appeared to realize that they now had back everything that we had fetched with so much trouble out of their damned wilderness. They let us get away,—and—here—here I sit, and my toupee's gone to hell too. Good God, good God, if only there were immutable justice! *Oleum et operam perdidi*†—the oil on that miserable path to the Rudolf Tower and the opportunity just now to thrash that ignorant milksop from Berlin. I'll not forget this day, if I live to be a thousand;—if a specimen that I lay rightful claim to as a dead specimen were to come back to life at the first incision of the dissecting scalpel, I could not weep bloodier tears. Ah, there is no justice—no justice in this world!"

Anatomist Zuckriegel laid his head onto his book on knavery, which he had left lying on the table as he marched off to the Celtic graves, and from now on was as good as dead to us. We took him along like a piece of baggage to Ischl, which we reached in the loveliest sunshine. Naturally, Roderich von der Leine here fell once again under the spell of the gentle sex, and I continued my journey to Salzburg alone.

Salzburg, too, lay roasting in its basin under the loveliest sunshine; but at all the street-corners, they had just posted the casualty lists from the first engagements in Italy, and that threw an ugly shadow over the charming city.

I had, I admit, neither relatives nor acquaintances in the Austrian army for whom I needed to worry, but it weighed heavily on my soul as I skimmed the mournful rows of dead and wounded, so that I

---

*"Cattle."
†"I wasted oil and effort," cited from Plautus, *The Little Carthaginian.*

quite justifiably took an interest in that brave lad from Hallstatt, Seppel Schönrammer. I would have felt very sorry to have found that death had snatched him away in the flower of his youth; fortunately, however, his name was merely in the list of the lightly wounded. The young hero had suffered no more than a slight contusion from a shot that had passed through his mess tin and into his knapsack. Which meant that at the moment of this rather inconsequential accident he was already in retreat homeward.

Translated by John E. Woods

Aquis submersus

Theodor Storm

In our "Palace Garden,"* which used to belong to the ducal palace
but had been wholly neglected since time immemorial, the
hawthorn hedges that had once been planted in the old French style
had even in my boyhood grown out to thin, spooky borders along
the avenue, but since they still bore a few leaves, we who live here
and are not spoiled by too much tree foliage can still appreciate
them even in this form, and especially one or another of the most
thoughtful among us will be found there. Then we are accustomed
to stroll in the meager shadows to the so-called "Mountain," a little
rise in the northwestern corner of the garden above the dry bed of a
fishpond, where nothing impedes the broadest view.

Most people may well look toward the west in order to enjoy the
light green of the marshes and beyond them the silver surface of the
sea, on which the shadow play of the long, stretched-out island
floats;† my eyes turn involuntarily to the north where, scarcely four
or five miles away, the grey, pointed church tower** rises from the
more elevated but desolate coast country; for there lies one of the
locales of my youth.

The pastor's son††from that village attended my hometown
grammar school with me, and countless times we walked out together on Saturday afternoon, to return on Sunday evening or Mon-

---

*All the places and structures in the story are in and around Storm's hometown of
Husum, as the persons mentioned in the frame were his acquaintances and a number
of the art works described are known or existed at one time. Placing a fiction within
an empirically recognizable setting is characteristic of Storm's realism.

†The island of Nordstrand opposite Husum.

**In the town of Hattstedt, a few miles north of Husum.

††Johann Matthias Ohlhues (1815–83), a school friend of Storm, who later
became pastor in Duisberg.

day morning to our Nepos* or later to our Cicero in the town. In those days there was still midway an unbroken stretch of heath, such as in the past had reached on the one side almost to the town, on the other almost to the village. Here the honeybees and the grey-white bumblebees buzzed on the blossoms of the fragrant heather while the beautiful, golden-green ground beetles ran under its thin stems; here in the aromatic clouds of the heather and the resinous bayberries hovered butterflies that were to be found nowhere else. My friend, impatiently heading home, often had trouble enough dragging his dreamy companion through all this splendor; however, once we had reached the tilled field we advanced all the more energetically, and soon, when we had waded through the sand up the long path, we already spotted, above the dark green of a lilac hedge, the gable of the pastor's house, from which the master's study with its opaque little windowpanes greeted the familiar guests.

At the home of the pastor and his wife, whose only child my friend was, we always had, as we say here, four feet to the yard, quite apart from the wonderful things to eat they provided. Nothing but the silver poplar, the only tall tree of the village and therefore the only enticing one, its branches rustling a good way above the mossy thatched roof, was forbidden to us like the apple tree of Paradise and therefore we climbed it only secretly; otherwise, as far as I can recall, everything was allowed and was well exploited appropriately to our age.

The main theater of our deeds was the large "priest's field," to which a little gate led from the garden. Here, with the congenital instincts of boys, we were able to hunt out the nests of larks and buntings, which we then visited repeatedly in order to see how much the eggs or the young had matured in the last two hours; here, as I now think, no less dangerous than that poplar, was a deep water-ditch, the edge of which was densely surrounded with old willow stumps, where we caught the nimble black bugs that we called "water Frenchmen" or, another time, floated the navy we had built out of walnut shells and boxtops on a wharf made expressly for the purpose. In the late summer it sometimes happened that we made a raid from our field to the sexton's garden, which lay across from the

---

*The Roman historian Cornelius Nepos (99–24 B.C.), whose works were often used as school texts.

pastor's on the other side of the water-ditch, for there we had our tithes to collect from two crippled apple trees, with the consequence, to be sure, that we sometimes earned a friendly threat from the good humored old man. So many youthful joys grew on this priest's field, in whose dry sand other flowers would not thrive; today, when those times come alive in me again, I still sense in my memory only the sharp aroma of the golden-budded tansy that stood in clusters on every mound.

But all this occupied us only temporarily; it was rather something else that aroused my continuing interest, something with which even we in the town had nothing to compare. I do not mean the tubular structures of the mason wasps that jutted out everywhere from the wall joints of the stall, although it was pleasant enough to watch the little beasts busily flying in and out in tranquil midday hours; I mean the much bigger structure of the old and uncommonly stately village church. From the foundation up to the shingle roof of the high tower it was constructed of granite blocks and, rising on the highest point of the village, it commanded a wide view over heath, shore, and marshes. Still, what attracted me most was the interior of the church; my imagination was already aroused by the huge key that seemed to have come down from the Apostle Peter himself. And, indeed, when we had succeeded in extracting it from the old sexton, it opened the portal to many wondrous things from which times long past looked upon us living persons, here with sinister, there with piously childlike eyes, but always in cryptic silence. Hanging down in the middle of the church was a terrible, larger-than-life crucifix; blood had dripped all over the gaunt limbs and distorted face of the figure; beside it, stuck to a wall pillar like a nest, was the brown, wood-carved pulpit, on which all sorts of grimacing beasts and animals seemed to be forcing themselves out of coils of fruit and leaves. But most enticing of all was the great carved altarpiece in the choir of the church, on which the passion of Christ was depicted in painted figures; one did not get to see, outside in daily life, such strangely wild faces such as that of Caiaphas* or of the soldiers who, in their golden armor, played dice for the robe of the crucified Christ. The only consoling contrast was the sweet countenance of Mary, collapsed at the base of the cross; in fact, she might easily have

---

*The high priest before whom Jesus was tried, Matt. 26:3ff.

ensnared my boyish heart into a fanciful inclination if something
else, with an even greater appeal of the mysterious, had not constantly distracted my attention from her.

Among all these strange or even eerie things there hung in the
nave of the church the innocent portrait of a dead child, a beautiful
boy of about five, resting on a pillow decorated with lace and
holding a white water lily in his small, pale hand. His delicate
expression, as though pleading for help, spoke, alongside of the
horror of death, of a last sweet trace of life; I was beset by an
irresistible feeling of compassion whenever I stood before this picture.

But it was not hanging alone here; close beside it a grim, black-
bearded man in a clerical collar and cap looked out of a dark
wooden frame. My friend told me that it was the father of that
beautiful boy, who, as the story still ran to the present day, was
supposed to have met his death in the water-ditch of our priest's field.
On the frame we read the date 1666; that was a long time ago.
Again and again I was drawn to these two pictures; a fantastic
longing came over me to obtain some more intimate information,
however scanty, of the life and death of the child; I tried even to read
it out of the gloomy countenance of the father, who despite his
clerical collar almost reminded me of the soldiers on the altarpiece.

After such studies in the twilight of the old church, the home of
the good pastor's family seemed all the more hospitable. To be sure,
it, too, was very old, and my friend's father had been hoping for as
long as I could remember for a new building; but since the sexton's
house was suffering from the same debility of age, nothing was built
here nor there. And yet how friendly the rooms of the old house
were: in winter the little room to the right of the hall, in summer the
larger one to the left, where pictures cut from Reformation alma-
nacs hung in mahogany frames on the whitewashed wall, where one
could view from the west window, besides a distant windmill, the
whole broad sky that in the evening was transfigured in rose red
splendor making the whole room gleam! The dear pastor and his
wife, the armchairs with their red plush cushions, the deep, old sofa,
the cosily whistling teakettle on the table at supper—it was all a
bright, friendly present. Only one evening—we were already fifth-
formers—it occurred to me what a past might cling to these rooms,

whether that dead boy might have once run about here in person with ruddy cheeks, the boy whose portrait now filled the gloomy space of the church as with a sweetly melancholy legend.

The occasion for such ruminations might have been my discovery, on the afternoon when we revisited the church at my suggestion, in a dark corner at the bottom of the picture, of four letters written in red paint that I had up to now failed to notice.

"They read C. P. A. S.," I said to my friend's father, "but we can't decode them."

"Well," he replied, "I am quite familiar with the inscription, and, if we appeal to rumor, the two last letters might be interpretable as *'Aquis submersus,'* that is, 'Drowned' or literally, 'Submerged in the water'; but then we would still be in difficulty with the preceding C. P.! Our sexton's young assistant, who had once passed the third form, thinks that it might mean *'Casu Periculoso,'* 'Through a dangerous accident'; but the old gentleman of those days thought more logically; if the boy drowned, the accident was not only dangerous."

I had been listening intently. *"Casu,"* I said; "it might also mean *'Culpa'?"*

"Culpa?" repeated the pastor. "Through guilt?—but through whose guilt!"

Then the grim portrait of the old preacher appeared before my soul, and without thinking I blurted out: "Why not: *Culpa Patris?*"

The good pastor was almost shocked. "Oh, oh, my young friend," he said and raised a warning finger to me. "Through the fault of the father?—Let us not accuse my late colleague despite his somber appearance. Furthermore, he would hardly have written such a thing about himself."

This last made sense to my youthful understanding, and so the actual meaning of the inscription remained a secret of the past as much as ever.

That both those pictures, by the way, distinguished themselves in their artistic quality in comparison to a few old portraits of preachers hanging just beside them had already become clear to me; but that experts wanted to see in the painter an able pupil of the old Dutch masters I only learned now from my friend's father. As to how he might have wound up in this poor village, or where he came from and what his name might have been, even the pastor was not able to tell me anything. The pictures themselves contained neither a name nor a painter's mark.

The years passed. While we were attending the university the good pastor died, and my school comrade's mother later followed her son to the curacy he had meanwhile obtained elsewhere; I no longer had any occasion to walk out to that village. Then, when I was settled myself in my hometown, it happened that I had to arrange for school quarters with good folks for the son of a relative. Thinking about my own youth, I was strolling through the streets in the afternoon sunshine when, at the corner of the marketplace, above the door of an old high-gabled house, an inscription in dialect caught my eye, which, translated, would sound something like this:

As smoke and dust will vanish again,
So must also the sons of men.

The words were probably not visible to young eyes, for I had never noticed them, as often as I had got my hot roll from the baker dwelling there during my school days. Almost automatically I went into the house; and in fact, here there was a lodging for my young cousin. The room of their old maiden aunt—so the friendly master baker told me—from whom they had inherited the house and the business, had been standing empty for years; for a long time they had wished a young guest for it.

I was led up a staircase, and we then entered a rather low room furnished in an old-fashioned way, both of whose windows with their little panes looked out on the spacious marketplace. In the past, the baker related, there had been two ancient lindens in front of the door, but he had had them cut down because they made the house too dark and also would have blocked the fine view here.

We were soon agreed on the terms in all details; but while we were still talking about the furnishings for the room, my eye had fallen upon an oil painting hanging in the shadow of a wardrobe, which suddenly absorbed my whole attention. It was still well preserved and depicted an elderly man with a serious and mild gaze, in a dark costume such as had been worn in the middle of the seventeenth century by men of the better classes who were more occupied with public affairs or learned matters than with the military calling.

Yet the old gentleman's head, as fine and attractive as it was and as felicitously as it may have been painted, would not have aroused this excitement in me; but the painter had put a pale boy in his arm, whose little, limply hanging hand held a white water lily—this boy I had long known. Here too it was doubtless death that had closed his eyes.

"Where does this picture come from?" I finally asked, as I suddenly realized that the baker, who was standing in front of me, had concluded his explanation.

He looked at me in surprise. "The old picture? That's from our maiden aunt," he replied: "it came from her great-granduncle, who was a painter and lived here more than a hundred years ago. There are some other things of his there."

With these words he pointed to a little chest of oak, on which all kinds of geometrical figures had been quite delicately carved.

When I took it down from the cupboard on which it stood, the lid fell back, revealing the contents to me: some heavily yellowed sheets of paper with very old script.

"May I read these pages?" I asked.

"If it gives you pleasure," replied the baker, "you may take the whole thing home. It's just old papers; they have no value."

However, I requested and obtained permission to read these worthless papers right there; and while I sat down in a huge old wing chair across from the old picture, the baker left the room, still astonished, to be sure, but nevertheless leaving the friendly promise that his wife would soon refresh me with a good cup of coffee.

But I was reading, and in reading I soon forgot everything around me.*

* * *

So now I was home again in our Holstein country; it was on the fourth Sunday after Easter in the year 1661! I had left my painting

---

*Storm endeavored to give a sense of the antiquity of the document with a moderate employment of archaic vocabulary and grammatical forms. No effort has been made to reproduce this effect in the translation. The loss is perhaps not too great, for, despite the meticulousness of the historical setting, Johannes's mentality seems more Romantic than characteristic of the seventeenth century.

equipment and other baggage in the town and was now walking cheerfully along the road through the May green beech wood that rises from the sea into the country. A couple of little forest birds flew before me and slaked their thirst in the water that stood in the deep wheel ruts, for a light rain had fallen over night and into the early morning, so that the sun had not yet risen above the forest shadow.

The bright song of the thrush sounding to me from the clearings found its echo in my heart. The commissions that my dear master Van der Helst* had put in my way during my last year in Amsterdam had relieved me of all cares; I was still carrying a good supply of traveling money and a bill of exchange on a Hamburg bank in my pockets; beyond that I was sumptuously attired; my hair fell to the shoulders of a short cloak trimmed in miniver, and a sword made in Liège was not lacking from my side.

But my thoughts hurried on ahead of me; constantly I saw Lord Gerhardus, my noble, most gracious patron, as, from the threshold of his room, he would stretch his hands out to me with his gentle greeting: "May God bless your entry, my Johannes!"

With my dear father, who had, oh, much too soon been taken to eternal bliss, he had at one time studied law at Jena and afterwards continued to pursue the arts and sciences with diligence, so that he had been a perceptive and zealous advisor to the most blessed Duke Friedrich† in his efforts, frustrated by the events of war, to found a state university. Although a nobleman, he had remained always loyally devoted to my dear father, after whose lamented passing he had taken care of my orphaned youth more than one might have expected and had not only increased my sparse means but, through his distinguished acquaintance among the Dutch nobility, so arranged it that my dear master Van der Helst took me on as his pupil.

I thought I knew that the honored gentleman was dwelling safely on his estate, for which the Almighty was never sufficiently to be thanked; for while I was applying myself to art in a foreign land, the atrocities of war had come over my homeland**—in such a way, however, that the troops supporting the king against the belligerent

---

*Bartholomeus van der Helst (1613–70), Dutch portraitist.

†Friedrich III, Duke of Holstein-Gottorf (1616–59), a powerful figure in both Holstein and Schleswig. The university in question was founded by his son, Duke Christian Albrecht, at Kiel in 1665.

**The Polish-Swedish War of 1655–60.

Swede* had laid waste to the land almost worse than the enemy, even condemning several of the servants of God to a wretched death. To be sure, owing to the sudden demise of Swedish Charles, peace had now come; but the grisly traces of war lay all around; many a peasant's or cottager's house, where I had been treated as a boy with a drink of sweet milk, I had seen on my morning walk burned down by the side of the road, and desolate weeds were on many a field where otherwise at this time the rye would have put out its green sprouts.

But such things did not weigh too heavily on me today; I only longed to prove by my art to the noble gentleman that he had not squandered gifts and favors on someone unworthy of them, and I also was not thinking about the vagabonds and roaming marauders that might still be left over from the war in the forests. But something else was bothering me, and that was the thought of Junker Wulf.† He had never been well disposed toward me; he even looked upon what his noble father had done for me as theft from himself, and many a time, when, as was often the case after my dear father's death, I spent the summer vacation on the estate, he soured and embittered the lovely days. Whether he was now in his father's house I had not heard; I had learned only that even before peace had been made he had kept company with the Swedish officers at gaming and drinking, which is not consistent with true Holstein loyalty.

While I was considering this, I had passed through the beech wood onto the footpath through the little fir wood that is close to the estate. The spicy aroma of resin surrounded me like a lovely memory, but soon I stepped out of the shadow into full sunshine, where meadows hedged with hazel bushes lay on both sides, and it was not long before I was walking between the two rows of mighty oak trees that lead to the lord's seat.

I know not what sort of an anxious feeling suddenly came over me, without any cause, as I thought at the time; for there was naught but sunshine around, and a right hearty and encouraging song of

*Karl X Gustav, king of Sweden 1654–60.

†*Junker*, from *Jung-Herr*, "young lord," is a north German term for the son of a lord and then for a landowning lord in general. Since no English equivalent seems to capture the tone of arrogance and crudity Storm clearly means to attach to the term, it has been retained in the translation.

larks sounded from the sky above. And behold, there on the field where the steward kept his beehives, the old wild pear tree still stood and whispered with its young leaves in the blue air.

"God greet you!" I said quietly, but was thinking less of the tree than of the sweet creature of God in whom, as it later turned out, all the happiness and sorrow and also all the gnawing penitence of my life was to be decided, for now and all time. This was the little daughter of the noble Lord Gerhardus, his only other child besides Junker Wulf.

In short: it was soon after my dear father's death when for the first time I spent the whole vacation here. At that time she was a nine-year-old girl who made her brown braids fly about gaily; I was a couple of years older. One morning I stepped out of the gatehouse; the old steward Dieterich, who lived above the entrance and next to whom, as a faithful man, my little bedchamber had been set up, had made me a crossbow of ash and also cast the bolts for it from sound lead. Now I wanted to attack the birds of prey, enough of whom screamed around the manor house; then she came skipping up to me from the courtyard.

"You know, Johannes," she said; "I will show you a bird's nest, there in the hollow pear tree; but those are thrushes, you musn't shoot them!"

With that she had already skipped on ahead of me; but before she had come to within twenty paces of the tree, I saw her suddenly stop. "The bogey, the bogey!" she cried and shook both her little hands in the air as though terrified.

But it was a big hoot owl that was sitting above the hole in the hollow tree and looking down to see whether it might catch a small bird flying out of it. "The bogey, the bogey!" cried the little girl again. "Shoot, Johannes, shoot!" The owl, however, made deaf by his gluttony, still sat and stared into the hole. Then I cocked my ash bow and shot, so that the bird of prey lay twitching on the ground; but from the tree a twittering little bird soared into the air.

Since that time Katharina and I were good companions with one another; in the forest and the garden, wherever the little girl was, there was I. But as a consequence I soon acquired an enemy; this was Kurt von der Risch, whose father lived an hour away on a rich estate. In the company of his learned tutor, with whom Lord Gerhardus liked to converse, he often came to visit. Since he was younger than Junker Wulf, he was left to me and Katharina, although he seemed especially to like the lord's brown-haired daughter. But that was all in vain; she only laughed at his crooked bird's nose, which, like almost all of his family, sat under bushy hair between two remarkably round eyes. Indeed, if she were only to see him from afar, she would lean her little head forward and call: "Johannes, the bogey! the bogey!" Then we hid behind the barns or ran straight into the forest that forms a bend around the fields and comes right up against the wall of the garden.

Consequently, when von der Risch became aware of this, we often got into hair-pulling contests, in which, however, since he was more hotheaded than strong, the advantage was usually on my side.

When I stayed here the last time for but a few days, in order to say farewell to Lord Gerhardus before my departure for a foreign land, Katharina was almost a maiden. Her brown hair was now captured in a golden net; in her eyes, when she raised her eyebrows, there was a play of light that made me quite uneasy. Also she had been given a fragile old maid to watch over her, who was called only "Coz Ursel" in the house; she did not let the child out of her sight and walked beside her everywhere carrying a long piece of knitting.

When I was walking with the both of them one October afternoon in the shadow of the garden hedges, there came up the walk to us a long, lanky fellow, dressed quite in fashion with a lace-trimmed leather jerkin and a feathered hat, and behold: it was Junker Kurt, my old adversary. I noticed at once that he was still courting his beautiful neighbor; also, that this seemed to please the old maid. Now it was "My Lord Baron" at his every word; at the same time she laughed most obsequiously with a repellently refined voice and lifted her nose immoderately into the air. But whenever I managed to slip in a word, she always spoke to me in the third person or just called me "Johannes," whereupon the junker squinted his round eyes and did his best to look down on me, although I was half a head taller.

I looked at Katharina, but she paid no attention to me; instead she walked demurely beside the junker, politely returning answers to him. But her little red mouth wrinkled now and then into a scornfully proud smile, so that I thought: "Console yourself, Johannes; his young lordship is causing your stock to rise!" Defiantly I hung back and let the other three go on before me. When they had gone into the house, however, and I was standing in front of it next to Lord Gerhardus's flower beds, brooding about engaging in a lively hair-pulling contest with von der Risch as in the past, Katharina suddenly came running back, plucked an aster from the flower bed beside me and whispered to me: "Johannes, you know what? The bogey looks like a young eagle; Coz Ursel said it!" And then she was gone before I knew what had happened. But all my defiance and anger was as though blown away. What did I care about von der Risch now! I laughed loudly and happily into the golden day, for the high-spirited words had been accompanied again with the sweet play of light in her eyes. But this time it had shone directly into my heart.

Soon afterward Lord Gerhardus had me called to his room; he showed me on the map one more time how I was to make the long journey to Amsterdam, gave me letters to his friends there and talked with me for a long time, as the friend of my dear, late father. For the same evening I had to go to the town, whence a townsman would take me to Hamburg in his carriage.

As the day was ending I took my leave. In the room below Katharina was sitting at her embroidery frame; I had to think of Greek Helen, as I had recently seen her in a copper engraving; the young neck that the girl bent over her work appeared to me that beautiful. But she was not alone; Coz Ursel sat across from her and was reading aloud from a French history book. As I came closer, she raised her nose to me: "Now," she said, "Johannes wishes to say adieu to me? Then he can at the same time pay his respects to the young lady!" At this Katharina had already stood up from her work, but as she extended her hand to me, Junker Wulf and Junker Kurt came into the room with a great noise, and she said only: "Farewell, Johannes!" And so I went away.

In the gatehouse I shook hands with old Dieterich, who had my staff and knapsack ready for me; then I walked between the oak trees toward the forest road. But I felt as though I could not rightly go away, as though a farewell were still owing to me, and I frequently stopped and looked behind me. Also, I had not gone on the footpath between the firs, but rather, as though instinctively, the much longer way on the main road. But the evening glow was already visible over the forest, and I had to hurry if I were not to be caught by nightfall. "Adieu, Katharina, adieu!" I said softly, and vigorously set my pilgrim's staff in motion.

Then, in the place where the footpath leads into the road—my heart stood still in a storm of joy—out of the darkness of the firs she was suddenly there; with glowing cheeks she came running up, she jumped over the dry ditch at the side of the road so that the cascade of her silken brown hair fell away from the golden net, and I caught her in my arms. With shining eyes, still gasping for breath, she looked at me. "I—I have run away from them!" she finally stammered; and then, pressing a package into my hand, she added softly: "From me, Johannes! And you shall not despise it!" Suddenly her little face grew downcast; her small, bowed mouth wanted to say something, but tears welled out of her eyes, and sorrowfully shaking her head, she quickly tore herself away. I saw her dress disappear in the dark fir path; then I heard the twigs rustle in the distance, and then I was standing alone. It was so quiet that one could hear the leaves falling. When I unfolded the package, it contained her golden christening coin that she had often shown me; a slip of paper was enclosed with it, which I read in the glow of the setting sun. "So that you will not suffer need," was written on it. Then I stretched my arms into the empty air: "Adieu, Katharina, adieu, adieu!" I called out perhaps a hundred times into the silent forest, and I reached the town only as night was falling.

Since then almost five years had gone by. How would I find things today?

And I was already standing at the gatehouse, and saw down in the courtyard the old lindens, behind whose light green leaves the two pointed gables of the manor house were now hidden. But as I tried to pass through the gateway, two pale grey bulldogs with spiked collars came at me quite wildly; they raised a terrifying howl and one leapt at me and bared his white teeth right in front of my face. I had never experienced such a welcome here. Then, to my good fortune, a rough voice well known to me called out of the chambers above the gate: "Hallo!" it called; "Tartar, Turk!" The dogs let me alone, I heard someone coming down the steps, and in the door under the gateway old Dieterich appeared.

When I looked at him, I could see that I had been abroad a long time; for his hair had become white as snow and the eyes that used to be so merry looked at me with a dull and distressed gaze. "Master Johannes!"* he said finally and extended both his hands to me.

---

*It is difficult to capture the nuances of this extremely class-conscious society in

122 • Theodor Storm

"God greet you, Dieterich!" I responded. "But since when do you keep such bloodthirsty beasts on the estate, attacking guests like wolves?"

"Yes, Master Johannes," said the old man, "the junker brought them."

"Is he home?"

The old man nodded.

"Well," I said: "maybe the dogs are necessary; there are many fellows left running loose from the war."

"Oh, Master Johannes!" And the old man was still standing there as though he did not want to let me into the courtyard. "You have come in bad times!"

I looked at him, but only said: "Certainly, Dieterich; the wolf looks out from many a broken window instead of the peasant. I have seen the like myself; but peace has been made, and the good gentleman in the manor will help, his hand is open."

With these words I wanted to go into the courtyard, although the dogs growled at me again, but the old man stepped into my path. "Master Johannes," he cried, "before you go further, listen to me! Your letter arrived all right with the Royal Post from Hamburg, but it could no longer reach the right reader."

"Dieterich!" I cried. "Dieterich!"

"Yes, yes, Master Johannes! Here the good days are gone, for our dear Lord Gerhardus is lying upon his bier in the chapel and the candles are burning beside his coffin. Now it will be different on the estate; but—I am a bondman, and it behooves me to be silent."

I wanted to ask: "Is the young lady, is Katharina still in the house?" But the words did not want to pass my tongue.

Across the way, in a rear wing of the manor house, was a little chapel, which I knew had not been used for a long time. So there I was to seek Lord Gerhard.

I asked the old steward: "Is the chapel open?" and when he

English. *Herr,* when applied to Gerhardus, is properly rendered "Lord," for he is a nobleman and a baron. But when applied to Johannes it is a sign that he has been lifted from his plebeian status, in his own eyes and those of others, by his skill as an artist. I have opted for "master." Coz Ursel's persistent habit, by the way, of addressing Johannes in the third person singular is not an affectation but a form of address used to inferiors from the seventeenth to the early nineteenth century, as though they were barely present. It is her way of insisting on his inferiority.

replied in the affirmative, I asked him to hold the dogs. Then I crossed the courtyard, where no one encountered me; only the song of a warbler came down from the tops of the lindens.

The door to the chapel was ajar, and I went in softly and quite anxiously. There stood the open coffin, and the red flame of the candles threw its flickering light on the beloved gentleman's noble countenance; the strangeness of death that lay upon it told me that he was now the denizen of another land. But as I started to kneel in prayer next to the corpse, there emerged above the edge of the coffin across from me a young, pale face looking at me through black veils almost in terror.

But it was only as a fleeting breath, then the brown eyes looked cordially up to me, and it was almost a cry of joy: "Oh, Johannes, it's you! Oh, you came too late!" And our hands grasped one another in greeting across the coffin; for it was Katharina, and she had become so beautiful that here, in the face of death, a hot pulse of life went through me. To be sure, the light playing in her eyes now lay frightened down in the depths; but the brown locks squeezed out of her black bonnet and the bowed mouth was all the redder in her pale face.

And, looking at the dead man almost in confusion, I said: "Indeed I came in the hope of thanking his living image with my art, to sit opposite him for many an hour and listen to his gentle and instructive words. Let me try, then, to capture his soon fading features."

And when she silently nodded to me, in tears that streamed over her cheeks, I sat in a pew and began to copy the dead man's countenance on a piece of paper that I had with me. But my hand trembled; whether if only before the majesty of death, I do not know.

While I was sketching I heard a voice from the courtyard outside that I recognized as that of Junker Wulf, immediately afterward a dog yipping as though after a kick or a blow with a whip, and then laughter and a curse from another voice that also seemed familiar to me.

When I looked at Katharina, I saw her stare at the window with utterly terrified eyes, but the voices and the footsteps passed by. Then she got up, came to my side, and watched as her father's countenance appeared under my pencil. It was not long before the footsteps of a single person returned outside; in the same moment Katharina lay her hand on my shoulder, and I felt her young body trembling.

Immediately the door to the chapel was torn open and I recognized Junker Wulf, although his usually pale face now seemed red and swollen.

"Why are you squatting all the time at the coffin!" he called to his sister. "Junker von der Risch was here to offer his condolences; you might have served him his drink!"

At the same time he had noticed me and pierced me with his little eyes. "Wulf," said Katharina, going up to him with me; "it is Johannes, Wulf."

The junker did not find it necessary to give me his hand; he only assessed my violet-colored jerkin and remarked: "You are wearing some fine feathers there; we'll now have to call you 'Sieur.' "

"Call me what you like!" I said, as we went out into the courtyard. "Although where I come from, they did not neglect to put 'Master' before my name. You well know that your father's son has great claims on me."

He looked at me somewhat surprised, but then only said: "Well, well, let's see what you have learned for my father's money; the wages for your work shall not be kept from you."

I replied that, as far as the wages were concerned, I had received them long in advance, but when the junker replied that he would conduct himself as behooves a nobleman, I asked him with what sort of work he wished to commission me.

"Now, you know," he said, and then stopped, looking sharply at his sister, "when a noble daughter leaves her house, her portrait must remain behind."

At these words I felt Katharina, who was walking beside me, grasp at my cloak as though she had lost her balance, but I replied calmly: "The custom is well-known to me, but what do you mean, Junker Wulf?"

"I mean," he said harshly, as though he were expecting to be contradicted, "that you are to make a portrait of the daughter of this house!"

This went through me almost like dread, whether more at the tone or the significance of the words, I don't know. I was also thinking that this was hardly the right time for such an undertaking.

Katharina was silent, but, since a pleading glance flew from her eyes to me, I answered: "If your noble sister will allow it, I hope to bring no shame to your father's patronage and my master's teaching. If you will clear out my chamber again above the gateway next to old Dieterich, what you wish shall be done."

The junker was content with this and also told his sister to have me served some refreshment.

I still wanted to ask a question about the start of my work, but I held my tongue, for the commission I had received suddenly aroused a rapture in me that I was afraid might break out with every word. Thus I had not noticed the two fierce watchdogs who were sunning themselves on the warm stones near the well. But as we came nearer, they leapt up and rushed at me with their jaws open, so that Katharina cried out; then the junker let out a shrill whistle, whereupon they crawled howling to his feet. "Hell's bells," he shouted, laughing, "two crazy fellows; it's all the same to them, a pig's tail or Flemish cloth!"

"Now, Junker Wulf"—I could no longer refrain from speaking—"if I am to be a guest in your father's house again, you can teach your animals better manners!"

His little eyes flashed at me and he tugged at his short, pointed beard a couple of times. Then he said, "That's only your welcome greeting, Sieur Johannes," bending over to pat the beasts. "So that everyone will know that a new regimen has begun here; for whoever crosses me I will drive into the jaws of the devil!"

With these last words, violently ejaculated, he had drawn himself up to his full height; then he whistled to his dogs and strode across the courtyard toward the gate.

I looked after him for a little while; then I followed Katharina, who silently, with bowed head, climbed the steps to the manor house under the shade of the lindens; just as silently we went together up the broad stairs into the upper house, where we entered the room of the late Lord Gerhardus. Here everything was as I had seen it before: the gold-flowered leather wall coverings, the maps on the wall, the clean parchment-bound volumes on the shelves, above the desk the beautiful forest scene of the elder Ruijsdael,* and in

---

*Salomon van Ruijsdael (ca. 1600–70), Dutch painter, teacher of his more famous nephew, Jacob van Ruijsdael.

front of it the empty chair. My eyes remained fixed on it; like the body of the deceased down below in the chapel, so this room, too, seemed to me now rendered lifeless and, despite the early spring shining through the window from the forest outside, as though filled with the silence of death.

In this moment I had almost forgotten Katharina. When I turned around, she was standing quite motionless in the middle of the room, and I saw how her breast was heaving violently under her delicate hands, which she held pressed against it. "It's true, isn't it" she said softly, "no one is here any more; no one but my brother and his fierce dogs?"

"Katharina!" I cried; "what is the matter with you? What is wrong in your father's house?"

"What is it, Johannes?" and almost wildly she grasped both my hands; and her young eyes flashed as though in anger and pain. "No, no; first let my father come to rest in his crypt! But then, you are to paint my picture, you will stay here a while—then, Johannes, help me; for the sake of this dead man, help me!"

At such words, quite overcome with pity and love, I fell to my knees before the beautiful, sweet Katharina and pledged myself and all my powers to her. Then a gentle flow of tears was released from her eyes, and we sat beside one another and spoke for a long time in memory of the deceased.

When we were going back down to the lower house, I also asked about the old maid.

"Oh," said Katharina, "Coz Ursel! Would you like to greet her? Yes, she is still here; she has her room down here, for the steps have long since become too burdensome for her."

So we came into a little room that looked out on the garden, where the tulips were just breaking out of the ground in the beds in front of the green hedge walls. Coz Ursel, looking in her black costume and crepe bonnet like nothing more than a vanishing heap, was sitting in a high-backed chair and had a board game in front of her that, as she told me later, the Lord Baron—after his father's death he really was such now—had brought her as a present from Lübeck.

"So," she said, when Katharina had spoken my name, while carefully inserting the ivory pegs around the board, "back again,

Johannes?—Oh, it's not coming out! *Oh, c'est un jeu très-compliqué!**

Then she threw the pegs into a pile and looked at me. "My," she said, "he is quite sumptuously dressed; but doesn't he know that he has entered a house of mourning?"

"I know it, my lady," I replied, "but I did not know it when I came into the gate."

"Well," she said and nodded in quite a conciliatory way, "actually, he doesn't really belong to the servants."

A smile flickered across Katharina's pale face, which was supposed to relieve me of any reply. Instead I praised the charm of the old lady's room, for even the ivy of the little tower, climbing the wall outside, had reached the window and waved its green tendrils in front of the panes.

But Coz Ursel said, yes, if only it weren't for the nightingales that were already starting with their noise at night; she couldn't sleep anyway; and then it was much too isolated here; she couldn't keep her eye on the servants from here; but nothing ever happened in the garden except when the gardner's boy trimmed the hedges or the boxwood beds.

And with that our visit ended, for Katharina reminded me it was high time to refresh my travel-weary body.

I was now lodged in my little chamber above the gate, to the particular joy of old Dieterich, for when we had finished work we sat on his coffer and I had him tell me stories just as in my boyhood. He then smoked a pipeful of tobacco, a habit that the soldiers had started here, too, and drew forth all sorts of stories of the hardships that they had had to suffer from the foreign troops on the estate and down in the town. But when I had once turned the conversation to good Lady Katharina, he at first couldn't find a stopping place but then suddenly broke off and looked at me.

"You know, Master Johannes," he said, " 'tis a sorry shame that you don't have a coat of arms like von der Risch over there!"

And since such talk brought the blood to my face, he patted me on the shoulder with his hard hand, saying: "Now, now, Master

*"Oh, it's a very complicated game."

Johannes; 'twas a fool thing to say; to be sure, we must remain where the Lord God has placed us."

I don't know whether I agreed with that sort of thing then, but I only asked what sort of a man von der Risch had turned out to be.

The old man looked at me right slyly and puffed on his short little pipe as though the expensive weed grew on the edge of the field. "Do you want to know, Master Johannes?" he then began. "He belongs to the lusty junkers who shoot the pommels off townspeople's houses on the Kiel marketplace; you can believe that he has splendid pistols! He doesn't know how to play so well on the fiddle, but since he likes a merry tune, one midnight not so long ago he rousted out the town musician, who lives above the Holstein Gate, with his sword, didn't even give him time to put on his jerkin and breeches. Instead of the sun the moon was in the sky; it was Epiphany and freezing cold; and the musician, the junker with his sword behind him, had to go fiddling through the streets in his shirtsleeves! Do you want to know more, Master Johannes? On his estate the peasants count themselves lucky if the Lord God has not blessed them with daughters—but he has money since his father's death, and our junker, as you know, had already gone through some of his inheritance."

I now knew enough, to be sure; anyway, old Dietrich had already closed his remarks with his maxim: "But I am only a bondman."

My clothes had come with my painting equipment from the town, where I had left everything in the Golden Lion, so that now, as was proper, I went about in dark dress. But I put the daylight hours to good use. Up in the manor house, next to the late lord's chamber, there was a gallery, roomy, with high ceilings, whose walls were almost completely hung with life-size pictures, so that there was only a place open for a pair next to the fireplace. These were the forebears of Lord Gerhardus, mostly men and women with serious and secure expressions, with countenances that one could well trust; he himself in the most vigorous manhood and Katharina's early deceased mother came at the end. The last two pictures were right exquisitely painted by our countryman, Georg Ovens of Eiderstedt,* in his powerful manner; and I now tried to trace with my brush the

---

*Georg Ovens (1623–78), painter from Holstein who was trained in Holland, possibly by Rembrandt.

features of my noble protector, in reduced scale, to be sure, and only for my own pleasure; but later it served me for a larger portrait, which is still my most precious company here in my lonely chamber. But the portrait of his daughter lives inside me.

Often, when I had set down my palette, I stood for a long time before the fine pictures. I found Katharina's countenance in both her parents: the father's forehead, the mother's charm around the lips; but where was the hard corner of the mouth, the little eye of Junker Wulf? That must have come from farther back in the past! Slowly I went along the row of the older portraits, almost a hundred years farther back. And behold, there hung a picture, in a black, already worm-eaten wood frame, that, even when I was a boy, made me stop as though it were holding me. It depicted a noblewoman of about forty years of age; the little grey eyes looked with cold penetration out of a hard face, only half of which was visible between the white collar and her veiled bonnet. I felt a shudder before the soul that had passed away so long ago, and I said to myself: "Here, this is the one! What mysterious paths nature takes! For a century and more something runs secretly, as though under cover, in the blood of the generations; then, long forgotten, it suddenly emerges to make trouble for the living. I must protect Katharina not from the son of noble Gerhardus, but from this woman here and the descendant born of her blood." And again I stepped up to the two most recent pictures, which refreshed my spirit.

So I passed the time in the quiet gallery, where around me only the dust particles played in the sun's rays, among the shades of those who had been.

Katharina I only saw at the midday meal, the old maid and Junker Wulf at her side; but unless Coz Ursel was talking in her high-pitched tones, it was always a silent and gloomy meal, so that I often gagged on the food in my mouth. The cause of this mood was not mourning for the departed; it lay rather between brother and sister, as though the tablecloth had been cut between them.* Katharina, after having hardly touched her food, always left early, scarcely greeting me with her eyes, but the junker, when he was in the mood, tried to keep me drinking with him; I had to defend myself against

---

*This is a common German idiom for an irreparable breach between persons, but Storm almost literalizes the metaphor here.

all sorts of taunts directed against me if I did not want to exceed my customary limit.

In the meantime, after the coffin had been closed for several days, the burial of Lord Gerhardus took place, down in the church of the village, where the family burial ground is located and where his bones now rest with those of his forebears, to whom the Supreme Being may one day grant a joyful resurrection!

Although many people from the town and the neighboring estates came to this funeral, there were few relatives and only distant ones, especially as Junker Wulf was the last of his line and Lord Gerhardus's lady had not been of a local family; so, in consequence, everyone left again after a short time.

Now the junker himself pressed me to begin my commissioned work, for which I had already chosen a place in the portrait gallery at a window facing north. To be sure, Coz Ursel, who could not climb the stairs on account of her gout, came and said it might better be done in her room or in the chamber next to it for the entertainment of us both. But I, only too gladly sparing myself such company, objected to the western sun there as the wrong kind of background for painting, and all her talking did her no good. Rather I was already busy the next morning curtaining the side windows of the gallery and setting up the high easel that I had made myself during the last few days with Dieterich's help.

When I had just laid down the stretcher with the canvas on it, the door from Lord Gerhardus's room opened and Katharine entered. For what reason, it would be difficult to say, but I felt that this time we were almost frightened as we faced one another. From her black attire, which she had not given up, the young face looked up to me in the most sweet confusion.

"Katharina," I said, "you know that I am supposed to paint your portrait; are you willing to put up with it?"

Then a veil came over her brown eyes and she said softly: "How can you ask, Johannes?"

Her answer brought happiness into my heart like a dew. "No, no, Katharina! But tell me, how can I be of service to you? Sit down so that we are not caught doing nothing, and then speak! Or rather, I already know. You don't need to tell me!"

But she did not sit down, she came up to me. "Do you remember, Johannes, how once you shot down the bogey with your bow? That is not necessary this time, although he is again lurking around the nest; for I am not a little bird that will let itself be torn to pieces by him. But, Johannes, I have a kinsman; help me against him!"

"You mean your brother, Katharina!"

"I have no other. He wants to marry me to a man I hate! During our father's long illness I fought the foul battle with him, and not until Father was in his coffin did I extort a promise from him to let me mourn Father in peace; but I know he won't even keep that."

I thought of a canoness, Lord Gerhardus's only sibling, and wondered if she should not be approached for protection and refuge.

Katharina nodded. "Will you be my messenger, Johannes? I have already written to her, but her answer got into Wulf's hands and I never found out what was in it; I heard only my brother's rage breaking out, such that would have filled even the ear of the dying man if it had still been open for the sounds of the world, but merciful God had covered his dear head with his last earthly slumber."

Katharina had now sat down across from me at my request, and I began to sketch out outlines on the canvas. So we were able to have a calm consultation; and since I had to go to Hamburg when the work was further advanced to order a frame from the wood-carver, we determined that at that time I would take the long road through Preetz* and deliver my message that way. The main thing now, however, was to get busy on my work.

There is often a strange contradiction in the human heart. The junker must already have known how I stood toward his sister; all the same, whether his pride obliged him to hold me in low regard or he believed he had frightened me sufficiently with his first threat, what I feared did not occur; Katharina and I were as undisturbed on the following days as on the first. Once he came in and scolded Katharina for wearing mourning, but then slammed the door behind him, and soon we heard him in the courtyard whistling a cavalry song. Another time he had von der Risch at his side. When Katharina made a violent movement, I asked her to remain at her

---

*A town between Kiel and Lübeck. After the Reformation the convent there became a home for noblewomen.

place, and continued calmly painting. Since the day of the funeral, when I had exchanged a distant greeting with him, Junker Kurt had not shown himself on the estate; now he came closer and examined the picture and spoke very fine words, but wondered why the young lady was so wrapped up and did not instead let her silken hair flow down her back in loose locks, as an English poet has so excellently expressed it: "locks which make such wanton gambols with the wind."* But Katharina, who up to now had said nothing, pointed to Lord Gerhardus's picture and said: "You don't seem to remember anymore that that was my father!"

What Junker Kurt replied to this I no longer recall, but my person did not seem present to him at all or only like a machine by which a picture was painting itself on the canvas. He started to say this and that about the picture over my head; but since Katharina no longer made any answer, he soon took his leave, wishing the lady pleasant amusement.

At this remark, however, I saw a swift glance flash toward me from his eyes like the point of a knife.

We suffered no further disturbance, and the work progressed with the season. On the forest pastures yonder the rye already was in silver-grey blossom and down in the garden the roses were already opening; but we two—I think I may write it today—we would now gladly have made time stand still; neither she nor I dared to touch upon my messenger journey with the slightest word. I would hardly know how to say what we talked about: only that I told her about my life in foreign lands and how I had always thought of home; also that her golden penny had once preserved me from need during an illness, as her child's heart had foreseen, and how I had later struggled and worried until I had recovered the treasure from the pawnshop. Then she smiled happily; and at the same time her dear face blossomed out of the dark ground of the picture ever more sweetly; it seemed to me as though it were hardly my own work. Occasionally it seemed as though something very warm were looking at me out of her eyes, but if I tried to capture it, it shied away, and yet it flowed secretly through the brush onto the canvas, so that, almost without my knowing it, a sensuously captivating picture came into being, like nothing else that came from my hand either before or

*Shakespeare, *The Merchant of Venice*, act 3, scene 2.

after. And finally it was time, and I was set to begin my journey the next morning.

When Katharina handed me the letter to her aunt, she sat in front of me one more time. Today there was no playing with words; we talked seriously and worriedly with one another. Meanwhile I applied the brush here and there, from time to time casting an eye on the silent company on the walls, whom otherwise I had hardly thought about in Katharina's presence.

There, while I was painting, my eye fell on that old portrait of a woman that hung at my side and directed its penetrating grey eyes at me out of the white lawn veil. I shuddered, nearly shifting my chair.

But Katharina's sweet voice came into my ear: "You have almost grown pale; what came over your heart, Johannes?"

I pointed at the picture with my brush. "Do you know her, Katharina? These eyes have looked at us here every day."

"Her? Even as a child I was afraid of her, and even during the day I would run through here as though blind. It is the wife of an earlier Gerhardus; she dwelt here well over a hundred years ago."

"She does not resemble your beautiful mother," I returned; "this face would have been able to say no to every plea."

Katharina looked at me quite seriously. "That's the way she is supposed to have been," she said; "she is said to have cursed her only child, but the next morning they pulled the pale young lady out of the garden pond, which was dammed up afterward. Behind the hedge, toward the forest, they say it was."

"I know, Katharina; today horsetails and rushes are still growing out of the ground there."

"Do you know also, Johannes, that one of our family is always supposed to show herself as soon as danger threatens our house? She is seen first here gliding along the windows, then disappearing in the garden bog."

Unwittingly my eyes turned again to the immovable ones of the picture. "And why," I asked, "did she curse her child?"

"Why?" Katharina hesitated a moment and looked at me almost in confusion with all her charm. "I believe that she did not want her mother's cousin as a husband."

"Was he such a very bad man?"

A look almost like a plea flew across to me, and a deep rose red covered her face. "I don't know," she said anxiously; and more softly, so that I could hardly hear it, she added: "It is said that she loved another; he was not of her class."

I had lowered my brush, for she sat before me with lowered eyes; if she had not raised her little hand from her lap and placed it on her heart, she herself would have been like a lifeless picture.

As lovely as it was, I finally said: "I can't paint this way; don't you want to look at me, Katharina?"

And when she lifted the lashes from her brown eyes, there was no longer any concealment; the beam of light went warmly and openly to my heart. "Katharina!" I had sprung to my feet. "Would that woman have cursed you, too?"

She took a deep breath. "Me, too, Johannes!" Then her head lay on my breast, and we stood in a close embrace before the portrait of the ancestress, who looked down on us with coldness and hostility.

But Katharina drew me gently away. "Let us not be intimidated, my Johannes!" she said. At the same moment I heard a noise in the staircase, and it was as though something with three legs were painfully laboring up the stairs. When Katharina and I had seated ourselves again at our places and I had picked up my brush and palette, the door opened, and Coz Ursel, the last person we would have expected, came coughing in on her cane. "I hear," she said, "that he wants to go to Hamburg to see to the frame: it is high time that I take a look at his work!"

It is widely known that old maids have the keenest faculties in matters of love and thus often bring affliction and misery into the world of the young. When Coz Ursel had hardly cast an eye on the picture, which she had not yet seen, she pulled herself up right proudly with her wrinkled face and asked me at once: "Did the young lady look at him as she appears there in the picture?"

I replied that it was just the noble art of painting not to give merely a copy of the face. But something unusual in our eyes or cheeks must already have struck her, for her eyes searched back and forth: "The work will soon be finished?" she then said in her most high-pitched voice. "Your eyes have an unhealthy gleam, Katharina; sitting so long seems not to have served you well."

I replied that the picture would soon be finished; there was only a little more to do here and there on the drapery.

"Well, then he won't need the young lady's presence any longer! Come, Katharina, your arm is better than this stupid stick here!"

And so I had to see the lovely treasure of my heart abducted by the withered lady, just as I thought I had won it; the brown eyes were barely able to send me a silent farewell greeting.

On the next morning, the Monday before Midsummer Day,* I set off on my journey. On a horse with which Dieterich had provided me, I trotted out of the gateway in the early morning; as I rode through the firs, one of the junker's dogs broke out and snapped at my animal's hamstrings, even though the horse was from their own stable—well, he who was sitting up in the saddle had always seemed suspicious to them. All the same, we escaped without injury, the horse and I, and arrived in Hamburg early in the evening.

The next morning I roused myself and soon located a wood-carver who had many finished patterns, so that it was only necessary to put them together and apply the decorations to the corners. Thus we came to terms and the master promised to send everything to me well packed up.

Now for a curious person there was much to be seen in the famous city, for example, in the Seamen's Society the pirate Störtebeker's silver goblet,† which is called the second emblem of the city, and no one, it says in a book, who has not seen it can say that he has been in Hamburg; then the miraculous fish with the real claws and wings of an eagle, which had been captured around this time in the Elbe and which the people of Hamburg, as I heard later, interpreted as a sign of victory over the Turkish pirates.** But, although a true traveler should not pass such rarities by, my spirit was too weighed down by both worry and my heart's longing. Therefore, after a merchant had cashed my bill of exchange and I had settled the score in my hostelry, I mounted my horse again at noon and soon had all the noise of great Hamburg behind me.

On the next afternoon I arrived in Preetz, announced myself in the convent to the reverend lady, and was soon admitted. In her imposing person I recognized immediately the sister of my dear departed

---

*June 24.

†Klaes Störtebeker, a notorious pirate executed in Hamburg in 1401. He is the model for a leader of rebellious youth in Günter Grass's novels *The Tin Drum* and *Cat and Mouse*. The cup was allegedly made from silver found on Störtebeker's ship and depicted his capture.

**Possibly a flying fish caught in the Elbe in 1662.

Lord Gerhardus; only, as often appears with unmarried women, the features of her face were, despite the resemblance, more severe than those of her brother. Even after I had handed over Katharina's letter I had to withstand a long and hard examination; but then she promised her assistance and sat down to her writing materials, while the maid was obliged to lead me into another room, where I was very well refreshed.

It was already late in the afternoon when I rode away again, but I calculated that, although my horse was already feeling the many leagues behind us, I would knock on old Dieterich's door around midnight. I carried the letter that the old lady had given me for Katharina well secured in a leather pouch on my breast under my jerkin. So I rode on into the deepening twilight, soon thinking but of her, the only one, and again and again thrilling my heart with lovely new thoughts.

It was a balmy June night; the aroma of the meadowflowers rose from the dark fields; the honeysuckle exhaled its fragrance from the windbreaks; the little nighttime insects hovered unseen in the air and the foliage or flew buzzing around the nostrils of my gasping horse, but above in the huge, blue-black bell of the heavens over me the constellation of the Swan in the southwest gleamed in its virginal magnificence.

When I was finally on Lord Gerhardus's territory again, I resolved at once to ride over to the village that lies to the side of the high road behind the wood. For I recalled that the innkeeper Hans Ottsen had a suitable handcart. Tomorrow I wished him to send a messenger with it into the town in order to pick up the Hamburg crate, and I wanted only to knock on his chamber window in order to arrange this with him.

So I rode along the edge of the wood, my eye almost dazzled by the greenish glowworms that flew about me with their playful lights. And the church was already rising large and dark before me, in whose walls Lord Gerhardus rested with his own people; I heard just as the hammer was drawn back in the tower and the bells rang midnight down into the village. "They are all sleeping," I said to myself, "the dead in the church or under the high, starry heavens down here in the churchyard, the living under their low roofs lying dark and silent before you." So I rode on. But when I came to the pond from which one could see Hans Ottsen's inn, I saw a misty reflection of light thrown out of it onto the path, and the sound of fiddles and clarinets met me.

Since I wanted to talk with the tavern-keeper all the same, I rode up and stabled my horse. When I then came out onto the threshing-floor, it was packed full of people, men and women, and such shouting and dissolute goings-on as I had never observed in earlier years, even at dances. The light of the tallow candles, which swung under a beam on a crossbar, lifted out of the darkness many a bearded and scarred face that one would sooner not have met in the forest. But not only vagabonds and peasant lads seemed to be enjoying themselves here; among the musicians who were standing in front of the main room on their tubs stood Junker von der Risch; he had a cloak over one arm and a robust girl on the other. But he didn't seem to like the piece, for he tore the violin out of the fiddler's hands, threw a handful of coins on his tub, and demanded that they play the newly fashionable two-step. When the musicians quickly obeyed him and madly played the new melody, he shouted for room and vaulted into the thick crowd, and the peasant lads scowled at him as the girl lay in his arms like a dove before a vulture.

But I turned away and went into the back room to talk with the innkeeper. There sat Junker Wulf with a tankard of wine and had old Ottsen next to him, embarrassing him with all sorts of jests; thus he threatened to raise his rent and shook with laughter when the frightened man pleaded most abjectly for mercy and leniency. When he caught sight of me he did not let up until I had made a third at the table. He asked about my journey and whether I had enjoyed myself well in Hamburg, but I only answered that I had just come back from there and that the frame would shortly arrive in the town, where Hans Ottsen might easily get it with his handcart.

While I was negotiating this with Ottsen, von der Risch came storming in and shouted at the innkeeper to get him a cool drink. But Junker Wulf, whose tongue was already wallowing heavily in his mouth, grasped him by the arm and pulled him down onto the empty chair.

"Now Kurt!" he cried. "Have you not yet had your fill of your girls! What will Katharina say to it? Come, let us be in fashion and play an honorable game of hazard with one another!" As he said this he pulled a pack of cards from under his jerkin. *"Allons donc!—Dix et dame!—Dame et valet!"**

I was still standing and watching the game that had just become fashionable, only wishing that the night would pass and morning would come. But this time the drunkard seemed to be the superior of the sober man, for every card fell badly for von der Risch one after the other.

"Cheer up, Kurt!" said Junker Wulf, smirking, as he scraped the talers into a pile: "Lucky in love, unlucky at play! Let the painter here tell you about your beautiful betrothed! He knows her by heart; you'll learn something about her from art."

But the other, as I knew better than anyone, did not seem very aware of his good fortune in love, for he pounded on the table, cursing and looking at me right fiercely.

"Ooh, you are jealous, Kurt," said Junker Wulf with amusement, as though he was tasting every word with his heavy tongue; "but cheer up, the frame for the picture is already finished; your friend the painter is just now returning from Hamburg."

At these words I saw von der Risch tense like a pointer who has scented his prey. "From Hamburg today? Then he must have used Faust's cloak;† for my groom saw him today in Preetz! He paid a visit to your aunt in the convent."

My hand went involuntarily to my breast where I had secured the pouch with the letter, for Junker Wulf's drunken eyes rested on me, and I could only feel that he saw my whole secret lying open before him. And it was not long until the cards were slapped on the table. "Oho!" he cried. "In the convent, with my aunt! I guess you're engaged in two trades at once, fellow! Who sent you on this errand?"

"Not you, Junker Wulf!" I returned, "and this is enough for you to know!" I wanted to reach for my sword, but it was not there; it now occurred to me that I had hung it on the saddle horn when I took my horse into the stable.

And the junker was already shouting again to his younger crony: "Tear open his jerkin, Kurt! I'll bet the whole pile here that you'll find a fine correspondence that you would not like to see delivered!"

---

*"Come on!—Ten and queen!—Queen and jack!"
†In the first *Faust Book* of 1587, well-known in the seventeenth century, Faust flies to a wedding on his cloak.

At the same moment I already felt von der Risch's hands on my body and we began to wrestle furiously with one another. I could tell that I would not find it so easy to beat him as in our boyhood, but then it fell out to my good fortune that I grasped both his wrists and so he stood before me as though shackled. Neither of us had uttered a word, but when we now looked into one another's eyes, each knew that he had his mortal enemy before him.

Junker Wulf seemed to think the same; he struggled up from his chair, as though he wanted to come to von der Risch's aid, but he must have partaken of too much of the wine, for he staggered back to his seat. There he shouted as loudly as his stammering tongue would permit: "Hey, Tartar! Turk! Where are you! Tartar, Turk!" And I knew that the two fierce curs, which I had seen earlier idling about the threshing-floor at the serving counter, were to spring at my bare throat. Already hearing them panting up through the crowd of the dancers, with a sudden heave I threw my enemy to the ground, leapt out of the room through a side door, slamming it with a crash behind me, and thus escaped to the outside.

And suddenly the quiet night and the glimmer of the moon and stars were around me again. I didn't dare at all to go to my horse in the stable, but jumped immediately over a wall and ran over the field toward the wood. As I soon reached it, I tried to keep the direction toward the estate, for the wood comes almost up to the garden wall. The light of the moon and stars was, to be sure, blocked by the foliage of the trees, but my eyes soon got used to the darkness, and, feeling the pouch secure under my jerkin, I groped my way stoutly forward. Since I saw that I could stay here no longer, I thought I would rest for the remainder of the night in my chamber, then discuss with Dieterich what should be done.

From time to time I stood still and listened, but on my way out I must have thrown the door into the latch and thus gained a good lead on them; not a sound could be heard from the dogs. I did hear, however, when I stepped out of the shadow into a clearing lit by the moon, the nightingales singing not far away, and I directed my steps toward their song, for I well knew that they had their nests around here only in the hedges of the manor garden; I now knew where I was and that I was not far from the courtyard.

I therefore followed the sweet song that sounded ever more brightly out of the darkness before me. Then something else struck my ear that suddenly came nearer and made my blood freeze. I could no longer doubt that the dogs were breaking through the underbrush; they held fast to my trail, and I already could clearly hear their panting behind me and their mighty leaps in the dry leaves of the forest floor. But God gave me his gracious protection; out of the shadows of the trees I plunged against the garden wall and pulled myself over on the branch of a lilac. The nightingales were still singing in the garden; the boxwood hedges threw deep shadows. It was in such a moonlit night that I had walked here with Lord Gerhardus before my journey into the world. "Look at it one more time, Johannes!" he had said then; "it could happen that upon your return you will find me no longer at home, and that there will be no welcome for you written on the gate; but I would not like for you to forget this place."

This now flew through my mind and I had to laugh bitterly, for now I was here as a hunted animal, and I already heard Junker Wulf's dogs running right fiercely outside the garden wall. As I had seen in earlier days, it was not everywhere so high that the raging beasts could not get over it, and round about in the garden there was no tree, nothing but the thick hedges and over near the house the flower beds of the late lord. Then, just as the barking of the dogs sounded a howl of triumph inside the garden wall, I saw in my peril the strong old ivy stem that climbed up the tower, and when the dogs came raging out of the hedge into the moonlit space, I was already far enough up that they could not jump high enough to reach me; they only tore down my cloak, which had slipped from my shoulder, with their teeth.

I, however, clinging in this way and fearful that the weaker branches farther up would not be able to hold me for very long, looked searchingly around to see if I could not find a better grip, but there was nothing to be seen but the dark ivy leaves around me. Then, in such peril, I heard a window open above me, and a voice called down to me—may I hear it again, when Thou, my God, wilt soon summon me from this earthly vale! "Johannes!" it called; softly but clearly I heard my name, and I climbed higher on the increasingly weak branches, while the sleeping birds fluttered up around me and the dogs sent up their howling from below. "Katharina! Is it really you, Katharina?"

But a trembling little hand already was coming down to me and pulling me toward the open window, and I looked into her eyes that stared full of horror into the drop.

"Come!" she said. "They will tear you to pieces." Then I pulled myself up into her chamber. But when I was inside, the little hand let go of me, and Katharina sank down on a chair standing by the window and tightly closed her eyes. The thick braids of her hair lay over her white nightdress down to her lap; the moon, which had risen over the garden hedges, shone through the window and fully illuminated everything. I stood still before her as though enchanted, she seemed to me so charmingly strange and yet so completely my own; only my eyes drank their fill of all her beauty. Not until a sigh lifted her breast did I speak to her: "Katharina, dear Katharina, are you dreaming?"

Then a pained smile ran over her face: "I almost think so, Johannes! Life is so hard; dreaming is sweet!"

But when the howling rose anew from down in the garden, she started up in fright. "The dogs, Johannes!" she cried. "What is going on with the dogs?"

"Katharina," I said, "if I am to serve you, I think it will have to happen soon, for there is little likelihood that I will get into this house again through the door." With that I took the letter out of my pouch and also related how I had got into a quarrel with the junkers down at the inn.

She held the letter into the bright moonlight and then looked at me openly and with a full heart, and we discussed how we would meet tomorrow in the fir wood, for Katharina was first to find out what day was fixed for Junker Wulf's departure for the midsummer market in Kiel.

"And now, Katharina," said I, "don't you have something that looks like a weapon, an iron measuring stick or something, with which I can defend myself against those two dogs down there?"

But she started up as though from a dream: "What are you saying, Johannes!" she cried, and her hands, which up to now had been resting in her lap, reached for mine. "No, don't go, don't go! Down there is death, and if you go, there will be death here, too!"

Then I knelt before her and laid my head on her young breast, and we embraced in great affliction. "Oh, Kate," I said, "what can poor love do? Even if it were not for your brother Wulf—I am not a nobleman and may not court you."

She looked at me very sweetly and anxiously; but then she spoke almost roguishly: "Not a nobleman, Johannes? I should have thought you were that, too! But—oh no! Your father was only the friend of mine—that probably does not count with the world!"

"No, Kate; that doesn't, and certainly not here," I replied and held her innocent body still more tightly; "but over there in Holland, there an able painter is regarded as the equal of a German nobleman; to pass over the threshold of Mynheer Van Dyck's* palace in Amsterdam is doubtless an honor to the most highborn. They wanted to keep me there, my master Van der Helst and others! If I were to go back there for a year or two, then we shall get away from here; only stand firm against your dissolute junker!"

Katharina's white hands stroked my locks; she hugged me and said softly: "Since I have let you into my chamber, I shall have to become your wife, too."

She probably did not imagine what a stream of fire these words poured into my veins, in which my blood was already warmly throbbing. A man beset by three terrible demons, by anger and mortal fear and love, my head now lay in the lap of the deeply beloved woman.

Then came a shrill whistle; the dogs below suddenly fell silent, and when the whistle was repeated, I heard them madly and wildly running away.

Footsteps sounded from the courtyard; we listened so intently that we stopped breathing. But soon a door there was first torn open, then slammed shut, and then bolted. "That is Wulf," said Katharina softly; "he has locked the two dogs into the stable." Soon we heard the door of the main corridor under us open and shut, the key turn, and afterwards footsteps in the lower hall that faded where the junker had his chamber. Then everything was quiet.

It was now safe, quite safe, but our chat with one another was suddenly quite at an end. Katharina had leaned back her head; I only heard our two hearts beating. "Shall I go now, Katharina?" I said finally.

But her young arms drew me silently up to her mouth; and I did not go.

---

*Presumably Anton van Dyck (1599–1641), Flemish painter. He did not live in Amsterdam but was a native of Antwerp and spent much of his career in England. The mention of him here is an anachronism, as he had been dead for twenty years.

There was no more sound but the singing of the nightingale out of the depth of the garden and from afar the murmuring of the little stream that flowed behind the hedges.

This was a night such as we hear of in the songs, when the beautiful pagan Lady Venus sometimes arises in the night and goes about to confound pure human hearts. The moonlight was extinguished in the sky, a sultry aroma of flowers wafted through the window, and there above the forest silent lightning flashes played in the night. —Oh, guardian, guardian, was your call so far from me?*

I still remember well that suddenly the cocks crowed sharply from the courtyard and that I held a pale and weeping woman in my arms who did not want to let me go, notwithstanding that morning was dawning over the garden, throwing a red gleam into our chamber. But then, when she became aware of it, she drove me away, terrified by mortal fear.

One more kiss, a hundred more; one more fleeting word; when the bell was rung for the servants at noon we were to meet in the fir wood; and then—I hardly knew myself how it happened—I stood in the garden, down below in the cool morning air.

One more time, while I picked up my cloak that had been ripped to pieces by the dogs, I looked up and saw a pale hand waving farewell to me. But I became almost terrified as I accidentally looked back for a moment from the garden step and glanced at the lower windows beside the tower; for I thought that I also saw a hand behind one of them; it threatened me with a raised finger and seemed to me colorless and bony like the hand of death. It was only for a fleeting moment, however, that this passed before my eyes; I thought at first of the tale of the spectral ancestress, but then told myself that it was only my own disturbed senses that had deluded me.

So, paying no further attention to it, I walked quickly through the garden, but soon noticed that in my haste I had got into the reed bog; one of my feet sank into it above the ankle as though something wanted to suck it in. "Ah," I thought, "the phantom of the

---

*The meaning of this line, which occurs again later in the text, has been an object of some interpretive disagreement. The best guess may be that Johannes here conflates the figure of the watchman in the medieval morning song, who warns the lovers to part at dawn, with the notion of a guardian angel. In the second occurrence the religious sense appears to have displaced the secular one.

house is grabbing you after all!" But I extracted myself and jumped over the wall down into the wood.

The darkness of the thick trees suited my dreamy mood; here it was still the blessed night around me from which my senses did not want to part. Only after some time, when I stepped out into the open field from the edge of the wood, did I become fully awake. A little group of deer stood not far away in the silver-grey dew, and above me from the sky sounded the morning song of the lark. Then I shook off all idle dreams, but in the same moment the question arose in my brain like hot anguish: "What now, Johannes? You have taken a dear life to yourself; know now, that there is nothing of value in your life but hers!"

But no matter how I thought about it, it constantly seemed to me best that, if Katharina were to find a safe refuge in the convent, I would then return to Holland, there secure the help of friends, and return at once to bring her with me. Perhaps she would have softened the heart of her old aunt, and, if worst came to worst—we would have to succeed without that!

I already saw us on a cheerful bark sailing over the waves of the green Zuider Zee, I already heard the carillon from the tower of the Amsterdam town hall and saw my friends break out of the crowd at the harbor and greet me and my beautiful wife with a loud cry and accompany us in triumph to our small but dear home. My heart was full of courage and hope, and I strode more vigorously and swiftly as though I might thus reach my happiness all the sooner.

But it was to be otherwise.

While engrossed in my thought I had gradually come to the village and here entered Hans Ottsen's inn from which I had had to flee so suddenly in the night. "Well, Master Johannes," the old man on the threshing-floor called to me; "what was your trouble yesterday with our gracious junkers? I was just outside at the serving-counter, but when I came in again they were cursing you right cruelly, and even the dogs were raging at the door you had slammed shut behind you."

Since I gathered from these words that the old man had not understood the quarrel, I replied only: "You know that von der Risch and I often used to tussle with one another when we were boys; yesterday there was just an aftertaste of it."

"I know, I know!" said the old man; "but today the junker is sitting on his father's estate. You should be careful, Master

Johannes; you want to take a long spoon when you sup with such gentlemen."

In this I had no reason to contradict him, so I ordered bread and a morning drink and went into the stable where I got my sword and also took my pencil and sketchbook out of my knapsack.

But it was still a long time until the noon bell, so I asked Hans Ottsen to have his boy bring my horse to the estate, and when he agreed to this, I walked out again to the wood. But I only went as far as the place on the pagan mound where one can see the two gables of the manor house rising over the garden hedge, a scene I had already chosen for the background to Katharina's portrait. Now I thought that, though she herself will be living before long in a foreign land and probably will never again enter her father's house, she ought not to be entirely bereft of a view of it, so I took out my pencil and began to sketch most carefully every little corner where her eye might once have rested. I intended to finish it in Amsterdam in color so that it would immediately greet her when I brought her into our chamber there.

After a couple of hours the drawing was finished. I made a twittering bird fly over it as though in greeting; then I sought the clearing where we were to meet and stretched out next to it in the shadow of a thick beech, longingly craving for the time to pass.

I must nevertheless have fallen asleep, for I awakened from a distant sound and became aware that it was the noon bell on the estate. The hot sun was blazing down and spread the aroma of the raspberries with which the clearing was covered. It recalled how Katharina and I, during our walks in the woods, had found sweet provender here, and now a strange play of the imagination began: now I saw her delicate figure as a child amidst the shrubs; now she stood before me, looking at me with blissful woman's eyes as I had seen her last, as I would enclose her in person on my beating breast immediately, in the next moment.

But suddenly I was overcome with alarm. Where was she? It was a long time since the bell had sounded. I jumped up, I walked around, I stood and peered through the trees in all directions; anxiety crept into my heart; but Katharina did not come; no footstep rustled in the foliage; only the summer wind whispered now and again in the treetops above.

Full of evil premonitions, I finally went away and took a round-about path to the estate. When I came between the oaks not far from the gate, I encountered Dieterich. "Master Johannes," he said, coming quickly up to me, "you have spent the night in Hans Ottsen's inn; his boy brought me your horse back. What did you intend to do with our junkers?"

"Why do you ask, Dieterich?"

"Why, Master Johannes? Because I should like to prevent a misfortune between you."

"What is that supposed to mean, Dieterich?" I asked again; but I felt tense as though the words were sticking in my throat.

"You know yourself, Master Johannes!" returned the old man. "I have just got wind of it a little—it might have been an hour ago. I wanted to call the lad who trims the hedges in the garden. When I came to the tower where our lady has her chamber, I saw Coz Ursel in close conversation with our junker. He had his arms crossed and spoke not a word, but the old lady was talking a blue streak and properly complaining in her high voice. She was pointing now down to the ground, now up into the ivy that grows on the tower. I understood nothing, Master Johannes, of any of it; but then—and now pay attention—she held something with her bony hands before the junker's eyes as though she were threatening with it, and when I looked more closely, it was a scrap of miniver such as you wear on your cloak."

"Go on, Dieterich!" I said; for the old man had his eyes on my torn cloak, which I was carrying on my arm.

"There is not much else," he replied; "for the junker turned suddenly to me and asked me where you were to be found. You can believe me, if he had been in reality a wolf, his eyes could not have blazed more bloodily."

Then I asked: "Is the junker in the house, Dieterich?"

"In the house? I think so, but what do you have in mind, Master Johannes?"

"I have in mind, Dieterich, that I have to talk with him at once."

But Dieterich had grasped me with both hands. "Don't go, Johannes," he said urgently; "at least tell me what has happened—your old friend has always had good advice for you!"

"Later, Dieterich, later!" I replied. And with these words I tore my hands out of his.

The old man shook his head. "Later, Johannes;" he said, "the Lord only knows!"

But I strode across the courtyard to the house. A maid, whom I asked in the corridor, said that the junker was in his room.

Only once before had I entered this room, which lay in the lower house. Instead of books and maps, as in his late father's room, here there were all sorts of weapons, hand cannons and arquebuses, also all kinds of hunting equipment on the walls; otherwise it was without decoration and showed that no one stayed here for long and with his whole attention.

I almost retreated from the threshold when I had opened the door at the junker's "Come in"; for, as he turned to me from the window, I saw a cavalry pistol in his hand, with the wheel lock of which he was fidgeting. He looked at me as though I had come from the lunatics. "So!" he drawled; "verily, Sieur Johannes, if it is not his ghost!"

"You thought, Junker Wulf," I returned, coming closer to him, "that I might have taken other roads than the one leading into your chamber!"

"I thought so indeed, Sieur Johannes! How good you are at guessing! But all the same, you've come just at the right time; I had people looking for you!"

There was something quivering in his voice that was like a beast of prey about to lunge, so that my hand went unconsciously to my sword. Nevertheless I said: "Hear me and allow me to say something calmly, Sir Junker!"

But he interrupted my speech: "You will be good enough to hear me out first! Sieur Johannes"—and his words, which at first came slowly, gradually turned into something like bellowing—"a couple of hours ago, when I woke up with a groggy head, I remembered and like a fool was sorry that in my inebriation I had set the wild dogs at your heels; but since Coz Ursel had shown me the scrap that they tore out of your plumage—hell and damnation! I am only sorry now that the beasts left the job undone!"

Once again I tried to get a word in, and, as the junker was silent, I thought he might listen. "Junker Wulf," I said, "it is true that I am not a nobleman, but I am no insignificant man in my art and I hope someday to equal the greater ones; so I ask you in propriety, give me your sister Katharina for a wife—"

Then the words froze in my mouth. From his pale face the eyes of the old portrait stared at me; a shrill laugh struck my ear, a shot—

then I collapsed and only heard my sword, which I had involuntarily almost drawn, falling with a clatter to the floor.

It was many weeks later that I sat in the already-dimming sunshine on a bench in front of the last house of the village, gazing with dull eyes toward the wood on the opposite side of which the manor house was located. My foolish eyes kept seeking the point where, as I imagined, Katharina's chamber looked out upon the already autumn yellow treetops; for of herself I had no news.

I had been brought with my wound into this house, which was occupied by the junker's forester; and, except for this man and his wife and a surgeon unknown to me, no one had come to me during my long convalescence. Where I had got the shot in my breast no one inquired, and I told no one about it; to appeal to the duke's courts against Lord Gerhardus's son and Katharina's brother could never occur to me. His mind might be at ease about it, and all the more since he always defied anything of the sort.

Only once had good Dieterich been there; he brought me at the junker's order two rolls of Hungarian ducats as wages for Katharina's portrait, and I took the money, thinking that it was a part of her inheritance of which, as my wife, she would probably not receive much later. I was not able to manage a confidential talk with Dieterich, which I greatly desired, for the yellow, foxy face of my host looked into my chamber every moment. But I found out so much, that the junker had not gone to Kiel, and since then Katharina had not been seen by anyone, neither in the courtyard nor in the garden; I was barely able to ask the old man to convey my greetings to the lady if there was an opportunity, and to tell her that I thought of soon traveling to Holland, but of returning even sooner, all of which he promised faithfully to transmit.

But afterwards I was beset by the greatest impatience, so that, against the will of the surgeon and before the last leaves had fallen from the trees in the forest, I set off on my journey. I arrived after a short time in good condition in the Dutch capital, where I was most affectionately received by my friends, and furthermore was able to recognize as a fortunate sign that two pictures I had left behind had both been sold at respectable prices through the helpful mediation of my dear master Van der Helst. Nor was this indeed all; a merchant who had previously been well-disposed toward me sent me a message that he had only been waiting for me so that I might paint the portrait of his daughter, who was married in The Hague, and a rich fee was immediately promised me for it. Then I thought, if I were to complete this, there would be enough of the helpful metal in my hands to enable me to bring Katharina into a well-ordered home without any other means.

As my friendly patron was of the same opinion, I went avidly to work, so that I soon saw the day of my departure coming nearer and nearer, ignoring the bad circumstances I still had to contend with over there.

But the eyes of man do not see the dark that is before him. When the portrait was completed and I had received rich praise and gold for it, I could not leave. In my labor I had not considered my weakness; the poorly healed wound overthrew me again. Just as the Christmas waffle stands were being set up at all the street intersections, my illness began and kept me confined longer than the first time. To be sure, there was no lack of the best medical art and the loving care of friends, but anxiously I saw day after day pass by, and no news could come from her or get to her.

Finally, after a hard winter, when the Zuider Zee once again made its green waves, my friends accompanied me to the harbor, but instead of good cheer I now took heavy cares on board with me. Still, the journey went quickly and well.

From Hamburg I traveled with the Royal Post; then, as almost a year before, I went on foot through the forest, in which barely the first tips were turning green. To be sure, the finches and buntings were already practicing their spring songs, but what did I care about them today! I did not go directly to Lord Gerhardus's estate; instead, as hard as my heart was beating, I turned to the side and walked along the edge of the wood to the village. There I soon stood in Hans Ottsen's inn and face to face with the innkeeper himself.

The old man looked at me strangely, but then said I looked quite fit. "Only," he added, "you mustn't play with muskets any more; they make worse stains than your paintbrush."

I was glad to leave him in this opinion, which I observed had been generally disseminated here, and for the present asked about old Dieterich.

Then I was obliged to hear that, before the first snow, as tends to happen to such strong people, he died a sudden but painless death.

"He is happy," said Hans Ottsen, "that he has joined his old master up there, and it is better for him, too."

"Amen!" I said; "my dear old Dieterich!"

But while my heart only, and ever more fearfully, sighed for news of Katharina, my timid tongue took a detour, and I said uneasily: "How is your neighbor, von der Risch, doing?"

"Oho," the old man laughed; "he has taken a wife, and one that will soon straighten him out."

Only in the first moment did I take fright, for I said to myself at once that he would not speak of Katharina this way, and when he mentioned the name, it was an elderly but rich maiden lady from the neighborhood; therefore I inquired bravely how things were in Lord Gerhardus's house and how the young lady and the junker were getting along with one another.

Then the old man threw me one of his strange looks. "You may think," he said, "that old towers and walls can't talk!"

"What's that supposed to mean?" I cried, but it fell like a hundredweight on my heart.

"Well, Master Johannes," and the old man looked me quite confidently in the eye, "you yourself will know best what has become of the lady! You were, after all, not here for the last time in the fall; I'm only surprised that you have come again, for Junker Wulf, I should think, will not have made the best of a bad bargain."

I looked at the old fellow as though I had become daft myself, but suddenly I had a thought. "You wretch!" I shouted, "you don't think that Lady Katharina has become my wife?"

"Now let me go!" replied the old man—for I was shaking him by both shoulders. "What business is it of mine! It's what people say! In any case: since New Year's the lady has not been seen in the manor."

I swore to him that I had lain ill in Holland all that time; I knew nothing of all this.

Whether he believed it I am unable to say, but he informed me that once an unknown clergyman is supposed to have come to the estate at night and in great secrecy. Although Coz Ursel had driven the servants into the quarters in time, one of the maids, who was listening through the crack in the door, claimed to have seen me going across the corridor to the stairs; later she had clearly heard a carriage driving out of the gatehouse, and since that night only Coz Ursel and the junker were in the manor.

Everything I undertook from then on, always in vain, to find Katharina or even just a trace of her, shall not be recorded here. In the village there was only the foolish gossip of which Hans Ottsen had given me a taste; therefore I went off to the convent to Lord Gerhardus's sister, but the lady would not admit me. Otherwise I was told that no sort of young woman had been seen with her. Then I journeyed back and so far demeaned myself that I went to von der Risch's house and appeared as a supplicant before my old adversary. He said scornfully that maybe the bogey had caught the little bird; he hadn't looked to see; besides he had no further connection with the people of Lord Gerhardus's estate.

Junker Wulf, for his part, who may have heard about it, sent a message to Hans Ottsen's inn that if I should dare to force myself on him, he would have me chased by the dogs again. Then I went into the forest and lay in ambush for him like a highwayman; the steel was bared from its sheath; we fought until I wounded his hand and his sword flew into the bushes. But he only looked at me with his evil eyes; he did not speak. At last I came for a long sojourn to Hamburg, where I hoped to pursue my researches conveniently and with greater circumspection.

But it was all in vain.

Now I will rest my pen for the present. For your letter is lying before me, my dear Josias; I am to stand godfather to your little daughter, the granddaughter of my late sister. On my journey I shall pass by the forest behind which Lord Gerhardus's estate lies. But all that belongs to the past.

* * *

Here the first part of the manuscript ends. Let us hope that the author celebrated a joyful christening and refreshed his heart in the bright presence of his friends.

My eyes rested on the old picture across from me; I could not doubt that the handsome, earnest man was Lord Gerhardus. But who was that dead boy Master Johannes had so gently set in his arm? Thoughtfully I took the second and last part, the handwriting of which seemed a bit more insecure. It read as follows:

As smoke and dust will vanish again,
So must also the sons of men.

The stone on which these words are carved was set over the doorframe of an old house. When I passed by it I always had to turn my eyes to it, and for a long time this same saying had often been my companion on my lonely walks. When they tore down the old house last fall, I purchased this stone from among the ruins, and today it has been similarly embedded over the door of my house, where after I am gone it may remind many who pass by of the vanity of earthly things. But to me it shall be an admonition, before the hand stops on my clock, to continue with the account of my life. For you, son of my dear sister, who will soon be my heir, may take, along with my small amount of earthly goods, also my earthly sorrow, which during my lifetime I have never been able to confide to anyone, not even to you, all my love notwithstanding.

Well, then; in the year 1666 I came for the first time to this town on the North Sea, the reason being that I had received a commission from the rich widow of a brandy distiller to paint the resurrection of Lazarus,* which picture she intended to donate as an obligatory and friendly memorial to her late husband and as an ornament to the local church, where yet today it is to be seen above the baptismal font with the four apostles. Besides, the mayor, Master Titus Axen,† who previously had been canon in Hamburg, where I had been acquainted with him, wanted me to paint his portrait, so that I had work to do here for a long time. I had my lodging with my only and elder brother, who had long filled the office of secretary of the town. The house in which he lived as an unmarried man was high and roomy, and it is the same house with the two lindens on the corner of the marketplace and Merchant Street in which, after having inherited it by my dear brother's passing, I now still live as an old man and submissively await reunion with the dear ones who have gone before.

I had set up my studio in the widow's large parlor; there was a good light from above for working and everything I might require

*John 11.
†A historical personage, mayor of Husum 1641–62.

was arranged for me. Only that the good lady herself was too much present, for every moment she came trotting into me from her serving-counter with her measuring cups in her hand, pressed with her portliness against my mahlstick, and sniffed around my picture. Indeed, one morning, when I had just backgrounded the head of Lazarus, she demanded with many superfluous words that the resurrected man should display the face of her late husband, although I had never seen this late husband face to face, and had heard from my brother that, as is customary with distillers, he carried the sign of his trade in the form of a bluish red nose on his face; so, as one may easily believe, I had to keep the unreasonable woman tightly under my thumb. When new customers called for her from the outer room, banging on the bar with their measures, and she finally had to let up on me, my hand with the brush sank into my lap and I had suddenly to think of the day when I copied with my pencil the face of quite another deceased man, and of her who stood so quietly beside me in the little chapel. And so, thinking back, I applied my brush again, but after it had gone back and forth for quite a while, I noticed to my own amazement that I had introduced the features of noble Lord Gerhardus into Lazarus's face. From his shroud the dead man's face somehow looked at me in silent accusation, and I thought: this is how he will receive me one day in eternity!

I could not paint any more today, but went away and crept into my chamber above the front door, where I sat at the window and looked down on the marketplace through the opening in the linden trees. There was a great crowd there, and everything from the weigh house across the way and further on to the church was full of carriages and people, for it was a Thursday and still the hour when outsiders may trade with outsiders, so that the constable and the market watchman were sitting idly on our neighbor's stoop, there being no fines to collect for the moment. The Ostenfeld women with their red jackets, the girls from the islands with their kerchiefs and fine silver jewelry, in between the grain wagons piled high and on them the peasants in their yellow leather breeches—all this might well make a picture for a painter's eye, especially when he had gone to school to the Dutch as I had; but the heaviness of my spirit made the colorful picture melancholy for me. Still, it was not remorse, such as I had experienced before; a yearning sorrow came ever more powerfully over me, tearing my flesh with wild claws and yet looking at me with lovely eyes. Down below the bright noon lay upon the swarming marketplace, but before my eyes a silvery moonlit night met the dawn, a couple of pointed gables rose like shadows, a window rattled, and as though in a dream the nightingales sang softly in the distance. Oh, my God and my Redeemer, Who art mercy itself, where was she in this hour, where was my soul to seek her?

Then from below, under the window, I heard a harsh voice speaking my name, and when I looked out, I observed a tall, lean man in the customary costume of a preacher, although his black hair, his haughty and dark countenance with a deep crease above the nose might have been more appropriate to a soldier. With his walking stick he directed to our front door another, thickset man of peasant appearance, but like him in black wool stockings and buckled shoes, as he himself strode away through the marketplace crowd.

Since immediately afterward I heard the doorbell ring, I went down and invited the stranger into the parlor, where from the chair I had offered him he observed me quite exactly and attentively.

He turned out to be the sexton from the village north of the town and I soon learned that they needed a painter there, as they wanted to donate the pastor's portrait to the church. I inquired a little as to what sort of credit he had earned with the congregation that it intended so to honor him, for, given his age, he could not have been in office very long, but the sexton said that the pastor had once brought suit against the congregation over a piece of farmland, otherwise he did not know of anything special that had happened. But his three predecessors were already hanging in the church, and since, as he was obliged to say, they had heard that I knew how to do the thing well, it was a good opportunity to get the fourth pastor in as well; the latter, to be sure, did not himself care much about it one way or the other.

I listened to all this, since I was very willing to interrupt work on my Lazarus for a while, but could not begin the portrait of Master Titus Axen on account of illness, so I began to inquire further about the commission.

What I was offered as a fee for such a task was small enough, so that I thought at first: they are taking you for a twopenny painter, one of those who travels in the baggage train to draw pictures of the soldiers for their girls at home, but the idea suddenly pleased me of walking out every morning for a time in the golden autumn sun over the heath to the village, which was only an hour away from our town. So I agreed, only with the condition that the painting would be done out in the village, since there was no suitable place here in my brother's house.

The sexton seemed quite delighted with this, saying that all that had been thought out in advance; the pastor had also insisted on it. The schoolroom in the sexton's own house had been chosen; this was the second house in the village and lay close to the parsonage, only divided from it in the back by the pastor's field, so that the pastor could easily walk over. The children, who didn't learn anything in the summer anyway, would be sent home.

So we shook hands, and since the sexton had also had the foresight to bring the measurements of the picture, all the equipment I needed could be sent already that afternoon with the priest's wagon.

When my brother came home—not until late in the afternoon, for the Honorable Council had had much trouble from the corpse of a knacker that respectable people did not want to carry to the cemetery*—he said that I was getting a head to paint such as was not often found over a clerical collar, and I should supply myself well with black and brownish red. He told me also that the pastor had come here into the land as a military chaplain with the Brandenburg troops, with whom he is supposed to have behaved even more wildly than the officers, but now he was a mighty warrior before the Lord who was a master at impressing his peasants. My brother also remarked that noble influence is supposed to have had an effect on his appointment in our area, as people said, from over there in Holstein; the archdeacon is supposed to have dropped a word about it while auditing the cloister. More than this, however, my brother had not heard about it.

---

*Knackers (flayers of dead animals), like executioners, were regarded as dishonorable and other citizens shunned any contact with them. Cf. in this volume the dishonoring of Tede Haien's table with the dead cat in Storm's *The White Horse Rider*.

Thus the morning sun of the next day saw me striding vigorously over the heath, and I was only sorry that it had already shed its red dress and its spicy aroma, so that the landscape had lost its whole summer adornment; for far and wide there were no green trees to be seen. Only the pointed church tower of the village I was aiming for—built, as I could already see, entirely of granite blocks—rose ever higher before me into the dark blue October sky. Between the black straw roofs that lay at its feet only low bushes and trees crouched feebly, for the northwest wind that blows here fresh from the sea brooks no hindrance on its way.

When I had reached the village and soon found my way to the sexton's house, the whole school immediately raced toward me with a joyful shout, while the sexton bid me welcome at his front door. "Observe how gladly they run away from their primers!" he said. "One of the rascals already saw you coming through the window."

In the preacher, who immediately afterwards came into the house, I recognized the same man I had seen the day before. But today, so to speak, a light had been set on his dark appearance; this was a handsome, pale boy, whom he led by the hand. The child might have been about four years old and looked almost tiny compared to the tall, bony figure of the man.

Since I wanted to see the portraits of the previous preachers, we went together into the church, which is on a high rise, so that on three sides one can look out over marshes and heath, but toward the west to the not far distant seashore. It must have been just high tide, for the mudflats were under water and the sea was bright silver. When I remarked how, beyond it, the point of the mainland and from the other side that of the island reached toward one another, the sexton gestured toward the water surface lying between them. "There," he said, "my parents' house once stood; but in '34 during the great flood it was driven like a hundred others into the fierce waters; on the one half of the roof I was thrown onto this shore, on the other father and brother went out into eternity."*

I thought: "So the church is probably standing in the right place; even without the pastor, God's word is preached here audibly."

The boy, whom the pastor had taken onto his arm, tightly held

---

*The flood of November 11–12, 1634, destroyed an island in the Bay of Husum; smaller islands were later reclaimed by dikes.

his neck with both little arms and pressed his delicate cheek against the man's black-bearded face, as though finding there protection from the terrifying infinitude that lay spread out before our eyes.

When we had entered the nave of the church, I looked at the old pictures and saw a head among them that would have been worth a good brush, but it was all twopenny painting, and thus the pupil of Van der Helst was getting into quite peculiar company here.

As I was just considering this in my conceit, the harsh voice of the pastor spoke beside me: "It is not my idea that the illusion of dust should endure when the breath of God has left it, but I did not want to oppose the wish of the congregation; only, master, make it short; I have better use for my time."

After I had promised my best efforts to the gloomy man, whose face I nevertheless liked for my art, I asked about a wood carving of Mary that my brother had praised to me.

An almost scornful smile passed over the pastor's face. "You have come too late for that," he said; "it broke into pieces when I had it removed from the church."

I looked at him almost in shock. "And you did not want to tolerate our Savior's mother in your church?"

"The features of our Savior's mother," he returned, "have not been transmitted."

"But do you wish to begrudge art the effort to seek them in a pious spirit?"

He looked down grimly at me for a while; for, although I am not numbered among the short, he stood half a head taller than I. Then he said vehemently: "Did not the king summon the Dutch papists onto that destroyed island, only to defy the judgment of the All High with the human work of the dikes?* Did not the vestrymen over there in the town recently have two of the saints carved into their pew? Watch and pray! For even here Satan is going from house to house! These images of Mary are nothing but the wet nurse of voluptuousness and papism; art has always dallied with the world!"

A dark fire glowed in his eyes, but his hand lay caressingly on the head of the pale boy who clung to his knee.

The child made me forget to reply to the pastor's words, but I

---

*Duke Friedrich III brought in Catholic dike-builders from Holland and Brabant.

reminded them that it was time to return to the sexton's house, where I began to try my noble art on its very adversary.

So I walked almost one morning after the other across the heath to the village, where I always found the pastor already waiting for me. Little was spoken between us, so the picture progressed all the more quickly. Usually the sexton sat next to us and carved all sorts of utensils quite neatly out of oak, a domestic skill that is pursued all around here; I bought the little chest he was working on at that time and years ago put the first pages of this document into it, as these last ones, God willing, shall also be enclosed in it.

I was not invited into the preacher's dwelling and never entered it. The child was always with him in the sexton's house; he stood at his father's knees or played with pebbles in the corner of the room. When I once asked him his name, he answered: "Johannes!"— "Johannes?" I returned; "that's my name too!" He looked at me with big eyes but said nothing more.

Why did these eyes touch my soul so deeply? Once a grim look of the pastor surprised me when I let my brush rest idly on the canvas. There was something in this child's face that could not have come out of his short life, but it was not a happy trait. This is how a child looks, I thought, who has been raised by a heart heavy with care. I should often have liked to reach my arms out to him, but I was hesitant in the presence of the hard man, who seemed to guard the child as though he were a precious object. I did often think: "What kind of woman may have been this boy's mother?"

I had once asked the sexton's old maidservant about the preacher's wife, but she gave me a short reply: "No one knows her; she hardly comes to the farmhouses for christenings and weddings." The pastor himself did not speak of her. Out of the garden of the sexton's house, which ends in a thick group of lilac bushes, I once saw her walking slowly over the priest's field to her house, but she had her back turned to me, so that I could only catch sight of her slender, youthful form, and besides that a couple of curled locks such as are only worn by the higher born, which the wind blew from her temples. The image of her gloomy husband appeared to my mind, and it seemed to me that this couple did not fit together well.

On the days when I did not go out I had taken up work on my

Lazarus again, so that after a time these pictures were completed almost simultaneously.

Thus I was sitting one evening after having finished my day's work with my brother down in our parlor. On the table at the stove the candle was almost burned down and the Dutch clock had already struck eleven o'clock. But we were sitting at the window and had forgotten the present, for we were recalling the short time that we had lived together in our parents' house; we also thought of our dear little sister, who had died in her first childbirth and now had long been awaiting a joyful resurrection with father and mother. We had not closed the shutters, for it did us good to look through the darkness that lay on the earthly dwellings of the town into the starry light of eternal heaven.

In the end we both fell silent in our own thoughts, and, as though on a dark stream, mine floated to her with whom they always found rest and unrest. Then, like a star from invisible heights, a thought suddenly befell me: the eyes of the handsome, pale boy, they were her eyes! Where had I had my senses! But then, if it were she, if I had already seen her herself! What terrible thoughts came storming over me!

Meanwhile my brother laid one hand on my shoulder, while with the other he pointed out to the dark marketplace, where a bright light now flickered over to us. "Just see!" he said. "What a good thing that we patched the pavement with sand and heather! They are coming from the bell-caster's wedding, but you can see from their lanterns that, even so, they are staggering around."

My brother was right. The dancing lights gave clear evidence of the excellence of the wedding celebration; they came so close to us that the two stained-glass panes, which my brother had recently purchased as a glazier's masterpiece, glowed in their deep colors as though on fire. But when the loudly talking crowd turned by our house into Merchant Street, I heard one of them say: "Ah, to be sure; the devil spoiled that for us! All my life I have wanted just once to hear a real witch singing in the flames!"

The lights and the merrymakers went by, and the town outside lay silent and dark again.

"Alas!" said my brother; "he is sorry about what relieves me."

Only then did I recall that the town was awaiting a grisly spectacle the next morning. To be sure, the young person who was supposed to be burned to ashes for having admittedly been in league with Satan had been found dead this morning in her cell by her jailer, but strict justice still had to be done to the dead body.

For many people this was like a soup served cold. After all, the bookseller's widow Liebernickel, who keeps the green bookstall under the church tower, had bitterly complained to me at noon, when I had come in for the newspaper, that the song she had had written and printed in advance now would fit the case like a square peg in a round hole. But, just like my beloved brother, I had my own thoughts about witchcraft, and I rejoiced that our Lord God—for doubtless it had been He—had so graciously taken the poor young person into His bosom.

My brother, who had a soft heart, began to complain about the duties of his office, for he had to read the judgment from the steps of the town hall as soon as the knacker had driven the dead body up, and afterwards had to assist with the carrying out of the sentence. "It's already cutting into my heart," he said, "the atrocious howling when they come down the street with the cart, for the schools will let out their children and the masters their apprentices. In your place," he added, "since you are a free bird, I would go out to the village and work some more on the portrait of the black pastor!"

Now it had been settled that I was not to come out again until the following day, but my brother tried to persuade me, not knowing how he was inciting the impatience in my heart; and so it happened that everything had to be fulfilled that I will faithfully write down in these pages.

The next morning, when across the way from my chamber window the cock on the church tower was barely gleaming in the red early light, I had already jumped out of bed, and soon I strode over the marketplace, where the bakers, awaiting many customers, had already opened their bread-stalls. I also saw that at the town hall the watchman and his footmen were already in motion, and one of them had already hung a black carpet over the railing of the great staircase, but I hurriedly went out of town through the arch under the town hall.

When I was on the stile behind the palace garden, I saw near the clay pit where the new gallows had been erected a mighty stack of wood piled up. A couple of people were still fussing with it. They may have been the jailor and his underlings putting inflammable material between the logs; the first boys were already running toward them over the fields from the town. I paid no further attention to this, but walked on vigorously, and when I came out from the trees I saw on my left the sea blazing in the first sunbeam that rose over the heath in the east. Then I had to fold my hands:

> Oh my God, Father and Son,
> Be Thou gracious to us all,
> Sinful children of the Fall,
> Thou who lovest us every one!

When I was out in the open, where the broad highway goes through the heath, I met many groups of peasants; they had their little boys and girls by the hand and pulled them along.

"Where are you going so eagerly?" I asked one crowd; "there is no market day in town today."

Well, as I had known in advance, they wanted to see the witch, the young disciple of Satan, burn.

"But the witch is dead!"

"True, that is an annoyance," they said: "but it's the niece of our midwife, old Mother Siebenzig; we can't stay away, and we must make do with the remains."

And more crowds kept coming, and now even wagons emerged from the morning mist, laden today with people instead of grain. Then I went to the side over the heath, although the night dew was still running from the plants, for my feelings required solitude, and from afar I saw that it seemed the whole village was on its way to town. When I stood on the pagan mound that lies here in the middle of the heath, I had a feeling that I, too, ought to return to town, and perhaps go down to the left toward the sea, or to the little village that lay down there close to the shore, but something like a feeling of luck, like a crazy hope, hovered before me in the air, and it shook my bones, and my teeth chattered. "If it was really she that I saw with my own eyes, and then if today—" I felt my heart beating like a hammer on my ribs; I made a large detour through the heath; I did not want to see if the preacher, too, were going to town on one of the wagons. But I nevertheless finally walked toward his village.

When I had reached it I walked quickly to the door of the sexton's

house. It was locked. For a while I stood indecisively; then I began
to knock with my fist. Inside everything remained quiet, but when I
knocked more loudly, the sexton's old, half-blind Trienke came out
of a neighbor's house.

"Where is the sexton?" I asked.

"The sexton? Gone to town with the priest."

I stared at the old woman; I felt as though I had been struck by
lightning.

"Is something wrong with you, Sir Painter?" she asked.

I shook my head and said only: "I suppose there is no school
today, Trienke?"

"Heavens, no! The witch is being burned!"

I had the old woman unlock the house, got my painting equipment and the almost-completed portrait out of the sexton's bedchamber, and, as usual, set up my easel in the empty schoolroom. I
daubed a little at the drapery, but I was only trying to deceive myself.
I was in no mood for painting; that is not why I had come here.

The old woman came running, groaned about the bad times and
talked about peasant and village matters that I did not understand; I
was longing to ask her one more time about the preacher's wife,
whether she was old or young, and also where she had come from,
but I couldn't get the words off my tongue. Instead the old woman
began a long yarn about the witch and her relatives here in the
village and about Mother Siebenzig, who had second sight, and she
told how the latter, in a night when gout had kept her awake, had
seen three shrouds flying over the pastor's roof. Such visions always
presage something, and pride goes before a fall, for the Madame
Pastor, despite all her elegance, is, after all, only a pale and feeble
creature.

I did not want to hear any more such chatter, so I went out of the
house and around on the path where the front of the parsonage
faces the village road. With fearful longing I turned my eyes toward
the white windows, but could not perceive anything behind the
opaque panes except a couple of flowerpots such as are seen everywhere. I might well have turned back, but went on all the same.
When I came to the churchyard, the wind carried a moaning of bells
from the direction of the town to my ear, but I turned and looked
down to the west, where again the sea flowed like bright silver at the

hem of the sky, and yet there had been a raging disaster there, when in one night the hand of the All High had thrown away many thousands of human lives. Why, then, was I writhing like a worm? We do not see whither His paths lead!

I no longer know where my feet still carried me then; I only know that I walked in a circle, for when the sun had almost reached its midday zenith, I arrived again at the sexton's house. Yet I didn't go into the schoolroom to my easel, but through the back door out of the house again.

I still have not forgotten the poor little garden, although my eyes have not seen it since that day. Like the one of the parsonage on the other side, it protruded as a broad strip into the priest's field, but in the middle between them was a group of thick willow bushes, which may have served as the border of a water pit, for I had once seen a maid climbing out of it with a full bucket as though out of a hollow.

As I went by the sexton's harvested bean beds without thinking very much, my mind filled only with irrepressible restlessness, from the field yonder I heard a woman's voice of sweetest sound, and how she lovingly spoke to a child.

Involuntarily I walked toward this sound; thus the pagan Greek god may have led the dead with his staff.* I was already on the far side of the lilac bushes that there run into the field without any fencing, when I saw little Johannes walking behind the willows with his arms full of the moss that grows here in the meager grass; he may, in the way of children, have made a little garden there. And once again the lovely voice came to my ear: "Just go ahead; now you have a whole pile! Yes, yes, I will look some more; there is enough growing there by the lilac!"

Then she herself stepped out of the willows; I had long since had no more doubts. Searching the ground with her eyes, she walked toward me, so that I was able to observe her undisturbed; and it seemed to me that she strangely resembled again the child she had once been, for whom I had once shot down the "bogey" from the tree. But her child's face of today was pale and neither happiness nor courage could be read in it.

She had gradually come closer to me without noticing me, for she

---

*Hermes, who led the dead to the underworld.

knelt at a strip of moss that ran under the bushes, but her hands did not pick any of it; her head sank to her breast, and it seemed as though she only wanted to rest in her suffering unseen by the child.

Then I called softly: "Katharina!"

She looked up; I took her hand and pulled her like one bereft of will into the shadow of the bushes. But when I had now finally found her and stood before her, unable to utter a word, her eyes turned away from me, and almost with the voice of stranger she said to me: "This is the way it is, Johannes! I knew that you were the foreign painter; I just didn't think that you would come today."

I heard this, and then I said it aloud: "Katharina—then you are the preacher's wife?"

She didn't nod; she looked at me rigidly and painfully. "He got his appointment for it," she said, "and your child got an honorable name."

"My child, Katharina?"

"And don't you feel it? He sat on your lap, one time, anyway; he told me about it himself."

May no man's breast be torn by such grief! "And you, you and my child, you are to be lost to me!"

She looked at me, she did not weep, she was only pale as death.

"I don't want that!" I cried; "I want . . ." And a wild sequence of thoughts raced through my brain.

But she had laid her little hand on my forehead like a cool leaf, and her brown eyes in the pale face looked at me pleadingly. "Johannes," she said, "you won't be the one who will make me even more miserable."

"And can you live like this, Katharina?"

"Live? But there is some good fortune in it; he loves the child; what more can one ask?"

"And does he know about us, about what once was?"

"No, no!" she cried vehemently. "He took the sinner to wife; no more. Oh God, is it not enough that every new day belongs to him!"

At this moment a faint singing could be heard from a distance. "The child," she said. "I must go to the child; something might happen to him!"

But my senses were concentrated only on the woman they desired. "Please stay," I said; "he is playing happily over there with his moss."

She had walked to the edge of the bushes and listened. The golden autumn sun shone so warmly; only a light breeze came up from the sea. Then we heard the little voice of our child singing from the other side of the willows:

> Two angels that spare me,
> Two angels that care for me,
> And two that will guide me
> Till Heaven abide me.

Katharina had stepped back, and her wide and ghostly eyes looked at me. "And now farewell, Johannes," she said softly; "never to meet again here on earth."

I wanted to pull her to me; I stretched both my arms toward her, but she warded me off and said gently: "I am another man's wife, don't forget."

But at these words I was overcome with an almost-wild rage. "And whose, Katharina," I said harshly, "were you before you became his?"

A sorrowful sound of grief broke from her breast; she put her hands before her face and cried: "Woe is me! Oh, woe, my poor, desecrated body!"

Then I completely lost control of myself; I tore her violently to my breast and she was finally, finally, mine again! And her eyes sank into mine and her red lips tolerated mine; we embraced fervidly; I could have killed her if we could have died together. As my eyes blissfully feasted on her face, she said, almost smothered by my kisses: "It is a long, fearful life! Oh, Christ Jesus, forgive me this hour!"

An answer came; but it was the harsh voice of the man from whose mouth I now heard her name for the first time. The voice called from the garden of the parsonage, and it called once again and more harshly: "Katharina!"

With that my happiness was at an end; she looked at me with an expression of despair. Then she was gone as silently as a shadow.

The sexton was already there when I entered the house. At once he began to talk to me of the judgment executed on the poor witch. "You don't seem to think much of it," he said; "otherwise you would not have come out to the village today, where the pastor drove even the peasants and their wives into the village."

I had no time to answer—a shrill scream pierced the air; I shall have it in my ears all my life.

"What was that, sexton?" I cried.

The man tore open the window and listened, but nothing more happened. "God help me," he said, "it was a woman who screamed like that; it came from the priest's field over there."

Meanwhile old Trienke had come in the door. "Well, sir?" she cried to me. "The shrouds have fallen on the pastor's roof!"

"What is that supposed to mean, Trienke?"

"That is supposed to mean that they are just now pulling the pastor's little Johannes out of the water."

I plunged out of the room and through the garden to the priest's field; but under the willows I found only the dark water and traces of wet mud next to it on the grass. Without thinking, quite automatically, I went through the white gate into the pastor's garden. Just as I wanted to go into the house, he himself came up to me.

The tall, bony man looked completely desolate; his eyes were red and his tangled black hair hung into his face. "What do you want?" he said.

I stared at him, for I was at a loss for words. Indeed, what did I want?

"I know you!" he continued. "The woman has finally told me everything."

This released my tongue. "Where is my child?" I cried.

He said: "His parents let him drown."

"Then let me see my dead child!"

But when I tried to get past him into the hall, he pushed me back. "The woman," he said, "is lying beside the corpse and cries to God from out of her sins. You shall not go in, for the sake of her poor soul's salvation!"

What I myself said then I have entirely forgotten, but the preacher's words engraved themselves in my memory. "Hear me!" he said. "As much as I hate you from the bottom of my heart, may God in His grace make me atone for it one day, and as much as you must hate me, we have one thing in common. Now go home and prepare a panel or a canvas! Return with it tomorrow in the early morning and paint on it the face of the dead boy. Not for me or my house; you may donate the portrait to the church here, where he lived his short, innocent life. May it there warn people that everything is dust before the bony hand of death!"

I looked at the man who shortly before had called the noble art of painting a strumpet of the world, but I agreed that it would be done.

Meanwhile news was awaiting me at home that suddenly illuminated the guilt and atonement of my life out of the darkness as though by a stroke of lightning, so that I saw the whole chain gleaming before me link by link.

My brother, whose weak constitution had been seriously undermined by the horrible spectacle in which he had had to take part today, had taken to his bed. When I came into him, he sat up. "I must rest for a while," he said, handing me a page of the weekly newspaper, "but read this! You will see that Lord Gerhardus's estate has come into the hands of strangers, since Junker Wulf has died a miserable death, without wife or child, from the bite of a mad dog."

I grabbed for the page that my brother held out to me, but I was almost reeling. I felt at this fearful news as though the gates of Paradise had sprung open before me, but at once I saw the angel with the flaming sword standing at the entrance, and again there was a cry from my heart: O guardian, guardian, was your call so distant? This death could have meant life for us; now it was only one horror added to the others.

I sat up in my chamber. Twilight came, night fell; I looked at the eternal stars, and finally I went to bed. But the refreshment of sleep was not to be mine. In my excited senses it seemed to me strangely as though the church tower out there had come close to my window; I felt the bell strokes droning through the wood of the bedstead, and I counted them all the whole night long. But finally morning dawned. The beams of the ceiling were still hanging like shadows over me, I leapt up, and before the first lark rose from the stubble fields, I already had the town at my back.

But, as early as I had gone out, I met the preacher already standing on the threshold of his house. He accompanied me to the hall and said that the wooden panel had arrived, also my easel and other equipment had been brought over from the sexton's house. Then he put his hand on the latch of a room door.

But I held him back and said: "If it is in this room, then permit me to be alone with my heavy task!"

"No one will disturb you," he replied and withdrew his hand. "What you need for bodily refreshment you will find in that room over there." He pointed to a door on the other side of the hall, then he left me.

My hand now lay on the latch instead of the preacher's. It was deathly still in the house; I had to collect myself a moment before I opened the door.

It was a larger, almost empty room, probably intended for the instruction of confirmation classes, with bare, whitewashed walls; the windows looked out on desolate fields toward the distant shore. But in the middle of the room a white bed had been set up. On the pillow lay a pale child's face, the eyes closed; the little teeth shimmered like pearls from the pale lips.

I sank at my child's corpse and recited a fervent prayer. Then I prepared everything necessary for the work, and then I painted—quickly, as one must paint the dead, who do not show the same face twice. From time to time I was as though frightened by something in the continuing great silence; but when I stopped and listened I knew that it had been nothing. Once it seemed to me as though I felt soft breaths on my ear. I stepped to the bed of the dead boy, but when I bent over the pale little mouth, only the chill of death touched my cheeks.

I looked around—there was another door in the room that might lead to a bedchamber; perhaps it had come from there! But, as intently as I listened, I heard nothing more; my own senses had probably played a trick on me.

So I sat down again, looked at the little corpse and painted some more; and when I contemplated the empty little hands lying on the linen, I thought: "You must at least give your child a little present!" And I painted into his hand on the portrait a white water lily, as though he had fallen asleep playing with it. Such flowers are rare around here, and so it might be a desirable gift.

Finally hunger drove me from my work, my tired body required refreshment. So I set down brush and palette and went across the hall to the room the pastor had indicated to me. Upon entering, however, I almost retreated in surprise, for Katharina stood before me, in black mourning, and yet in all the magic glow that happiness and love can arouse in a woman's face.

Oh, I realized only too soon: what I saw here was only the portrait I had once painted myself. Then for this, too, there had been no more room in her father's house. But where was she, then, herself? Had they taken her away or were they holding her prisoner here? For a long, long time I looked at the portrait; the old days rose up and tormented my heart. Finally, since I had to, I broke a piece of bread and swallowed a couple of glasses of wine; then I returned to our dead child.

When I had come back into the room and was about to sit down to my work, it appeared that the eyelids in the little face had opened a little. Then I bent over, in the delusion that I might once again catch my child's glance, but, as the cold pupils lay before me, I shuddered; I imagined that I saw the eyes of that ancestress of the family, as though she wanted to announce from the dead face of our child: "My curse has caught you both after all!" But at the same time—I could not have resisted for all the world—I embraced the little, pale corpse with both arms and lifted it to my breast and with bitter tears hugged my beloved child for the first time. "No, no, my poor boy, your soul, which forced even that grim man to love, did not look out of such eyes; what is looking out here is nothing but death. It has not surfaced from the depths of a terrible past. Nothing else is there but your father's guilt; it has plunged us all into the black flood."

Carefully I laid my child back into his pillows and gently closed both his eyes. Then I dipped my brush into a dark red and wrote below in the shadow of the picture the letters: C. P. A. S. That was to mean: *Culpa Patris Aquis Submersus,* "Sunken into the flood by fault of the father." And with the sound of these words in my ear, which pierced my soul like a sharp sword, I finished the painting.

During my work the silence in the house had continued; only in the last hour did a soft noise penetrate through the door behind which I had presumed a bedchamber. Was Katharina there in order to be invisibly near me during my heavy labor? I could not make it out.

It was already late. My picture was finished, and I wanted to turn to leave, but it seemed to me that I must still say a farewell without which I could not go away.

So I stood hesitantly and looked through the window to the

desolate fields outside, where twilight was already spreading; then the door from the hall opened and the preacher came in to me.

He greeted me silently; then he stood with folded hands and looked alternately at the face on the picture and that of the little corpse in front of him, as though he were making a careful comparison. But when his eyes fell on the lily in the boy's painted hand, he raised both his hands as if in pain and I saw how a stream of tears suddenly poured from his eyes.

Then I, too, reached out my arms to the dead boy and cried too loudly: "Farewell, my child! Oh, my Johannes, farewell!"

But in the same moment I heard soft footsteps in the next room; there was a sound as though little hands were feeling at the door. I clearly heard my name called—or was it that of the dead child?— then there was a rustling as though of women's clothes behind the door, and the sound of a falling body was audible.

"Katharina!" I called. And I had already leapt over and was shaking the latch of the firmly locked door; then the pastor laid his hand on my arm: "That is my office!" he said. "Go now! but go in peace, and may God be gracious to us all!"

Then I really did go away; before I realized it I was walking outside on the heath on the way to the town.

Once more I turned around and looked back at the village, which rose out of the evening darkness only as a shadow. There lay my dead child—Katharina—everything, everything! My old wound burned in my breast; and strangely, I suddenly became conscious of something that I had never heard here before: that I was hearing the surf roaring from the distant shore. I met no one, I heard no bird calling, but from the dull surging of the sea I heard constantly, like a grim lullaby: *Aquis submersus—aquis submersus!*

* * *

Here ended the manuscript.

What Master Johannes had once presumed to hope in the fullness of his strength, that he would one day equal the greater ones in his art, those were to be words spoken into empty air.

His name does not belong to those that are named; one would hardly be likely to find him in a dictionary of artists; even in his local region no one knows of a painter by his name. The chronicle of our town does mention the large Lazarus picture, but at the beginning of our century the picture itself was sold off along with the other art treasures when our old church was torn down, and it disappeared.

Aquis submersus.

Translated by Jeffrey L. Sammons

The White Horse Rider

Theodor Storm

The tale I want to tell you is one I chanced upon well over half a century ago when I was staying with my great-grandmother. She was an old lady, the wife of Senator Feddersen,* and I used to sit by her armchair, engrossed in a volume of magazines, bound in stiff blue covers. I cannot now recollect whether it was the "Leipzig" collection, or the Hamburg series called "Pappe's Selected Readings"† but I still feel a faint thrill as I remember the way her gentle hand would glide fondly over my hair now and again while I read. She was in her eighties then and she and the old times with her are long since dead and buried. More recently, however, I have hunted high and low for a copy of that story, but without success. And so I must admit that I can as little vouch for its authenticity as defend my account of it if anyone should choose to challenge what I have written. All I know for certain is this. Although there is no objective reason why the details should have remained so vividly in my mind, it has haunted my memory for the best part of my life.

It was an October afternoon in the third decade of the present century—so the storyteller began—and I was riding along a dike in northern Friesland. The weather was abominable and for more than an hour, there had been nothing to gaze at on my left but a desolate polder, from which even the cattle had been called in. On my right, uncomfortably close, were the mudflats of the North Sea. It should, indeed, have been possible to sight several low-lying islands and sandbanks from the dike, but all I could see were the livid grey waves which beat against the dike with an angry roar and from time

---

*Elsabe Feddersen (1741–1829), Storm's maternal great-grandmother, the matriarch of the family in his boyhood.

†Periodical anthologies of current German and foreign literature. The 1838 issue of the second of these contains one of Storm's main sources for the story.

to time, spattered me and my horse with muddy flecks of foam. In the eerie twilight, I could not tell the sky from land, for even the half-moon which had already risen was, for the most part, covered with dark, driving cloud. It was icy cold. My hands were so numb that they could hardly grip the reins and I could not blame the crows and sea gulls, driven inland by the storm, for their incessant cawing and screaming. It was growing dusk and I could no longer make out my horse's hoofs distinctly when I looked down. I had not met a soul nor had I heard anything but the raging of wind and sea and the cry of the wheeling birds as they almost touched me and my faithful mare with the tips of their outstretched wings. I will not deny that there were moments when I longed for nothing so much as to be safely indoors.

This stormy weather had now been going on for the past three days, and I had already stayed longer than I should at a farm in one of the northern parishes. It belonged to one of my relations, a cousin for whom I had a particular affection, but today I decided I could postpone my departure no longer. I had business to attend to in the town, which was a few hours' ride away to the south. So in spite of all the persuasive pleas of both my cousin and his good lady, in spite of the fact that I had not yet sampled their delicious homegrown apples—their fruit trees included both the Perinette and the Grand Richard varieties—I had set off that same afternoon. "Wait till you get to the sea!" my cousin had called as he waved good-bye to me from his front door. "You'll turn back then if not before, I'll be bound. We'll keep your room ready for you!"

And indeed, there was an instant when he was almost proved right. An inky pall of cloud descended, turning everything pitch-dark and at the same time, howling squalls of wind tried to sweep me and the mare clean off the dike. "Don't be a fool," said an inner voice. "Go back to your kind friends and toast yourself by their snug fireside." But by then, since I was more than halfway to my destination, it was more sensible to continue my journey. So I trotted on once more and drew my coat collar closer about my ears.

It was just then, however, that I observed something coming towards me along the dike. I could hear no sound, but whenever the pale moon cast its feeble light, the object grew clearer and clearer until I thought I could make out the dark figure of a man. As he approached, I saw that he was riding a gaunt, high-stepping white horse and a dark cloak swung from his shoulders. He darted past me and two burning eyes stared at me out of a pallid countenance.

Who was he and what did he want? I was struck by the fact that I had heard neither the beat of the horse's hoofs nor the panting of its breath, and yet it had galloped hard by me along the dike. That's odd, I thought as I rode on, but I was given little time to puzzle it out, for the rider turned back after a short while and soon overtook me from behind. I felt as if the flying cloak had actually brushed against me as he passed and still the apparition had made no sound, exactly as on the first occasion. The distance between us gradually increased and all at once, I had the impression that the shadow of man and horse were plunging down the slope against the inner wall of the dike.

With some misgiving, I followed in their wake. When I reached the place where they had disappeared, I saw in the polder below the gleam of a pond; for in these parts, the high tides cut deep channels into the land and as the water ebbs, it leaves behind a number of standing pools which are usually small but can be quite deep.

Even allowing for the shelter of the dike, the surface of the water was remarkably still. The rider could certainly not have ruffled it in the least. But he had gone for good and I saw nothing more of him. However, I did see something else, and this time it was a sight to rejoice my eyes. Ahead of me there were beams of light which flickered up towards me from the fields below. They seemed to be coming from one of those Frisian farmhouses which dot the landscape, long straggling buildings erected on man-made mounds of earth of varying height, as a precaution against flooding. It was indeed a big house of this type which lay before me, and it stood, I would have said, at about half the height of the inner wall of the dike. All the windows were lit up on the southern side, that is, to the right of the entrance. I thought I could see people within and in spite of the storm I fancied I could hear their voices. Of its own accord, my horse had already taken the path down from the dike which led to the front door. I could tell at once that it was an inn for I noticed the hitching posts in front of the windows. These consisted of heavy beams resting on two stands, with big iron rings driven into them so that livestock and horses could be safely tethered when the traveler made a halt.

I tied my horse to one of the rings and handed over its care to the servant who came to meet me as I stepped inside the hallway. "Is there some gathering here tonight?" I asked, for now I could hear plainly the sound of human voices and the clink of glasses.

"Yes, you might say so," replied the fellow. He spoke Low German, or Plattdeutsch, as it is called, a dialect which had been common locally for the last hundred years or so, side by side with Frisian. "The dike reeve and his wardens are here, keeping an eye on things for them as owns the land hereabouts. They're waiting for high tide."

As I entered the room I saw about a dozen men sitting at a table that ran the length of the windows. A bowl of punch stood on the table and a man of imposing appearance appeared to be presiding over the company. I bade them good evening and asked leave to join them at the table, which was willingly granted.

"I hear you are keeping vigil," I said, turning to the man I have mentioned. "It's foul weather out of doors and I imagine the dikes will be hard put to it tonight."

"Yes, indeed," he replied. "But there is no danger for us here on the east bank nowadays, we feel. It's over the other side, in the west, that there may be trouble. You see, their dikes are mostly the old-fashioned kind, whereas our main dike was rebuilt during the last century on quite a different pattern. As a matter of fact," he went on, "we were up on the dike ourselves until a short while ago. But it turned so much colder, as I expect you noticed for yourself, that we came in here and we shall wait up for several hours yet. We have men on duty at all key points and they can be relied on to let us know if need arises." And before I could place my order with the landlord, a steaming glass of punch was pushed in front of me.

I soon learned that my friendly neighbor was the dike reeve, as he is called. As we got into conversation, I began to describe my strange encounter on the dike. He listened attentively and all at once I became aware that the hum of conversation around us had died away completely. "The white horse rider!" cried a voice and a shudder of fear ran through the room.

The reeve got to his feet. "There's no cause for alarm," he said firmly, and looked round the table. "It need not be a warning for us. Last time, in the year '17,* it was the folk across the water who caught it. Let us hope that they are prepared."

---

*If the reference is to the great flood at Christmas 1717, it is an anachronism, as the inner story takes place in the middle of the eighteenth century. There was no flood

A cold shiver ran down my spine. "Forgive me for asking," I said, "but what does it mean? Has the man on the white horse some special significance?"

On the far side of the room, behind the stove, sat a thin little man in a threadbare black jacket. He held himself a trifle hunched, as though one shoulder were higher than the other. He had taken no part in the general conversation so far, but even so he did not look as if he had dropped in for the sake of a little nap, as one could tell clearly by the alertness of his eyes. They were fringed with dark lashes which stood out in striking contrast to the sparse grey hair on his head.

It was to this man that the dike reeve now pointed. "Our schoolmaster by the stove there is the best person to let you have the story," he declared, raising his voice. "Of course he has his own version, although personally I think my old housekeeper Antje Vollmers used to tell it better, many years ago."

"Oh come, you must be joking," came the somewhat querulous voice of the schoolmaster from behind the stove. "Surely you don't encourage such foolish gossips with their old wives' tales."

"But I do," retorted the reeve. "These foolish old gossips as you call them are the ones who hand such tales down from one generation to the next and so keep them alive."

"Obviously we must agree to differ on this subject," said the little man, and a superior smile flitted over his fine-drawn features.

"You can see for yourself he thinks he's a cut above the rest of us," the reeve whispered in my ear. "Although he was born in these parts, he studied theology in his youth. But then he was crossed in love and ever since he has been stuck in a rut here, as the village schoolmaster."

Meanwhile, the latter had emerged from his chimney corner and seated himself beside me at the long table. "Come on, sir!" called one or two of the younger men present. "Let's all hear the story."

"By all means," said the little man and, turning to me, he went on: "I am happy to be of service to you. But there is so much superstition mixed up with the facts that it requires some little skill to tell the tale without these trimmings."

"I beg you, sir, leave nothing out," I answered. "You can trust me

---

in 1817, but one did occur during Storm's boyhood in 1825 that remained vividly in his memory.

to sift the wheat from the chaff for myself."

The old man looked at me with an understanding smile. "Very well, then," he began, "in the middle of the last century, or rather, to be a little more precise, both before and after the middle of the century, there was a dike reeve here who knew more about dams and sluices than do most of our farmers and landowners. Yet even that was scarcely enough, since he had read hardly any of the learned works written on the subject by those whose business it is to know such things. Such knowledge as he possessed he had worked out for himself, for dikes were a passion with him, literally from his boyhood onward.

"I expect you have heard for yourself that Frisians are said to have a gift for mathematics and you must surely have been told about one of our greatest sons, Hans Mommsen.* He was an ordinary farmer from Fahretoft, yet he invented compasses, chronometers, telescopes and organs. Now in a small way, the reeve's father was a man of the same stamp, although admittedly nothing like Mommsen in stature. This man, Tede Haien, had a smallholding where he grew rape and beans and grazed a cow, but in autumn and in spring, he was occasionally asked to do some surveying. So when winter arrived and the nor'wester rattled his shutters as it blew in from the sea, you might have seen him sitting in his living room, busy with dividers and compasses. His son would be there too, more often than not, and he would look up from his copybook or his Bible and watch his father calculating and measuring, and burying his fingers in his shock of fair hair.

One evening, the lad ventured to ask his father why he had written down such and such a thing. He wanted to know why it had to be just so and not something different and he volunteered his own opinion of what the answer should be.

The old man was taken aback and did not know what to say. "I cannot give you a reason," he replied at last, shaking his head. "All I know is that I am right and that you are wrong. If you want to know more about it, then go up to the loft in the morning and look in the chest there for a book by a man called Euclid. That will tell you all about it."

The very next morning the boy hurried up to the loft and he soon

---

*Or Momsen (1735–1811), a peasant mathematician from Fahretoft, north of Storm's home town of Husum. Several motifs, such as Hauke's teaching himself geometry from a Dutch translation of Euclid, are taken from Momsen's life.

found what he wanted, for there were not many books in a house like that. But his father laughed when his son laid the volume on the table before him, for it was a Dutch edition and even if Dutch is half German, neither of them could understand it. "Why of course, I had forgotten," he said. "That book belonged to my father and he could read Dutch. Wasn't there a German one?"

The boy, who was never one for wasting words, looked at his father in his quiet way. "No, there wasn't. May I keep this?"

And when the old man nodded, his son produced a second book, which was so tattered it was all but falling apart. "This one too?" he asked abruptly.

"Take them both," said Tede Haien, "for all the good they'll do you."

Now the second book was a little Dutch grammar and since the winter had only just begun, by the time the gooseberries were ripening in their garden, the boy had mastered almost the whole of his Euclid, which was a popular study in those days.

"I am not unaware," the narrator interrupted himself, "that this anecdote is often related about Hans Mommsen too, but it was told in these parts about Hauke Haien—for that is the name of the boy I have been speaking about—long before Mommsen was born. But you know how it is, I am sure. Whenever a man achieves fame, he becomes something of a legend in his hometown and everything his forerunners did whether flattering or otherwise, is eventually attributed to him.

The father soon realized that the boy was not interested in cattle or sheep rearing. He hardly even noticed when the beanfields started flowering although that is what our fenmen look forward to most all winter. Tede Haien, then, began to think about his son's future, for his own smallholding could support only himself and a boy, but not a bookish scholar and a foreman as well. He realized too that with all his mathematics, he had never got on in the world himself, so he decided to send the growing lad to work on the dikes, where he had to shift barrowloads of earth from Easter until Martinmas.* "That'll cure him of all this Euclid nonsense," he muttered to himself.

So the youth wheeled his barrow like the rest of the gang, but he always kept his Euclid in his pocket and when the other laborers got

*November 11, the day on which peasants celebrated the end of the harvest.

down to their breakfast or dinner, which they had brought with them, he would sit on an upturned wheelbarrow with the book in his hands. And when in the autumn the tides were higher than usual and sometimes the men had to be laid off, Hauke Haien did not go home like the others. Instead he stayed on the site, sitting on a ridge of the steep dike wall facing the sea, with his hands folded on his knees. As the tide came in, he watched the dreary North Sea waves dashing higher and higher against the grass sods of the dike and it was only when the water splashed his feet and the spray broke in his face, that he would climb a few feet higher up the bank and then sit down again to watch. He did not hear the pounding seas nor the scream of the gulls and the marsh birds, as they flew round and above him, almost touching him with their wingtips and flashing their beady black eyes into his. Neither did he notice the autumn evening spreading gradually over the vast wastes of the sea. All he saw was that at high tide, the surf on the crest of the waves beat away remorselessly against the selfsame spot in the dike, eating away the turf inch by inch before his very eyes.

When he had stared at it for a long time, he would slowly nod his head and, without looking up, he would sketch a gentle curve in the air with one hand as if he would have liked to modify the slope of the dike wall and make it less steep. Only when it grew too dark to make out anything at all, and there was nothing but the tide roaring in his ears, did he stand up and trot along home, his clothes half-drenched with spray.

On one such evening, he came straight into the living room where his father was busy polishing his mathematical instruments. "What were you doing out there on the dike?" he asked. "You might have been drowned. The sea is cutting right into the dike today."

Hauke only looked at his father stubbornly.

"Don't you hear what I say? I'm telling you you might have been drowned."

"I heard you," said Hauke, "but I didn't get drowned, did I?"

"No," answered the father after a pause, looking at his son with an absentminded air. "Not this time."

"All the same," Hauke persisted, "those dikes of ours are no good."

"What are you talking about?"

"The dikes, I say."

"And what about the dikes?"

"I say they're not much use," replied Hauke.

Tede Haien laughed in his face. "So that's your opinion, is it? And this infant prodigy* of mine, knows better than the men who built them, of course!"

But the boy stood his ground. "The sea face is much too steep," he said. "If there's a really high sea one day—and these things have happened more than once—we could all be drowned, even here, behind the dike."

The old man took his tobacco out of his pocket, twisted off a plug and popped it in his mouth. "And how many barrowloads did you shift today?" he asked angrily, for he could tell at once that the rough manual work had in no way discouraged the boy from thinking.

"I don't know, father," he answered. "As many as the others, maybe half a dozen more. . . But all the same, the dikes will have to be rebuilt."

"In that case," said the father," and he gave a short laugh, "perhaps they'll make you dike reeve one day. Then you can alter them yourself."

"Yes, father," was the reply.

The old man looked at his son again and swallowed hard. Then he got up and went out of the room. He had no idea what to say next.

Even when the maintenance work was over towards the end of October, Hauke liked nothing better than to take a walk in a northerly direction towards the open sea. He was waiting for All Souls' Day,† which some call Friesland's day of woe, for it is then that the equinoctial storms are usually at their worst. But Hauke waited for it as eagerly as a child looking forward to Christmas. Whenever an exceptionally high tide was expected, you could be certain that, come wind or weather, he would be out there on the dike, all by himself. And when the gulls screamed, when the water hurled itself against the dike and then retreated, tearing away whole

---

*The original has "prodigy of Lübeck," a reference to Christian Heinrich Heineken or Heiniken (1721–25), who at the age of four is supposed to have mastered several foreign languages and branches of knowledge.

†November 1.

sods of turf as it withdrew, you could have heard his infuriated laughter. "You're no good!" he would shout at the boiling seas before him. "You're useless, like human beings too." And at last, often when it was pitch-dark, he would trudge home from the bleak wastes along the dike until he came to his father's thatched cottage. He had shot up into a gawky youth and he had to stoop beneath the low doorway.

Often as he entered the living room he produced a handful of soft clay which he had brought in from the fields. He would sit down near his father, who left him alone these days, and by the light of the thin tallow candle he would knead the clay into various models of dikes. Then he would place them in a shallow dish of water and try to imitate the dash of the waves against them, or else he took his slate and drew the profile of a dike as it faced the sea, as he considered it ought to be built.

It never occurred to him to go out and meet the boys he had known at school and they in turn had little interest in such a dreamer of dreams. When the winter came and frost set in, he would wander out along the dike farther than he had ever been before until the ice-covered surface of the mudflats stretched out before him as far as the eye could see.

One February, when the land was still in the grip of a hard frost, several corpses had drifted in from the open sea and were washed up on the frozen shore. A young woman, who had been standing by as they carried them into the village, met Tede Haien and she was so full of it, she had to tell him all about it there and then. "Don't think for a minute that they looked human any more," she declared. "No, they looked like sea devils. Their heads were as big as this"—and here she held her outstretched hands wide apart—"and they were as black as tar and as shiny as the crust on a new baked loaf. The crabs had been at them too and when the children saw them, they screamed aloud."

Old Haien, however, had seen such sights for himself. "They must have been drifting in the sea since November," he replied indifferently.

Hauke stood there silent, but as soon as he could, he slipped away to the dike. There's no saying if he was hoping to find more corpses, or if he was drawn to the deserted spot by the horror which must have been brooding over it still. On he went until he stood alone in the midst of desolation, where only the wind swept over the dike, where there was nothing to be heard but the complaint of the big birds as they wheeled swiftly by. To his left was the broad, deserted marshland. On the other side, the shore stretched away into the distance and a glittering surface of ice covered the mud. It seemed as if the whole world lay in the white grip of death.

Hauke stood there on the dike and his keen eyes searched far and wide, but there were no more bodies to be seen. Only the ice rose and fell in sinuous curves where invisible currents thrust their way below the frozen surface.

Hauke ran home, but an evening or two later he was back again. At that very spot, the ice had begun to split. Clouds of vapor were escaping from the fissures which crisscrossed the surface, so that a network of steam and mist arose, mingling weirdly with the twilight. Hauke stared and stared for there were dark figures of adult height striding about in the haze, with dignified but strangely terrifying movements. They had long noses and they craned their necks as they paced up and down by the edges of the cracks where the stream came belching forth.

All at once and for no apparent reason, they began jumping up and down in a senseless frenzy, with the big ones leaping over the smaller ones and they in turn bumping into the larger ones. Then they spread out and gradually their outlines grew blurred. "What are they doing? Are they the spirits of men drowned at sea?" wondered Hauke. "Ho there!" he cried aloud into the darkness. But there was no response to his shouting and they continued to behave in the same eerie manner.

Then Hauke remembered an old sea captain who had told him about the terrifying Norwegian sea-spirits, who have a thick tuft of seaweed growing out of their necks in place of a head. But Hauke did not run away. He dug his heels more firmly into the mud of the dike and gazed at the fantastic figures cavorting in the falling darkness. "Have you come to haunt us?" he shouted hoarsely. "You'll not drive me away, never fear!"

It was only when night had blotted out the scene that he strode home again with stiff unhurried steps. Behind him there came a noise like the rushing of wings and echoing cries. He neither turned round nor would he hasten and it was very late when he got home. He never told his father nor indeed anyone else about what he had seen that evening. It was only many years later, on a similar day and at the same time of the year, that he visited the spot again, taking with him his only child, a feebleminded daughter with whom the Lord had seen fit to afflict him. Creatures like those he had seen that day in his boyhood were hovering about the mudflats and he told the child that she must not be frightened, for they were nothing but herons and crows, trying to catch fish in the cracks in the ice. It was only the mist that made them loom so large and seem so frightening.

"Heaven knows, sir," added the schoolmaster as an aside, "there are many things on this earth to confuse an honest Christian, but Hauke Haien was neither a fool nor one of your country bumpkins."

As I made no comment, he was about to resume his narrative, but among the guests who had so far listened in silence, filling the low room with an ever-thickening pall of tobacco smoke, there was a sudden ripple of movement. One by one they turned their heads until everyone was looking out of the windows, which were uncurtained. We could see the clouds scudding across the sky and the shifting play of light and darkness. But I, too, fancied I had seen something, a haggard horseman galloping past on a white steed.

"Wait a moment, Schoolmaster," said the reeve softly.

"There's no cause to be afraid," answered the schoolmaster. "I have said nothing to offend him and, indeed, why should I? I have every respect for the man." And he looked up at the reeve with his small but intelligent eyes.

"Good, good," said the reeve. "Let us fill up your glass for you." When this was done, the listeners still, for the most part, looking slightly anxious, turned their faces back to his, and he proceeded with his story.

And so Hauke grew up into a tall, thin young man, always alone, preferring the company of the wind and the sea to that of his fellow men, forever seeking solitude. About a year after he had been confirmed, however, his whole life changed its course and it all came about because of a white Angora cat. Now this cat belonged to Trin Jans, whose sailor son had brought it with him from Spain on the last voyage he ever made, just before his accidental death. Trin Jans lived in a hut right out along the dike and as the old woman pottered about indoors, this old monster of a tom used to sun itself by the front door, blinking at the black-headed gulls as they flew overhead. If Hauke passed that way, the cat would miaow after him and the youth would nod to it as if there were some tacit understanding between them.

One day in spring, Hauke lay basking in the sun which was already strong for the time of year. He had chosen a spot towards the foot of the dike, down by the shore where sea pinks and fragrant beach wormwood grew. A few days before when he had been up near the church, he had filled his pockets with pebbles from the higher stony ground beyond the marshes. Then, as the ebb tide laid bare a stretch of mud and the little grey sandpipers darted across it, crying, he would suddenly pull a stone from his pocket and throw. It was a sport he had practiced since early childhood and more often than not one of the birds was left lying in the slime. But just as often, he was unable to fetch it in and he had even thought of taking Trin's cat along with him and training it as a retriever. All the same, he could sometimes find a few spots firm enough to bear his weight and then he would make a dash for it and collect his booty for himself. If the cat were still sitting outside the door on his return, it would start up such a caterwauling at the sight of his modest gamebag, that Hauke was obliged to throw it one of the birds.

As Hauke went home on this particular day with his jacket over one shoulder, he was carrying only one bird in his hand. It was not a species which he recognized but its iridescent feathers shone, silky and metallic, and the cat miaowed as usual when it saw him coming. But this time Hauke had no intention of giving up his prey—it might have been a kingfisher, he thought—so he refused to satisfy the cat's awakened lust.

"One for me and one for you!" he called out. "Today it's my turn. You'll have to wait until tomorrow for yours. This is too good for cat's food."

The tom stalked after him warily. Hauke stopped and eyed it stonily, the bird still in his hand. The cat paused too, with one paw raised. But the boy had underestimated his feline friend it seemed, for as he turned his back to go on his way again, he felt the bird ripped out of his hand and at the same time, a sharp claw dug into his arm. The lad saw red. With the fury of a wild beast he turned and pounced on the cat, clutching it by the throat. He lifted the huge creature high in the air and he kept it in a stranglehold until the eyes bulged out of the shaggy fur. He did not even notice that its powerful hind claws were slashing his arm to ribbons. "Oho!" he cried, tightening his grip. "Let's see who can hold out the longest!"

All at once, the hind legs went limp and Hauke walked back a few steps and flung the body against the wall of the old woman's hovel. It did not move so he turned away and started off home.

Now this Angora cat was the apple of its mistress's eye. It was her sole companion and all her sailor son had had to bequeath to her when he lost his life so suddenly, as he helped his mother to catch crabs in the mud during a storm. Hauke had hardly gone a hundred paces, mopping the blood from his scratches with a rag as he walked, when a great hue and cry assailed his ears. As he turned back, he saw the old woman crouching on the ground. Wisps of white hair escaped from her red kerchief and fluttered in the wind. "Dead!" she shrieked and raised her skinny arm to shake her fist at him. "It's dead, I tell you. My curse on you for this! You've killed it, you good-for-nothing loafer. Why, you weren't fit to brush its tail!" She threw herself over the corpse and with her apron she wiped its head tenderly where the blood still oozed from its nose and mouth. Then she raised her head once more and a torrent of abuse broke out afresh.

"Have you finished?" Hauke shouted. "If only you'd be quiet for a moment you'd hear what I have to say. I'll find you another cat, I tell you, one that will be satisfied with mice and rats for food."

Then he strode off as if that was the end of the affair. But the incident must have upset him, nevertheless, for when he came to the huddle of houses where his father lived, he walked straight past them and along the dike southwards in the direction of the town.

Meanwhile, Trin Jans had set off in the same direction. In her arms was a bundle wrapped in an old blue-check pillowcase and she carried it as carefully as a mother holding her baby. Her white hair fluttered in the mild spring breeze.

"What's that you're carrying, Trina?" asked a young farmer whom she met coming the other way. "A treasure worth more than all your house and land," retorted the old woman, hurrying on. When she reached the height above Haien's cottage, she turned off and trotted down the steep footpath which led from the dike to the houses below.

Tede Haien happened to be standing at his door, looking at the sky. "Hello there, Trin," he said as she stood before him leaning hard on her crook and panting for breath. "What have you got there in that bag of yours?"

"Let me come in, Tede Haien, and then you'll see." And her eyes had a peculiar gleam in them as she looked at him.

"Come in then," said the man. What did he care about the look in the eyes of a silly old woman like that?

When they were both indoors, she went on: "Clear away that old tobacco tin and the writing things from the table. Why must you be always scribbling anyway? That's better. Now wipe the top and make sure it's clean."

The old man, whose curiosity was roused a little by then, did as he was bid. When he had finished, Trin Jans took the blue cover by the two corners and shook out the dead cat on the table. "There you are!" she screeched. "It was your Hauke who killed it!" Thereupon she began her bitter weeping again, stroking the dead animal's thick fur and laying its paws together. She put her long nose close beside its head and whispered incomprehensible words of tenderness into its ears.

Tede Haien looked at it blankly. "I see," he said. "So it was Hauke's doing was it?" He was at a loss to know what to do with the old woman, who was crying her eyes out.

Trin Jans nodded grimly. "Yes, it was Hauke. I swear by God that he did it." She wiped away the tears from her eyes with her gnarled old hand, which was crippled with rheumatism. "And now I've neither chick nor child left!" she keened. "And you know as well as I do what it's like to be old and how cold it is by yourself in bed. Your legs freeze and you can't get to sleep and you have to listen all night to the nor'wester instead, rattling at the shutters. I hate the sound of it, Tede Haien. It reminds me of the night my lad was trapped in the mud."

Tede Haien nodded and the old woman stroked the fur of her dead tomcat. "But when I sat by my spinning wheel in the winter," she began again, "then the cat sat by my side and purred along with it. It would look at me with its big green eyes, and when I got cold and crept into my bed, it wouldn't be long before puss jumped up too. There it lay across my frozen legs and the two of us slept as warm and cosy as if I were young again with my sweetheart by my side." The old woman looked slyly at Tede Haien as if her reminiscence ought to rouse some response in him and again her eyes glinted.

Tede Haien thought for a while. "I'll help you, Trin Jans," he said, going to his cash box and taking a silver coin from one of the drawers. "You say that Hauke killed your cat and I know you don't tell lies. So here is a crown piece with the head of Christian the Fourth* on it. Buy yourself a tanned lambskin with it to warm your cold feet. And the next time our cat has kittens, you may choose the biggest one for yourself. I think that's fair compensation for a decrepit old tomcat like yours. And now, get this thing out of my sight! You can take it to the knacker's yard in the town for all I care. But hold your tongue and don't go telling everyone that you brought it to my house and let it lie on an honest man's table."†

The old woman had already grabbed at the taler as he spoke and she tucked it away in a pocket she kept hidden under her skirt. Then she stuffed the cat back in the pillowcase, wiped the bloodstains off the table with her apron and stalked towards the door. "Don't forget about the kitten," she called back.

It was some time later, as old Haien was pacing up and down the narrow living room, that Hauke came in and threw the brightly plumed bird on the table. But he saw the remains of bloodstains on the scrubbed white wood and he asked casually: "What's this?"

The father paused. "That is blood, blood which you shed."

The boy flushed hotly. "Has Trin Jans been here with her old cat?"

Tede Haien nodded. "Why did you kill it?" he asked.

Hauke bared his mauled arm. "That is why," he said. "He snatched the bird out of my hand."

The old man made no answer. Again he paced the room and it was some time before he stopped in front of his son and looked at him as if his mind were elsewhere. "I have settled the business with the cat," he said, "but it seems the cottage here is too small for us both. You cannot have two masters in a house. It is time you found yourself a place, Hauke."

"Yes, father. I was thinking the same thing."

---

*(1588–1648), king of Denmark. The duchies of Schleswig and Holstein, including North Friesland, where the story occurs, were in personal union with the Danish crown from 1460 to 1864.

†Dead animals were regarded as dishonorable. Trin has made Tede's table dishonorable by dumping the dead cat on it.

"Why?" asked the old man.

"Well, a kind of devil comes over you, if you haven't a proper job to tackle. You need to work to get things out of your system."

"I see," said the old man. "And that is how you came to kill the cat, is it? In that case, there might easily be worse to come."

"You may be right, father, but they say the dike reeve has dismissed his farm lad. That's something I could do."

The old man had begun pacing up and down again, spitting black tobacco juice. "The dike reeve is a fool. He has no more sense than a goose. He's only reeve because his father and his grandfather held office before him and because he owns more land than the rest of us. Come Martinmas, and the accounts for the dikes and sluices are due, he has to ply the schoolmaster with roast goose and mead and wheaten biscuits to help him out. There old Volkerts sits and nods his head as the teacher runs down the columns of figures with his pen and says, 'Bless my soul, schoolmaster, what a good head you have for sums.' But if the schoolmaster is too busy or refuses to come, then there the reeve sits, sweating, writing away and crossing it all out again. His silly fat face goes red and hot and his eyes bulge like marbles, as if his bit of a brain was trying to push its way out that way."

The boy, who was standing in front of his father, was amazed at such a torrent of words. He had never heard the old man speak like that before. "Yes, God help him, he is a fool, I know. But his daughter Elke can reckon well enough."

The old man glanced at him sharply. "What's that, hey?" he remarked. "And what do you know about Elke Volkerts, pray?"

"Why nothing, father. It was only that the schoolmaster mentioned her."

The old man did not reply. He shifted the tobacco quid pensively from one cheek to the other.

"And I suppose you thought you could sit down and do your sums together. Is that it?"

"Oh yes, father, that might be a good idea," replied the son, and his mouth twitched gravely.

Tede Haien shook his head. "Well, I shan't stand in your way. Go and try your luck."

"Thank you, father," said Hauke and went up to the loft where he slept. He sat down on the edge of the bed and wondered why his father had taken him up so sharply about Elke Volkerts. Of course he knew her by sight, a slender, dark-skinned girl of eighteen, with a thin face and black eyebrows that bridged a pair of defiant eyes and a delicate nose. So far he had hardly ever spoken to her but if he went round to see Tede Volkerts, he would be able to have a good look at her and find out what kind of girl she was. And suddenly he felt he must go there right away and see about the job, to make sure that no one else got in first. It was hardly evening yet, so he put on his Sunday coat and his best boots and set off in high heart along the road.

The long sprawling house which belonged to the dike reeve could be seen from far away. Not only did it stand on a high embankment but beside it to the east of the front door grew the tallest tree in the village, a mighty ash which the first reeve of the family, the present holder's grandfather, had planted in his youth. Previously two saplings had died without taking; but on his wedding morning he had planted a third tree, and this one had thrived. Its great crown of leaves was still spreading with every year that passed and it rustled in the constant wind as in the old days.

The sloping banks on either side of the path were planted out with turnips and cabbages and presently, as Hauke's tall gangling figure climbed the mound towards the house, he saw that the owner's daughter was standing near the low doorway. One thin arm hung limp by her side and the other hand seemed to be groping behind her for one of the iron rings which were let into the wall on either side of the door, so that visitors could tie up their horses. The girl seemed to be looking out over the dike and across the sea to where, on that quiet evening, the sun was just sinking below the horizon; its last rays gave a golden glow to the girl's dark skin.

Hauke slowed down a little. "She's no fool at any rate," he thought to himself. Then there he was at the top of the bank. "Good evening, Miss Elke," he said walking towards her. "What's that you're staring at with such big eyes?"

"Something that happens every evening, though not always like this." She let go the iron ring which clanged against the wall. "And what brings you here, Hauke Haien?" she asked.

"I hope you won't object," he said, "but I heard that your father has got rid of his farmhand and I thought he might take me into service."

She looked him up and down. "You're on the slight side for the job, Hauke," she answered. "Still, a steady pair of eyes is worth more to us than two strong arms." She looked at him almost frowning, but Hauke held her gaze without flinching. "Come in," she said. "My father is in the sitting room. Let's go in and see him."

The next day, Tede Haien and his son were standing in the large living room at the dike reeve's house. The walls were covered with glazed tiles, some of which had pictures on them, a ship in full sail, a fisherman sitting by a riverbank, or an ox grazing beside a farmhouse. This highly durable wall covering was interrupted by a great bed let into an alcove with folding doors which were now closed. A glass-fronted cabinet nearby displayed a variety of porcelain and silverware. In a niche near the door leading to the best parlor stood a Dutch chiming clock in a glass case.

The dike reeve was a stout man with a florid complexion. He was seated on a brightly colored woollen cushion in his armchair at the head of a wooden table which had been scrubbed until it was spotless. His hands were loosely clasped over his belly and his round eyes gazed contentedly at the skeleton of a fat duck. Fork and knife lay on the plate before him.

"Good day to you, Reeve," said old Haien and slowly the big man turned his head to see who was addressing him.

"Is it you, Tede?" he remarked, and his voice positively oozed with the fat of the duck he had just demolished. "Sit down, sit down. It's a fair step from your house to mine."

"I have come about my boy," said Tede Haien, as he sat down on the bench which ran the length of the wall, so that he was opposite the reeve. "I hear you have had some trouble with your farm lad and that you have agreed to take Hauke in his place."

"That's right, Tede, although I don't know what you mean by 'trouble.' Bless my soul, we fenmen know how to cure most of our ills." And he picked up the knife before him and parted the bones of the duck affectionately. "That was my favorite bird," he chuckled. "She used to eat out of my hand."

"I thought the fellow had played havoc with your livestock," said Haien, ignoring the last remark.

"Yes indeed, Tede. He certainly did. The fat blockhead forgot to water the calves. There he lay, dead drunk in the hayloft and the poor beasts bellowed all night with thirst and kept me awake so long I had to make up for it by sleeping till noon. You can't run a farm like that."

"No, Reeve. Indeed you can't. But there's no danger of that happening with my boy."

Hauke was still standing by the doorpost. His hands were in his pockets and he held his head high, studying the window frames in the wall opposite. The dike reeve raised his eyes to look at him again. "No, no, Tede," nodding first at the son and then at the father. "Your Hauke won't ruin my night's sleep. The schoolmaster told me some time ago that he'd rather sit at his slate doing sums than over a glass of brandy."

Hauke was not listening, however, for Elke had come into the room and as she quietly removed the remains of the meal from the table, she glanced at him for a moment. His eyes met her dark ones. "By all that's holy," he told himself, "she's no fool, that's for certain."

The girl went out again.

"You know of course," old Volkerts began speaking again, "that the Lord has not granted me a son."

"True, but don't let that grieve you," replied Tede Haien. "They do say that the brains in a family wear out by the third generation and it was your grandfather, as we all know, whom we have to thank for protecting the land."

The reeve pondered over these words for some little time and then looked up, bewildered. "What do you mean by that, Tede Haien?" he asked, rousing himself in his armchair. "I am the third generation, aren't I?"

"Why so you are!" declared Tede Haien and his thin face looked at the stout old dignitary with a glint of malice in his eyes. "But I meant no offense, Reeve. It's only a saying."

"Don't repeat all the old wives' tales you hear, Tede Haien," the reeve went on. "If you knew my daughter, you'd soon see she can run rings round me when it comes to reckoning. All I wanted to say was that since I have no son of my own, your Hauke will be able to learn a lot here in my house with his pen and pencil, as well as out in the fields, and that won't come amiss."

"Yes, yes, I'm sure he will. You are quite right there," said old Haien, and then he began to haggle for some concessions in the articles of apprenticeship which had not occurred to the boy the evening before. By the time Tede was finished, Hauke would be entitled to receive eight pairs of woollen stockings in the autumn as well as linen shirts in addition to his wages. His father would have a right to his son's services at home for eight days every spring and so forth and so on. But the reeve complied readily with every request. Hauke Haien seemed to him to be just the lad he wanted.

"Well, my boy," said his father when they had left the reeve's house, "may the Lord help you if yon's the man to teach you your trade."

"Don't worry, Father," replied Hauke calmly. "It will be all right in the end."

And in this, Hauke was not far wrong. The longer he stayed in the reeve's service, the more he learned about the ways of the world, at least insofar as they concerned him. Perhaps it was all to the good that he had no enlightened person to guide him, for he was thrown back on his own resources as, indeed, he had been all his life. There was, however, one person in the house who resented his presence and that was the foreman, Ole Peters, who was a good worker but too quick with his tongue. The previous farmboy had been lazy but easygoing and as strong as a horse. He was very much more to the foreman's taste, for Peters could load a big barrel of oats on to his back without any hesitation, and he could order him about to his heart's content. But he could not bully the silent Hauke like that, for Hauke was much his superior intellectually. He had a way of looking at Peters which the latter found most disconcerting. All the same, the foreman lost no opportunity getting his own back. He made a point of finding work which might be harmful to a growing lad, not yet toughened by hard manual labor. "You ought to have seen that fat boy, Niss," Peters would tell Hauke. "Why, he would have done that without turning a hair." Then Hauke would brace himself and summon all his strength to do as he was told, although it sometimes required a painful effort.

It was fortunate for him that Elke often intervened, either personally or by prompting her father, and so was usually able to protect him from the worst. One may well ask what it is that forges a bond between two such strangers. Perhaps it was nothing more than their common gift for mathematics and the girl could not bear to sit by and see a fellow spirit coarsened by such rough work.

The rift between the two employees had not lessened when Martinmas was over, and with the coming of winter much time had to be spent in preparing the various dike accounts for audit.

One evening in May in the following year the weather turned so bad it was more like November out of doors. Even inside the house, one could hear the surf thundering away behind the dike, "Hey there, Hauke," said the reeve. "Come into the sitting room. Here's a chance for you to show if you're any good at figures."

"But master," he replied, "I've just been told to go and feed the calves."

"Never mind about that," was the answer. "Elke! Where have you got to, girl? Go and find Ole and tell him he's to feed the cattle. Hauke's needed here to do the books."

And Elke hurried into the stable and gave the foreman his orders.

Peters was busy putting away the horses' harness which had been in use during the day. He had the snaffle in his hand and when he heard Elke's message, he struck the rack such a blow with it, it looked as if he would have liked to smash it to smithereens. "The devil take that damned scribbler!" he fumed.

The words reached Elke as she closed the stable door.

"Well?" asked her father as she came back into the parlor."

"Ole will see to it," answered Elke, biting her lips a little. She sat down opposite Hauke on a clumsily carved wooden chair, of a kind that people here used to make for themselves in those days, during the long winter evenings at home. She had taken her knitting from a chest of drawers and she got on with her work. It was a white stocking with a pattern of red birds on it, long-legged creatures, herons perhaps, or maybe they were storks. Hauke, at the other side of the table, was immersed in the accounts and the reeve relaxed peacefully in his armchair, his eyes blinking sleepily as they followed Hauke's quill. Two tallow candles burnt on the table, as always in the reeve's house. The shutters had been put up outside and the catches on the leaded windows were secured on the inside. Let the wind beat against them as hard as it might! Now and again Hauke would look up from his work and eye the birds on the knitted stocking or glance at the girl's thin, serene face.

A sudden loud snort came from the armchair and the two young people exchanged a lightning glance and a smile. Gradually the snores subsided, the breathing grew more quiet and even. At last it was safe to speak to each other; only Hauke could not think of anything to say.

Elke lifted her knitting in the air to see how far she had got and the birds on it could be seen at full length. "Where did you learn that, Elke?" Hauke whispered across the table.

"Learn what?" retorted the girl.

"How to knit birds, I mean."

"Oh, that. Trin Jans who lives out along the dike showed me. She knows all kinds of things. She used to be in service here many years ago, in my grandfather's day."

"But you weren't born then," objected Hauke.

"No, I don't suppose I was, but she often came to see us after she had left."

"Is she fond of birds, then?" asked Hauke. "I thought she only liked cats."

Elke shook her head. "She rears ducks and sells them too. But last year, after you killed her Angora cat, the rats got into the coop and ate them. Now she wants to build another coop, in front of the house this time."

"So that's it," said Hauke and he whistled softly between his teeth. "So that's why she's been dragging loads of clay and stones from the uplands. But then she'll be obstructing the pathway. Has she been given a permit?"

"I don't know," said Elke, but Hauke had spoken the last words so loudly that the reeve was startled from his slumbers. "Permit?" he asked and looked from one to the other, mystified. "What's that about a permit?"

But when Hauke had explained it to him, he only laughed and clapped the boy on the shoulder. "Never mind about that. The path is wide enough in all conscience. Heaven help the reeve if he has to bother his head about little things like poultry coops."

Hauke felt a twinge of conscience. If he was really to blame for the loss of the old woman's ducklings, he would not argue the point. "All the same," he persisted, "there's one or two folk round here who could do with pulling up, and if you'd rather not do it yourself, you can always get the wardens to tackle it. After all, they're responsible for keeping the dikes in good order."

"What's that? What's the boy saying?" The reeve sat up with a jerk and Elke left off her knitting and let it lie in her lap, so that she could listen properly.

"Yes," Hauke went on. "I know you have completed the spring inspection but all the same, Peter Jansen has still not cleared his land of weeds. The goldfinches will have a high old time among the purple thistles when summer comes. And close by, I don't know whose land it is, but there's a great hollow in the dike on the far side. When the weather's fine, the children play roly-poly in it, but the Lord help us if there's a flood tide."

The reeve's eyes grew bigger with every word that Hauke spoke.

"And then . . .," Hauke hurried on.

"And then what?" interrupted the reeve. "Haven't you finished yet?" And you could tell by his voice that the boy had already said too much for his liking.

"Well, then there's that buxom lass Vollina, Warden Harder's daughter, who fetches her father's dun mare from the fens every day. Once she's up on its back with those plump calves of hers, she says, 'Giddy up!' and rides straight up the slope of the dike and never bothers to use the track."

It was only then that Hauke noticed Elke's intelligent eyes seeking his and she gently shook her head. Hauke stopped abruptly, but the reeve's fist came down on the table with such a thump that it made him jump. "And what if the weather strikes there?" he shouted and Hauke was taken aback at the sudden bearlike growl in his voice. "Fine her, I say! Serve a summons on her. Have that fat hussy fined, I tell you. She's the minx who made off with three of my young ducks last summer. Yes, yes. Have a summons served, I tell you. Actually, I believe it was four ducks."

"Oh Father," said Elke, "surely it was the otter that stole the ducks?"

"A fine otter!" snorted the old man. "I can tell the difference between that fat wench and an otter, thank you. No, there were four ducks, Hauke. And as for the rest of your prattle, let me tell you that the head reeve and I did the rounds together in the spring after we'd had breakfast here in my house. We rode side by side and we saw nothing of these weeds or this hollow of yours either. Ah well," he sighed, "a fellow has only two eyes when all's said and done, but a reeve needs a hundred. You ought to thank God, both of you," and here he nodded energetically towards Hauke and his daughter, "that you haven't my responsibility. Now get out those bills from the straw merchants, Hauke, the ones for layering and mattressing the new dikes. And check them carefully, young man. Their adding up can be very shaky."

Then he leaned back in his chair, settled his heavy body comfortably and was soon sound asleep once more.

A similar scene occurred on many evenings. Hauke had sharp eyes and whenever they were together, he did not hesitate to bring to his master's attention any cases of damage to the dikes or negligence in their upkeep. And as the reeve could hardly ignore everything, the whole administration became suddenly much more efficient. Those who had jogged along in the same old way for many years, now found their sins of commission or omission were catching up with them. Knuckles were rapped all round and the bewildered owners were forced to look about them, wondering what had hit them. Ole Peters, the foreman, lost no time in broadcasting to all and sundry who it was who was really responsible for these activities and he tried to stir up resistance not only to Hauke but to his father as well, who was held to be equally to blame. But others who were not affected, or who had actually benefited by Hauke's intervention, only laughed and were delighted that the boy had managed to rouse the old man to take some action at last. "Only it's a pity that the young monkey hasn't a respectable slice of land to call his own. Then in time to come, we might get a reeve of the old breed, as in days gone by. But the few square yards he'll inherit from Tede Haien aren't enough for that."

The next autumn when the chief inspector of dikes, who was known as the head reeve, came on his rounds, he looked old Volkerts up and down, as the latter pressed him to begin his breakfast. "Do you know, Reeve, on my word, you look ten years younger since my last visit. It does me good to hear all these suggestions of yours. I only hope we can deal with them all today."

"We'll manage, we'll manage, Your Honor," replied the old man, smiling smugly. "The roast goose before us will fortify us for the work ahead. Yes, thank God, I keep pretty fit and strong." Here he glanced round to make sure Hauke was not within earshot, and then added with pompous complacency, "And I trust the Lord will allow me to carry on with my duties for a few years longer."

"Let us drink to that," replied the inspector, rising.

Elke, who had been serving breakfast, left the room as the glasses clinked and she gave a soft laugh once she had closed the door. She took a dish of poultry scraps from the kitchen and she had to pass through the stable on her way to the yard. Hauke was in there, forking hay on to the racks for the cattle which had been brought in early because of the bad weather. When he saw the girl coming, he stopped and stuck the fork in the ground. "Hello Elke," he said.

She stopped too and nodded to him. "You ought to have been in the sitting room just now," she told him.

"Why?" he asked.

"The head reeve was praising my father so."

"Your father? What has that to do with me?"

"He was complimenting him for his work on the dikes."

The young man's face flushed dark red. "I can guess what you're hinting at."

"Don't blush, Hauke. Of course the praise was really due to you."

Hauke looked at her, half-smiling. "You too, Elke," he said.

But she shook her head. "No, Hauke. When my father and I were on our own and I gave him what little help I could, the reeve never commended us. I can only give a hand with the bookkeeping, but you notice everything that's going on out of doors, things which my father should see for himself. You have cut me out completely."

"I did not intend to, you least of all," said Hauke, embarrassed. And he pushed aside the head of one of the cows. "Now then, Rosy, don't eat the fork out of my hand. You'll get as much as you want presently."

"Don't think I regret it, Hauke," said the girl after a moment's reflection. "It's a man's business, when all's said and done."

Hauke stretched out his arms towards her. "Give me your hand on it, Elke."

This time it was the girl whose face colored, up to her dark eyebrows.

"Why should I? I don't tell lies!" she exclaimed.

Hauke wanted to answer but she had already disappeared. He stood there, pitchfork in hand, but there was nothing to be heard

except the ducks and hens quacking and cackling in the yard outside.

It was in the January of the third year of Hauke's apprenticeship
that a winter festival took place, a contest in a game rather like
curling, which is called *Eisboseln* in these parts. The frost had held
for a long time and there had been no onshore winds, so that all the
ditches that drained the fens were covered with a firm smooth
surface of ice. The land which was normally parceled up into small
lots was now transformed into a wide course and perfect for the
game, which was played with small wooden balls weighted with
lead. Day in, day out, a gentle breeze blew from the northeast.
Conditions were ideal. The previous year, the villagers from the high
ground to the east had been the winners and now they had accepted
the fenmen's challenge to a return match.

Each team consisted of nine players. A referee was selected and
there was also a marker for each side. These latter were required to
pit their wits against each other whenever there was a doubtful
throw. So it was important to pick men who knew how to present a
dubious case in the best possible light. The most likely to be chosen
were men not only with a reputation for a good deal of common
sense but who were also considered to have the gift of gab. Preemi-
nent among them was Tede Volkert's headman, Ole Peters. "As long
as the team does the throwing, you can leave the arguing to me, and
I'll do it free of charge at that."

It was the day before the match and getting on for evening. In the
inn parlor, the organizers were gathered together, for the team was
one man short and they had to decide who should fill the vacancy
from among the latest applicants. Hauke Haien's name was one of
those now under consideration. At first, he had been reluctant to
take part, although he had every confidence in his skill at throwing.
But as Ole Peters was one of the honorary officials, Hauke was afraid
he would have him rejected and he wanted to spare himself such
humiliation. It was only Elke who had persuaded him to volunteer
at the last moment. "He is only the son of a day laborer," she had
said, "whilst your father owns a cow and a horse, and besides, he's
the wisest man in the village."

"But suppose he does get them to turn me down all the same?"

Her dark eyes were half-smiling as she looked at him. "Then he'd better be prepared for a shock when he asks the reeve's daughter to dance with him in the evening."

And so Hauke felt encouraged and he finally consented.

Now the three rivals for a place in the team were gathered outside the inn in the freezing cold. They stamped their feet and kept looking up to the stone steeple of the church tower, which stood hard by the inn. The pastor's doves, who had gorged themselves all summer in the fields, were winging their way home from the farm-yards and barns in the neighborhood where they had to seek their food during the winter. One by one they disappeared beneath the shingles of the tower where they had built their nests. In the west, the sunset glowed deep red over the sea.

"It will be a fine day tomorrow, but cold," said one of the lads, and he began stumping up and down. "I'll say it will be cold!" A second youth, who had seen that all the doves were home, went inside the inn and stood listening outside the door of the parlor from which there came the sound of a lively argument. Hauke joined him. "Listen," said the first young man, "they're calling for you." Then they heard Ole Peters's husky voice barking out: "We're having no boys or farm lads in our team, I say."

"Come closer," whispered the other and he tried to drag Hauke nearer the door by his coat sleeve. "Now you can find out just what they think of you."

But Hauke tore himself away and went out of doors again. "If they wanted us to hear what they have to say, they wouldn't have locked us out," he called back.

Outside stood the third contender. "I don't think I'm in the running," he declared to Hauke. "I'm barely eighteen. If only they don't call for our birth certificates! But you're lucky. You have your foreman there to talk them round."

"Yes, but which way?" muttered Hauke and he kicked a stone viciously across the path. "Into getting me disqualified."

The noise inside the parlor rose to a climax and then their voices gradually died down. Once more the lads waiting out of doors heard the nor'easter blustering softly past the church spire. Then the lad who had been eavesdropping rejoined the others. "Who is it to be?" asked the eighteen-year-old.

"Him," was the reply and a finger pointed to Hauke. "Ole Peters was all for ruling him out as only a farmer's boy, but the others were on his side. 'And his father has land of his own and livestock,' argued Jess Hansen. 'You call that land?' shouted Peters. 'Why you could cart it all away in a few barrowloads!' Then Ole Hensen intervened. 'Be quiet a moment,' he ordered, 'and I'll tell you something. Now who is the first man in the village?' There was silence for a moment as if they had to think before they answered. Then a voice said, 'The dike reeve, of course' and the others all echoed 'Why yes, of course, it's the reeve.' 'And who is that pray?' cried Ole Hensen. 'But think before you answer!' Then someone started chuckling and another fellow joined in until you could hear nothing but loud laughter. 'Very well,' said Hensen. 'Call him in then. You wouldn't show the reeve the door, would you?' And I imagine they're still laughing in there. But there wasn't another squeak from Ole Peters," added the lad, concluding his report.

Almost at that very moment, the parlor door was flung open and a loud cheerful voice rang out in the cold night air. "Hauke!" it cried. "Hauke Haien!"

So Hauke went inside and no more was said about who, in fact, was the dike reeve. But what was going on inside Hauke's head, no one ever knew.

As he approached his master's house later that evening, he saw Elke standing by the hedge at the foot of the slope and the moonlight shimmered over the broad meadows, which were white with rime. "You here, Elke?" he asked.

She nodded. "What happened? Did he dare?"

"Of course he did. Why shouldn't he?"

"Well? What was the outcome?"

"It's all right, Elke, I can play tomorrow."

"Good night, Hauke." And she darted up the bank and disappeared into the house.

He followed her, slowly.

The next afternoon, a dark mass of people could be seen gathered on the open fields which lay to the east of the dikes on the land side. One moment the crowd would be motionless. Then, after a couple of throws which sent the wooden balls hurtling over the ground, now freed from frost by the afternoon sun, the whole body would move off downhill, leaving the long low houses farther and farther behind. In the midst of the throng were the two teams of competitors and surrounding them was the entire population, everyone old or young, who lived either in the fenlands or in the upland village. The older men wore long jackets and they pulled thoughtfully at their short-stemmed pipes. The women wore shawls and jackets and pulled children by the hand or carried them on their arm. As one by one the frozen ditches were crossed, the sharp tips of the reeds could be seen sparkling in the pale gleam of the afternoon sun. It was bitterly cold but the game went on without a pause and all eyes followed the flight of the balls, for the honor of each side depended on them today. The markers carried iron-tipped staves, a white one for the fenmen and a black one for the village. As the ball came to rest, the appropriate stick was rammed into the frozen ground to mark its position, to the silent approval of the one side or the scornful laughter of the other. Whichever ball reached the target first would be the winning throw for that team.

There was little spoken throughout the game. Only a really masterly shot would bring a shout from the lads or from the women. Or one of the old men might take his pipe from his mouth and tap the thrower on the shoulder, exclaiming: "Now that was a fine throw, as old Zacharias said when he heaved his wife out of the window!" Or "That was worthy of your late father, God rest his soul!" or some such word of encouragement.

Hauke was out of luck when he made his first throw. Just as he swung his arm back to bowl, a cloud which had been covering the sun, suddenly moved away and a dazzling beam of light shone straight in his eyes. The throw fell short and landed in a ditch, stuck in the hollow ice at the edge.

"That doesn't count!" called his teammates. "He can have it again."

The marker from the other side rushed in to disagree. "Of course it counts. It was a perfectly good throw."

"Ole Peters!" cried the fenmen. "Where's Ole? Where the devil's he got to?"

But Peters was there on the spot. "There's no need to shout so. I suppose it's Hauke in trouble and you want me to get him out of it. Just as I thought."

"Rubbish! It was a no ball and Hauke must have his throw again. Show us what you can do for him with that great mouth of yours."

"Just wait and see!" cried Ole and, walking up to his counterpart from the opposing team, he started spouting a stream of nonsense, chattering away nineteen to the dozen. But there was none of his usual fire or wit in his arguments and Elke, standing close by, her dark brows frowning, flashed her furious eyes at him. But she did not dare to interfere, for women had no voice in such matters.

"I suppose you're talking such twaddle because you haven't a leg to stand on," replied the marker from the village. "The sun, moon and stars are a fair risk. They don't favor one side more than the other. No, admit it. It was a clumsy throw but a perfectly valid one, and it has to count like any other bad shot."

The debate went back and forth but the upshot was that the referee's decision went against Hauke Haien.

"Let's get on with the game then," called the villagers. Their marker drew his black stick out of the ground and the player whose turn it was stepped forward and threw. As Peters moved on to follow the shot, he had to pass Elke Volkerts. "And what made you leave your wits at home today, pray?" she whispered angrily as he approached.

Peters glowered at her and the expression on his broad face was devoid of all humor. "I wanted to keep you company," he retorted, "since you seem to have done the same."

"Don't try to fool me. I know what you're up to," she answered, drawing herself up proudly. But he turned away and behaved as if he had not heard her.

So the game went on and the black and white sticks were moved, one at a time, farther and farther along the ice. With Hauke's next throw, the ball flew so far that the big white-washed barrel which was the target came clearly into sight. Hauke had grown into a sturdily built young man, who had worked away at both mathematics and the art of throwing since boyhood. "Oho," came a voice from the crowd. "That was a good throw, Hauke, worthy of the archangel Michael himself, I do declare." An old woman with a tray of cakes and spirits pushed her way through the crowd and came up to Hauke. She poured out a full glass and offered it to him. "Come on lad. Let's make it up. You're doing a better job today than when you killed my cat." As he looked at her, he saw it was Trin Jans. "Thank you, old lady," said he. "But I don't drink hard liquor." He dipped into his pocket and pressed a freshly minted mark piece into her hand. "Take this, though, and drink it up yourself, Trin. Now we're friends again."

"You're quite right, Hauke," replied the old woman, promptly taking his advice. "It's better for old folks like me."

"How are your ducks?" he called out to her as she moved away with her basket over her arm. She did not turn but shook her head and threw up her hands. "I can't do anything with them, Hauke. Those ditches of yours breed too many rats. No, God help me, I must find another way to earn a living." And she worked her way through the thronging crowd and offered her schnapps and honey cakes for sale.

By now the sun had dropped below the dike and where it had been the sky was flooded with a purple glow. Black crows were flying overhead and for a fleeting moment they were changed to gold as evening fell. But across the fens, the dark mass of people left the distant houses far behind and drew closer and closer to the white barrel. One really good throw might just reach it by now. It was the fenmen's turn and Hauke was the next man to throw. The dike cast its broad evening shadow across the wastes and the distempered cask shone white against it. "You can't possibly win," jeered the villagers, for although the contest was close, they had the advantage by at least ten feet.

Hauke's lean figure emerged from the crowd. His gray eyes, set in his long Frisian face, gazed towards the barrel. The ball rested in his hand as he balanced it at arm's length.

"What's the matter?" Ole Peters's voice croaked in his ears. "Is the barrel too big? Shall we change it for a kitchen saucepan?"

Hauke turned and looked Peters straight in the eyes. "I'm playing for the honor of the fens. Whose side are you on?"

"You wouldn't be throwing for Elke Volkerts as well, would you?"

"Out of my way!" shouted Hauke and took up his stance. Peters pushed his head up closer, but before Hauke could ward him off, a hand shot out from the crowd and pulled Ole back, so that he staggered against his laughing comrades. It was not a particularly powerful hand that had done the trick, for as Hauke glanced back for a moment, he saw Elke close by, smoothing her sleeve. Her dark eyebrows made angry lines across her flushed face.

Hauke felt his arm had acquired the strength of tensile steel. He leaned forward a little, swung the ball once or twice in his hand then, as he drew back his arm, a deathly silence descended on all sides. Everyone's eyes followed the flight of the ball as they heard it swish through the air. It was a long way away when a white gull flew up from the dike, calling, and its outstretched wings hid the ball from sight. An instant later, though, came the impact of the ball, and they heard it crash into the barrel. "Hurrah for Hauke!" cried the fenmen and there was great jubilation among the crowd. "Hauke!" they cheered. "Hauke Haien has won!"

As they all gathered round him, he groped to one side for a certain hand. And when the people cried, "Why are you standing there Hauke? The ball is safely home!" Hauke merely nodded and did not move. Only when he felt that the little hand responded to his own firm clasp, did he answer: "I believe you're right. I think I've won."

Then everyone turned to go back and Elke and Hauke were parted in the surge towards the village inn. The crowd had to pass close by the reeve's house and here they both escaped from the crush. Elke went up to her room immediately and Hauke stood on the embankment in front of the stable door and watched the people gradually making their way uphill to the inn where a room had been prepared for dancing. Darkness was spreading over the whole countryside. The silence grew all about him and only the cattle stirred in the stable. From the village inn, he fancied he could hear the sound of clarinets. Then round the corner of the house came the rustle of a gown and small firm footsteps sounded along the path that led from the fens to the village. In the twilight, Hauke made out a moving figure. It was Elke, off to the dance. The blood shot up in his face. Should he not run after her and go with her? But he was no ladies' man and he stood there, hesitating, until she had disappeared into the night.

It was only when there was no longer any danger of catching her up, that Hauke followed in her footsteps until he reached the inn by the church. There was such a babble and hullaballoo going on both outside the inn and in the hall, as everyone tried to push their way inside, such a shrilling of violins and clarinets, that the noise bewildered and deafened him. Unobserved, he squeezed his way into the hall known as the Guild Room. It was not very large, and it was so full, one could hardly see a yard ahead. Silently Hauke posted himself by the doorway and watched the swirl of dancers. What fools they looked, he thought. There was no need to worry that anyone would embarrass him with praise. Everyone had forgotten about the afternoon's contest and who had won the game hardly an hour before. The lads had eyes for nothing but their girls as they whirled them round and round. Hauke's eyes sought one person and one person only. At last, there she was—dancing with a cousin of hers, one of the younger dike wardens. But a moment later she was swallowed up in the crowd again and he could see only the other lasses from the fens or the village, and none of them interested him in the least.

The violins and clarinets stopped abruptly and the dance was over. But another started with scarcely a pause for breath and the words Elke had spoken a day or two before flashed through Hauke's mind. Would she keep her word, he wondered, or would he have to watch her dancing past him with Ole Peters? The thought of it made him want to cry out. He wished . . . Well, what did he wish? But Elke did not seem to be taking part in this dance and when it was over at last, another one followed it. This time it was a two-step which was all the rage just then. The musicians played like fury, the young men grabbed at their girls and the wall lights flickered. Hauke all but dislocated his neck trying to make out the dancers as they passed him and he suddenly realized that the man of the third pair near him was Ole Peters. But who was his partner? A broad-shouldered lad blocked his view and Hauke could not see the girl's face. But the dancers whirled on and Ole and his partners spun round. "Vollina, Vollina Harders!" Hauke almost shouted the name aloud and gave a great sigh of relief. But where was Elke? Had she no partner, or had she refused them all because she did not wish to dance with Peters? Once more the music stopped and yet another dance began, but still it brought no sign of Elke. Ole came into sight again, still dancing with Vollina. "Well, well," thought Hauke. "It looks as though old Jess Harders will soon be expected to hand things over and retire." But where was Elke?

Hauke left his place by the doorpost and made his way into the room. And all at once he was standing in front of her. She was sitting in a corner, talking to an older girl who was a friend of hers. "Hauke!" she exclaimed, and her oval face looked up at his. "Are you here? I didn't see you dancing."

"I haven't been dancing," he replied.

"Why ever not?" And, half rising from her seat, she added, "Will you dance with me? I refused Ole Peters, you know. He won't ask me again in a hurry."

Hauke made no move. "Thank you, Elke, but I don't know much about dancing. People might laugh at you and besides . . ." He stopped short and his grey eyes looked at her so tenderly, that it seemed he had left it to them to finish the sentence for him.

"What do you mean, Hauke?" she asked softly.

"I mean Elke, that the end of the day can hardly improve on the beginning, as far as I'm concerned."

"Yes," she said, "you won the game."

"Elke!" His reproach was so mild it was barely audible:

The girl flushed hotly.

"Get along with you," she said, dropping her eyes. "What are you trying to say?"

At this point, her friend was swept off to dance by some young man or other so that Hauke could speak up a little more boldly. "I thought I had won something better!"

For a few seconds her eyes remained fixed on the ground. Then she raised them slowly, so that they revealed all the serene strength of her character. It was a look which warmed Hauke through and through, like a gentle breeze on a summer's day. "Do as your heart bids you, Hauke. We should know each other well enough by now."

Elke did not dance any more that evening and when she and Hauke returned home, they walked hand in hand. The stars twinkled from the depths of the sky above the silent marshes. A light wind sprang up from the east and it turned bitterly cold. But the two of them walked home side by side with never a thought for shawls and wraps, as if it had suddenly turned to spring.

Immediately after the dance, Hauke set about making a certain purchase, although there was no prospect of his using it for a long time to come. All the same, it was something of a solemn occasion, even if he had to celebrate it quietly and alone. The next Sunday, therefore, he went into the town and called on old Andersen, the goldsmith. There he asked to see a broad gold ring. "Give me your hand and we'll measure you," said the goldsmith, reaching for the ring finger. "You don't need a big size. It's not as thick as that of most lads round here." "I'd rather you measured my little finger," answered Hauke and held it out to him.

Andersen was somewhat surprised but a young man's whims were his own business, after all. All he said was: "We'll have to look among the ladies' rings for one as small as that," and Hauke felt himself blushing. But the small gold ring which Andersen produced fitted his little finger admirably and he took it hastily, paying for it in bright new silver. Then, with his heart thumping, and as if he were performing some special ceremony, he deposited it in his waistcoat pocket. From that day on, he always carried it about with him, diffidently and yet with pride, as if that waistcoat pocket had been made for the sole purpose of holding his ring.

Hauke Haien carried it about for many a year, so that presently, when the waistcoat had to be replaced, the ring was transferred to a new pocket, still awaiting an opportunity which would release it from its confinement. Occasionally, he felt a sudden impulse to go up to his master and speak straight out. After all, Hauke's father was a man of property too. But on sober reflection he had to admit that the reeve would simply laugh such presumption out of court. So he and the reeve's daughter continued to live under the same roof and although she too kept silence as befitted a modest young lady, they felt they were still walking hand in hand as on the night of the dance.

A year after the throwing contest, Ole Peters gave his master notice and married Vollina Harders. Hauke had been right. Her father, old Jess Harders, was forced to retire and it was no longer the fat daughter who rode the dun mare into the fens but the boisterous son-in-law. And it was rumored that he, too, rode back home down the side of the embankment, just as the girl had done. Hauke was now promoted to foreman and a younger boy was taken on in his own place. The reeve had been opposed to this at first. "He's better as an apprentice," he had grumbled. "He won't have time to do the books." "If you don't promote him, Hauke will leave too," Elke had pointed out to him. The old man was so terrified at such a prospect that he gave Hauke the job after all and in spite of the extra responsibility, Hauke still helped the reeve with the administration and maintenance of the dikes as he had done before.

At the end of another year, however, Hauke had to tell Elke that his father's health was failing fast. The few days in the summer when the reeve allowed him to go home and help were not nearly enough to do all that was necessary. The old man was worrying too and Hauke did not like to see this. It was a summer's evening. The two young people were standing in the gathering dusk beneath the big ash tree in front of the house. The girl looked up into the branches without speaking for a while. "It was not for me to say anything, Hauke, although I knew of this, of course," she replied at last. "I thought you would know for yourself what was the right thing to do." "Then I must leave your house," he said, "and I can never come back."

Again she was silent and looked into the sun setting red behind the dike and sinking into the sea. "I want to tell you something," she continued. "I went to see your father this morning and I found him fast asleep in his armchair. He had his pen in his hand and the drawing board was on the table with a half-finished sketch on it. He woke up presently and he made a great effort to chat with me for a little while and when I wanted to go he tried to detain me, holding my hand as if he feared this would be our last meeting. But all the same . . ."

"All the same what, Elke?" asked Hauke as the girl hesitated.

A few tears ran down her cheeks. "I was only thinking of my own father," she said. "Believe me, he will find it hard to manage without you." And as if it needed great self-control to say more, she added, "I often have the feeling he is not far from death's door himself."

Hauke did not answer, but all at once, he felt as if the ring in his pocket had stirred of its own accord. Before he could even reproach himself for such wishful thinking, Elke went on, "No, no. Don't be angry, Hauke. I know you will never forsake us, even then."

He took her hand impulsively and she did not pull it away. For a little while they stood there in the failing light until at last their hands slipped apart and then went their separate ways. A gust of wind sprang up, rustling the ash leaves and rattling the shutters at the front of the house. But as night descended slowly, silence once more covered the whole countryside.

Again, it was Elke who persuaded the dike reeve to release Hauke from his service, although he had not given due notice, and it meant that both farmhands were new to the job. A few months later, Tede Haien passed away, but before he died, he called his son to his bedside. "Sit down, my son," said the old man in a tired voice. "Come closer, there's no need to be afraid. It is only the dark angel of the Lord who is with me, come to call me to His presence."

Deeply moved, the son sat down at the edge of the bed in the dark alcove where his father had always slept. "Speak, father. Tell me, is there still something you have to say?"

"Yes, my son, there is," answered the old man, spreading his fingers over the coverlet. "When you were hardly more than a boy and you went into service with the dike reeve, you had a notion in your head you might like to be reeve yourself one day. I never forgot that and bit by bit, I came to see that you might well be the right man for it. But the little land I could leave you when I died was not enough for such high office. So once you had left home, I lived very frugally so that I could bequeath you a few more acres."

Hauke seized his father's hands and the old man tried to sit up so that he could see his son better. "Yes, yes," he said. "In the top drawer of my cash box you will find a document. You know old Antje Wollmers has a fen of five and a half acres. When she grew old and crippled she could not live on the rent it brought in. So every year at Martinmas, I gave her an agreed sum and indeed, when I had anything over, I gave the poor old soul a little extra. In return she made over the title deeds to me and it has all been signed and sealed legally. Now she too is dying. It's the curse of these marshes, cancer,* that has got her. You won't have to pay her any more, of that you can be sure."

Tede Haien closed his eyes for a few moments before he went on. "It isn't much, I know, but it's more than you were used to when you went into service. May it help you, my son, throughout your days on this earth."

Before Hauke could thank him properly, the old man dropped off to sleep. His mind was free of cares and in a few days' time, when the dark angel of the Lord shut his eyes for ever, Hauke came into his father's estate.

The day after the funeral Elke came to see Hauke at his cottage. "Why Elke!" he exclaimed. "How kind of you to look in."

"I'm not looking in," she answered. "I have come to tidy up the house for you so that you can live decently. Your father was too busy with figures and drawings to pay much attention to the way he lived, and in any case, the housework is always neglected when there's a death in the house. I want to make the place habitable for you."

---

*While writing the story, Storm was suffering from stomach cancer, from which he died a few months after finishing it.

His grey eyes were full of gratitude as he looked at her. "Please do," he said. "I like to see it tidy."

She set about her self-appointed task at once. The drawing board, which was still lying about, was dusted and stored away in the loft; the pens, pencils and chalk were put away carefully in a drawer under lock and key. Then the young servant girl was called in to help and all the furniture was rearranged, so that when they had finished the whole room looked lighter and larger than before. "It needed a woman's touch," said Elke smiling, and in spite of his grief at his father's death, Hauke was happy watching her at her work and giving a hand himself when necessary.

As dusk approached—it was the beginning of September—and everything was as she wished it, she took his hand and turned her dark eyes to his. "Now come home with me and have supper with us this evening, for I promised my father I would bring you with me. Then you can come back here with an easy mind."

As they entered the reeve's spacious living room, the shutters were already up and the customary two candles on the table were lit. The reeve tried to rise and greet his former employee but his heavy body sagged back into the big armchair and he could only give him words of welcome. "Nice of you to come, Hauke. I'm glad you seek out an old friend. Step closer, lad, here where I can talk to you." And as the young man approached his chair, the reeve's plump old hands closed round one of Hauke's. "Now, now, my boy," he said, "don't grieve, for we all must die, and your father was a man of whom no one spoke ill. But hurry up, Elke, and serve the roast. We need to fortify ourselves for there's a heap of work waiting. What with the autumn inspection due, and the bills for work on the dikes and sluices piling up sky-high, to say nothing of the recent damage to the dike round the western polder, I don't know if I'm on my head or my heels these days. But you're a sight younger, and you've got a clear head on your shoulders. You're a good lad, Hauke."

This was a long speech for the old man, but it revealed all that was on his mind. When he had done, he fell back in his chair and his eyes gleamed wistfully towards the door as Elke came in with the roast on a dish. Hauke stood by his side, smiling.

"Hurry up and sit down," said the reeve. "There's no time to waste. You lose all the flavor if you let it get cold."

Hauke sat down. It never occurred to him to refuse to help. And when the autumn inspection was over and a few more months had elapsed, he had indeed finished the bulk of it for old Tede Volkerts.

The schoolmaster paused and looked around him. A gull screamed as it swerved past the inn window and out in the hall there was the stamping of feet as if someone was shaking the thick clay soil from his heavy boots.

The reeve and the wardens turned their heads to the door of the inn parlor as a burly man wearing a sou'wester entered the room.

"We've both seen him, sir, Hans Nickels and I. It was the man on the white horse and he rode down the embankment and into the gap."

"Where was that?" asked the reeve.

"There's only the one, sir, that pond on Jensen's land where the Hauke Haien polder begins."

"You only saw it once, you say?"

"Yes, just the once. It passed like a shadow. But there's no saying it hadn't been that way before."

The reeve got to his feet. "You must excuse me," he said turning to me. "We must go out and see where the mischief threatens." Then he went out with the man who had brought the message and the rest of the company broke up and followed them.

I remained in the big bleak room alone with the schoolmaster. Now that the uncurtained window was no longer obscured by a row of backs, one could see outside and watch the dark clouds scudding across the sky, driven by the wind.

The old teacher remained seated and the smile on his lips was both condescending and yet compassionate too. "I don't care to stay down here now that everyone has gone," he said. "May I invite you to my room? I lodge here and believe me, I know this kind of weather. We have nothing to fear on this side of the dike."

I accepted gratefully for the room was growing chilly. Carrying a candle, we mounted the stairs to an attic room whose windows looked out westward, although they were now curtained with dark woollen hangings. I noticed a modest collection of books on a shelf, the portraits of two elderly professors on the walls, and in front of the table stood a big wing armchair. "Make yourself at home," said my kindly host and threw some peat on the little stove which was still glowing, and which was crowned by a tin kettle. "It'll only take a little while and then I'll make a nip of grog to keep you awake."

"I don't need anything for that," I said. "I find the life story of your Hauke Haien too absorbing to fall asleep."

"Really?" he said, nodding towards me with his clever eyes once I was comfortably esconced in his armchair. "Now where had I got to? Oh yes, I know. Well then:"

Hauke had inherited his father's property and as the sufferings of old Antje Wohlers had also come to an end, the total area had been extended. But since his father's death, or rather, since his father had spoken to him as he lay dying, the ambition Hauke had nursed secretly since his childhood began to grow within him. He told himself, more often perhaps than was fit and proper, that when the time came to appoint a new reeve, he was the right man for the job. After all, his father, who was a good enough judge—everyone used to say he had the best brains in the village—had told him so, and his last words seemed like an extra and a precious legacy which he had bequeathed to his son. The old woman's land that his father had acquired would be the first stepping stone towards this achievement. For admittedly, even the combined estate was not enough. A reeve had to own property on a much larger scale than that. Yet if his father had pinched and scraped during his last lonely years and so had been able to increase his holding, then Hauke could do the same. Nay, Hauke could do even better, for Tede Haien's strength was already past its peak when he began saving, whereas his son was capable of immensely hard work for many years to come.

It must be admitted, however, that as Hauke pursued his objective, he used the same ruthlessness which he had brought to the administration of the reeve's affairs in the old days and this won him few friends in the village. To make matters worse, his old enemy, Ole Peters, had recently come into an inheritance of his own and was beginning to be looked to as a man of substance. In his mind's eye Hauke kept seeing a row of faces and they all viewed him with rancor and hostility. Then bitter resentment would seize him. He would stretch out his arms as if he was itching to get his hands on these people who wanted to exclude him from this office, when, he was quite convinced, only he was fitted for it. And these thoughts would not leave him alone. They haunted him and there grew in his young heart, side by side with love and a sense of honor, ambition and hatred. But these he locked away deep within himself, and not even Elke suspected their existence.

At the beginning of the following year, there was a wedding in the village and the bride was a relation of the Haiens. Hauke and Elke were both invited and as a result of the unforeseen absence of a near kinsman, they found themselves sitting side by side at the wedding breakfast. Only a smile on both their faces betrayed their pleasure at this stroke of good fortune. Nevertheless, Elke sat without saying a word amid the gaiety and laughter and the clinking of glasses.

"Is there anything wrong?" asked Hauke.

"Not really. It's only that there are too many people here for my liking."

"But you look so sad."

She merely shook her head and they both relapsed into silence.

Elke seemed so reserved that Hauke felt a surge of emotion that was not far removed from jealousy and beneath the concealment of the overhanging tablecloth, he reached furtively for her hand. She did not withdraw it but clasped her own confidingly round his. Did she feel herself very much alone in the world as she watched her father growing weaker day by day before her eyes? Hauke would not have thought of asking himself such a question, but he took a deep breath and drew the gold ring from his waistcoat pocket. "Will you wear it for me?" he asked, his voice trembling as he slipped it on the ring finger of her slim hand.

The pastor's wife was sitting opposite. Suddenly she put down her fork and turned to her neighbor. "My goodness, look at that girl," she remarked. "Why, she's turned as white as a sheet."

But the blood came coursing back into Elke's cheeks. "Can you wait, Hauke?" she whispered.

The young man pondered for a moment. "What for?" he asked.

"Oh, you know well enough. I don't have to tell you."

"That's true, Elke," he said. "Yes, I can wait, if only one can see an end to the waiting."

"Dear God, I fear the end is very near. Don't say such things, Hauke. You know it means my father's death." Then she placed her other hand to her breast. "Until then, I shall wear your ring round my neck, here. Don't be afraid though. You will never get it back as long as I live."

Then they both smiled and he squeezed her hand so hard that in any other circumstances she would have cried out.

The pastor's wife had been eyeing them closely all the time and she watched Elke's eyes glowing with dark fire beneath the lace edge of her gold embroidered cap. The noise was too great for her to hear what had been said but she did not turn to her neighbor again. She was not likely to meddle if there was to be a wedding by and by— and as far as she could tell this looked very likely—if only because of the fee her husband would collect when he performed the ceremony.

Elke's forebodings were soon fulfilled. One morning not long after Easter, Tede Volkerts was found dead in his bed. His expression, however, assured everyone that he had died peacefully. In recent months he had often observed how weary he was of living. His favorite dishes had ceased to give him any pleasure. Even roast duck failed to rouse his appetite.

There was to be a grand funeral for the dead reeve. In the churchyard up on the rising ground stood an impressive grave with wrought iron railings round it. It lay to the west of the church itself and a weeping willow tree grew by its side. Leaning against the tree was a broad blue tombstone bearing a skull with prominent jaws, which were bristling with teeth. Below it, the following verse was engraved in large letters:

> Into the hungry maw of Death
> Goes every creature drawing breath,
> A wise old man has passed away,
> Have mercy, Lord, on Judgment Day.

It was the grave of the former dike reeve, Volkert Tedsen, and now a fresh one had been dug nearby for his son, Tede Volkerts.

The funeral procession had wound its way up from the house in the fens and was already nearing the churchyard. It consisted of a stream of wagons from all the neighboring villages and at their head was the heavy coffin drawn by two glossy black horses from the reeve's own stable. As they toiled up the sandy slope to the village, their manes and tails tossed in the keen spring wind. The graveyard was packed to the walls, and there were even urchins squatting on top of the walled gateway, holding smaller children in their arms; they all wanted to watch the burial.

In the reeve's house down on the marsh Elke was laying the tables, set out in the best parlor and the living room ready for the funeral feast. Old wine stood waiting by the side of every setting; for the head reeve—for he, too, was present that day—and for the pastor, there was a bottle apiece of the very best. When everything was finished, she went through the stable to the courtyard entrance. She saw no one, for the farm lads were driving two of the wagons in the funeral cortege. At the gate, with the wind fluttering her black dress, she stood and watched the last vehicles as they reached the church. Presently she could hear a burst of sound which seemed to be followed by a deathly hush. Elke folded her hands together. No doubt they were lowering the coffin into the ground. "Earth to earth, ashes to ashes, dust to dust." Softly, as if she could actually hear the words being spoken, she repeated them to herself. Then her eyes filled with tears and she dropped her hands to her lap. "Our Father, which art in Heaven . . .," she prayed, her heart overflowing with emotion. When she had finished the Lord's Prayer, she stood quite still for a long time, she who was now mistress of this great property, and within her heart thoughts of death and of life wrestled for mastery.

A distant noise roused her. When she opened her eyes, she saw one farmcart after another hurrying down the hill in the direction of the reeve's house. She straightened her shoulders, gave one more keen glance towards the approaching vehicles and then returned the way she had come through the stable and into the house, where everything was prepared for the solemn feast. Again there was no one about but through the wall she could hear the maids whispering in the kitchen. The set tables looked so still and deserted. The mirror between the windows and the brass knobs on the stove had been covered with white cloths. There was no brightness anywhere in the room. Elke noticed that the doors of the wall bed where her father had slept his last sleep had been left open, so she went and closed them. Absentmindedly, she looked up and read the gilded rhyme carved above, which was wreathed with roses and carnations:

> The man who does his day's work right
> Will sleep untroubled through the night.

It had been put up in her grandfather's day. Her eyes fell on the wall cupboard. It was almost empty, but it still contained a cut-glass goblet which, her father had loved to tell her, he had won once in a riding contest when he was a young man. She took it down and placed it by the head reeve's setting. Then she went to the window for she could hear the wagons rumbling up the slope to the house. One by one they stopped and the guests jumped down, more cheerful now than when they had left only a short while before. Rubbing their hands and chatting away, they crowded indoors. Soon they were seated at the table, arrayed with steaming dishes of well-cooked food. The best parlor had been reserved for the head reeve and the pastor. A loud hubbub ran the length of the big table in the living room, as if the dread stillness of death had never reigned within those walls. Silent, giving all her attention to her guests, Elke waited at table with the maids, making sure that nothing was lacking. Hauke Haien was one of those at the long table, together with Ole Peters and other smallholders.

When the meal was over, the guests rose and the gathering broke up into small groups. White clay pipes were fetched from the rack in the corner and as they were lit, Elke was busy once more, serving cups of coffee to her guests, for no expense had been spared that day. In the living room, near the late reeve's desk, stood the head reeve, talking to the pastor and an elderly dike warden, Jewe Manners. "Well, gentlemen," the head reeve began, "the old reeve has been laid to rest with all due honor, but where are we to find a new one? I believe you will have to assume the office, Manners."

The old man smiled and raised his black velvet skullcap to show his head of white hair. "It would hardly be worth while for so short a spell, Your Honor. I was made a warden when Tede Volkerts was appointed reeve and that's a good forty years ago."

"Well, that's no disadvantage. With your long experience you would find it all plain sailing."

The old man shook his head. "No, no, sir. Let me stay as I am. That way, I may be on hand for a few years yet."

The pastor was of the same opinion. "Why don't you appoint the man who has been reeve in fact if not in name for several years past?"

The head reeve looked at him inquiringly. "I don't understand, Pastor. Whom do you mean?"

The latter pointed to the parlor where Hauke was gravely explaining some matter or other to a couple of men who were much his senior. "There he is," said the pastor. "Look at that long Frisian face, the shrewd gray eyes, the thin nose and those two bumps above the eyebrows. He used to be Volkert's headman and now he has a smallholding of his own. Mind you, he is rather young."

"In his thirties, I'd say," observed the chief inspector, scrutinizing the man in question.

"He's barely twenty-four," Manners informed him. "But the pastor is right. All the good suggestions that came from the reeve's office during recent years, came from Hauke Haien. The old man was not up to much towards the end, you know."

"Really!" remarked the head reeve. "And you think he's the right man to take over his late master's office?"

"He has proved himself already," answered Manners. "All he lacks is a sizable property of his own. His father left him about fifteen or maybe twenty acres, but in the past that has never been considered enough for a dike reeve."

The pastor opened his mouth as if he were about to reply, but Elke Volkert, who had been hovering near them for some time, stepped forward impulsively. "Will Your Honor allow me to say a word?" she asked. "It is only that I would not like anyone to commit an act of injustice out of ignorance."

"Speak up, Miss Elke," answered the chief inspector. "It is always good to hear words of wisdom from a pretty girl!"

"I don't know about wisdom, sir, I only want to tell you the truth of the matter."

"Then we certainly ought to listen."

The girl glanced round hastily, as if she wanted to be sure that no busybody was eavesdropping. "Well, sir," and her breast rose and fell under the stress of her strong emotion, "my godfather Jewe Manners has told you that Hauke Haien's land amounts to no more than twenty acres. That is true at the moment, but as soon as it can be arranged, Hauke will have the whole of my father's estate to call his own as well. I imagine that the two properties together would be quite enough for his appointment as reeve."

Old Manners poked his head towards her as if he had first to make sure who it was who had spoken. "What's that, child?" he said. "What's that you're saying?"

Elke drew from her bodice the shining gold ring which she wore on a black ribbon round her neck. "I am betrothed, Godfather. Here is the ring, and the man I am to marry is Hauke Haien."

"And when may I ask—since I am your godfather, I can claim the right, I think—when did all this happen?"

"It was a little while ago, but I was of age, Godfather," she replied. "Only my father was already failing in health and knowing him as I did, I did not wish to upset him by announcing it publicly. Now that he is with God, he will surely see for himself that his child will be in good hands with such a man for a husband. I intended to keep silence for the year of mourning, but now for Hauke's sake and for that of all of us who live in the fens, I had to speak out." And, turning to the head reeve, she added, "I hope you will forgive my being so bold."

The three men looked at each other. The pastor laughed, Elke's godfather confined himself to a noncommittal "Hm, hm," and the chief inspector rubbed his forehead as if the decision he had to make was a very important one. "And how do the marriage laws on property run in this part of the world, my dear? I confess I am not well versed in these complicated legalities."

"Nor do you need to be," answered the reeve's daughter. "I shall have the title deeds transferred to my future husband before the marriage ceremony. After all, I too have my pride," she added mischievously. "I want to marry the richest man in the village."

"Well, Manners?" declared the pastor. "I don't think that you as godfather will raise any objection if I marry the old reeve's daughter to the new reeve?"

The old man shook his head gently. "May the Lord bless them," he said solemnly.

The inspector held out his hand to the girl. "You have spoken wisely and well, Miss Elke. Thank you for explaining the situation to such good effect. I trust that I may continue to be a guest in your house for many years to come, although in happier circumstances than today's. But the truly remarkable feature of today's business is that such a very young lady has been responsible for the creation of a new dike reeve."

"Well, sir," replied the girl, and she looked at the kindhearted dignitary with those grave eyes of hers, "surely even a woman may be allowed to help the right man." Then she went into the nearby parlor and without a word, she placed her hand in Hauke Haien's.

Several years went by. Tede Haien's little cottage was now occupied by a robust laborer, his wife and their child. The young reeve, Hauke Haien, lived with his wife, Elke Volkerts, in the farm-house which had belonged to her father. In summer the leaves of the big ash tree rustled just as they had always done, but on the bench which now stood beneath it, it was usually the young mistress who sat there alone in the evening, busy with some domestic task in her hands. For they had had no children, and the man had something better to do of an evening than sit idle out of doors. In spite of the assistance he had given the late reeve in the past, there were a great many matters outstanding which, for one reason or another, Hauke had not wished to press in those days. Gradually, however, he was clearing up the arrears and he had to be ruthless in so doing. In addition, there was the administration and the running of his own greatly enlarged estate and at the same time, he tried to economize by doing without a second farmhand. So apart from Sunday, when they went to church together, and at their hasty midday meal during the week, the young couple scarcely saw each other from early morning until late at night. It was a life of continuous toil, and yet they were content.

Then the troublemakers got busy. Some of the younger generation of property owners from both the fens and the village met at the inn one Sunday after church. They were a group of rather hotheaded young men who drank hard, and after the fourth or fifth glass, they began grumbling, not about the king and the government—they were not so presumptuous in those days—but about their local and regional officials and the local taxes and impositions. The longer they talked, the less good they had to say of anything, especially the new dike levies. The sluices and drains which had functioned well enough for many years past, suddenly appeared to be all in urgent need of repair. They were forever finding fresh weak spots in the dikes and hundreds of barrowloads of earth were needed to shore them up. To hell with it all!

"That all comes of your smart new dike reeve," said the villagers. "He's always thinking up some new scheme or other and he pokes his nose into everything."

"You're right there, Marten," said Ole Peters, who was sitting opposite the last speaker. "He goes behind our backs and he's always showing off, trying to impress the chief inspector. But it looks as if we're saddled with him all the same."

"Why did you let them foist him on you?" Marten wanted to know. "Now you have to pay for it, and in hard cash too."

"Yes, that's how we're placed," laughed Ole Peters, "and we can't alter it either. But things have come to a pretty pass when the old reeve was only appointed because of his father before him, and the new one because of his wife." The laughter which greeted this witticism showed what a popular point of view it was.

But the words spoken so publicly at the inn did not remain unrepeated and soon the joke was being circulated in village and fen. Inevitably, Hauke came to hear of it as well. And again the row of malicious faces passed before his inward eye and the laughter at the inn sounded in his ears, even more contemptuous than it had been in fact. "The dogs!" he shouted and his eyes glanced grimly to one side as if he would like to have them all whipped.

Elke laid her hand on his arm. "Let them be," she soothed him. "They are only jealous."

"That's just it," he growled.

"And what about Ole Peters himself," she went on. "Didn't he acquire his own property through his marriage?"

"That he did, Elke, but Vollina's portion wasn't big enough to make him reeve."

"Say rather, that he was not big enough to do the job." And Elke turned her husband round so that he had to see himself in the mirror, for they were standing between the two windows in the living room. "There stands the reeve," she said firmly. "Take a good look at him. The only man fit for the office is the one who holds it."

"You may be right," he answered thoughtfully. "And yes . . . well, I must be off. I have to see about the east sluice again. The gates still don't shut properly."

She pressed his hand. "Look at me first and tell me what's the matter. Your eyes seem so far away."

"It's nothing, Elke. I told you you were quite right."

Hauke went out, but he had not gone far before he forgot all about the sluice gates. Another idea was hammering in his brain, one he had only half thought out, although he had been carrying it about in his head for several years. It had been pushed into the background by his new official duties, but suddenly it took possession of him and soared into flight on mighty wings.

Hardly aware of how he had got there, he found himself up on the sea dike a good distance south and in the direction of the town. The village that sprawled away to his left had long since disappeared from view, and still he strode on, his eyes fixed on the expanse of unreclaimed foreshore which stretched out on his right hand towards the sea. If anyone had been with him, they would have observed a penetrating intellect at work behind those eyes. At last he stopped. The foreland had narrowed to a strip which ran parallel to the dike. "I must do it," he said to himself. "Seven years in office and they still say I am dike reeve only because I married Elke. I must put a stop to that."

Still he stood there and his keen gaze took in the grassy foreshore in all its aspects. Then he retraced his footsteps until he reached the spot where a narrow ribbon of reclaimed land merged into the broad expanse lying at his feet. Close by the dike, however, a fast running creek cut straight across the ground, cutting off the foreshore so that it was turned virtually into an island. A crude wooden bridge spanned the stream for cattle or haywains and farm wagons to be driven across from one side to the other. Now the tide had ebbed and the golden September sun made the extensive mudflats glitter. Yet one could still see the current flowing in the deep stream in the middle, even though the tide was out. "It could be dammed," said Hauke to himself as he watched the flow. Then after a while he gazed straight ahead beyond the creek, and from the dike on which he stood, he drew in his mind's eye the sketch of a dike which would enclose the whole of the foreshore. He could imagine it running first south and then veering to the east, recrossing the creek farther along and finally joining up with the existing dike. But it had to be more than a new dike. He wanted it to be a new design of dike, a shape which until then had been no more than a notion at the back of his mind.

"There must be roughly a thousand acres in all, a new polder," he smiled to himself. "Not an enormous area to reclaim, but still . . ."

Another factor suddenly occurred to him. This stretch of foreshore belonged to the community, and every landowner was allotted shares in it either in proportion to his other holdings in the region, or they could be acquired in accordance with duly recognized legal procedure. Hauke Haien began to calculate how many shares he possessed, firstly in his own right, and then on account of old Volkert's estate. But he had also bought land for himself since his marriage, partly on a hunch that it might be of advantage to him at some time in the future, partly because he was extending his sheep breeding. It came to quite a large amount, for he had bought up the whole of Ole Peters's shares in the foreshore. The latter had lost his best breeding ram during a partial flooding of the area, and Peters, in a fit of disgust, had wanted to be rid of all his shares. But that had been an isolated incident, for as far as Hauke could remember, even during the highest flood tides, only the edges of the land had ever been inundated. Once it was all protected by his new dike, however, what excellent pasture and arable land it would provide, and think what a price it would command! The mere thought of it was intoxicating, but Hauke kept his head. He dug his nails into his palms and forced himself to see clearly and soberly what actually lay before him. It was just a large, flat stretch of coast, unprotected from the sea, liable to erosion in every storm and at every high tide, sustaining little more than a flock of draggle-tailed sheep which were grazing listlessly. As for him, the prospect was one of unrelenting toil, constant battles and inevitable aggravation. And yet in spite of it all, as he came down from the dike and trod the footpath to his home, he felt he was bringing with him a treasure of unestimable value.

Elke met him in the hall. "What was wrong with the sluice?" she asked.

He looked at her with an enigmatic smile. "We shall soon need another sluice altogether," he said, "and gates, and a new dike into the bargain."

"I don't understand," she answered as they went into the living room. "What are you going to do, Hauke?"

"I intend," he began slowly and then paused for a moment: "I intend," he repeated, "to build a dike which will enclose the whole of the foreshore, from where it begins opposite our own land and then juts out to the west. I want to reclaim it for good. I know that even the worst tides have left us in peace for a generation or more, but one of these days there will be a really bad storm and if it is submerged, everything growing on it will be destroyed and it will lose all its value. Letting it lie in its present state has been sheer negligence. It should have been tackled years ago."

She looked up in amazement. "But now you are blaming yourself and no one else," she protested.

"I am indeed," he said, "but until now, there has been so much else which had to be seen to first."

"Surely you have done enough already," she pleaded.

Hauke had seated himself in the old reeve's chair and his hands gripped the armrests.

"Have you the courage to see it through?" his wife went on.

"Yes, I have," he answered without hesitation.

"Don't be hasty, Hauke. This is a matter of life and death. Nearly everyone will oppose you and no one will say thank you in the end for all your trouble and care. And suppose it does not succeed? Ever since I was a child, I remember people saying the creek can't be dammed and it was better to leave it alone."

"That was just an excuse for their laziness. Why shouldn't the creek be dammed?"

"That I can't say. Perhaps because it runs so straight and the current is too strong." But it struck a chord in her memory and an almost mischievous smile came into her serious eyes. "When I was small," she said, "I once heard the farmhands talking about it. They believed that if a dam was to stand, something must be buried alive in it during the building, and only then would it hold. They say that over on the other bank, a dam was built over a hundred years ago and they buried in it a gypsy child which its mother had sold for a small fortune. But you wouldn't get a mother to sell her child these days."

Hauke shook his head. "It is a good thing we have no children or I would not put it past them to ask us straight out for one of ours."

"They should never have it," said Elke, and she hugged her body instinctively, as if suddenly afraid.

Hauke smiled, but Elke went on with her probing, "And what about the tremendous cost of it all? Have you thought of that?"

"Yes, I have, Elke, but the value of the income from it once the work is done will more than offset the cost. And, in addition, the expense of maintaining the old dike will be substantially reduced by the new construction. There are more than eighty teams of horses in the community and there is no shortage of strong young arms, so we can do the work ourselves. At least it will prove to everyone that you did not make me dike reeve for nothing, Elke. I have to show them what I am made of."

She had been kneeling before him and now she looked into his face anxiously. Then she got up with a sigh. "I must get on with my work," she said and slowly stroked his cheek. "You must do yours too, Hauke."

"Amen to that, Elke," he smiled earnestly. "There's work for both of us."

There was indeed, plenty for them both, although the heaviest burden now fell on the husband's shoulders. On Sunday afternoons and often in the evenings too, when the day's work was done, Hauke sat down with a competent surveyor and they buried themselves in calculations, designs and sketches. It was the same whenever he was alone and he often went on until long after midnight. Then he would creep into their bedroom, for the stuffy old folding beds in the sitting room were no longer used when Hauke took over the house, and his wife, to make quite sure he would get some rest at last, lay there with her eyes shut as if she were asleep, although she had been waiting for him with throbbing heart for many hours past. He would gently kiss her brow and whisper a few loving words as he stretched himself out beside her, but often the cock had crowed before he dropped off to sleep.

When the winter storms were raging, he would often rush off to the dike and stand there, pencil and paper in hand, sketching and making notes, while a gust of wind blew his cap off and his long straw-colored hair flew round his flushed face. Sometimes he took one of the farmhands out in a boat across the shallows, as long as the ice did not prevent their passage, and there, with plumb line and rod, he measured the depths of the currents where he was not yet certain of them.

Elke used to tremble for his safety, but once he was back he could only have guessed her relief from the extra pressure of her hand or the way her somber eyes would light up at the sight of him. "Be patient, Elke," he said to her once, when she clung to him as if she would never let him go. "I must have everything clearly worked out in my own mind first before I submit my project."

Then she nodded and let go his arm.

The rides into the town to see the chief inspector grew more and more frequent, and all the day-to-day tasks in the house and on the farm were followed by still more toil at night. He hardly spoke to a soul except in the way of business and he had less time than ever to spend with his wife. "These are difficult days," Elke told herself, "and there's no saying how long it will go on."

At last, when the spring sunshine and the strong winds had banished the ice everywhere, the preliminary work was finally completed. The report was ready for the head reeve to submit to higher authority. It described itself as "a proposal to build a dike round a specified portion of the foreshore, to the furtherance of the public good, particularly insofar as it affects not only the community but also the Treasury, since public funds were bound to be increased in years to come by the yield from approximately one thousand additional acres of farmland." It had all been written out in a neat hand and attached were the necessary designs and plans of the places involved immediately and also at some future date, together with suggestions about sluices and drainage and all the relevant details. Finally, they were rolled securely into a firm bundle and sealed with the dike reeve's seal of office.

"There it is, Elke," said Hauke Haien, "give it your blessing."

She placed her hand in his. "We'll stand together, come what may."

"Aye, that we will."

Then the application was sent to the town by a messenger on horseback.

"You will note, my dear sir," the schoolmaster interrupted his recital, fixing me with a friendly gaze from his penetrating eyes, "that what I have told you so far is information I have gathered together in the course of some forty years spent in this neighborhood. It comes from reliable contemporaries or from what their descendants learned from their lips. What follows, and I say this so that you can reconcile the two parts of the story, was more in the nature of common gossip at the time and indeed, it is still a topic for conversation in these parts, as soon as All Saints' Eve starts the spinning wheels humming for the winter.

Now in those days, if you stood on the old dike at a point about five or six hundred yards north of the reeve's farm and looked out over the mudflats, you could see a low-lying islet known as Jevers Sands, or Jevers Isle. It lay perhaps a mile or so away, roughly midway between this coast and the opposite shore, although a little nearer to us, as far as one can judge. A couple of generations earlier it had been in use as good pasture for sheep, but in Hauke Haien's day all this had stopped, for once in a while the low-lying island was completely inundated and always just at the height of summer. The sea water destroyed the growth completely and it became unusable for grazing. So it happened that no one ever visited the isle except for the gulls and similar birds and occasionally a sea eagle. On moonlit evenings, if you looked out from the dike, there would always be sea mists hovering round it. Sometimes it was thick fog, at other times there was only a thin haze, but when the moon was in the east, it was said that one could make out the bleached bones of drowned sheep and the skeleton of a horse too, although how that got there, no one could understand.

One evening towards the end of March, two men were standing on the dike, their day's work done. One was the laborer who now lived in Tede Haien's cottage and the other was Iven Johns whom the reeve employed as a groom. The island itself could scarcely be seen at all for the floating haze which dimmed the light of the moon, but the two men fixed their eyes on it all the same. Something peculiar seemed to rivet their attention and they stood there, glued to the spot. The laborer was the first to shake himself and thrust his hands in his pockets. "Come along, Iven," he said. "There's something evil about it. Let's go home."

Iven laughed, although his voice betrayed a trace of fear. "Oh, it's nothing, just an animal of sorts and a big one at that. But how in the devil's name did it get across the mud? Look, it's stretching out its head towards us. No, it isn't. It's bending its neck and grazing. Why, I thought there was no pasture over there. What on earth can it be?"

"It's none of our business," replied the other. "I'm going home even if you won't come. Good night to you, Iven."

"Oh, it's all right for you, with a wife waiting for you at home to warm your bed at night. My garret is cold and empty."

"Good night, then," called the laborer and trudged off down the embankment and home. Iven turned his head once or twice and watched him as he went, but the fascination of the uncanny sight held him fast. A dark, thickset figure now approached from the direction of the village. It was the odd-job boy whom the reeve also employed.

"Do you want me, Carsten?" asked Johns.

"I? I don't want you," said the lad, "but the master does. He says he wants a word with you."

Johns's eyes had wandered back to the island once more. "I'm coming," he said. "I'll be there in a moment."

"What's that you're staring at so hard?" asked Carsten.

Iven raised his arm and pointed in silence to the island.

"Oh," whispered the boy. "There's a horse over there, a white one.

It must be the devil's own. How does a horse come to be out there on Jevers Isle?"

"I don't know, Carsten. If it is a horse, that is."

"Of course it is, Iven. You've only to watch how it grazes. But who took it over there? There isn't a boat in the village big enough to ferry it across. Perhaps it's only a sheep after all. Peter Ohm says that by moonlight a dozen stacks of turf look like a whole village. But no, look! It's prancing now. It must be a horse after all."

Both men stood there for a while in silence, with eyes only for the blurred scene in the distance. The moon was high in the sky and as the tide came in, the water glittered as it crept up over the mud. Only the soft lapping of the water could be heard, there was no sound of any living thing in all that vast wilderness of water. The fens beyond the dike were deserted. The cattle were all in their stalls. Nothing moved except the creature they took to be a horse, a white horse far out on Jevers Isle. "It's getting clearer," declared Iven, breaking the silence. "I can see the sheep bones white in the moonlight."

"So can I," said Carsten, craning his neck. Then a sudden thought struck him and he plucked at his companion's sleeve. "Iven," he whispered, "you know that horse's skeleton that's been lying out there for years. Where's it gone? I can't see it any more."

"No more can I," breathed Iven. "That's queer."

"Not as queer as you think. They do say that on some nights—though I don't know which—those bones pick themselves up and come to life again."

"You don't believe that, do you? Why, that's just an old wives' tale."

"Perhaps you're right," said the boy.

"But I thought you had come to fetch me, Carsten. Come on, we'd better go back. There's nothing more to see here." But the boy would not budge until Iven tugged at his sleeve and dragged him away along the footpath.

"Now listen, Carsten," he said when the sinister island was already a goodish distance behind them. "They do say you're a bit of a daredevil. I bet you'd like to go over there and find out for yourself just what's going on."

"Well yes," replied Carsten, although he shuddered a little at the idea. "I'd like to go and see."

"Are you quite sure? All right then," he went on, after the lad had firmly given him his hand on it, "we'll get out the boat tomorrow evening. You row out to Jevers Sands and I'll stay and watch from the dike."

"All right," replied the lad. "It's a deal. And I'll take my whip along."

"Yes, do."

They walked on in silence and slowly climbed the bank leading up to their master's house.

At the same time on the following evening, Johns was sitting on the big boulder that stood outside the stable door when along came Carsten, swishing his whip through the air. "It's got a fine crack to it," said Iven.

"That it has, but look out for it," answered the boy. "I've fixed a few nails in the lash."

"Let's be off then."

As on the previous evening, the moon was in the east and it shone with a clear light. Soon they were out on the dike once more, looking towards Jevers Isle which seemed to rest on the water like a patch of mist. "There goes the horse again," said Iven. "Do you know, I was here this afternoon and it had disappeared, but then I saw the white skeleton lying there quite plainly."

The boy peered forward. "The skeleton's not there now," he muttered.

"Well then, how do you feel about it now? Are you still itching to find out?"

Carsten thought it over for a moment, then he flicked his whip once more. "Let's get the boat out," he said.

The creature on the island, whatever it was, seemed to raise its head and look towards the mainland. They did not see it, however, for they had already gone down to the shore to the place where the boat was lying, "In you get," said Iven and loosened the painter. "I'll stay here till you get back. Make for the eastern tip of the island. That was where they always used to land." The boy nodded, and without another word he rowed out into the moonlight, the whip lying by his side. Iven strolled back along the shore and then climbed up to the top of the dike until he reached the spot where they had stood before. Soon he saw the boat pull in at a steep and gloomy cove at the mouth of a creek and a stocky figure jumped out on to the land. He thought he could hear the crack of the whip too, but perhaps it was only the noise of the incoming tide.

A few hundred yards to the north, he saw what they had taken to be the white horse and yes! there was Carsten making straight for it. Now the animal raised its head uneasily and the boy—this time there was no mistake about it, Johns could hear it clearly—cracked his whip with a flourish. But what was the matter with Carsten? He was returning to the boat, going the way he had come. The creature went on peacefully grazing, as if it had never been disturbed. It made no sound, but white streamers like foam on the crest of the waves seemed to shimmer across the apparition. Johns stared at the fantastic sight, spellbound.

Soon he heard the boat grounding on the shore below him and in the half-light, he could make out the figure of the boy climbing up the seawall towards him. "Well, Carsten?" he asked eagerly. "What was it?"

"There was nothing there," answered Carsten, shaking his head. "I could see it until just before I landed, but once I had actually set foot on the island, the devil knows where the beast got to, for the moon was bright enough. But when I reached the spot where we had seen it, there was nothing but those whitened sheep bones and a bit farther along, lay the horse's skeleton. It had a long white skull and the moonlight shone through the empty eye sockets."

"Hm," said Iven. "Are you sure you looked properly?"

"Yes, of course. I was standing right on the spot where we'd seen it. But I must have startled some damn peewit or other, which had settled down for the night behind the skeleton, for suddenly it shot up into the air and gave me quite a turn, so that I cracked my whip at it once or twice."

"And that was all?"

"Yes, Iven, that was all."

"And quite enough too," said Iven taking the lad by the arm and pointing towards the island. "Look again, Carsten. Can you see anything now?"

"By all that's holy, it's back again!"

"Again!" said Iven. "I was watching the whole time and it's never left the spot. You walked right up to the brute, so close I thought you were going to touch it."

The boy stared at him. His usually cheeky face was aghast and Iven was equally shaken. "Come," he said. "Let's go home. From here, you'd think it was alive, and when you go out to it, there's nothing but old bones. There's more to this than folks like us can fathom. But don't you breathe a word of this to anyone. There are times when it's better to hold your tongue."

They turned away and hurried home side by side. They did not speak and the silent fens spread out beneath them.

So the full moon waned and the nights grew darker and then something else occurred which was difficult to explain, and this is how it happened.

Hauke Haien had occasion to go into the town on business, on a day when a horsefair was being held. Although he had no intention of visiting the fair, nevertheless, when he came home that evening, he was leading a second horse by the halter. The new horse was ungroomed and so thin one could count its ribs and its eyes lay dull and sunken in their sockets. Elke was waiting at the door to greet her husband. "Heavens above!" she exclaimed. "What are we to do with an old nag like that?" For Hauke had ridden right up to the house, and before they halted beneath the ash tree, she had seen that the creature was lame into the bargain.

The young reeve, however, jumped down laughing from his chestnut gelding. "Don't worry, Elke. I got it very cheap."

"But you know that the cheapest goods always cost you dearest in the end," she answered sensibly.

"Not always, Elke. The beast is not more than four years old. Take a good look at it. Oh, it's been starved and ill-used, admittedly, but there's nothing that our good fodder won't put right in time. I shall look after it myself and make sure it isn't overfed to start with."

Meanwhile, the animal stood there with lowered head and its long mane drooping over its neck. As Hauke called for the groom, Elke walked all round the horse, and scrutinized it thoughtfully. "We've never had a creature like that in these stables before," she said, shaking her head.

As the odd-job boy came round the corner of the house, he stopped short, as if rooted to the spot, with terror in his eyes. "What's wrong, Carsten?" asked the reeve. "What's got into you? Don't you like my new white horse?"

"Yes, oh yes, master. Why shouldn't I?" the boy managed to say.

"Well, lead it into the stable for me, but don't feed it. I'll be along presently and I'll see to it myself."

The boy took the white horse's halter very gingerly and then, as if for protection, he grasped at the bridle of the gelding he knew so well. Then Hauke went with his wife into the living room where there was mulled ale waiting for him and a plate of bread and butter.

It did not take him long to satisfy his appetite and he soon got up and paced the room, back and forth. His wife joined him. "Let me tell you how I got hold of the brute, Elke," he said, as the setting sun played on the tiles of the wall. "I had spent a good hour with the head reeve, for he had some splendid news for me. They want to modify a few details in my design, but the most important thing, my profile, has been fully accepted in principle and any day now we should receive orders to go ahead with the scheme."

Elke could not help sighing, "And what will happen next?" she asked anxiously.

"Oh, it will be hard going, I know," answered Hauke, "but I believe that was why the Lord brought us together. The farm is running so smoothly that you can take a big share of its administration on your own shoulders. Just think, ten years from now, we shall have doubled our estate."

As he started speaking, Elke had taken her husband's hand and pressed it reassuringly. But his last words brought no joy to her heart. "But for whose benefit is it? You will have to find another wife, since I have given you no children."

Tears spurted into her eyes but he took her firmly in his arms. "Let us leave that to the Almighty," he said. "We're not old, Elke, and even in ten years' time we shall still be young enough to enjoy the fruits of our labors ourselves."

As he held her close, she looked at him with her dark eyes. "Forgive me, Hauke. It's silly of me, I know, but sometimes I get so despondent."

He bent down and kissed her face. "You are my woman and I am your man, Elke. That's how it will always be. There'll never be anyone else."

She clasped her arms round his neck. "How right you are, Hauke. Whatever fate may bring, we shall share it." Then she freed herself from him, blushing. "You were going to tell me about the white horse," she reminded him softly.

"So I was, Elke. I want you to hear. I have already told you how overjoyed I was at the good news about the dike, so I rode off out of town the moment the head reeve had finished with me and away along the causeway. Just beyond the harbor I saw a gypsy fellow* dressed in rags. I've no idea who or what he was, a vagabond or a tinker, or so I took him to be. He was leading the white horse on a halter, but as I passed, the animal raised its head and looked at me piteously with its dull eyes, just as if it were asking me for help. Perhaps I was in a generous mood, so I spoke to the man. 'Hey my man,' I said, 'where are you going with a jade like that?'

"The man halted, and the horse too. 'I'm going to sell it,' was his answer and he winked slyly.

"'But not to me,' I smiled.

"'Oh yes, I think you'll buy it,' he replied. 'It's a fine horse and cheap at a hundred taler.'

"For answer, I laughed in his face.

"'There's nothing to laugh at,' said he. 'I don't expect you to pay that much. But I don't need it and it's only going to rack and ruin. It would be a different animal if you took it in hand.'

"So I jumped down from my chestnut and when I looked in the nag's mouth, I saw that it was still a youngster. 'How much then?' I cried, for the horse stood there as if imploring me to take it.

"'You can have it for thirty talers, sir,' was the fellow's reply, 'and I'll throw in the halter as well.' And there and then, he stretched out his brown claw of a fist and we shook hands on it. So that's how I came to buy it, and dirt-cheap too. The peculiar thing was, though, that as I rode away with my purchase, I heard a great guffaw, and turning my head, I saw the gypsy standing there, legs apart, hands behind his back, and laughing away like the devil himself."

"Oh dear! I'd rather the horse didn't take after such a master! I only hope it will thrive here, Hauke."

"Well, for my part, I'll do all I can to make it so." And the reeve went into the stable as he had told the boy he would.

And it was not only on that first evening that he fed the horse personally. Every day from that time on, he looked after it himself. He wanted to show what a bargain he had got and in any event, he

---

*In the original he is called a "Slovak," a popular term for a gypsy. The gypsies were notorious in Germany as tricky horse-dealers. This "gypsy," however, may well be a being of more unearthly provenance.

was determined that it should not suffer any further neglect. In a very few weeks, the animal's whole appearance had improved. Gradually the rough hairiness gave way to a smooth glossy coat dappled with bluish flecks, and when Hauke led it round the yard one day, it stepped out surely on its slender legs. He remembered the strange ragamuffin who had sold it to him. "He must have been either a fool, or else a rogue who had stolen it," he muttered to himself. Soon, whenever the horse in the stable heard his footsteps outside, it tossed its mane and whinnied and Hauke saw, too, that it possessed those qualities one looks for in an Arab, a lean muzzle and a pair of fiery brown eyes.

One day he led it from the stable and placed a light saddle on its back. Hardly was he in the stirrups and when it let out a neigh from its throat like a cry of pleasure and darted off down the bank and along the path in the direction of the dike. Hauke sat firm and when they reached the dike, the horse quietened down and stepped out daintily, almost dancing along, tossing its head towards the sea. He patted and stroked its smooth neck, but it no longer needed such soothing. It seemed to be wholly one with its rider and when they had traveled northwards along the dike for a stretch, he turned its head with the merest tug at the rein and was soon back home once more.

The farmhands were waiting for his return at the end of the path. "Here you are, Johns," called the reeve, jumping to the ground. "Ride it out to the fens with the other horses. You'll find it carries you like a babe in a cradle, it's so gentle." The white horse shook its mane and neighed loudly across the sunlit fens as the groom loosened the girths and then hurried off with harness and saddle to hang them up in the stable. The horse laid its head on it's master's shoulder and patiently allowed him to fondle it. But when Johns came back and tried to mount it, the horse sheered abruptly to one side and then stood still again, with its fine eyes still fixed on its master.

"Iven!" exclaimed Hauke, "are you hurt?" And he tried to help the groom to his feet.

Iven got up, rubbing his haunch. "No, master, I'm all right. But that's a horse only the devil can ride."

"And I," added Hauke laughing. "Perhaps you'd better lead it out to pasture."

The groom obeyed, somewhat shamefaced, and the white horse allowed itself to be led quietly away.

Some evenings later, Johns and Carsten were standing by the stable door. Behind the dike the red sunset glow was fading rapidly and already the fields below were in darkness. Now and then one could hear a cow lowing in the distance as if it had been disturbed, or a lark gave a dying shriek as a weasel or water rat made a sudden pounce. Johns leaned against the doorpost and pulled at his short pipe, although it was already too dark to see the smoke. Neither the man nor the boy said anything, but something was obviously bothering Carsten and he racked his brain for words to broach the forbidden subject, "I say, Iven," he blurted out, "you know the horse's skeleton on Jevers Isle?"

"What about it?" asked Iven.

"That's what I'd like to know. It just isn't there any more, neither by day nor at night. I must have been out along the dike looking for it twenty times or more."

"I should think the bones are so old they've just fallen apart."

"But I went to have a look by moonlight, I tell you. There's nothing there any more, and nothing moving either."

"Well, if the skeleton's fallen to pieces, it can't get up, can it?"

"It's no joke, Iven. I know what I know. I can tell you where it is."

Iven Johns turned on him roughly. "Well, then, where is it?"

"Ah, where?" echoed the boy impressively. "It's standing in our stable. That's where it is since it left the island. Oh, the master wouldn't be tending it himself without good reason. I know what I'm talking about, Iven."

The latter puffed away hard into the night. "You must be crazy, Carsten," he said. "The master's white horse? Why, if ever a horse was alive, it's that one. It beats me how a smart lad like you can believe such fairy stories."

But Carsten was stubborn. If the devil was in it, why shouldn't it be alive? Indeed, that made it so much the worse. Whenever he had to go to the stable in the dark—for even in the summer, the horse was kept stabled—it gave him a turn, the way it jerked its head and stared at him so fiercely. "The devil take it," he mumbled to himself. "I'm damned if I'm going to stay with a creature like that around. I'll go as soon as I can."

So behind his master's back, he started looking about for fresh employment and it was not long before he gave the reeve notice. On

All Saints' Day he left and went to Ole Peters as a farmhand. Here he found credulous listeners to his story of the reeve's horse which, he swore, belonged to the devil himself. Fat Vollina and her father, Jess Harders, who had been a warden once but was now becoming senile, lent their willing ears. They enjoyed a tale that made their flesh creep and they quickly repeated it to everyone else who relished such nonsense or who had a grudge against the dike reeve.

Meanwhile, the authorities had given permission for the new dike to be started at the end of March. The first thing that Hauke did was to call a meeting of the dike wardens and on the day fixed, they all turned up at the inn by the church. They listened as he went over the main points from the documents so far drawn up. He described his original proposals, the chief inspector's comments, and finally the government's decision, which supported the principal feature of the scheme, namely that the dike should be built with a new type of profile. Instead of rising almost vertically from ground level, it would slope very gradually on its sea face. The response was far from enthusiastic. Everyone looked disgruntled.

"Well, well," said one of the older men. "This is a pretty mess we're in, and it's no use protesting either, if the powers that be are hand in glove with our dike reeve here."

"You're right there, Detlev Wiens," said another. "Just when we've got our hands full with all the spring work to be done, we're expected to drop everything and build a dike as long as the Great Wall of China.*

"The spring work should hardly be affected," Hauke answered. "After all, it will take a little time before we start. You can't rush a thing like this."

Few of those present had been convinced by his arguments. "And what about the construction of this new profile of yours?" protested a third speaker. "Why, your dike will be as broad as it's long on the sea face. Where's all the material to come from, I should like to know, and when will it be finished?"

"If not this year, then next perhaps. It mainly depends on how much work we're prepared to put in."

Ironic laughter greeted this remark. "But why all this unnecessary

*The original has "as long as Lawrence's son was tall," a reference to a son of one Laurentius Damm of Hamburg, who around 1600 was supposed to have been nearly ten feet tall at his confirmation.

effort? The new dike will be no higher than the old one," cried a fresh voice, "and that has held for a good thirty years."

"That's true," Hauke admitted, "but it was breached thirty years ago, and also thirty-five years before that; and going back another forty-five years there was a disaster yet again. Since then, we have been spared any of the really high tides, but that was due to luck. The present profile is still too steep and the dike is a poor design, I tell you. Now this new dike will stand up to any tide there might be. It will stand for centuries, because with such a gentle slope the angriest sea will find no point of attack. So the land we reclaim now will be safe for you and your descendants for hundreds of years to come, and that is why the government and the chief inspector are all behind me. And that is why you too should see it in a favorable light, as a project which will benefit everybody."

As no one present could think of a suitable reply for the moment, a white-haired old man rose from his chair with some effort. It was Elke's godfather, Jewe Manners, who, at the reeve's special request, had remained in office as warden in spite of his age. "Well, Reeve," he said. "There's no disputing it. You're upsetting the whole community and putting us all to considerable expense, and I must say I wish you had waited until the Lord had called me to my eternal rest before you embarked on such a scheme. But when all's said and done, you are doing the right thing and only a fool would think otherwise. We ought to thank the Almighty every day of our lives that, in spite of our negligence, He has spared this precious piece of foreshore from storm and flooding. But now the eleventh hour has struck and we must put our hand to the work with all the knowledge and skill at our disposal. We must not try God's patience too hard. I am an old man, my friends, and I have seen dikes built and dikes breached. But this is one which the Lord Himself has inspired. The dike which Hauke Haien has devised and which has now been approved by the authorities will outlast everyone alive today. And if you yourselves are not grateful to him, then your grandchildren at least will never hesitate to pay tribute to his memory."

Jewe Manners sat down again, pulled his blue kerchief from his pocket and mopped his forehead. The old man had always been recognized as a person of great capacity and irreproachable integrity and although those present disagreed with him, no one spoke. Then Hauke Haien took up the word again and they saw that he had turned very pale.

"I am grateful to you, Jewe Manners," he began. "I am glad that you are still with us and that you have spoken your mind. Perhaps the rest of you gentlemen will be able to regard the new construction, for which I take full responsibility, as something which cannot be altered now. Therefore let us get on with the business of deciding what needs to be done."

"Speak up then," said one of the wardens, and Hauke spread out the plan of the new dike on the table before them.

"A few moments ago, someone asked where all the earth needed is to come from. If you take a look at this plan, you will see that where the foreshore juts out into the mudflats, I have left a strip of land beyond the proposed line of the dike. Most of the earth we can take from there and also from the edge of the foreshore which runs north and south of the new polder. As long as we have a good facing of clay towards the water, we can use sand for the inner side or for filling in the middle. But first we need to appoint a surveyor to mark out the precise course of the new dike. The man who helped me to draw up the initial plans will probably be the best man for this. Next, we shall have to have horsedrawn tip-up carts specially made, for transporting earth and the various materials to the site. We must also provide for damming the creek and for the land face, where we shall probably have to make do with sand; we shall need I don't know how many hundreds of cartloads of straw for binding and layering, maybe more than we can spare from our own output. We must therefore discuss how we are to obtain all we need and how the work is to be organized. Later on, we shall have to employ an experienced carpenter to put up the new sluice here, on the western side."

The wardens gathered round the table and glanced halfheartedly at the papers before them. One by one they said a word or two, but only because they felt they had to say something. "You must have thought it out, reeve," one of the younger men declared when it came to finding a surveyor. "Surely you know who is the best man for the job."

"But it is your duty as wardens to give your own opinions and not merely to echo mine, Jacob Mayen," retorted Hauke. "If you have a better suggestion, I shall withdraw mine in favor of yours."

"Oh, I suppose it'll be all right," answered Mayen.

It was then that one of the older men raised an objection. He had a nephew, it seemed, who was superior to any surveyor they had ever had in these parts, not excepting even the reeve's late father, Tede Haien.

So the claims of the two surveyors were compared and disputed and eventually it was decided to commission them jointly. Similar arguments arose over the tip-up carts, the straw deliveries and everything else, and when Hauke finally trotted home on his chestnut gelding, which he still rode regularly at that time, it was very late and he was almost exhausted. He dropped into the old armchair which had belonged to his predecessor, who had been of a much heavier build but also more easygoing. His wife came to his side.

"How tired you look, Hauke," she said and her slender hand stroked the hair from his forehead.

"I am a bit tired," he admitted.

"But things are settled, aren't they?"

"Oh yes," he answered with a wry smile, "they're settled, but I'll get no help from anyone. Indeed, I'll be thankful if no one puts a spoke in the wheel."

"But surely, not all of them were obstructive?"

"No, Elke. Your godfather Jewe Manners is a good man. I only wish he were thirty years younger."

A few weeks later, when the building line of the dike had been agreed and the majority of the carts had been delivered, all those who had a claim on the area to be enclosed, as well as anyone who owned property immediately behind the present dike, were called to a meeting at the inn. There the reeve told them that its purpose was to lay before them his proposals concerning their respective contributions to the cost of the scheme both in money and in labor, and to hear what they thought of them. The smallholders with property behind the dike were concerned insofar as the new dike and the proposed sluice would reduce the cost of maintaining the old one and so they could also be expected to pay their share in cash and in kind. It had been a tremendous task for Hauke to get this scheme worked out so quickly and indeed, it would not have been possible if the head reeve had not procured for him the services of a clerk and a messenger boy, although he was once again working regularly far into the night. When he sought his couch at last he was dog-tired, but his wife no longer had to pretend to be asleep these days. She, as well as he, had so much to do during the day that she dropped off at once as soon as her head touched the pillow, and she slept so heavily, it would have needed a great deal to wake her.

Hauke had read aloud his suggestions, and the papers which had, in fact, been on view at the inn for the past three days for anyone who was interested, were spread out for all to see. There were some serious-minded men present who appreciated the reeve's painstaking efforts, and after calm reflection they concluded that his intentions were just and reasonable. But there were others who had no title to the new land, because it had been relinquished by themselves or their forefathers or the former owners, and they complained that they would gain no benefit from the contributions demanded of them, ignoring the fact that the new construction would in the long run substantially reduce the burden on their own property. Others again, who were lucky enough to own shares in the new polder, begged to be relieved of them. They would sell them for a song, they declared, for the costs were so high that ownership was a liability they simply could not afford.

Ole Peters was leaning against the doorpost with a set face. "Think hard before you sell," he intervened in his hoarse voice, "you know you can trust the reeve as far as arithmetic is concerned—he's always been good at figures! He had the biggest share in the foreshore anyway, but he managed to buy me out, and as soon as he had mine too, he decided we needed a new dike!"

A shocked silence followed. The reeve was standing by the table on which his papers were spread and he raised his head and looked at Ole Peters. "You know perfectly well that that's a foul calumny, Ole Peters, but you make the accusation all the same because you know that mud sticks. The truth is that you wanted to be rid of your shares several years ago, at a time when I needed some extra land for sheep breeding. And if you want to know, it was the slur you cast on me here in this inn, that I should never have been reeve but for my wife, that roused me to action. I had to show you all that I hold office in my own good right. Actually, I am only doing now what the reeve before me should have done. But if you still bear me a grudge for the land I bought from you, there are plenty of shares going cheap tonight, as you have heard for yourself. People are anxious to sell because it means more hard work than they're prepared to give!"

A few of those present murmured their approval and old Jewe Manners, who was standing close by, applauded him loudly. "Bravo, Hauke Haien! The Lord will bless your work and bring it to a successful conclusion."

But their business did not get finished that day, although Ole Peters said no more and they continued until it was suppertime. It needed a second meeting before everything was arranged, and even that would have come to nothing, had not Hauke agreed to supply four teams of horses in the next month instead of the three which should have been his contribution.

The Whitsuntide bells were ringing across the land by the time the dike was finally begun. Back and forth plied the carts between the foreshore and the site, tipping out the heavy earth they had fetched and then going back to reload. Along the building line itself, there were men ready to shovel the clay into position and then level it off with spades. Vast quantities of straw were used, but not only to give body to the lightweight materials such as sand and loose earth which were used for the inner wall of the dike. In addition, as single stretches were completed one by one, the sods of turf which comprised the outer layer were firmly mattressed with straw against the erosion of the waves. Foremen were appointed who paced up and down, and when gales blew up, they had to open their mouths wide and bellow their orders in the teeth of the wind and weather. And among them rode the reeve on his white horse, for he used no other from that time on, and the steed darted back and forth with its rider as he rapped out his brusque orders, as he praised a good workman or, as sometimes happened, ruthlessly dismissed another for being careless or idle. "That won't do," he would storm. "We're not having the whole scheme ruined because you're too lazy to do your share properly." As he approached from the fens, the men could hear the galloping horse snorting from a long way off and that was the signal to attack their task with extra zeal. "Get on with it!" ran the word. "Here he comes on his white horse!"

During midmorning the workers would knock off and sit around in threes and fours, eating the food they had brought with them. If Hauke happened to arrive at that time, he would ride along the line of the dike which was temporarily deserted, and his eyes were quick to spot a slovenly piece of work. If he then went over to the men and explained to them how the job should be done, they looked up at him, chewing away stolidly, but they never replied, either to agree with him or indeed, to make any comment whatsoever. Once, about this time of day, when he was particularly pleased with the way a certain section had been tackled he approached the nearest group of workmen and jumped down from his horse, asking them in a cheerful voice who was responsible for such excellent workmanship. But they remained on their guard and gave him only sullen looks, until finally someone muttered a name or two with obvious reluctance. His horse stood there as quiet as a lamb, but the man to whom he had given it clutched the reins with both hands and gazed nervously at the animal's handsome eyes which were, as usual, directed towards its master.

"Why Marten," exclaimed Hauke. "You look as if you'd been struck by a thunderbolt!"

"It's your horse, sir. It's so quiet, it seems to be thinking up some mischief."

Hauke only laughed and himself took the horse by the bridle. At once it started rubbing its head affectionately on his shoulder. A few of the men glanced warily at horse and rider but most of them chewed away in silence, ignoring the reeve completely. Now and again they tossed crumbs to the sea gulls who had observed where the men took their food and swooped down on slender wings to within a few feet of the ground. His mind elsewhere, Hauke watched the birds for a while as they begged for scraps and their ready beaks snapped up the morsels of food in midair. Then he sprang into the saddle and rode off abruptly without a backward glance. The few words they spoke amongst themselves as soon as he had gone sounded like mockery in his ears. "What is wrong?" he asked himself. "Is Elke right when she says they are all against me, even these hired hands and simple people, many of whom are taking home good money because of this dike of mine?"

He spurred on his mount, so that it darted along the meadow as if it had wings. Of course he knew nothing of the sinister gloss to the story of the white horse which his former employee Carsten had given to all and sundry. But what would people have thought if they had seen him at such moments, with his eyes staring out of his haggard face, his cloak flying and the horse that seemed to be breathing fire?

So summer and autumn went by and the work continued until the end of November, when frost and snow brought it to a halt. They had not finished yet and decided to leave the area open for the present. The dike now stood about eight feet above ground level but a gap had been left in the west, where the sluice gates were to be built later. Beyond the old dike, the creek had not been touched at all, so that the tides could flow in and out as they had done for the past thirty years without doing any serious damage to either the new or the old dike. And so they commended their human endeavors to God's care, until the spring sunshine would make it possible to complete the undertaking.

Meanwhile, a happy event was awaited at the reeve's house. In the ninth year of the marriage, a child was born. It was red and wrinkled and weighed seven pounds, which is as it should be for a newborn infant, when it happens to be a girl, as this one was. Only its cry was not as lusty as it should have been and the midwife did not feel too happy about the sound of it. There was worse to come, however. On the third day, Elke developed childbed fever and became delirious, recognizing neither Hauke nor the old nurse. The unbounded joy that Hauke had felt at the sight of the child was turned to ashes. The doctor was fetched from the town. He sat by the bedside, felt Elke's pulse and wrote out a prescription, but for all that he looked helpless. Hauke shook his head. "A doctor's no use," he thought, "only God can help." He would always have called himself a Christian, albeit an unconventional one, but there was something now which prevented him from praying. When the doctor had left, and Hauke stood staring out of the window at the dreary winter's day, the sick woman cried aloud in her delirium and he clenched his hands together. But he himself did not know if it was a gesture of piety or if it was only to keep a grip on himself in his terrible anguish.

"Oh the sea, the sea!" whimpered the sick woman. "Hold me, Hauke!" she cried. "Don't let me go." Then her voice sank and it sounded as if she were weeping. "Must he go to the sea, the open sea? Dear God, I shall never see him again!"

At that Hauke turned and thrust aside the nurse who was standing by the bed. He fell on his knees and clasped his wife in his arms. "Elke, say you know me! I am here with you, close." But she only opened her eyes which were glazed with fever and looked around her as if all hope had gone.

He laid her back on the pillows and clutched his hands in despair. "Oh, God, don't take her away from me. You know I cannot do without her." Then he seemed to think again and he added more softly: "I know that You cannot always do as You wish, not even You. And yet, You are all-wise. You must do as Your wisdom tells You. Only speak to me, oh Lord. Give me a sign."

A sudden stillness filled the room. He heard only the sound of gentle breathing. As he raised his head, he saw that his wife lay in a peaceful slumber but the nurse was looking at him with horror in her eyes. He heard the door close. "Who was that?" he asked.

"It was the maid, Ann Grete, going out. She brought in another warming pan."

"You look at me as if I had shocked you, Frau Levke. What is it?"

"It was your prayer which horrified me. That is no way to pray if you want to save a woman's life."

Hauke looked at her sharply. "Do you go to the conventicle then, at the house of the Dutch tailor, like Ann Grete does?"

"Yes sir, we both believe in the living faith."*

Hauke let the subject drop. At that time, the conventicle movement was flourishing and it had spread among the Frisians too. Its leading lights were apparently either craftsmen who had come down in the world, or schoolmasters who had been dismissed from their posts for drunkenness, and many people flocked to their secret meetings, where anyone could play the priest, young girls and married women of all ages, ne'er-do-wells and lonely old folk. Ann Grete used to spend all her free evenings there and so did the reeve's odd-job man, who was in love with her. Elke did not like it and she felt it her duty to tell Hauke what she thought about such goings on. But he believed it was wrong to try to persuade people in matters of conscience. These meetings hurt no one, he felt, and it was better for the servants to spend the evenings there than at the inn, drinking.

So the matter had rested there and even now he held his peace. But other tongues started wagging and the words of his prayer were repeated from house to house. He had denied God's omnipotence

---

*Storm is referring to the spread of pietist and fundamentalist sects from Holland in the eighteenth century. As a rational Protestant, Storm naturally disapproved of such religious movements, without perhaps fully perceiving their function in enabling members of the poorest class to provide themselves with spiritual solace and communal solidarity.

and what was God if he was not the Almighty? Hauke Haien was an atheist. Perhaps those whispers about the devil's horse he rode had some truth in them after all. But Hauke learned nothing of these rumors. In those dark days, he had eyes and ears only for his wife. Even the child did not exist for him.

The old doctor came every day, sometimes twice, and once he even stayed the night. He wrote out yet another prescription and Iven Johns galloped off with it posthaste to the apothecary's. Then the physician's face lost its strained look and he nodded more confidently to the reeve. "Things are improving," he told Hauke. "With God's help she may recover."

And one day, whether through his skill or whether the Lord had indeed answered Hauke's prayer, the doctor's old eyes began to beam when he was alone with his patient. "Well, my dear, this is a great day for me. Now I can speak with certainty," he told her. "Things looked very black at one time, but now you are back with us once more, in the land of the living."

Elke's dark eyes grew radiant. "Hauke, Hauke, where are you?" she called, and the moment he heard her clear voice he came running into the room and flung himself by her bedside. She put her arms around his neck. "Hauke, my husband," she cried. "My life has been saved. I shall not be taken from you."

The doctor took his silk kerchief from his pocket and wiped his forehead and cheeks. Then he went away, nodding with satisfaction.

Three evenings later, a pious preacher, a former shoemaker whom the reeve had had to dismiss, gave a sermon at the Dutch tailor's house, describing for his hearer's benefit, what he considered were the divine attributes. "Whosoever disputes the power of Almighty God, whosoever says, 'I know you cannot do as you wish,' has fallen from God's grace. We all know the wretched man, he weighs like a millstone on the community, and he seeks out God's enemy, the friend of sin, to be his comforter, for the hand of man must always seek some staff to lean on. But I tell you, beware of a man who prays in such fashion. His prayer is not a prayer. It is a curse!"

These words, too, flew from mouth to mouth, for nothing remains a secret long in such a small community. Even Hauke came to hear of it, although he did not speak of it, not even to his wife. He could only embrace her fervently and say: "Be faithful to me, Elke. Always stay true!"

He saw the surprise in her face as she turned to him. "Stay true to you? But who else could there be?" A moment or two later, she realized what he had meant. "Yes, Hauke," she added, "we must indeed be true to each other. And not only because we need each other so." Then they parted and went away to do their separate tasks.

Things might still have been all right with him even after that, but in spite of the constant demands of his work, there was a loneliness about him. A devil-may-care attitude lurked in his heart, so that he cut himself off from other men. Only towards his wife was he still the same, and to his child, when he knelt by its cradle every evening and morning, as if there alone he would find salvation. but he grew more severe than ever with his workmen and servants. The botchers and the idle whom he had formerly corrected with a mere reprimand were now terrified at the harshness of his castigation and Elke had to go among them afterwards, trying to undo the harm he had caused.

As spring approached, work on the dike was resumed. A temporary embankment was erected to protect the gap in the west from the sea until the new sluice was ready. It was semicircular in shape and a corresponding bank was put up to protect the inner face. Like the sluice, the main dike gradually grew in height and as it neared completion the pace was speeded up.

The reeve's work grew no lighter, though, for in the place of old Jewe Manners, who had died during the winter, there was now Ole Peters, who had been nominated a dike warden. Hauke made no attempt to prevent his appointment, but instead of an encouraging word and the friendly clap on the shoulder that went with it, such as he had so often received from his wife's old godfather, his successor was furtively obstructive, forever raising unnecessary objections which had to be rebutted by equally unnecessary explanations. For although Ole Peters had grown in importance these days, he still knew nothing about civil engineering and he still nursed a resentment against the "damned scribbler" who kept crossing his path.

Above sea and marsh stretched a brilliant sky when summer came, and the meadows were once more dotted with cattle whose occasional lowing broke the deep stillness all around. The larks sang tirelessly high in the blue, but one was only aware of it when, once in a while, for no more than it takes to breathe a sigh, the song was suddenly broken off. No storms interrupted the work, and except for a coat of paint, the sluice was already finished without the temporary dikes having been put to the test even for a single night. It seemed, indeed, as if the good Lord had shown His favor towards the new enterprise. Even Elke's eyes smiled as her husband came home from the dike on his white horse. "What a good creature you've grown into," she said and patted its glossy neck.

If she had the child on her arm, Hauke would jump down readily and dance his tiny daughter up and down. If the horse turned its brown eyes toward them, he said, "Come here. I'll let you have the honor too," and he placed the little Wienke, as she had been christened, in the saddle and led the horse round in circles on the grass. The old ash tree was also allowed to "have the honor." He placed the child on a low springy branch and bounced her up and down. The mother watched from the front door and her eyes were laughing. But the child never laughed. She had a delicate nose but the eyes on either side of it seemed to stare into the distance without expression, and the little hands never reached out to grasp the stick her father held out to her. It did not worry Hauke, for he knew nothing of how small children should develop, but when Elke saw her servant's bright-eyed daughter who had been born within a few days of her own, she could not help comparing the two children. "My little one is not as forward as yours, Stina," she said wistfully. The woman was holding her older child, a chubby little boy, by the hand. She gave him an affectionate shake and answered: "Oh well, ma'am, children are all different. Why, this one was stealing apples from the pantry before he was two years old." Elke stroked the curly hair out of the plump lad's eyes and then she pressed her silent child to her heart in secret sorrow.

As the year slipped by and October came, the new sluice in the west was firmly embedded, with the dike closing in on either side. It sloped gently towards the sea and now stood at about fifteen feet above the point reached by the ordinary high tides. Only the gaps where the creek flowed had still to be filled in. From the northwest corner, one could get a clear view of Jevers Isle and the shallows beyond, but it was also a very windy spot. If a spectator stopped to admire the prospect, his hair was blown about and he was wise to hold on to his hat.

At the end of November when the gales and the rain set in, there remained only the closing of the gap between the old and new dikes. It was on the northern side of the gap that the creek ran, through which the sea water had been allowed to flow into the polder. The walls of the dike towered on either side and the gulf between them, which had still to be filled in, was exceedingly deep. In dry summer weather, the task would have been easier, but if it had had to wait until the following year, the whole undertaking would have been jeopardized.

Hauke put everything he had into getting the job finished. The rain streamed down in torrents, the wind whistled, but his haggard figure on the mettlesome white steed stood out, and could be seen now here, now there, up among the figures on the dike or down among the dark swarm of workers, feverishly toiling at ground level on the north face. It was here that the tip-up carts unloaded the clay, which by now had to be fetched from a long distance, as the nearer supplies were used up. Through the drumming of the rain and the wind's roar, the reeve's sharp orders rang out, for he had taken complete charge of the operation that day. He called each cart forward by number and held back those who tried to push in and unload out of turn. "Stop!" he called and everything halted. "Straw! Tip a load of straw down!" he called to the men above and the straw came tumbling down on to the wet clay below. Those below rushed forward and raked it out, spreading it over the heavy soil, shouting up to the men above not to bury them. Then fresh supplies of earth arrived and Hauke was back again at the top of the embankment, looking down into the gap from his horse and watching the men shoveling away and finding it hard to keep their balance. Then he looked out to sea. It was blowing hard and the water's edge advanced inexorably until the waves were mounting the wall of the dike. He saw that the men were drenched to the skin and could hardly catch their breath for the keenness of the wind. The chill rain beat down relentlessly. "Keep at it men, don't give in!" he shouted encouragement to them. "One foot more and that will do for this tide."

Other noises, too, penetrated the howling of the storm, the men shouting, the slap of the clay as it met the ground, the creaking of the carts and the rustle of straw, slithering down the sides of the gap. And amongst it all was the yelping of a little fawn dog which ran hither and thither, cold and bewildered, lost among the welter of men and carts. All at once the pathetic creature gave a piercing howl which no one could fail to hear. Hauke looked down. He had seen it fly through the air, flung down into the gap as it was being filled in. His face blazed with fury. "Stop! Stop I tell you!" he thundered down to the men in charge of the carts, for they were still tipping wet clay into the gulf.

"Why?" a rough voice shouted back. "You don't mean us to stop on account of this miserable tike, do you?"

"Stop, I tell you!" boomed Hauke once more, "and bring that dog to me. I'll have no slaughter on our conscience."

But no one lifted a finger and a few more spadefuls of earth were thrown in the direction of the squealing puppy. Hauke dug his spurs so hard into his horse that it gave a shriek. He galloped down the bank and everyone stepped hastily aside, out of his path. "The dog!" he cried. "I want that dog."

A hand tapped his shoulder gently, like the touch of old Jewe Manners. But when he turned impatiently, it was only a friend of the old man's. "Have a care, Reeve," he whispered. "You have no friends here among these people. Let the dog go."

The wind whistled, the rain splashed. Most of the men had stuck their spades in the ground but a few had flung them aside. Hauke bent forward over the old man. "Will you hold my horse for me, Harke Jens?" he asked, and hardly had the latter got the reins in his hand than Hauke sprang into the gap and snatched up the whining little beast in his arms. A second later he was back in the saddle and riding up the bank. His eyes darted over the men who were standing by the carts. "Who was it?" he demanded. "Who threw the creature down there?"

For a moment all were silent, for anger flashed from the reeve's thin face and their fear of him was only heightened by their superstitious beliefs. Then one of the carters, a bullnecked fellow, stepped forward. "It was none of my doing, Reeve," he said and he bit off a plug of chewing tobacco and shoved it calmly in his mouth before he went on: "But whoever did it was quite right. If your dike is to hold something must be buried alive in it."

"Buried alive? What Sunday school taught you that?"

"None of them," answered the lout with an insolent throaty laugh. "It was our grandfathers who taught us and they were as good

Christians as ever you are. A child would be better still, but if you can't get one a dog will do."

"Stop spouting such barbarous teachings!" shouted Hauke. "It would be better if they buried you."

"Oho, oho!" the cry rose from a dozen throats, and before the reeve had time to think he found himself encircled by grim faces and clenched fists. He saw, indeed, that he was friendless, and the possible danger to his dike struck him with sudden terror. What would happen if they were all to down tools? Then he saw Harke Jens going among the workmen, speaking to one, laughing with another and smiling in a friendly way. One after the other, he clapped them on the shoulder, and one by one they reached for their spades again. A few moment later, the work was in progress once more on every side. What more did Hauke want? The creek must be dammed and the dog was securely hidden in the folds of his coat. With abrupt resolution, he steered his horse towards the nearest cart. "Straw over the edge now!" he barked in a tone of command and the driver obeyed him mechanically. Soon it was cascading down into the depths below and the others reached out as it fell and started working in it.

They went on for another hour until it was past six o'clock. It was almost dark but the rain had stopped. Hauke called the foreman to his side. "Have everyone on the job at four tomorrow morning. There will still be moonlight and with God's help, we shall finish it then. Oh, one thing more," he added, as they all prepared to go home. "Do you know whose dog it is?" And he took the trembling puppy out of his coat.

They shook their heads and only one man spoke: "It's been running round the village for days, begging. It's a stray."

"Then I shall keep it," replied the reeve. "Don't forget now. Four o'clock tomorrow morning!" And with that he rode away.

As he arrived home, Ann Grete was just going out. He met her at the door and as she had changed into clean clothes, it at once occurred to him that she was going to the conventicle at the tailor's. "Hold out your apron," he ordered her, and as she did so, reluctantly, he threw the puppy into it with the mud still clinging to it. "Take it to Wienke. It will be a playmate for her. But first wash it and rub it warm. That will please the Lord too, you know, for the poor creature is frozen stiff."

And Ann Grete, who could hardly refuse to obey her master, did not get to the conventicle that evening.

The next day, the last spadeful of earth was dug. The wind had dropped and the gulls and avocets flew in graceful curves back and forth over land and water. From Jevers Isle cawed the myriad voices of the wild geese, still content to linger on the North Sea coast on such a day, and out of the white morning mist which covered the fens there gradually dawned a golden autumn day which shed its light over the latest achievement wrought by man's hand.

A few weeks later, the head reeve and the civil commissioners arrived to inspect it for themselves. There was a banquet to celebrate the completion at the reeve's house, the first that had taken place there since old Tede Volkers' funeral. All the wardens were present as well as the more important title holders. After the meal, they and the reeve got into the various conveyances and Elke was helped into the gig by the head reeve himself, the brown chestnut gelding impatiently stamping its hoofs. Then he jumped up behind and took the reins in his own hands for the privilege of driving the reeve's wife, whom he had always considered such a sensible woman. So they drove merrily up the path to the new dike and along it to the newly reclaimed polder.

Meanwhile a light breeze had sprung up from the northwest and from both of these directions the tide was coming in fast. But there was no mistaking it. The gradual curve of the wall softened the impact of the waves just as Hauke Haien had predicted. The commissioners were full of praise for him, so that the halfhearted objections, which were fitfully raised by some of the wardens, were soon smothered in the general approval.

The great day passed but the reeve was accorded a further moment of gratification as he rode out one day along the new dike, lost in thought. Perhaps he was wondering why the area that would never have been enclosed but for him, which was born of his sweat and toil through the long night watches, had been named after one of the royal princesses and was now officially known as the New Caroline Polder. But so it was and the name appeared on all the appropriate documents, on some of them even in bold red letters. As he eyed the grassland, he saw two workmen with tools over their shoulders striding along, one about twenty paces behind the other. "Wait for me," he heard the more distant one call to the other. "Another time," was the reply as the man in front took the path leading down from the dike to the polder. "I haven't time now, Jens. It's getting late and I have to cut some turf."

"Where from?"

"Why from here, of course, from the Hauke Haien Polder."

He was shouting at the top of his voice as he trudged along the path, announcing it to the whole of the fens which lay before him. But Hauke felt that his name had been proclaimed aloud for all the world to hear. He rose in the stirrups and then spurred on his white horse, keeping his eyes fixed on the broad acres which stretched away to his left. "Hauke Haien Polder"—he repeated it under his breath. It sounded as if no other name would possibly do for it. What matter if they were all against him, they would never escape his name. As for the Princess Caroline, why, that title would soon survive only on paper. The horse galloped along proudly, but the words: "Hauke Haien Polder! Hauke Haien Polder!" still rang in his ears. In his mind, the new dike swelled in importance to become almost the eighth wonder of the world. There was nothing to compare with it in the whole of Friesland. He let the white horse dance along with him but he felt as if he was surrounded by all his fellow countrymen. Only he stood head and shoulders above the rest and his eyes darted over the crowd, keen but compassionate.

Three years had run their slow course since the dike was finished. It stood up well to the elements and the cost of repairs had been very small. White clover almost covered the new polder and as one walked through the sheltered meadows, a great cloud of sweet fragrance was borne across in the summer breeze.

The time had come to convert the theoretical shares in the polder into reality and the various title deeds were made out for the new owners in accordance with the recognized principles of allocation. Hauke was not slow to acquire any new shares which happened to come on to the market, but Ole Peters refrained sourly. He owned no land in the area reclaimed. There were, of course, the usual wrangles and disputes before the division was finally confirmed, but eventually a settlement was reached. Soon that, too, was over and done with, and the reeve was safely over yet another hurdle.

From that time on he lived a solitary life, managing his estate and carrying on his duties as dike reeve, seeing only those who were nearest and dearest to him. His old friends were no more and he had no gift for making new ones. But there was peace under his roof and the subdued child did nothing to disturb it. She spoke little and there was none of that constant stream of lively questioning which one expects from bright youngsters. When she did ask something, it was often put in such a way that it was difficult to know what she really meant. But her sweet, simple face seldom looked anything but contented. She had two companions and they were enough for her. When she wandered out on to the grassy bank round the house, the little fawn dog her father had saved from death was invariably in attendance. She had called it Pearl, and it was always fussing round her, so that if the dog came in sight, one knew that little Wienke was not far away. Her second playmate was a sea gull called Claus.

It was a very old woman who had brought Claus into the household, none other in fact than Trin Jans. She was eighty years old by now, and no longer capable of fending for herself in her hovel out on the dike. It was Elke's idea to offer her a home for the rest of her days, for she had been her grandfather's servant. She could spend the evening of her life under their roof and die decently when her time came. Elke and her husband went to fetch her, although they almost had to use force to get her to come back with them. They housed her in a little sitting room of her own attached to the new barn which Hauke had had to build when his expanding farm interests demanded extra space. There was another room there in which the maids slept and they could be on hand if the old woman needed attention during the night.

All Trin Jans's household possessions had been arranged round the walls. There was a chest of drawers made from old packing cases, two colored pictures of her dead son, a spinning wheel which had been silent these many years and a spotlessly clean four-poster bed before which stood a roughly made stool. It was upholstered with fur, the skin of the Angora cat which had been killed so long ago. She also brought with her her only pet and that was the sea gull, which had made its home with her for some time now. True, it flew away south each winter with the other gulls, but it returned each year as soon as the beach grew redolent with the scent of wormwood.

The barn had been built towards the foot of the bank on which the house stood and the old woman could not see the sea from her window, for the dike blocked the view. "You keep me here like a prisoner," she grumbled one day when Hauke came to see her. "Which way is it to Jevers Sands? Is it out over the brown cow or the black one? I can't see it from down here."

"What's Jevers Sands to you anyway?" asked Hauke.

"I don't care a fig for Jevers Sands," the old woman retorted, "but I want to see the spot where my boy was taken to meet his Maker."

"Then you should sit under the ash tree near the house. You can see right out to sea from there."

"That's all very well, but I haven't your young legs," she muttered. And that was all the thanks that Hauke and his wife got for their kindness to her, for several weeks at least. Then there was a sudden change, however. One morning, Wienke's little head peeped round the half-open door. "Well!" exclaimed the old woman, who was sitting in her wooden chair with her hands folded in her lap. "And what do you want?"

The child came nearer and stared at her solemnly with her apathetic eyes.

"Are you the reeve's bairn, then?" asked Trin Jans.

The child nodded.

"Then you may sit down on my stool here. The cover used to be my Angora tomcat. As big as this! But your father killed it. If it was still alive, you could have had a ride on it."

Wienke did not reply but turned her eyes to the white fur. Then she knelt down and her little hands began to stroke it, as children do with a living cat or dog. "Poor puss," she said and went on with her affectionate stroking.

"That's enough, now," said the old woman after a little while. "You can still sit on it, after all, and that's as good as a ride. Perhaps that's why your father killed it." She lifted the child in the air and plumped her down clumsily on the stool. The child sat there, neither speaking nor moving and her eyes never left the old woman, who began to shake her head. "How you're punishing him, Lord our God. Yes, you're punishing him all right." But pity for the child seemed to overwhelm her. Her crippled old hand reached out and stroked the child's wispy hair and Wienke seemed to like it.

From then on, the little girl came to see the old woman every day.

254 • *Theodor Storm*

Soon she could seat herself on the Angora stool and Trin Jans put into her hands some scraps of bread and meat which she had prepared, and told her to scatter them on the floor. In a trice the sea gull had shot out from some corner or other, with wings spread, and set to with a great squawking. At first the child had been startled and cried out in fright at the sight of the big, violent bird, but soon she got used to the game they played and the moment she put her head round the door, the gull would fly towards her and settle on her head or her shoulder, until the old woman came to her aid and the feeding could begin. Until then, Trin Jans had never let anyone so much as touch her Claus, but now she sat by patiently and watched the child gradually stealing all the bird's affection. Meekly it allowed the little one to catch it, and she carried it about with her, wrapped in her apron. If they went out into the field and the fawn dog was nearby, it would leap up at her in a fit of jealousy. "Not you, Pearl, not you!" she would cry and raise the gull as high as her arms would stretch, until it could free itself and fly off over the bank. Then the dog would wheedle her and jump up until it had taken the gull's place in her arms.

When Hauke or his wife happened to chance on this strange foursome, who had nothing in common but their deficiencies, they would glance tenderly at their daughter. But once they turned aside, their faces showed only grief, which each of them carried alone, for neither of them had yet spoken the words which would have brought relief.

One summer morning, Wienke was sitting with the old woman and the two animals on the big stones that stood outside the barn door. Her parents happened to pass that way, the reeve leading his horse with the reins over one arm. He had been to fetch it himself from the pasture and he was going out to the dike. Elke had seen him coming and slipped her arm through his as they walked together. The sun shone warmly. Indeed, it was almost sultry and a sudden gust of wind blew up from south-southeast. The child grew restless as soon as she saw her parents. "Wienke wants to come too," she said and, shaking the gull from her lap, she reached for her father's hand.

"Come on then," he answered.

"What? In this wind?" cried Elke. "Why, it will blow her away."

"Don't worry, I'll hold her tight. The air is warm and the sea is so lively she can watch the waves dancing."

Elke ran into the house and fetched a scarf and a little hood. "But there's a storm brewing," she cautioned. "Better be off at once and don't stay too long."

"We shan't get caught," laughed Hauke and lifted the child into the saddle before him. Elke remained for a while on the bank, shading her eyes with her hand as the pair trotted along the path and up on to the dike. Trin Jans sat on the stone muttering unintelligibly with her faded lips.

The child lay still in her father's arms. She seemed to find it difficult to breathe in the heavy atmosphere that precedes a storm. He bent down to her. "Well, Wienke?" he asked.

She looked at him. "Father," she said, "you can do everything, can't you, everything?"

"Such as?"

But she did not respond. Her own question appeared to mean nothing to her.

It was high tide when they reached the top of the dike and the sun's reflection struck the wide surface of the water and dazzled the girl's eyes. The wind whirled the crest of the waves and the tide came rushing in with a roar, beating against the shore. Wienke's little hands clutched in panic at her father's fist which held the reins, so that the horse was startled and jumped to one side. Her light blue eyes looked up in bewilderment and fear. "The water, Father, the water!"

He freed himself gently. "Be still, child, your father is here. The water won't hurt you," he soothed her.

She pushed the flaxen hair away from her eyes and ventured to look out at the sea once more. "It won't hurt me," she repeated trembling. "No, Father, tell it not to hurt us. If you tell it not to, then it won't."

"No, I can't do that," answered Hauke gravely. "But the dike we ride along protects us from it, and the dike was your father's idea and he had it built."

Her eyes looked at him, baffled. Then she hid her head, which was very small for her age, in the folds of her father's greatcoat.

"Why are you hiding, Wienke?" he whispered. "Are you still afraid?"

A tremulous little voice emerged from the ample folds. "Wienke doesn't want to see it any more. But you can do anything, can't you, Father?"

A roll of distant thunder rumbled against the wind. Aha, thought Hauke, here it comes! And he turned his horse. "Let's go home to mother," he said aloud.

The child gave a deep sigh of relief but it was only when they got back to the house that she ventured to raise her head from her father's chest.

Indoors, Elke took off her scarf and hood and the girl stood stiff as a block of wood while her mother did so. "Well, Wienke? Did you like the big sea?" she asked, giving the child a gentle shake.

Wienke opened her eyes wide. "It talks," she said. "Wienke was frightened."

"The sea can't talk, Wienke. It only rushes in and makes a noise." The child stared vacantly. "Has it legs? Can it get over the dike?"

"No, it can't do that. Your father is dike reeve and he takes care that it doesn't."

"Yes," said the child with a stupid smile and clapped her hands. "Father can do everything." Then she turned away from her mother impatiently. "Let Wienke go to Trin Jans. She has some red apples."

Elke opened the door and let the child go. When she had closed it again, those eyes of hers which had always comforted and encouraged her husband hitherto, now betrayed the depths of despair.

Hauke took her hand and pressed it, as if there was no need for words, but she said softly: "No, Hauke, let me say it. We waited so long for a child of our own and at last she was born. Now, oh my God, I am sure she is feebleminded. She will never be anything but a child. I had to say it aloud and not keep it to myself any longer. I had to tell you."

"I have known it for a long time," answered Hauke quietly and he held his wife's hand tightly, for she tried to take it away.

"So we are just as alone as ever we were," she went on.

At this, Hauke shook his head. "No, Elke. I love the child, and when she throws her little arms about me and clings close to my heart, I would not have missed it for all the gold in the world."

Elke's face was dark with anguish as she gazed into space. "But why has it happened? What has its poor mother done to be punished in this fashion?"

"I have asked that too, Elke. I have asked God, who alone knows why. But He does not tell us and maybe it is as well. Perhaps we should not understand if He did."

Then he took his wife's other hand and drew her tenderly towards him. "Never stop loving the child as you do. That she understands, you can be sure."

Elke threw herself on her husband's breast and wept her fill, for she was no longer alone in her suffering. Then suddenly she flashed a smile at him and gave his hand a squeeze. She ran from the room and fetched Wienke from the barn. She took her in her arms and hugged and and kissed the little lass until the child stammered: "Mother! Dear, dear Mother!"

So they lived their quiet life together at the dike reeve's house and had the child not been there, they would have been much the poorer for it.

Gradually the summer drew to its end, and the birds of passage had already taken wing. The air was no longer filled with lark song, but a few of the birds still lingered, pecking at grains near the barn during the threshing and one heard them squawk as they fluttered away. A hard frost had already set in.

One afternoon, old Trin Jans was in the kitchen of the big house. She sat by the stove on the wooden step of a staircase which went up to the loft. She seemed to have acquired a new lease of life during recent weeks and she liked to come into the kitchen quite often now and watch Elke busy with her tasks. She no longer grumbled about her old legs, for one day Wienke had made her come up to the house, and tugged her along by her apron. The child knelt by her side, watching the flames flickering through the opening in the stove. One small hand clung to the old woman's sleeve and the other played with her own fair hair.

Trin Jans started speaking, telling the child about her young days. "I was in service with your great-grandfather, you know, I was one of the maids and I had to feed the pigs. Oh, he was a clever man, was your great-grandfather, wiser than all the others put together. One moonlit night—it was a cruel long time ago, that it was—they happened to close the sluice gates, and a mermaid was trapped and couldn't get back to the sea. How she screamed and tore at her hair, which was as coarse as bristle. Yes, child, I saw and heard her for myself. How she shrieked! The ditches between the fens were full of water, and the moon shone so bright that it gleamed like silver. She swam from one ditch to the other and lifted her arms and she beat her hands—or what they have for hands, they're more like flippers—well, she beat them so hard you could hear the clap of it from a great way off. Then she clasped them together and you'd have thought she was praying, only creatures like that can't pray. I sat on a stack of wood outside the front door—they'd left it there to build something, I dare say—and I could see right out over the fens. And the mermaid swam about for a long time and her arms glittered like silver and diamonds whenever she raised them high. Then I lost sight of her and the wild geese and the gulls which I hadn't heard till then, began to wheel back and forth, squealing and cackling."

Trin Jans stopped. The child picked on a word she knew. "Could she pray? What did you say? Who was it?"

"It was one of the merfolk, child. They're monsters who can never go to Heaven."

"Never go to Heaven," Wienke echoed, and she heaved a deep sigh as if she understood.

"Trin Jans!" came a deep voice from not far away and the old woman gave a start. It was the reeve, Hauke Haien, and he was leaning against the kitchen doorpost. "What nonsense is that you're telling the child? I've told you before, keep such fairy tales to yourself, or else tell them to the geese and the hens."

The old woman looked at him resentfully, and pushed the child away. "They're no fairy tales," she mumbled half to herself. "My great-uncle told me about it."

"Your great-uncle? Why, I thought you said just now that you saw it yourself?"

"What's the odds? It's all one," the old crone retorted. "But you've no faith, Hauke Haien. You want to make out my great-uncle to be a liar." She huddled nearer the stove and stretched out her hands to the flames.

The reeve cast a glance through the window. "Come with me, Wienke," he said, for it was still light, and he drew the simple-minded creature towards him. "Come with me, I want to show you something from the dike. Only we shall have to walk. My horse is being shod." He took her into the living room and there Elke fastened a thick woolen shawl round the little one's throat and shoulders. A few minutes later, father and daughter were walking towards the northwest, out along the old dike and past Jevers Isle, where the mudflats stretched for miles, almost to the horizon.

Sometimes he carried her, sometimes he took her by the hand. Gradually the dusk came on and everything in the distance grew blurred and hazy. Close by the shore, turbulent streams forced their way beneath the surface of the ice and made it crack in places. Smoking mist emerged from these fissures as Hauke Haien had once seen in his youth, and along their edges were the same sinister figures, hopping about and bumping into each other as if they were demented, bowing and scraping and then without warning, swelling in breadth to a monstrous size.

The child clutched his hand in terror and tried to hide her face in it. "Sea devils," came an unsteady little whisper from between his fingers. "They're sea devils."

Hauke shook his head. "No, Wienke, they're neither sea devils nor merfolk. There are no such things. Who's been telling you such tales?"

She looked at him blankly without speaking and he stroked her cheeks tenderly. "Look again! They're only poor, hungry birds. See, there's a big one flapping its wings. They're trying to catch fish in the cracks where the mist is rising."

"Fish," repeated Wienke.

"They are God's creatures, just as we are. You mustn't believe in mermaids and monsters. The good Lord is with us, everywhere."

Little Wienke kept her eyes firmly on the ground and held her breath as if she was staring down into some terrifying abyss, and perhaps she was. Her father watched her for a long while and then bent down and gazed into her face. But there was no sign there of any emotion or understanding. He lifted her in his arms and when he found how cold her hands were, he put both of them into one of his thick woollen gloves. "That's better, my Wienke," he said, and in all probability, the child was oblivious to the passion and sincerity in his voice. "I have to keep you warm. You are our child, our only child and you love us . . ." His voice broke, but the little one pressed her face affectionately against his rough beard.

And so they walked home, content.

With the arrival of the New Year, the reeve's house was once more beset by care. Hauke was suddenly stricken down by a marsh fever and he in his turn hovered near death's door. When he recovered and was up and about again, thanks to his wife's loving care, he seemed a changed man. His physical weariness appeared to affect his spirits too, and Elke grieved when she saw how little he cared if things were done well or ill. All the same, towards the end of March, he insisted on mounting his white horse and riding it along the dike for the first time since his illness. It was afternoon and although the sun had been shining earlier, it now lay hidden behind a heavy haze.

There had been a few exceptionally high tides that winter, but none had done much harm. On the opposite bank, a flock of sheep were drowned on a low-lying island and some of the foreshore had been washed away. But here on this side, and as far as the new polder was concerned, there had been no damage at all to speak of. The previous night had seen the most severe gale of the season and the reeve decided to go and examine the situation for himself. He rode up from the fens towards the new dike and at the southeastern tip, he saw it had held well. But when he reached the northeast corner where the new and the old dikes met, he found a different story. The new one was indeed intact, but where formerly the creek had flowed beside the old dike, he saw that the turf bore signs of serious erosion and the tide had worn a hollow in the body of the bank, revealing a honeycomb of mouse-runs. Hauke dismounted and inspected the bank more closely. The field mice had tunneled deep into the earth and without a doubt, the damage must go much farther than one could see at a glance.

This came as a deep shock to the reeve. It should have been foreseen when the new dike was being built. As it had been overlooked then, they were paying for it now. The cattle had not yet been put out to pasture, for the new grass was uncommonly late for the time of year. Wherever he looked the ground seemed bare and trodden. He mounted his horse again and rode back and forth along the shore. The tide was on the ebb and it became obvious that the creek had changed its course. It had channeled a new bed for itself in the mud and was now attacking the old dike from the northwest. However, as far as he could judge, the new one, with its gentle slope, had been able to withstand the onslaught.

The prospect ahead was a gloomy one for the reeve. His heart sank as he thought of all the vexation there was to come, to say nothing of the work it meant for him before it was all put right. It was not only that the old dike would have to be reinforced. The slope would have to be altered as well to bring it into line with the new one. Most important of all, however, the dangerous course of the creek, which they believed they had dammed successfully, must be diverted either by further dams or by expensive brushwood fencing. Once more he walked the horse to the farthest point northwest and then back again, his eyes fixed on the new bed of the creek which he could see clearly enough, outlined in the exposed mudflats below him. The horse strained forward, snorting and pawing the ground impatiently with its forehoofs, but the rider held it in. He had to ride slowly to assess the situation, but also he wanted time to control the misgivings which were mounting inexorably within him.

Suppose there was a flood tide again, a great inundation as there had been in 1655, when vast stretches of the land were submerged and men's lives were lost too. Suppose it happened again as it had done in the past, and more than once at that. A fever of apprehension seized him. The old dike would give, it could not take the strain. What then? What would happen? There was only one way to save the old enclosure, to save the bulk of the land and people's lives. Hauke felt a clutch at his heart and his normally clear head grew giddy. His land, the Hauke Haien Polder must be sacrificed and the new dike pierced!

In his imagination, he could see the waters bursting through the beach, covering grass and clover with salt spume and spray. Savagely he dug his spurs in his horse's flanks and, with a cry of pain, he galloped along the dike and down the path which led to his house.

Shocked to the core and his mind awhirl with wild, uncoordinated plans, he flung himself into his armchair. When Elke came in with the child, he got up, lifted the child in his arms and kissed her. He slapped aside the little fawn dog who was trying to make a fuss of him. "I must go to the inn," he said and took down his cap from the hook on the door where he had hung it only a short while before.

His wife looked at him anxiously. "What takes you there?" she asked. "It will soon be dark."

"There's business to attend to," he murmured almost to himself. "I'll find some of the dike wardens there, I know."

Elke followed him and pressed his hand, for he was already at the door as he spoke. Hauke Haien, who had never consulted anyone in the past, was now in a hurry to seek advice from people whose opinions he had formerly despised. In the inn parlor were Ole Peters, two of the other wardens and a local farmer who owned land in the polder. They were having a game of cards.

"I suppose you've been out on the dike today," said Peters, as he swept up the cards halfway through the deal and threw them down on the table.

"Yes, I was there," answered Hauke. "It looks bad, Ole."

"Bad? Oh, a few hundred turves and a truss or so of straw will soon put things to rights. I was there about noon myself."

"We shan't get off so cheaply, I fear," replied the reeve. "The creek has reappeared. As it can't get at the dike from the north, it's trying again from the northwest, this time."

"You should have left it as you found it," remarked Ole dryly.

"You mean that because you have no interests in the new polder, it should never have come into existence at all!" Hauke retorted. "That's your own fault! Still, if we now have to put up hedging along the old dike to protect it, it's the green clover behind the new one that will provide the money to pay for it, and more."

"What's that?" cried one of the wardens. "Hedging? How much of it will be needed? You always like doing things the most expensive way, I must say."

The cards lay untouched on the table. Ole Peters leaned forward on both elbows. "I want to tell you something, Reeve. This new enclosure of yours is eating us out of house and home. We are still paying for the fact that you had to have it so wide, and now that it's attacking the old dike, we are expected to foot the bill again. Luckily, it's not as bad as you make out. It has held so far and it will do so again. Go out on your white horse again in the morning, and take another look."

Hauke had come to the inn from the tranquillity of his own home. The reply he received had been worded mildly enough, but he could not fail to detect a threat of tough resistance beneath it. He felt he was still too weak to do battle with them; he could not fight them all just now.

"All right, I shall do as you suggest, Ole," he conceded. "But I'm very much afraid I shall find it no better than I left it today."

A sleepless night followed. As Hauke tossed and turned restlessly on his pillow, Elke too lay awake, concerned for her husband. "What is the matter?" she asked at last. "If there is something on your mind, tell me. We have always confided in each other."

"It's no great matter," he replied. "There are some repairs needed to the dike by the side of the sluice. You know I always like to think things out during the night." That was all he said; he wanted to remain free to act as he thought fit; unawares, his wife's clear insight and strength of character were an obstacle in his present weakness, something he involuntarily avoided.

The next morning when he rode out along the dike, it all seemed like a different world from the one he had found the day before. As then, the tide was low, but the day was still young and the pale spring sunshine cast its rays almost vertically down over the expanse of mud. The white sea gulls skimmed smoothly this way and that and, invisible in the azure sky, the larks poured forth their eternal melody. Hauke, who did not know how the very beauty of nature can deceive us, stood at the northwestern corner of the dike and scanned the ground for the new bed of the creek which had so shaken him on the previous day. But with the sun's rays almost directly overhead, at first he could not even find it. It was only when he shaded his eyes with his hand against the dazzle, that he could just make it out. It looked as if the twilight shadows of the previous day had been misleading, for now the course was only faintly traced. It must have been the colony of mice that had done the damage, rather than the tide. Of course, something would have to be done about it, but with some careful excavation and the turf and straw which Ole Peters had suggested, the damage could easily be repaired.

"So it wasn't so bad after all," he told himself with relief. "Why, you nearly frightened yourself out of your wits." He summoned the wardens and for the first time in his experience, the work recommended was agreed without any opposition. The reeve felt a healing calm spreading through his veins, refreshing his enfeebled body, and a few weeks later, the work had been successfully completed.

The year progressed but as the weeks went by, Hauke passed that way with growing disquiet. Whether on horseback or on foot, he would eye suspiciously the tender new green sprouting from the newly laid turves undisturbed in their straw layering, and he found himself turning away his eyes or galloping along by the inner dike instead. On a few occasions when he should have gone there, he sent his horse back to the stable although it was already saddled. At other times, when he had no special business there, he hurried there furtively, leaving his home on foot and alone, as if on a sudden impulse. Sometimes even then, he turned back, as if he could not screw up sufficient courage to visit the ill-fated corner yet again. And presently he reached a point where he would have been glad to tear down the whole structure with his bare hands, for this portion of the dike haunted his mind's eye like the embodiment of a bad conscience. Yet his hand remained paralyzed, nor could he speak to anyone about it, not even to his wife.

One night in September, a storm sprang up which veered round to the northwest before its force was spent. It had not been a very violent one, however, and next morning, Hauke rode out to the dike at low tide beneath an overcast sky. As his eyes wandered over the mudflats, he had a premonition of what to expect. There to the northwest, he suddenly caught sight of it again. There was the new, the phantom bed of the creek but much more clearly visible and more deeply etched in the ooze. No matter how he strained his eyes, it did not recede or vanish.

When he arrived home, Elke rushed to grasp his hand as soon as she saw the despair in his face. "What is the matter, Hauke?" she asked. "Don't say something has gone wrong! Just when we were so happy and I thought the world was leaving you in peace."

The way she spoke made it impossible to express the irrational fear which held him in its grip.

"No, Elke," he said. "I have no enemies to worry about. It is only the weight of responsibility I bear that oppresses me. It is no easy task to protect the community from the sea which God created."

He freed his hand to evade any further questioning by the wife whom he loved so dearly. He went to the stable and the barn as if he had to inspect something there, but his eyes saw nothing. He was wholly preoccupied, finding a way to still his conscience, to convince himself that it was all hallucination, the exaggerated fantasy of a sick mind.

"The year I am telling you about," said my host, the schoolmaster, after a longish pause, "was the year 1756 and it will never be forgotten in this part of the world.* The reeve's household lost one

*The storm of October 1756 is a historical event.

of its members that month, for towards the end of September, Trin Jans lay dying in the little room they had set aside for her by the barn. She was nearly ninety years old and in accordance with her wishes they had propped her up on her pillows. Her eyes were fixed on the small leaded panes of the window, staring into the distance. There must have been a thin layer of haze lying above a heavier one that day, for a kind of mirage took place. All at once, the image of the sea was reflected by the sun and mirrored above the rim of the dike. It stretched out into a long silver ribbon, shining with a blinding light, and clearly visible in the sickroom. The southern tip of Jevers Isle could also be seen quite clearly.

At the foot of the bed cowered the reeve's daughter, holding tight to her father's hand, for he stood beside her. Death had already traced its unmistakable lines in the old woman's countenance, and little Wienke stared breathlessly at the uncanny and to her incomprehensible change in the homely but familiar features.

"What is she doing, Father? What is it?" she whispered fearfully and dug her fingernails into her father's hand.

"She is dying," answered the reeve.

"Dying," repeated the child, puzzled and confused.

The old woman moved her lips. "Jins, Jins!" and a croak like a cry for aid broke forth from her lips as she spoke her son's name. She stretched out her arms, which were nothing but skin and bone, in the direction of the glittering reflection. "Help me, help me! You are beyond the waters now. May God have mercy on the others!"

Her arms sank, the bedstead creaked softly. Trin Jans had breathed her last.

The girl gave a deep sigh and turned her pale eyes to her father. "Is she still dying?" she asked.

"No, it is over," said the reeve picking up the child in his arms. "She is a long way from us now. She is with God."

"With God," repeated the child and paused for an instant as if she had to think it over. "Is that good, to be with God?"

"Yes, that is the best of all." But the dying words which had been uttered still rang in Hauke's head. "May God have mercy on the others," he said softly to himself. "What did the old witch mean? Do the dying prophesy?"

It was soon after Trin Jans had been buried in the village churchyard that all kinds of rumors started. Disasters and strange happenings began to afflict the people of Friesland it was said, and it is certainly true that on Mid-Lent Sunday,* the golden cock on the church steeple was blown down by a whirlwind. And it is true too that in the middle of the summer a great plague of vermin descended from the sky like a blinding snowstorm, and layers of these insects covered the fens to a depth of several inches. No one had ever seen anything like it before.

At the end of September, the reeve's farm produce was taken to the market in the town and when his servants returned, having sold the butter and the corn, their faces were white with fright as they clambered down from the carts. "What is it? What is the matter with you?" asked the maids who had run out into the yard when they heard the wheels of the cart.

Ann Grete, still wearing her outdoor clothes, was gasping for breath as she entered the kitchen. "Tell us quick, quick," clamored the maids. "What on earth has happened?"

"Oh may sweet Jesus have mercy on us all!" cried Ann Grete. "You know old Mary from the farm across the water? Well, we always stand near each other with our butter, just by the corner where the apothecary lives. Now she told me and Iven Johns says so too, that something terrible is on the way, some disaster which will affect the whole of North Friesland. 'And that's the truth, Ann Grete,' said Johns to me and do you know"—here she lowered her voice—"they say there's something queer about the reeve's white horse."

"Hush, hush," chorused the other maids.

"I don't care, it's true anyway. But over there on the other bank, things are worse than with us. Not only flies and vermin, they say, but it's been raining blood. And on Sunday morning when the pastor looked in his washbasin, what do you think he found? Five little death's-heads in it, skulls no bigger than peas and everyone went to have a look at them. Then in August there was a plague of caterpillars, crawling about everywhere. They had bright red heads and they ate corn, flour and bread and whatever they could find. They couldn't even burn them out, either, for the fire did not harm them at all."

Suddenly the girl stopped. No one had noticed before that the

---

*Laetare Sunday, the third Sunday before Easter.

mistress of the house had come into the kitchen. "What nonsense," she scolded. "Don't let the master hear you." The maids all rushed to reply but Elke was firm. "There's no need to tell me. I have heard quite enough, thank you. Now get back to your work. That will please the Lord more than all this idle chatter." Then she bore off Ann Grete to the living room to render her account for the sale of the butter.

So this superstitious gossip got short shrift in the reeve's household, but elsewhere it spread like wildfire and with the longer evenings, it was repeated so often that it took a firm hold. It brooded over the countryside like thunder in the air and everyone felt in their heart of hearts that some terrible catastrophe was imminent.

It was just before All Souls' Day in October. All day long the wind had been blowing hard from the southwest, and that evening heavy brown clouds chased each other across the half-moon in the sky so that shadows and eerie light pursued each other over the ground. The wind was mounting. In the reeve's living room the supper dishes had not yet been cleared away. The lads had been sent to see to the cattle in the stalls and the maids had had to check the windows throughout the house and in the loft, and make sure that all the doors and shutters were secure, so that the wind could do no damage indoors.

Hauke and his wife were looking out of the window. He had just swallowed a hasty supper for he had been out on the dike. He had gone on foot quite early in the afternoon, to see that there were pointed stakes and sacks of clay or earth in readiness wherever there might be a weak spot in the dikes. He had posted men everywhere to ram in the stakes and heap the sacks as soon as the tide began to threaten the safety of the dike. The strongest contingent he had placed at the juncture of the old and new dikes and they had the strictest orders not to leave their posts except in case of dire necessity. Then, when all was arranged, he had returned to the house not a quarter hour before, drenched through and hair disordered. Now he stood listening to the squalls and gazing vacantly into the wild night as the wind rattled the leaded windowpanes. The wall clock in its glass case had struck eight. The child, standing beside her mother, suddenly gave a start and hid her face in her mother's skirt. "Claus!" she sobbed. "Where is my Claus?"

This was not such a foolish question as it appeared, for the gull had not migrated either this winter or the last. The father did not trouble to answer but the mother picked up the child. "Claus is in the barn," she soothed her. "He's nice and warm in there."

"Why?" asked Wienke. "Is that good?"

"Yes, it's good."

The master was still standing at the window. "This won't hold much longer, Elke. The wind will be blowing the panes in. Call one of the maids and tell her to go out and clamp down the shutters."

The mistress gave the orders and the maid ran out of doors. From within, they could see her skirts flying in the gale. But as she loosened the clamps the storm blew the shutter out of her hand and hurled it against the glass so that a few panes were shattered and the fragments fell inside the room. One of the candles was blown out, leaving a smell of smoke behind. Hauke had to go to her aid himself and it needed all their combined strength to get the shutter into position. As they tore open the door to return to the house, a sudden gust followed them in, so that all the pieces of glass and silver in the wall cabinet rattled against each other. The wooden beams in the upper story shivered and creaked as if the wind were about to rip the roof off. But Hauke did not come straight back into the living room. Elke heard him striding through the threshing shed and out to the stable. "My horse, Johns! Saddle it at once!" she heard him shout. When he came back into the room, his hair was disheveled but his grey eyes were blazing. "The wind has changed. It's a nor'wester blowing now and we're only halfway to high tide. This is not just a gale. It's going to be a hurricane, worse than anything we have known in our lifetime."

Elke had gone as pale as death. "And you must go out again?" He seized both her hands and gripped them convulsively. "Yes, I must, Elke." Slowly she raised her dark eyes to his and they looked at each other. It was only for a few seconds but it seemed like eternity. "Yes, Hauke," said his wife. "I do know. You have to go."

There was a stamping of hoofs outside the front door. Elke fell on his neck as if she would never let him go, but it lasted only for a moment. "This is our fight," said Hauke. "You are safe here. No floods have ever reached this house. Pray to God that He will be with me, too."

He wrapped himself in his cloak and Elke took a kerchief and wound it carefully round his throat. She wanted to speak but her trembling lips could not utter a sound.

Outside, the horse neighed like a trumpet blast in the howling wind. Elke went out with her husband. The old ash tree creaked as if it would fall. "Quick, master, into the saddle," shouted the groom. "The horse is straining like mad. The reins might snap." Hauke embraced his wife once more. "I'll be back by dawn," he told her.

He leapt into the saddle. The horse reared high and then, like a war-horse into battle, it charged off down the embankment, bearing its rider into the night and the teeth of the gale. "Father, my father," wailed a pitiful little voice. "Father dear."

Wienke had followed him out into the dark and was running after him. But a hundred yards away, she stumbled over the uneven ground and fell.

Iven Johns carried the weeping child back to her mother. Elke was leaning against the trunk of the ash tree, as the wind whipped the branches, staring in a trance into the night which had swallowed up her husband. When, for a moment, there was a sudden lull in the roaring of the gale and the pounding of the sea, she started in fright. It seemed as if the elements were poised, waiting to destroy Hauke, and if they were silent it must mean they had already seized him. Her knees trembled and the wind had loosened her hair, which was blowing free. "Here is the child, ma'am," shouted Johns. "You'd better hold her tight." And he pressed little Wienke into her mother's arms.

"The child? God forgive me, I had forgotten all about you, Wienke!" she cried. She lifted the infant in her arms and hugged her to her breast with all a mother's love. Then she dropped on her knees. "Oh Lord God, and you His son Jesus, do not snatch him from us and leave us a widow and an orphan. Protect him dear God. You and I alone know his secret heart." And the gale began again, thundering as if the whole world would be destroyed in the fury of its might.

"Don't stay here, ma'am," said Johns. "Come with me." And he helped her up and led them both indoors, into the living room.

The white horse galloped on. The narrow path to the dike was thick with mire for it had rained heavily all the previous day. But even the clinging mud sucking at its hoofs did not seem to hinder it.

They sped along as if they had the firm ground of a summer's day beneath them. The clouds raced across the sky like a pack of hounds in full pursuit. Below them the wide marshes were transformed into an unrecognizable wilderness, alive with fitful shadows. From beyond the dike, the sea roared ever louder, as if it would engulf the whole world. "Oh, on!" shouted Hauke to his horse. "This is the most terrible ride of our lives."

A cry like the agony of death broke out from beneath the horse's hoofs. The man tugged at the reins and looked round. To one side and quite close to the ground were a flock of white sea gulls. They were seeking shelter inland and they cackled in mockery as they flew. As the moon appeared for a brief moment through the clouds, Hauke saw that one of them lay crushed on the path, and he fancied he saw a red ribbon fluttering round its neck. "Claus!" he cried, "poor Claus!"

Was it Wienke's bird? Had it recognized horse and rider and sought them out for protection? Hauke could not tell. "Forward!" he shouted once more and again the horse reared and resumed its gallop into the night. Again the storm paused without warning and a deathly hush took its place, but in another instant, it had started again with renewed ferocity. In that breathing space, however, Hauke had heard the sound of human voices and the barking of dogs, borne across from the village. As he turned his head and looked back, he saw in the moonlight a scene of feverish activity with people bustling about heavily laden carts. Other wagons were scurrying towards the higher ground inland, fleeing for their lives. The sound of livestock bellowing came to his ears, as if they had been driven out of the warmth of their stalls. "Thank God," he breathed. "They are seeking safety for themselves and their cattle." The sigh of relief that went up from his heart was followed by a sudden clutch of fear. "My wife, my child! Who will remember them? But no, no. Our house stands high, it is safe as it is. No floods will rise to such a level."

But it all passed in a flash and the fleeting vision had gone for ever.

A fearful squall of wind greeted man and mount as they left the narrow path and reached the dike itself. Hauke pulled up his horse with a powerful tug at the reins. But where was the sea? Where was Jevers Isle? What had happened to the opposite shore? There were only mountainous waves before him, menacing against the night

sky, each vying to outtop the other in the livid twilight, before they
came crashing down with the howl of wild beasts in the jungle. The
white horse pawed the ground and snorted amidst the earsplitting
din. The rider was overwhelmed by the futility of human endeavor.
Now must come night, death and chaos.

He pulled himself together. This was a flood tide that had always
occurred in these parts from time to time, only he himself had never
seen one quite like this before. His wife and child were safe at home
in a well-built house that stood on high ground. As for his dike—
and his breast swelled with pride for everyone called it the Hauke
Haien Dike now—it would show them all how a dike should be
built.

But what was that? Hauke halted at the point where the two dikes
met. Where were the men he had posted here, with orders to keep
watch? He looked north along the old dike where he had also left a
few men on duty. At neither place was there a soul to be seen. He
rode a little farther but it was exactly the same. Only the blustering
of the gale and the pounding of the sea, stretching out into immea-
surable distance, deafened his ears. He turned back and rode until
he came once more to the abandoned corner. His eyes took in the
length of the new dike. He could make it out quite clearly now. The
waves were rolling in much more slowly here and with far less force.
It might have been a different sea altogether. "The dike should
hold," he muttered and wanted to laugh aloud.

But his laughter faded as his eyes traveled farther along still. What
was that at the northwest corner? A dark huddle of people was
engaged in frantic action. What were they working at? What were
they doing to the dike? The spurs bit into the horse's flanks and it
flew off with the reeve towards the throng. The storm met them
broadside on and the gusts were so strong that they were almost
whipped off the dike and hurled into the polder below. But man and
beast knew where they were going. Hauke could see already that
there were a few dozen men working away for dear life and he saw
that they were cutting a channel to breach the new dike. He pulled
up his horse by brute force. "Stop!" he yelled. "What devil's work is
this?"

In sheer panic they had stopped their digging when they saw the
reeve had arrived. The wind had carried his words towards them and
he saw that several of them were trying to answer him. But he could

only make out their excited gestures for they were all to his left and the words they spoke were blown away in the wind, which was now so strong that they would have been blown over if they had not huddled together for protection. Swiftly Hauke took the measure of the cutting which had been dug and gauged the height of the tide, for in spite of the new profile, the water was so near the rim of the dike that he and the horse were bespattered with foam. Another ten minutes' work and then the tide would come flooding through the channel and the Hauke Haien Polder would be buried beneath the sea.

The reeve motioned one of the workmen to the other side of his horse. "Now tell me," he barked. "What are you supposed to be doing and what does it mean?"

"We have to breach the new dike, master, so that the old dike doesn't give."

"What was that?"

"We're cutting through the new dike."

"And destroying the polder? What fiend gave you such orders?"

"It was Ole Peters, the dike warden. He told us to do it."

Anger flashed from the reeve's eyes. "Don't you know me?" he bellowed. "Ole Peters has no right to give orders when I am in charge. Back to your posts, I say, and quickly."

As they hesitated, he made the white horse canter through the crowd. "Be off I tell you, or you can all go to hell."

"Have a care there!" shouted one of the men and raised his spade against the prancing horse. One kick knocked the spade out of his hand and the other hoof felled him to the ground. A sudden cry arose from the throats of all present, a cry which men voice only when the fear of death strikes. For a moment everyone seemed paralyzed, even the reeve and his steed. Nothing could be heard above the raging of the storm and the crash of the waves. Hauke swung round in the saddle. His eyes dilated. 'My God! A breach! A breach in the old dike."

"And you are to blame, Reeve!" shouted a voice from the crowd. "On your head be it! You shall answer for that before the throne of God."

Hauke's face, which had been flushed with anger, turned white, so white that the light of the moon, which had now appeared, could not make it seem any paler. His arms hung limp, he was hardly aware that he held the reins. But that was only for a moment. Then he straightened his back with a jerk and a harsh groan escaped his lips. In silence he turned his horse and the white steed snorted and raced away eastwards carrying him along the dike.

Hauke's eyes darted from side to side. His head was on fire. What sin had he committed that he should answer for it before the Almighty? The piercing of the new dike—perhaps they would have finished it in time if he had not stopped them! But it was all one now and a hot stab of pain ran through his heart, for he realized his crime only too well. He should never have allowed Ole Peters's evil mouth to talk him out of repairing the old dike properly last summer. He alone had recognized how serious it was. He should have insisted on putting it right in spite of everything. "Oh God!" he cried into the storm. "I admit my guilt. I have failed in my duty!"

On his left and almost at the horse's hoofs, the seas raged. In front of him and now in total darkness lay the old polder with its mounds of earth and its humble cottages. The faint light from the sky became completely obscured and the single beam of a lantern penetrated the darkness, coming as it were, to comfort the reeve in his anguish. It must be shining from his own house, a token of love from his wife and child. Thank God their house was secure. The rest of the community, too, must surely be safe by now, away in the upland village. From it, there gleamed a forest of lights, more than he had ever seen before. One of them winked high in the air. It must have been coming from the church steeple and its twinkling rays fanned out into the night. "They must all have got away in time," Hauke told himself. "Of course, many a house will lie in ruins and there will be hard times ahead, with the fens ruined by sea water and so much repairing needed to dikes and sluices. But it is a cross we must bear and I will do all I can, even for those who have injured me in the past. Only be merciful, Lord, and spare our lives."

His eye was caught by the new polder. The sea frothed and foamed all round it but within, all was peaceful and still. A great exultation burst from his heart. "The Hauke Haien Dike will hold," he rejoiced. "It will hold for a hundred years and more."

A noise like the crack of thunder roused him from his reverie. The white horse refused to go on. What was wrong? The horse leapt back and in an instant he could sense that a portion of the dike had broken away and went plunging down out of sight. He opened his eyes wide. This was no time for musing. They had just reached the old dike and indeed, the horse had already placed its forefeet on the path. Instinctively, he pulled it back. Then the last of the cloud rolled away from the moon's face and the gentle orb illuminated the ghastly scene, for the turbulent sea was pouring into the old polder, hissing and foaming.

Hauke gazed at it, numb with horror. The water came flooding in as if it would swallow up everything, man and beast alike. Then the beam of light he had seen before seemed to strike him in the eye. There was still a lamp shining from his own house and thus reassured, he realized that beyond the whirlpool which swirled before him, only about one hundred yards of land had been inundated so far. Beyond it, he could still see the path leading out of the meadow. Then he saw something else too. There was a cart moving in the distance. No, it was not a cart, it was a two-wheeled gig and it was rushing along the dike in his direction. In it sat a woman and yes, there was a child by her side. And was that not the yapping of a little dog which reached his ears through the storm? God in Heaven, it was his wife and child coming towards him and the foaming waters of the flood surged implacably towards them. A cry, a cry of utter despair came from the rider's throat. "Elke!" he shouted at the top of his voice. "Elke! Go back, go back!" But the storm and the sea were pitiless. Their roaring drowned his words. The wind caught at his cloak so that he was almost dragged from the saddle and still the gig came on, paying not the least attention to the water flooding in. He saw that his wife was holding out her arms towards him. Had she recognized him? Had her love for him, her fear for his safety driven her from the shelter of their home? And now she was trying to shout something to him. One last word, was it? So many questions darted through his head and all remained unanswered. Not a word could either of them hear, all their shouting was in vain. Only the water thundered in their ears, drowning every other sound as if the end of the world had come.

"My child!" Hauke moaned into the storm. "Oh Elke, my faithful Elke!" Another huge piece of the dike broke away and the water came hurtling through the enlarged gap. Once more he saw below him the wheels of the gig and the head of the horse drawing it. For a moment they emerged from the seething cauldron and then they disappeared. The lonely figure on the dike could see nothing more.

"This is the end." he said softly to himself. He rode up to the edge of the landslide and saw how the waters were creeping forward towards the village where he had been born and heard the sinister rushing noise they made. He could see the light shining from his own house, but it was meaningless to him now. He straightened his back and jabbed his spurs so hard into the horse's soft parts that it reared violently and would have toppled over if he had not forced it down again. "Forward!" he cried, as he had so often done when the going was hard. "Take me, too, oh Lord, but spare the others." Again he applied the spurs and this time the horse gave a scream which could be heard above the wind and the surging waves. From the boiling torent there came a dull thud, a brief struggle. . . .

The moon shone in the sky but on the dike below no living thing could be seen. Only the wild waters remained and already the old polder was almost totally submerged. The embankment on which the reeve's house stood remained unscathed, high above the flood, and the lamp still shone in the window. Up in the village the houses grew dark one by one, but the sparkling rays of the lonely light from the church tower trembled over the foaming waves.

The narrator fell silent. I reached for the brimming glass which had been standing by my side untouched for a long time. But I did not raise it to my mouth. My hand remained resting on the table.

"That then is the story of Hauke Haien," my host concluded, "so far as my knowledge of it goes. No doubt our present reeve's housekeeper would have told it differently in many respects. For instance, some say that the white skeleton of a horse which used to lie on Jevers Isle could be seen again by moonlight as soon as the floods had gone down. Indeed, the whole population was ready to swear they had seen it. This much is certain, though. Hauke Haien, his wife and child lost their lives in the deluge. You will not find their graves in the churchyard. Their bodies must have been carried out to sea as the tide receded. I suppose their remains decomposed somewhere at the bottom of the sea, and so they found peace at last from their fellow men. But the Hauke Haien Dike still stands after a hundred years and if you are going into town tomorrow, and do not mind half an hour's detour, you can ride along it for yourself.

"You see that Jewe Manners was right when he promised its builder that future generations would pay him tribute, for that is the way of the world. They gave Socrates hemlock to drink and they crucified Our Lord. We may not go to such extremes these days, I suppose, but people still worship a man who performs deeds of violence or they canonize some coarse, bullnecked rogue of a priest. Or else they turn a decent man into a ghost, just because he had vision and could see a little father ahead than most of us do. Oh yes, that's still common enough."

When this earnest little man had finished speaking, he got up and listened. "There's been a change in the weather," he said and, going to the window, he drew aside the heavy curtain. It was bright moonlight. "Here are the dike wardens coming back. See, they are saying good night and going their separate ways. The breach must have been in the far bank. The water level has gone down already."

I stood by his side and looked out. The windows here were well above the rim of the dike and it was as he had said. I picked up my glass and drained it. "I am much indebted to you for this evening," I said. "I think we shall be able to sleep in peace."

"So we can," replied the little man. "And I wish you a very good night."

I went downstairs and met the reeve in the hall. He had come to fetch a map which he had left in the inn parlor. "It's all over now," he said, "but I suppose the schoolmaster has explained many things to you. He prides himself on being one of the enlightened."

"He appears to be a highly intelligent person."

"Yes, yes, of course, but seeing is believing you know. The dike was breached on the other bank, just as I declared it would be."

I shrugged my shoulders. "I shall have to sleep on it," I replied. "Good night, Reeve."

He laughed. "Good night," he answered.

The next morning, in soft golden sunshine which played over a landscape of widespread devastation, I rode along the Hauke Haien Dike and into the town.

Translated by Stella Humphries

Plautus in the Convent

Conrad Ferdinand Meyer

To enjoy the cool of evening after a hot summer day a company of cultivated Florentines had assembled, in front of a pavilion in the Medici gardens, about Cosimo de' Medici,* the "father of his country." The dusk crept by slow degrees over a gorgeous but delicately shaded, cloudless sky above the group of temperate revelers, in which a sharp-featured, gray-haired man† was conspicuous, whose eloquent lips held the listening circle spellbound. The expression of his animated countenance was a strange mixture: over the serene brow and the smiling corners of the mouth lay the shadow of a sad experience.

When a pause ensued, Cosimo, with the shrewd eyes in an ill-favored face, spoke out and said, "Poggio, my friend, I have lately been browsing again in the little volume of your *Facetiae*.** To be sure, I know it by heart, and this I could not but regret since I was now able to take pleasure only in the happy turns of a supple style, without the former sensation either of curiosity or of surprise. Fastidious as you are, it is impossible that you should not have excluded from the authorized edition of the book one or another of your droll and amiable pleasantries, whether because it was too spicy, or because it was not spicy enough. Try to recollect. Favor these friends, who will understand the most veiled allusion and excuse the boldest jest, with a *Facetia inedita*. Telling your story and

---

*(1389–1464), ruler of Florence and notable patron of arts, letters, and learning.

†Gian Francesco Poggio Bracciolini (1380–1459), humanist, polemicist, secretary to eight popes beginning with Boniface IX, and discoverer of many manuscripts of ancient authors, including twelve comedies of Plautus.

**A collection of satirical and licentious tales, 1438–52. Meyer apparently did not know this work at firsthand.

sipping your wine"—he pointed to the goblet—"you will forget your sorrow."

The fresh grief to which Cosimo alluded, as to a matter of common report about town, had befallen the venerable Poggio—present secretary of the Florentine Republic, past secretary to five popes, formerly a cleric and latterly a family man—at the hands of one of his sons, of whom all were brilliantly endowed and all worthless.* This miscreant had disgraced the gray hairs of his father by an act which came close to theft and robbery, and which, moreoever, imposed upon the thrifty Poggio, his bondsman, a serious financial sacrifice.

After a little reflection the old man replied, "Those and similar pleasantries which are to your liking, friend Cosimo, comport, like flowery wreaths, only with brown locks, and sound ill from the lips of a toothless graybeard." Smiling, he displayed a fine row of white teeth. "And," he sighed, "only with reluctance do I return to these youthful frivolities, harmless as in themselves they may be, now that I behold my openmindedness and my easygoing philosophy of life degenerate in my son—I know not by what uncanny law of increase—into tolerable impudence, even into profligacy."

"Poggio, you are preaching!" interposed a youth. "You, who have given back to the world the comedies of Plautus!"†

"Thank you for your warning, Romolo!" cried the unhappy father, collecting himself; for, as a good companion, he too thought it improper to burden the guests with his domestic troubles. "Thank you for reminding me. *The Discovery of Plautus* is the *Facetia* with which, indulgent friends, I will entertain you today."

"Call it rather *The Rape of Plautus*," interrupted a scoffer.

But Poggio, without deigning to look at him, continued, "May it please you, friends, and at the same time demonstrate how unjust is the reproach with which the envious pursue me, that in a dishonorable, reprehensible way I have appropriated to myself those clas-

*History records a bad character of only one of Poggio's sons, Giacomo, who was hanged in 1478 for participation in a political conspiracy. Meyer expands the motif in order to throw a questionable light on Poggio's character.

†Poggio's discovery of the Plautus manuscripts did not occur at the time of the inner story, but some years later, in 1429. In this work Meyer was not much concerned with historical accuracy.

sics of which they cannot deny I am the discoverer—that, to put it bluntly, I have stolen them. Nothing is farther from the truth."

A smile went about the circle, in which Poggio at first gravely declined to join, but in which finally he also participated; for as one who knew human nature he was aware that even the falsest prejudices can be uprooted only with difficulty.

"My *Facetia*," he said, with a parody of the inclusive summary usually prefixed to an Italian short story, "has to do with two crosses, a heavy and a light one, and with two barbarian* nuns, a novice and an abbess."

"Fit for the gods, Poggio," a neighbor interrupted him, "like those simple-minded German vestals with whom, in your admirable letters from abroad, you peopled as with naiads the healing springs along the Limmat†—by the nine muses, the best thing you have written! That letter circulated in a thousand copies all over Italy."* *

"I exaggerated, knowing your taste," said Poggio jocosely. "At any rate, Ippolito, you, as a lover of simplemindedness, will delight in my barbarian nun. And so I begin."

In those days, illustrious Cosimo, when we were lopping off the superfluous heads of our holy church, lately become a hydra, I found myself in Constance and actively devoted myself to the magnificent business of an ecumenical council.†† My leisure time, however, I divided between contemplation of the stimulating spectacle which had crowded upon the narrow stage of a German imperial city the piety, science, and statecraft of the century, with its popes, heretics, mountebanks, and courtesans, and the occasional search for manuscripts in the neighboring monasteries.

Following up various clues and trails, I came to the supposition, amounting to certainty, that in a nearby convent there was a Plautus in the hands of the barbarian nuns, having strayed thither as a legacy or as a pledge from some impoverished Benedictine abbey. A Plautus! Imagine, illustrious patron, what that meant at a time when our curiosity was being so unbearably goaded by the few fragments then extant of the great Roman comedian. That I could not sleep you may

---

*Poggio uses the word to mean non-Tuscan and nonhumanist, in this case, Swiss.
†Swiss river flowing from Zurich to Baden.
* *A famous letter on the baths of Baden.
††The Council of Constance, 1414–18, called to end the Great Schism.

well believe, Cosimo—you who share and encourage my enthusiasm for the relics of a greater world which has declined and fallen. Would that I had left everything in the lurch and had hastened to the spot where an immortal, instead of delighting the world, lay moldering in ignoble obscurity! But those were the days when the election of a new pope occupied the minds of all men and the Holy Spirit was beginning to turn the attention of the assembled fathers to the merits and virtues of Otto Colonna;* though this is not to say that the daily and hourly running about of his adherents and servants, of whom I was one, had thereby become any the less necessary.

Thus it happened that an inferior and dishonest searcher, unfortunately a fellow countryman of ours, in whose presence I had, in the joy of my heart, indiscreetly mentioned the possibility of so great a discovery, anticipated me, and—blunderer that he was—instead of getting the classic by fair means or foul, aroused the suspicion of the abbess of the convent in which it lay buried in dust, and directed her attention to the treasure which she unwittingly possessed.

Finally I got a free hand and, in spite of the impending papal election, mounted a sturdy mule, leaving orders that a messenger should be dispatched to me upon the occurrence of the great event. My mule-driver was a Rhaetian who had come to Constance in the retinue of the Bishop of Chur, and his name was Hans of Splügen. He had unhesitatingly accepted my first offer and we had agreed upon an incredibly low sum.

A thousand pleasantries passed through my mind. The blue ether, the summer air tempered by a cool, almost cold breath from the north, the inexpensive trip, the difficulties of the papal election happily overcome, the supreme satisfaction awaiting me in the discovery of a classic—these heavenly benefits disposed me to infinite good humor, and I heard the muses and the angels sing. My companion, on the contrary, Hans of Splügen, abandoned himself, as it seemed, to the most melancholy reflections.

Happy myself, I benevolently sought to make him happy also, or at least to cheer him up, and I gave him all sorts of riddles—mostly from biblical history, which is familiar to the people. "Do you know," I asked, "the manner in which the prince of the apostles was freed from his chains?"† And I received the answer that he had seen

*Oddone Colonna (1368–1431), elected Pope Martin V at the Council in 1417.
†Acts 12:6–11.

the miracle depicted in the church of the Apostles at Tosana.*
"Listen, Hänsel," I continued. "The angel said unto Peter, 'Bind on
thy sandals and follow me.' And they went, Peter not knowing that it
was an angel, past the first and the second ward, through the gate
and along a street. And forthwith the companion departed and then
Peter said, 'Now I know of a surety that an angel hath led me.' From
what circumstance, Hänsel, did this sudden knowledge, this incontrovertible certainty come to him? Tell me that, if you can guess
it." Hans thought a while and then shook the curly locks of his hard
head. "Listen, Hänsel," I said, "I will answer the question. From this
circumstance Peter recognized the angel, that he asked no gratuity
for his services. Such is not the way of this world. That is the way
only of the heavenly beings!"

But one ought not to jest with the people. Hänsel suspected in this
joke, born of nothing, a purpose or an allusion.

"It is true, sir, that I am conducting you for almost nothing, and
that, though I am not an angel, I shall ask you for no gratuity. Know,
then, that I also on my own account am drawn to Monasterling-
en"†—he mentioned the name of the nunnery which was the goal
of our expedition—"where tomorrow Gertrude will wind the rope
girdle about her hips, and her blond hair will be shorn from her
head."

Tears rolled down the sunburned face of the hardy youth who, I
may add—perhaps there was a drop of Roman blood in his veins—
possessed much natural dignity of speech and action. "By Cupid's
bow," I exclaimed, "an unhappy lover!" and bade him tell me his
story, which proved to be simple but by no means easy to understand.

Hänsel had, he said, come with his bishop to Constance, and
being without employment, had sought work in the neighborhood
as a carpenter. He had found it on some buildings in process of
erection for the nunnery, and had made the acquaintance of
Gertrude, who lived nearby. They had learned to like each other and
found favor in each other's sight. Gladly and often they had sat
together—"in all decency and honor," said he, "for she is a good
girl." Then suddenly she had withdrawn from him, without detri-
ment to their love, but peradventure as though a strictly limited time

*Now called Thusis, in eastern Switzerland.
†Münsterlingen on Lake Constance. The Latinized form of the name is Meyer's
invention.

had elapsed; and he had heard for certain that she intended to take the veil. Tomorrow she was to be invested, and he had in mind to attend this ceremony, in order to have the testimony of his own eyes to the fact that an honest and by no means impulsive girl could, for no conceivable reason, leave a man whom she confessedly loved, to become a nun—to embrace duties for which Gertrude, a natural woman and full of life, was as unsuited as she could possibly be, and for which, to judge from her own expressions, she had no desire, but rather recoiled from them with horror and dread.

"It is unexplainable," the melancholy Rhaetian concluded; and added that through the mercy of heaven his wicked stepmother had recently died, on whose account he had left his father's house; so that this and the arms of his aged father were again open to receive him. His love, accordingly, would now find a warm nest awaiting her; but she was incomprehensibly determined to nestle in a cell.

At the close of this speech Hänsel relapsed into his dark brooding and obstinate silence, which he interrupted only to answer my question concerning the kind of woman the abbess was. He said she was an ugly little person, but an excellent manager who had restored and rehabilitated from slovenliness the economic administration of the convent. She came from Abbatis Cella* and people called her simply "Brigittchen of Trogen."

Finally the convent appeared above the skyline of monotonous vineyards. Hänsel now asked me to leave him behind at an inn by the roadside, since he wished to see Gertrude only once more—at her investiture. I nodded assent and dismounted from the mule, in order to stroll at leisure toward the not distant convent.

There they were having a merry time. On the lawn of the convent yard an indistinguishable great object was being sold at auction or exhibited for some other purpose. A rough soldier, with his helmet on his head, blew from time to time a discordant trumpet, perhaps a piece of booty, perhaps an ecclesiastical instrument. About the abbess, with her nuns, and the questionable herald in a patched doublet and tattered hose, whose bare toes peered forth from his worn-out boots, laity and an aggregation of monks formed a motley group in the most free and easy attitudes. Among the peasants stood here and there a nobleman—in Turgovia, as this German district is

*Appenzell.

called, there is an overabundance of such small and petty crested fowl—but minstrels, gypsies, vagabonds, strumpets, and rabble of every sort, attracted thither by the Council, also mingled in the strange circle. One after another, they stepped forth and tried the weight of the object in which, upon nearer approach, I recognized a gigantic old horrible cross. It seemed to be extraordinarily heavy; for after a short while it began to sway back and forth in the wearying hands of even the strongest bearer; it threatened to fall, and would have come crashing down if other hands and shoulders had not tumultuously put themselves under the ponderous beams. Shouts and laughter accompanied the scandalous performance. To complete the ignoble scene, the boorish abbess danced about like one possessed upon the freshly mown lawn, inspired by the worth of her relic—the meaning of this country fair began to dawn upon me—and probably also inspirited by the convent wine which, without cups and without ceremony, passed in huge wooden buckets from lip to lip.

"By the tresses of the Virgin Mother!" shrieked the impious jade, "not a man of you, not even the stoutest, can lift and carry this cross of our blessed Duchess Amalaswinta;* but tomorrow our Gertrude will toss it like a shuttlecock. I only hope the mortal creature will not grow vain! To God alone the glory, says Brigittchen. People, the miracle is a thousand years old and to this day is brand new. It has always worked, and upon my word it shall go off tomorrow without a hitch." Manifestly the excellent abbess had had a drop too much in the course of this heavenly day.

Comparing these comical doings with similar events that I have witnessed in my own blessed country, I began to understand them and to estimate them at their true value—just as, an hour later, with fuller knowledge of the facts, I definitely solved the problem; but the trend of my thoughts was suddenly and unpleasantly interrupted by a shrill call of the clownish woman in the white cowl, with the flushed face, the blinking, crafty eyes, the scarcely discoverable pug nose, and the bestial mouth gaping at an enormous distance below it.

"Hi, there, Italian scribe!" she yelled at me. I was on this day clad

---

*This is no doubt part of the pious fraud, for the historical Amalaswinta, a daughter of Theoderich, king of the Visigoths, can have had nothing to do with this matter.

in a simple traveling costume and carry the evidence of my classical origin in my countenance. "Come a bit nearer and let me see you lift the cross of the blessed Amalaswinta!"

All eyes were turned in expectation of amusement at me, people made way for me, and with rude jolts in the Swiss fashion shoved me forward. I excused myself on the ground, well-known to you, my friends, of the shortness and weakness of my arms.—The narrator raised his arms enough to reveal the fact.

Then the shameless woman, looking me over, cried out, "Your fingers are all the longer for it, you smooth customer!"—and in fact, by the daily practice of writing, my fingers have become developed and pliant. The crowd of bystanders burst into a boisterous laugh, incomprehensible to me, but offensive, and I charged the abbess with it. In vexation I turned away, went around the corner of the church nearby, and finding the main portal open, I entered. The noble round arch of the windows and ceiling, instead of the new-fangled pointed arch and the foolish French filigree, restored my soul to peace and composure. Slowly I strode forward the length of the nave, attracted by a piece of sculpture which, lighted from above, stood forth in impressive solidity from the religious dimness and seemed, in its way, to be a thing of beauty. I went up to it and was not disappointed. The statuary consisted of two figures united by a cross, and this cross completely resembled in size and proportions the one exhibited on the lawn, whichever may have been imitated from the other. A powerful woman crowned with thorns was carrying it almost level in brawny arms and on her mighty shoulder, and yet was sinking beneath its weight, as was shown by her knees, roughly outlined on her gown. By the side and in front of this tottering giantess a smaller figure, with a little crown upon her lovely head, mercifully placed her more delicate shoulder under the unbearable burden. The old master had purposely—or more probably from lack of artistic resources—treated the forms and garments only in the rough, reserving his cunning and the ardor of his soul for the faces, which expressed despair and mercy.

Taken with the charm of this expression, I stepped backward to get a better light. Lo and behold, there knelt before me on the other side of the group a maiden, presumably a native, a peasant girl of the vicinity, almost as powerfully built as the sculptured duchess, and with the hood of her white cowl thrown back over heavy braids of blond hair and a sturdy neck unused to concealment.

She arose; for absorbed in meditation, she had not sooner become aware of my presence than I of hers; brushed away a flood of tears from her eyes, and made a move as if to depart. She was to all appearances a novice.

I detained her and asked her to explain the statue to me. I was one of the foreign fathers at the Council, I told her in my broken German. This information did not seem to make much impression upon her. She related to me in a simple way that the image represented an ancient queen or duchess, the founder of this convent, who, taking the vow here, had wished to proceed to the investiture, her head crowned with thorns and her shoulder laden with the cross. "They say," continued the girl doubtfully, "that she was a great sinner, heavy laden with guilt for the murder of her husband, but of such high station that secular justice could not reach her. Then God touched her heart and she fell into great distress, despairing of the salvation of her soul!" After a long and bitter atonement, craving a sign that she was forgiven, she had caused this great, heavy cross to be built, which the strongest man of her time was hardly able to lift alone; and she too would have succumbed beneath its weight, had not the Mother of God in visible form mercifully assisted her to bear it, placing her ambrosial shoulder beside the earthly one.

These words the blond German did not use, but simpler ones, indeed so crude and uncouth that they could not be translated from a barbarian speech into our cultivated Tuscan without becoming boorish and grotesque; and that, my lords, would in turn be inappropriate to the expression of large-mindedness in the defiant blue eyes and the bold but shapely features of the girl whom I then saw before me.

"The story is credible!" I said to myself; for this feat by a barbarian queen seemed to me befitting the times and the customs of the dark close of the first millennium. "It might be true!"

"It is true!" Gertrude asserted curtly and vehemently, with a gloomy glance of conviction at the statuary, and again made a move as if to depart; but I detained her for the second time, with the question whether she were the Gertrude of whom my guide of today,

Hans of Splügen, had told me. She replied in the affirmative, unabashed, not even embarrassed, and a smile like a wandering light spread slowly from the firm corners of her mouth over her brown face, now beginning to grow pale in the convent air.

Then she reflected and said, "I knew that he would come to my investiture, and I can have no objection. Seeing my tresses fall will help him to forget me. Since you happen to be here, Reverend Father, I will make a request of you. If the man returns with you to Constance, reveal to him the cause of my refusal to be his wife after"—and she blushed, though almost imperceptibly—"after I had been friendly with him in all honor, according to the custom of our country. More than once I have been on the point of telling him the story, but I bit my lip; for it is a secret compact between the Mother of God and myself, and secrets should not be disclosed. To you, however, who are versed in secrets of the soul, I can confide the compact without betrayal. You shall then acquaint Hans with as much of it as is fitting and to you seems meet. It is only that he may not deem me fickle and ungrateful, and remember me as such.

"This is how it is with me. When I was a mere child—I was ten years old and had already lost my father—mother was taken with a grave and hopeless sickness, and fear came upon me, lest I be left alone in the world. Out of this fear, and out of love for my mother, I dedicated myself to the Virgin Mary for my twentieth year, if she would preserve my mother's life until then, or nearly then. She did so, and mother lived until last Corpus Christi day, when she peacefully died, just at the time when Hans had work as a carpenter in the convent; so that he it was who made mother's coffin. Since I was now alone in the world, what wonder is it that I fell in love with him? He is honest and thrifty, as the Italians are for the most part; 'modest and discreet,' as they say on the other side of the mountains. Moreover, we could converse in two languages; for my father, who was a strong and courageous man, had repeatedly accompanied a puny, timid tradesman, not without profit, over the mountains, and had brought home a few bits of Italian from the other side. If now Hans called me *cara bambina*, I returned the compliment by calling him *poverello*,* and both ring true, though I will find no fault with

* "Dear child; poor fellow."

the words of endearment usual in our country, when they are honestly meant.

"But it was at this time also that I was due to keep my vow, and every ringing of the Angelus reminded me of it.

"On the other hand, thoughts came into my mind and whispered to me such things as 'The vow of an innocent child who does not know the difference between man and woman could have no power to bind you,' or 'Kind as she is, the Virgin Mother would likely have granted you your mother's life of her own mercy and as a free gift.' But I said in reply, 'A bargain is a bargain,' and 'Honesty is the best policy!' She has kept her part of the agreement, and I will keep mine. Without truth and faith the world cannot endure. What did my father say, who is no more? 'I would keep my word with the devil,' said he, 'not to mention the Lord our God!'

"Hear now, Reverend Father, what I think and believe. Since the Virgin Mother bore the cross for the queen, she has, recruiting her convent, from time immemorial helped all novices without distinction to bear it. It has become a habit with her; she does it unconsciously. With my own eyes I, a nine-year-old child, saw how Lieschen of Weinfelden, a sickly creature who took the veil here, carried the ponderous cross as if in sport on her drooping shoulder.

"Now I shall say to the Virgin, 'If thou wilt have me, take me!—although I—If thou wert Gertrude and I were the Mother of God—should perhaps not take a child at its word. But no matter: a bargain is a bargain!—only with this difference: the duchess, burdened with sins, felt relieved and happy in the convent; it will be pain and sorrow for me. If thou bearest the cross for me, lighten my heart also; else there will be trouble, Mother of God! If thou canst not lighten my heart, then let me a thousand times rather to my shame and before the eyes of all the people plunge down and fall flat upon the floor!"

As I watched these laboring thoughts slowly draw deep furrows in Gertrude's young brow I smiled and suggested cunningly, "An adroit and clever girl could extricate herself from the difficulty by stumbling!" Then fire flashed from her blue eyes. "Do you think, sir, I shall cheat?" she exclaimed wrathfully. "So help me God the Father, the Son, and the Holy Ghost in my last hour, as I will honestly bear the cross with all the strength and sinews of these my arms!" And she raised her arms convulsively, as though she were already carrying the cross, so that the sleeves of her cowl and smock fell far back. Then I, as the Florentine that I am, beheld the slender, powerful, feminine arms with artistic delight. She observed me, frowned, and indignantly turned her back upon me.

After she had gone I seated myself in a confessional, rested upon my elbow, and meditated—verily not upon the barbarian maiden, but upon the Roman classic. Suddenly my heart rejoiced and I cried out exultantly, "Thanks, ye immortal gods. A darling of the comic muse is restored to the world! Plautus is won!"

Friends, a conspiracy of circumstances guaranteed me this success.

I know not, Cosimo, what your views are on the subject of miracles. I myself am a tolerable believer, neither superstitious nor presumptuous; for I cannot endure those absolutists who, when an inexplicable fact has gathered an atmosphere of superstition about it, either summarily believe or just as summarily reject the whole phenomenon—moon and corona—without investigation and without distinction.

The marvel and the fraud, both I believed I had here discovered.

The heavy cross was genuine, and a magnificent sinner, a barbarian woman, might have lifted it with the superhuman strength of despair and fervor. But this deed had not been repeated; on the contrary, it had for centuries been imitated by jugglery. Who was guilty of the fraud? Was it mistaken piety? Calculating avarice? The answer to these questions lay hidden in the darkness of the times. But so much was certain: the horrible cross, black with age, which was exhibited to the people, and the one which had been borne by a succession of simple or compliant novices—and only lately by the feeble and wily Lieschen of Weinfelden at her investiture—were two distinct pieces of wood; and all the while that the heavy one was being shown and weighed on the lawn, a light counterfeit was carefully locked up in some secret place within the convent, in order on the morrow to change places with the true one and deceive the eyes of the people.

The existence of a counterfeit cross, of which I was as much convinced as of my own existence, afforded me one weapon. A recent event afforded me another weapon.

Three dethroned popes* and two heretics† burned at the stake did not suffice to reform the church; the commissions of the Council were busied, one with this, the other with that abuse to be corrected. One of the commissions, of which the most Christian doctor Gerson** and the stern Pierre d'Ailly†† were members and I for the time being was secretary, sought to restore discipline in the nunneries. Counterfeit miracles, dangerous in the unreliable hands of women, and the evil books read by the sisters came up for discussion. Be it said in passing: these matters were treated by the two Frenchmen with a degree of pedantry simply incomprehensible to us Italians, without the suggestion of a jest, howsoever readily one might have found the humor of the situation. Enough! The fact of these discussions formed the warp, sinful participation in a fraudulent miracle the woof of my fabric, and the net was woven which unexpectedly I cast over the head of the abbess.

Slowly I mounted the steps of the choir and from there turned to the right into the likewise lofty and boldly vaulted sacristy, in which, designated by self-glorifying inscriptions, the empty spot appeared where the heavy cross usually leaned against the wall, and whither it was destined presently to return from the convent lawn. Two small portals led into two side rooms. One proved to be locked. Opening the other, I stood in a room dimly lighted by a circular window obscured with cobwebs. Behold, it contained the convent library huddled together upon a few worm-eaten shelves.

My whole being throbbed with excitement, as though I were a youthful lover entering the chamber of Lydia or Glycera. With trembling hands and shaking knees I drew near to the parchments; and if I had found the Umbrian's comedies among them, I should have covered them with insatiable kisses.

But alas! I turned the leaves of naught but rituals and liturgies, the sacred contents of which gave cold comfort to my disappointment. No manuscript of Plautus! The report had been true. Instead of

---

*Gregory XII, Benedict XIII, John XXIII.

†Among them John Huss.

**Jean Charlier de Gerson (1363–1429), theologian and church statesman at the Council.

††(1350–1420), cardinal; teacher and colleague of Gerson. The commission here described is fictional.

finding the buried treasure, a stupid collector had, by clumsy importunity, caused it to sink into unfathomable depths. I came upon—as my only booty—a dust-covered copy of the *Confessions of St. Augustine,* and as I have always been fond of the subtle little volume, I mechanically thrust it into my pocket, thus providing myself, according to my habit, with reading matter for the evening. Lo, like a bolt of lightning from a clear sky, my little abbess, who had had the cross dragged back to the sacristy and, without my having noticed her in the all-absorbing keenness of my desire and my disappointment, had trailed me through the open door into the library—like a bolt of lightning, I say, the little woman, cursing and railing, descended upon me; nay more, she groped with unseemly searching about my toga and brought to light again the church father reposing in my bosom.

"Mannikin," she shrieked, "I saw at once by your long nose that you are one of those Italian martens which of late have been sniffing around after books in our convents. But I tell you there is a difference between a befuddled monk of St. Gall and a nimble woman of Appenzell. I know," she continued with a smirk, "what bacon draws the cats. They are watching for an opportunity to seize the buffoon's book which we have stored up here. No one of us knew what was in it until the other day an Italian scamp came to venerate our most holy relics and then tried to carry off the jester under his long priestly gown,"—she pointed to mine. "But I said to myself, 'Brigittchen of Trogen, don't be swindled! The pigskin must be worth its weight in gold, since the Italian risks his neck for it.' For in our country, man, we say, 'He who steals a rope's worth shall hang by the rope!' Brigittchen, who is up to snuff, privately consults a learned friend, a man without guile, the priest of Diessenhofen,* who is fond of our humble wine and at times plays merry pranks upon our sisters. After he had examined the odd scrolls, yellow with age, he exclaimed, 'Odsnigs, Lady Abbess, you can get something for that! You can build your convent a barn and a winepress! Take the book, my good woman, hide it under your pillow, lie with the podex—so it is called—beneath you, and by the crown of the Virgin stay there until an honest purchaser presents himself!' And so

---

*Town in Switzerland where Meyer as a boy had disagreeable experiences with a clerical friend of his father.

Brigittchen did, though she has lain somewhat uncomfortably ever since."

I suppressed a smile at the Umbrian's resting place, to which the three judges of the lower world may have consigned him for his sins, and, assuming the dignity which I possess when circumstances call for it, I reproved her with a stern glance.

"Abbess," I said in a solemn tone, "you do not know who I am. Before you stands an emissary of the council, one of the fathers assembled in Constance, one of the holy men commissioned to reform the nunneries." And I unfolded a splendidly engrossed bill of innkeeper's charges; for I was inspired by the nearness of the comic poet in hiding.

"In the name," I read, "and by authority of the seventeenth ecumenical council! Let no Christian vestal sully her hands with one of those works dangerous to good morals, whether composed in Latin or in one of the vulgar tongues, whereof the invention hath corrupted the souls of . . . Pious Mother Superior, I may not offend your chaste ears by reading the names of these reprobates. . . .

"Counterfeit miracles, traditional or once performed, we prosecute with inexorable severity. If intentional fraud can be proved, the guilty woman—though she were the abbess—shall without exception atone for the sacrilege by death in the flames."

The abbess became as white as a ghost. But with admirable presence of mind the hypocrite immediately recovered her composure.

"Glory and honor to God!" she cried, "for finally setting His holy church in order!" And with an ingratiating smirk she fetched from a corner of the bookcase a daintily bound little volume. "This," she said, "an Italian cardinal, our guest, left behind for us. He used to read himself to sleep with it after dinner. The priest of Diessenhofen, who examined it, pronounced the opinion that it was the grossest and most damnable thing that had been conceived since the invention of the alphabet—and that too by a cleric. Pious father, I confide this abomination to your keeping. Free me from its contagion!" And she handed over to me—my *Facetiae!*

Although this surprise was probably due to the malicious mischief-making of chance rather than of the Mother Superior, I felt hurt and indignant. I began to hate the little abbess. For our writings are our own flesh and blood, and I flattered myself that in mine

I walk demurely, offending neither the modest muses nor the infallible church.

"It is well," I said. "I only wish you might be found guiltless in the second and more essential point! To the assembled people you have, in the neighborhood and under the very eyes of the council," I remarked reproachfully, "promised a miracle with so much vulgar advertising that you cannot now withhold the performance. I do not know whether that was wise. Do not marvel, Abbess, that your miracle is going to be put to the test! You have invited your own doom!"

The woman's knees knocked together and her eyes wandered. "Follow me," I said sternly, "and let us inspect the instruments of the miracle!"

She followed in dismay and we entered the sacristy, to which the genuine cross had returned, and with its rifts and cracks and gigantic shadow in the spacious dimness of the noble room was resting as mightily on the wall as if only today a despairing great sinner had seized it and had sunk to her knees under its weight, touching the stone pavement with her forehead at the moment when the Queen of Heaven appeared and succored her. I tried to raise it, but could not lift it an inch. All the more ridiculous did the outrage appear, of replacing this crushing burden with a bauble. I turned resolutely toward the high narrow door behind which I suspected the latter to be.

"The key, Abbess," I commanded. The little woman stared at me with eyes of horror, but boldly answered, "Lost, my lord bishop, more than ten years ago."

"Woman," I rejoined with terrible seriousness, "your life is at stake! Yonder dwells a retainer of my friend the count of Doccaburgo.* Thither I shall send or go for help. If there be found here a counterfeit copy of the real cross, of lighter weight, you shall be consumed by flames of fire, you sinner, like the heretic Huss, and not less guilty than he!"

There was a moment of silence. Then the woman—I know not whether with chattering teeth or with gnashing of teeth—drew forth an antique key with complicated wards and opened the door. The

---

*Supposed to be an Italian form of Toggenburg, a valley near St. Gallen. Meyer attempted but did not complete a novella about a count of Toggenburg.

result was flattering—my intelligence had not deceived me. There against the wall of the high, chimneylike room leaned a black cross with rifts and cracks, which I at once grasped and in my feeble arms lifted without difficulty. In every one of its bumps and hollows, in all details the counterfeit conformed to the model of the genuine cross, and even for a sharp eye was indistinguishable from it—only that it was ten times lighter. Whether it was hollowed out or constructed of cork or some other light material, the rush and tumble of events never permitted me to ascertain.

I admired the perfection of the imitation and the thought dawned upon me that only a great artist, only an Italian could have brought this to pass; and, enthusiastic as I am for the fame of my native land, I exclaimed, "Perfect! Masterly!"—verily, extolling not the fraud, but the art expended upon it.

With a grin, the brazen woman, who had watched me attentively, shook her finger at me and said, "Crafty joker, you have outwitted me, and I know what there will be to pay! Take your jester, whom I will fetch at once, under your arm, keep your own counsel, and God be with you on your way!" Whenever, on one of the seven hills of Rome, two augurs met and, according to an ancient saying, smiled knowingly at each other, the play of features was surely more delicate than the gross laugh which distorted the face of my abbess and was translatable into the cynical words, "We all know where Bartolo gets his wine. We are rogues all together, and no one needs to put on airs."

But meanwhile I was pondering over a punishment for the worthless woman.

Then in the silence that had suddenly ensued we heard a tripping, a whispering and tittering in the adjacent choir and surmised that we were being watched by the idle and inquisitive nuns. "By my precious maidenhood," the woman implored me, "let us go, my lord bishop! Not for the wealth of the world would I have my nuns find me here with you; for you are a handsome man and my sisters' tongues are as sharp as scissors and knives!" This scruple seemed to me well founded. I bade her depart and take her nuns with her.

After a while I too left the sacristy. But I only carefully closed the door of the room in which the sham cross was concealed, without turning the key. This I drew out; put it beneath my cloak, and let it slip into a crevice between two stalls in the choir, where, for all I know, it may still repose to this very day. I did this, however, with no definite plan, but prompted by some whispering god or goddess.

When I sat in the low-studded prioress's room, alone with my abbess and an odor of sanctity, I experienced such a longing for the innocent play of the muse and such a repugnance for the twists and turns of entrapped mendacity that I determined to make short work of the matter. The Mother Superior had to confess to me how she had been initiated into the hoary swindle, and I closed the incident with few pretorian edicts. She confessed that her predecessor in office had, when at the point of death, called her and the father confessor into secret conference, and that both had commended the inherited sham miracle to her fostering care as the economic salvation of the convent. The confessor, she volubly related, had been inexhaustible in praise of the venerable age of the fraud, its deep meaning, and instructiveness. Better and more convincingly than any sermon, he said, the phantom miracle symbolized to the people the initial difficulty and the subsequent ease of a godly life. This symbolism had so turned the head of the poor woman that in one and the same breath she affirmed that she had committed no wrong and that as a child she too had once been honest.

"I will spare you for the sake of our Mother Church, upon which the flame of your burning at the stake would cast a false light"— with these words I cut short her rustic logic, and curtly commanded her to give the counterfeit cross to the flames after the loudly trumpeted miracle had been performed once more—from motives of prudence I did not venture to prevent this—but to deliver the Plautus without delay.

Scolding and reviling me, the abbess obeyed. She submitted to the decrees of the Council of Constance as they were formulated by me, not indeed with the foreknowledge of the assembled fathers, but certainly in their spirit and in conformity to their intention.

When Brigittchen, growling like a bear, brought me the codex—I had fled to a comfortable room in the visitors' quarters situated next the wall that encircled the convent—I forced her ill-bred ladyship out of the apartment and locked myself in with the Umbrian's comic characters. Not a sound disturbed me there, except the refrain of a children's song which some peasant girls were singing in the meadow beneath my window, and this made my solitude only the more enjoyable.

After a while, to be sure, the Mother Superior, highly excited, made a great pother outside, and with desperate fists pounded upon the heavy bolted oaken door, demanding the key to the open room of the counterfeit cross. I gave her, with my regrets, the brief and veritable information that it was not in my hands, paid no further attention to her, and, myself in the seventh heaven of delight, let the miserable woman wail and groan like a soul in Purgatory. But I reveled as one bidden to a wedding feast.

A classic author newly come to light—not an obscure thinker, nor a sublime poet—no, that which lies nearest at hand and eternally fascinates, the wide, wide world, the pulse of life, the hilarious marketplaces of Rome and Athens, wit, altercation, and equivocation, the passions, the effrontery of human nature in the extenuating exaggeration of the comic mirror. While I devoured one piece I was already keeping hungry watch over the next.

I had finished the witty *Amphitruo*, the *Aulularia* with the incomparable figure of the miser lay open before me—but I stopped and leaned back in my chair; for my eyes pained me. Twilight and darkness were coming on. The girls in the meadow outside had for at least a quarter of an hour indefatigably repeated the silly ditty,

Adam, he had seven sons . . .

Now they mischievously struck up a new refrain, and with droll resoluteness they sang,

To the convent I'll not go,
I'll not be a nun, no, no!

I leaned out in order to catch sight of these little foes of celibacy and take pleasure in the contemplation of their innocence. But their game was in no wise an innocent one. Nudging each other with their elbows, and exchanging knowing glances, they sang, not without invidiousness and malice, up at a grated window, behind which they supposed Gertrude to be. Or was she already kneeling in the sacristy yonder, under the pale glimmer of the ever-burning light, according to the custom of those about to take the veil, who pass in prayer the night before their marriage to heaven? But what was that to me? I lighted the lamp and began to read the comedy of the Pot.*

Not until my lamp burned out and the letters swam before my

*The *Aulularia* (The Pot of Gold).

weary eyes did I throw myself down upon my couch and fall into a restless slumber. Soon the comic characters were again hovering about me. Here a soldier boasted with high-sounding words, there the drunken youth caressed his sweetheart, who with a graceful turn of her head met his kisses halfway. Then, without warning, there stood in the midst of the merry antique rabble a broad-shouldered, barefoot barbarian maiden girdled with a rope, brought like a slave to the mart, staring at me, as it seemed, with reproachful and threatening eyes that gleamed forth from beneath her gloomy brow.

I was frightened and awoke with a start. The morning dawned. On account of the summer sultriness I had left one half of the little window open, and from the adjacent choir of the convent chapel I heard a monotonous orison that passed over into a smothered groan and then into a violent outcry.

Interrupting himself, the narrator turned to a grave man who sat over against him and, in spite of the summer heat, had after the manner of the ancients draped the folds of his mantle about him. "My learned and far-famed friend," said he, "my great philosopher, tell me, I beseech you, what is conscience?

"Is it a universal attribute? By no means. We have all known men who had none, and, to mention only one, our holy father, John XXIII* whom we dethroned at Constance, had no conscience, but on the contrary, such a happy heart, such a cheerful, I had almost said childlike spirit, that in the midst of his evil deeds no specter disturbed his slumbers and he awoke every morning more serene than he had lain down the day before. When at the castle of Gottlieben, where he was confined, I unfolded the scroll of complaints against him and with hesitant voice and flushed face read to him the sum of his sins—ten times greater than the number attached to his papal name, *scelera horrenda, abominanda*†—he picked up a pen and to while away the time adorned a St. Barbara in his breviary with a moustache.

"No, conscience is no universal attribute, and even among us, who have a conscience, it appears as a Proteus, in changing forms. In

---

*Baldassare Cossa (ca. 1370–1419), antipope as John XXIII, who had been obliged to convene the Council. Said in Meyer's sources to have been a pirate in his youth, he was notorious for his scornful spirit, choleric temper, and immoral conduct.

†"Crimes to be dreaded, abominated."

your humble servant, for example, it awakes every time that it can embody itself in an image or in a tone. When recently I was a guest at the court of one of those petty tyrants with whom our fortunate Italy swarms, and on that balmy evening sat to wine and music with fair women on an airy balcony that jutted out from the tower of the castle over a bottomless pool of cool water, I heard a sigh from below. It was the voice of a prisoner. Banished was my joy, and I could remain there no longer. It troubled my conscience to enjoy life, kissing, drinking, and laughing so near to misery."

In the same manner I could not now endure the cry of a woman in despair so close at hand. I threw a cloak about me and stole through the dim cloister to the choir, saying to myself that while I was reading Plautus a change must have come over Gertrude: on the threshold of a decision she must have come to the incontrovertible conviction that she should surely perish in this community, in the nothingness—or worse, the corruption of the convent, confined as she should be together with the common herd, despising it and hated in her turn.

In the portal of the sacristy I stopped to listen, and saw Gertrude wringing her hands before the genuine, heavy cross. Believe me, they were bleeding, and I daresay her knees were bleeding too; for she had been upon her knees in prayer the whole night long; her voice was hoarse, and her converse with God, after her heart had sunk within her and no new words came to her lips, was convulsive and brutish, like a dying effort.

"Mary, Mother of God," she cried, "have mercy on me! Let me fall beneath the weight of thy cross; it is too heavy for me! I shudder at the thought of a cell!" And she made a motion as if she were snatching or uncoiling a serpent from about her body; and then, in a paroxysm of anguish, even suppressing her shame, she exclaimed, "What befits me is sun and cloud, sickle and scythe, husband and child . . ."

In the midst of this misery I could not restrain a smile at this human confession made to the Blessed Virgin; but the smile died on my lips. Gertrude had suddenly jumped to her feet and fixed her great eyes, weirdly staring from out her blanched face, upon a spot in the wall which was marred by I know not what red stain.

"Mary, Mother of God, have mercy on me!" she cried again. "My limbs cannot abide in the cell and I shall strike my head against the ceiling. Let me sink under the weight of thy cross; it is too heavy for me! But if thou shouldst make it light upon my shoulder without being able to make light my heart, then beware"—and she stared at the uncanny spot—"lest some morning they find me lying with a crushed head at the foot of the wall!" Infinite compassion seized me—and not compassion alone, but anxious apprehension also.

Exhausted, Gertrude had seated herself upon a chest which contained some sacred relic, and was plaiting her blond hair which, during her wrestling with God, had loosened itself from the braids. At the same time she sang to herself half sadly, half playfully, not in her robust alto, but in a high-pitched child's voice not her own,

> To the convent I must run,
> Must be a poor, unhappy nun. . . .

paraphrasing that refrain with which the peasant children had derided her.

This was madness, which sought to waylay her and slip with her into the cell. But Optimus Maximus* availed himself of me as the instrument of his will and bade me save Gertrude at any cost.

Now I, too, addressed myself in unfeigned piety to that virgin goddess whom the ancients adored as Pallas Athena and whom we call Mary. "Whoever thou art," I prayed with uplifted hands, "Wisdom, as some say, Mercy, as others affirm—it is all one; Wisdom doth not record the vow of an inexperienced child, nor will Mercy hold an adult woman bound by the foolish promise of an infant. With a smile of clemency thou wilt annul this empty bond. It is thy cause I plead, goddess. Be gracious unto me!"

Since I had given the abbess, who feared treachery, my word that I should have no further speech with Gertrude, I determined after the manner of the ancients with three symbolical actions to bring the truth home to the novice, so manifestly that even the slow wits of a peasant girl could grasp it.

Paying no attention to Gertrude, I stepped up to the cross. "When I wish to recognize an object that I have once seen, I put my mark on it," I said pedantically; and drawing my sharp dagger, forged by our

---

* "The greatest best," i.e., God.

famous fellow citizen, Pantaleone Ubbriaco* the cutler, I cut a chip of some size out from under the head and the crossbeam, as it were the armpit of the cross.

Secondly, I took five measured steps. Then I burst out laughing and began with expressive gesticulation, "That porter in the hall at Constance cut a comical figure when my luggage arrived! He surveyed the biggest piece there was, an enormous box, rolled his sleeves above his elbows, spat upon his hands—the rude fellow—and, straining every muscle for a supreme effort, raised the trifling burden of an empty chest with ease to his deluded shoulder. Ha! Ha! Ha!"

Thirdly and lastly, I placed myself in mock solemnity between the real cross and the sham cross in its unlocked abiding place, and repeatedly pointing this way and that, I oracularly murmured, "Truth in the air, falsehood in there!"—presto! and I clapped my hands, "Falsehood i' the air, truth is in there!"

Out of the corner of my eye I looked over at the novice sitting in the twilight, in order to gather from the facial expression of the young barbarian the effect of these three oracles upon her. I perceived the tension of disquieting meditation and the first flicker of blazing wrath.

Then I repaired to my room, cautiously, as I had gone forth from it, threw myself without undressing upon my couch, and enjoyed the sweet slumber of a good conscience until aroused by the hum of the multitude proceeding to the convent and by the clangor of the festal bells above my head.

When I again entered the sacristy, Gertrude, deathly pale, as though she were being led to the scaffold, was just returning from a procession to a neighboring chapel, a traditional requirement no doubt instituted to give opportunity for the fraudulent exchange of crosses. The adornment of the bride of heaven began. In the group of psalm-singing nuns the novice girded herself with the coarse, thrice-knotted rope and slowly removed the shoes from her sinewy but well-shaped feet. Now they presented to her the crown of thorns. This, by contrast to the symbolical counterfeit cross, was a wreath of hard, real thorns, bristling with sharp points. Gertrude seized it eagerly and pressed it with voluptuous cruelty so firmly upon her

---

†A fictional name; it means "drunkard."

head that the warm rain of her young blood spurted forth and in heavy drops ran down her innocent brow. Sublime wrath, a present judgment of the righteous God, gleamed destruction in the blue eyes of the peasant girl; so that the nuns began to recoil from her in fear. Six of their number, whom the abbess had presumably initiated into the pious fraud, now laid the sham cross upon her honest shoulder, with clumsy grimaces, as though they were hardly able to lift the bauble, and with such stupid hypocrisy that I verily believed I saw the truth of God in the thorny crown, openly honored and glorified by human untruthfulness, but secretly reviled.

Now everything developed with the swiftness of a thunderstorm. Gertrude cast a quick glance at the place where on the genuine cross my dagger had cut a deep mark, and found the false one unscarred. Contemptuously she let the light cross glide from her shoulder, without clasping it in her arms. Then with a shriek of derisive laughter she seized it again, and triumphantly smote it to pieces upon the stone pavement. And with a bound she stood before the door of the room in which the real, the heavy cross was concealed, opened the door, found and lifted the cross, shouted wildly for joy, as though she had discovered a treasure, raised the cross unaided to her shoulder, embraced it exultantly with her valiant arms, and turned with her burden slowly toward the choir where, as upon an open stage, she was to appear before the multitude. Breathlessly waiting, nobility, clergy, peasantry, a whole people, crowded the spacious nave of the church. Lamenting, reproving, threatening, imploring, the abbess with her nuns threw herself in the way.

But she, with gleaming eyes lifted up to heaven, cried out, "Now, Mother of God, do thou conclude this business honestly!" And then with a loud voice, "Make way!"—like a workman carrying a piece of timber through a press of people.

All gave way before her and she entered the choir, where, with a vicar of the bishop at their head, the rural clergy awaited her. All eyes were focused upon the heavy-laden shoulder and the blood-besprinkled countenance. But the true cross proved too heavy for Gertrude and no goddess made it lighter. She strode with panting bosom, ever more bent and more slowly, as though her bare feet were implanted and rooted in the floor. She stumbled a little, re-covered her balance, stumbled again, sank down upon her left knee, then upon her right, and endeavored with all her might to rise again. It was in vain. Now her left hand let go the cross and, stretched forward to reach the floor, supported for a moment the weight of her entire body. Then the arm bent at the elbow and doubled up. The head with its crown of thorns fell forward heavily and struck the stone pavement with a thud. Over the body of the exhausted victim the cross rolled ponderously, released by the right hand only after Gertrude had been stunned by the fall.

That was bloody truth, not the illusion of jugglery. One sigh rose from the breasts of a thousand witnesses.

The horrified nuns drew Gertrude forth from beneath the cross and lifted her to her feet. She had swooned in her fall, but consciousness soon returned to the sturdy maiden. She passed her hand over her forehead. Her eye fell upon the cross which had overwhelmed her. A smile of thanks flitted across her face, to the goddess whose help had not been forthcoming. Then with heavenly humor she spoke the roguish words, "Thou dost not wish me, Virgin pure! Then another will have me!"

Still wearing the crown of thorns, without appearing to feel the bloody pricks, she now set her foot upon the first of the steps that led from the choir down into the nave. At the same time her eyes wandered searchingly about the congregation, and found him, whom they sought for. A profound silence ensued. "Hans of Splügen," Gertrude began in clear and audible tones, "wilt thou take me for thy wedded wife?" "Indeed, I will, with joy a thousandfold. Come down and see!" answered a happy and convincing masculine voice from the back of the nave.

She did so and descended calmly, but radiant with joy, one step after another, once more the simple peasant, who no doubt was glad soon to forget the affecting spectacle that in her despair she had given the multitude, now that her modest human desire was granted and she was permitted to return to the everyday sphere of her humble existence. Laugh at me, if you will, Cosimo; I was disappointed. For a short space the peasant girl had appeared to my excited senses as the incarnation of a higher being, as a demonic creature, as Truth exultantly unmasking Falsehood. But "What is truth?" asked Pilate.

Pondering this and following Gertrude from the choir down into the nave, I was plucked in the sleeve by my messenger, who informed me of the sudden election of Otto Colonna to the papacy by enthusiastic acclamation, and of sundry remarkable circumstances.

When I looked up again, Gertrude had vanished. But the excited multitude was shouting and clamoring with divided opinion. From yonder group of men the words resounded, "Hag! Witch!" They meant the abbess. Here women's voices shrilled, "Sinner! Impudent hussy!" That was Gertrude. Whether the former surmised the pious fraud, or the latter believed the miracle to be desecrated by Gertrude's worldliness—no matter; in either case the spell of the relic was broken and the career of the miracle closed.

Coarsely reviled by the people, the valiant Brigittchen began to retort in kind, and the dumbfounded faces of the attending priests showed a complete scale of expressions from sly complicity down to the most incorruptible stupidity.

I felt my dignity as a cleric and put an end to the abomination. Mounting the pulpit, I solemnly announced to assembled Christendom, *"Habemus pontificem Dominum Othonem Colonna!"** and struck up a resounding Te Deum, in which first the chorus of nuns and then the entire congregation lustily joined. After the hymn had been sung, nobles and peasants hastened to mount their horses or to set out afoot on the way to Constance, where, after the *triregnum*† had come to an end, the blessing conveyed to the city and to the world must be trebly strong.

I, for my part, slipped back into the cloister in order with all secrecy to get the Plautus that was in my room. Going furtively away again, with the codex under my arm, I happened upon the abbess who, economical as she was, was carefully carrying the pieces of the sham cross in a great basket to the kitchen. I congratulated her upon the denouement. But Brigittchen believed herself swindled and yelled at me in fury, "Go to the devil, you two Italian scoundrels," meaning, so far as I could judge, the Umbrian Marcus Accius Plautus and the Tuscan Poggio Bracciolini, your fellow citizen. A pretty blond boy, another curly-head, whom Hans of Splügen, before his departure with Gertrude, had thoughtfully engaged for me, then led out my mule, which carried me back to Constance.

---

*"We have a Pontiff, Lord Otho Colonna!"
†The schismatic reign of Gregory XII and the two antipopes.

*Plaudite amici!** My story is at an end. When the Council of Constance, which lasted longer than this little narrative, was likewise at an end, I returned with my gracious master, His Holiness Martin V, over the mountains, and found as our host and hostess in the inn at Splügen, to the north of the dangerous pass, Hänsel and Gertrude in health and prosperity—she not in a stifling cell but in a windswept rocky valley, with a child at her breast and the conjugal cross resting lightly upon her shoulder.

"Let this *Facetia inedita,* illustrious Cosimo, be a not unwelcome supplement to the codex of Plautus which at this hour I present to you, or rather to our native land, whose Father you are, and to learning, to which your halls with their store of treasures are always open.

"It was my intention to bequeath the unique manuscript to you, lest, as a living donor, I should invite the tenfold greater recompense with which you are wont in your incorrigible generosity to reward every gift presented to you in homage. But who knows"—Poggio sighed resignedly—"whether my sons would respect my last will?"

Cosimo replied amiably, "I thank you for both, your Plautus and your *Facetia*. Without a scruple you lived this and accomplished it, young as you then were. As a mature man you have recounted it to us in the wisdom of your years. This toast"—he lifted a noble bowl enclasped by a laughing satyr—"I pledge to my honest Poggio and his blond barbarian maiden!"

They drank and laughed. Then the conversation passed quickly from Plautus to the thousand discovered treasures and unrolled parchments of antiquity, and to the greatness of the century.

Translated by William Guild Howard

*"Applaud, friends!"

Flagman Thiel

Gerhart Hauptmann

1

Every Sunday Thiel, the flagman, was to be seen sitting in a pew in the church at Neu Zittau.* If he was absent, you might be sure he was on Sunday duty or else—as happened twice in the course of ten years—at home ill in bed. Once a great lump of coal from the tender of a passing locomotive had struck his leg and sent him rolling into the ditch at the bottom of the embankment. The second time the trouble was a wine bottle that had come flying from an express and had hit him in the middle of his chest. Nothing but these two mishaps had ever succeeded in keeping Thiel from church the instant he was off duty.

The first five years he had had to come alone to Neu Zittau from Schön-Schornstein, a small collection of homes on the Spree. Then, one fine day, he appeared in the company of a delicate, sickly looking woman. The people thought she ill suited his herculean build. And on a later Sunday afternoon, at the altar of the church, he solemnly gave her his hand and pledged his troth.

So, for two years, the delicate young creature sat beside him in the pew. For two years her fine, hollow-cheeked face bent over the ancient hymnal beside his weather-tanned face.

And suddenly the flagman was to be seen sitting alone, as of old.

On one of the preceding weekdays the bell had tolled for the dead. That was all.

---

*All the place names are locations on the Spree River, southeast of Berlin, near the railroad line to Frankfurt on the Oder and Breslau, where Hauptmann lived at this time in the village of Erkner.

Scarcely any change, so the people declared, was to be observed in the flagman. The brass buttons of his clean Sunday uniform were as brightly polished as before, his red hair as sleekly pomaded and as neatly parted, military fashion. Only he held his broad, hairy neck a little bent, and sang more eagerly, and listened to the sermon more devoutly. The general opinion was that his wife's death had not hit him very hard. A view that was strengthened when in the course of the year he married again. The second wife was a strong, stout milkmaid from Altegrund.

Even the pastor felt free to express his doubts when Thiel came to announce his engagement.

"So soon again? You really want to marry so soon again?"

"I can't keep my house running, sir, with the wife who's gone."

"To be sure. But I mean—aren't you in a bit of a hurry?"

"It's on account of the boy."

Thiel's wife had died in childbirth. The boy had lived and been named Tobias.

"Yes, yes, to be sure, the boy," said the pastor, with a gesture clearly revealing that he had not thought of the infant until that moment. "That throws a different light on the matter. What have you been doing with him until now while you are at work?"

Thiel explained that he left Tobias in the care of an old woman. Once she had nearly let him get burned, and another time had let him roll from her lap to the floor. Fortunately the child had not been badly hurt—only a big surface bruise. Such a state of things could not continue, the flagman said, especially as the child, being delicate, required particular attention. For that reason and also because he had sworn to his wife on her deathbed that he would always take exceedingly good care of the child, he had decided to marry again.

The people found absolutely nothing to cavil with in the new couple that now visited the church regularly on Sundays. The milkmaid seemed to have been made for the flagman. She was but a few inches shorter than he and exceeded him in girth, while her features were just as coarsely molded as his, though, in contrast, they lacked soul.

If Thiel had cherished the desire for an inveterate worker and paragon of a housewife in his second wife, then his hopes were surprisingly fulfilled. However, without knowing it, he had purchased three other qualities, too, a hard, domineering disposition, quarrelsomeness, and brutal passion.

Within half a year the whole place knew who was lord and master in the flagman's little house. Thiel became the object of general pity. It was a piece of good luck for the "creature," the exercised husbands said, that she had got such a gentle lamb as Thiel for a husband. With other men she wouldn't come off so easy, she'd receive some hard knocks. An animal like that had to be managed— with blows, if need be—a good sound thrashing to make her behave herself.

But Thiel, despite his sinewy arms, was not the man to thrash his wife. What got the people so annoyed seemed to cause him no perturbation. As a rule, he let his wife's endless sermonizings pass without a word, and when he did occasionally make a response, the slow drag of his speech and the quiet coolness of his tone contrasted oddly with her high-pitched bawling.

The outside world seemed scarcely to touch him. It was as though he carried something within him that heavily overbalanced all of the evil it brought by good.

Nevertheless, for all his phlegm, there were occasions on which he would not allow things to pass—when little Toby was concerned. Then his childlike goodness, his yieldingness took on a dash of determination that even so untamed a temperament as Lena's did not dare to oppose.

The moments, however, in which he revealed this side of his character became rarer and rarer, and finally ceased completely. During the first year of his marriage he had shown a certain suffering resistance to Lena's tyranny. In the second year this also ceased completely. After a quarrel he no longer left for his work with his earlier indifference in case he had not previously placated her. Often he even stooped to beg her to be kind again. His solitary post in the heart of the Brandenburg pine forest was no longer, as it had been, the place where he would rather be than anywhere else on earth. The quiet devout thoughts of his dead wife were crossed by thoughts of the living wife. It was not with repugnance, as in the first months of his marriage, that he trod the homeward way, but often with passionate haste, after having counted the hours and minutes till the time of his release.

He who had been united to his first wife by a more spiritual love fell into his second wife's grip through the power of crude impulses. He became almost wholly dependent upon her.

At times he experienced pangs of conscience at this turn, and resorted to a number of unusual devices to bring about a change. For one thing, he declared his hut and his beat to be holy ground, dedicated exclusively to the shades of the dead. And he actually succeeded by all sorts of pretexts in preventing Lena from accompanying him there. He hoped he should always be able to keep her off. The very number of his hut and the direction in which it lay were still unknown to her.

Thus, by conscientiously dividing the time at his disposal between the living and the dead, Thiel actually succeeded in soothing his conscience.

Often, to be sure, especially in moments of solitary devotion, when he felt the tie between him and his dead wife deeply and warmly, he beheld his present condition in the light of truth, and he experienced disgust.

If he was doing day duty, his spiritual intercourse with her was limited to dear recollections of their life together. But in the dark, when a snowstorm raged among the pines and along the embankment, his hut at midnight, by the light of his lantern, became a chapel.

With a faded photograph of the departed before him on the table, and the hymnal and the Bible turned open, he alternately read and sang the whole night long, interrupted only at intervals by the trains rushing past. He would attain a state of ecstasy in which he had visions of his wife standing there in person.

In its remoteness this post, which Thiel had held for ten years, contributed to the intensification of his mystic inclinations. To the north, east, south and west, it was separated by a walk of at least three quarters of an hour from the nearest habitation. It lay in the very heart of the forest. But there was a grade crossing there, and Thiel's duty was to lower and raise the gates.

In the summer days passed, in the winter weeks, without a single person except other railroad workers setting foot on Thiel's beat. Almost the only changes in the solitude came from the weather and the periodic mutations of the seasons. It was not difficult to recall the events—besides the two mishaps to his body—that had broken into the regular course of the hours of service.

Four years previous the imperial special bearing the Kaiser to Breslau had gone dashing by. Once on a winter's night an express had run over a stag. And once on a hot summer's day, as Thiel was making an inspection of his beat, he had found a corked bottle of wine. It was scorching hot to the touch, and Thiel had esteemed its contents because when he uncorked it a geyser spouted out, showing that the stuff was well fermented. Thiel had laid the bottle on the edge of a pond in the woods to cool off. Somehow it had disappeared from the spot, and even after the passage of years Thiel never thought of that bottle without a pang of regret.

A bit of diversion was provided by a spring behind the hut. From time to time men at work on the road bed or on the telegraph lines came for a drink, and stayed, of course, to talk a while. Sometimes the forest ranger would also come when he was thirsty.

Tobias developed slowly. It was not until he was two years old that he learned to walk and talk. For his father he displayed unusual affection, and as he grew more understanding Thiel's old love for his child was reawakened. Accordingly Lena's love for the child decreased, turning into unmistakable dislike when the next year a baby boy was born to her, too.

After that bad times began for Tobias. In his father's absence he was particularly made to suffer. He had to dedicate his feeble powers unrewarded to the service of the little cry-baby. He became more and more exhausted. His head grew too large round, and his fiery red hair, with the chalky face beneath, on top of his wretched little body, made an unlovely and pitiful impression. When the backward mite was seen dragging himself down to the Spree with his baby brother bursting with health in his arms, curses were muttered behind the windows of the cottages. But no one ever ventured to utter the curses in the open.

Thiel, who was most of all concerned, seemed to have no eyes for what was going on, and refused to understand the hints of well-meaning neighbors.

2

Once Thiel returned from night duty at seven o'clock of a June morning. Directly Lena had greeted him, she burst into her usual complaining.

A few weeks before notice had been given that they could no longer cultivate the piece of land which they rented for planting potatoes for their own use, and no other land had been found to replace it. Though everything pertaining to the land was part of Lena's duty, Thiel nonetheless had to listen to a hundred iterations that he would be to blame if they had to buy ten sacks of potatoes for dear money. Thiel merely muttered a word or two. Paying slight attention to Lena's tirade, he went straight over to Tobias's bed, which he shared with the boy on nights when he was off duty.

He sat down and watched the sleeping child with an anxious expression on his good face. For a while he contented himself with chasing away the persistent flies, then he woke him up. A touching joy lighted up the boy's blue, deep-set eyes. He snatched for his father's hand, and a pitiful smile drew the corners of his mouth. Thiel helped him put on his few bits of clothing. Suddenly a shadow chased across his face. He noticed that his son's right cheek was slightly swollen and bore finger marks designed white on red.

At breakfast Lena brought up the same subject again, pursuing it with even more vigor. Thiel cut her off by telling her that the railroad inspector had given him for nothing the use of a stretch of land alongside the tracks not far from his hut, probably because it was too distant for the inspector to use for himself.

Lena was incredulous, then gradually her doubts melted away and she became noticeably good-humored. How big was the lot? How good was the soil? She plied him with questions. And when she learned that there were actually two dwarf fruit trees on the land, she fairly lost her head. At length the questions were all asked, and as the shopkeeper's bell, which could be heard in every house in the place, kept ringing incessantly, Lena ran forth to ferret out the latest news.

While she remained in the dark shop crowded with wares, Thiel occupied himself at home with Tobias, who sat on his knee playing with pinecones that his father had brought from the woods.

"What do you want to be when you grow up?" asked Thiel. The stereotyped question was invariably answered by the equally stereotyped reply, "Railroad inspector." It was not asked in fun. The flagman's dreams actually soared so high. It was in all seriousness that he cherished the hope that with God's help Tobias would become something extraordinary. The instant "railroad inspector" left the child's bloodless lips, Thiel's face brightened, fairly radiated bliss.

"Go play now, Tobias," he said soon afterward, lighting his pipe with a shaving kindled at the hearth fire. The boy showing shy pleasure went out.

Thiel undressed and got into bed. For a long while he lay staring up at the low, cracked ceiling. Finally he fell asleep and woke up shortly before twelve o'clock. While Lena in her noisy fashion prepared the midday meal, he dressed and went out on the street to fetch Tobias, whom he found scratching plaster out of a hole in the wall and stuffing it into his mouth. Thiel led him by the hand past the eight houses that constituted the hamlet down to the Spree. The stream lay dark and glassy between sparsely foliaged poplars. Thiel sat down on a block of granite close to the water's edge.

Every fair day the villagers were accustomed to see him on this spot. The children were devoted to him. They called him Father Thiel. He taught them games that he remembered from his own childhood, reserving, however, the best of his memories for Tobias. He whittled him arrows that flew farther than those of the other boys, he carved him willow pipes, and even deigned to sing ditties in his rusty bass, and tap the beat with the horn handle of his knife against the bark of a tree.

The people thought him silly. They blamed him. They could not understand how he could go to so much trouble for the little brats. Though they should have been richly content, seeing that the children were well taken care of when in his charge. Besides, Thiel did more than play with them. He took up serious things, too. He heard the older ones recite their lessons, helped them study their Bible and hymn verses, and spelled out c-a-t and d-o-g with the younger ones.

After the midday meal Thiel rested again a while, drank a cup of coffee, and began to prepare for work. It took him a lot of time, as for everything he did. Each move had been regulated for years. The objects carefully spread out on the walnut dresser went into his various pockets always in the same order—knife, notebook, comb, a horse's tooth, an old watch in a case, and a small book wrapped in red paper. The last was handled with especial care. During the night it lay under Thiel's pillow, and by day was carried in his breast pocket. On a label pasted on the cover was written in Thiel's awkward yet flourishing hand, "Savings Account of Tobias Thiel."

The clock on the wall with the long pendulum and sickly yellow face indicated a quarter to five when Thiel left. A small boat, his own property, ferried him across the Spree. Arrived at the further side, he stood still a moment and listened back in the direction he had come from. Then he turned into a broad path through the woods and within a few moments reached the depths of the deep-booming pine forest, its mass of needles like a dark green undulating sea.

The moist layers of needles and moss made a carpet as inaudible to the tread as felt. Thiel made his way without looking up, now past the rusty brown columns of the older trees, now between the thickly enmeshed younger growth, and farther on across broad stretches of nursery, overshadowed by a few tall slim pines for the protection of the young saplings. A transparent bluish haze rising from the earth laden with mingled fragrances blurred the forms of the trees. A heavy, drab sky hung low over the tops. Flocks of cawing crows seemed to bathe in the gray of the atmosphere. Black puddles filled the depressions in the path and cast a still drearier reflection of a dreary nature.

"Fearful weather,"* thought Thiel when he roused out of deep reflection and looked up.

Suddenly his thoughts were deflected. A dim feeling came to him that he must have forgotten something. And surely enough, when he searched his pockets, he discovered that he had not brought along the sandwich that he required on account of the long hours on duty. For a while he stood undecided. Then turned and hurried back.

In a short while he reached the Spree, rowed himself across in a few powerful strokes, and without delay, perspiring from every pore, ascended the gradual slope of the village street. The shopkeeper's old, mangy poodle lay in the middle of the road. On the tarred board fence around a cottager's yard perched a hooded crow. It spread its feathers, shook itself, nodded, uttered an earsplitting caw, caw, and with a slapping sound of its wings rose in the air and let the wind drive it in the direction of the forest.

Nothing was to be seen of the villagers—about twenty fishermen and lumbermen with their families.

---

*This is a reading that was introduced into modern editions *(furchtbares Wetter)*. The first edition reads "fruitful weather" *(fruchtbares Wetter)*, which is probably to be preferred.

The stillness was broken—by a high-pitched voice. The flagman involuntarily stopped. A volley of violent, jangling tones assailed his ears. It seemed to come from the open dormer window of a low house that he knew only too well.

Treading as silently as possible, he glided nearer. Now he quite clearly recognized his wife's voice. Only a few steps more, and he could understand almost everything she said.

"You horrid little beast, you! Is the poor baby to scream its belly inside out from hunger? What? Just you wait—just you wait. I'll teach you to mind. You'll never forget."

For a few moments there was silence. Then a sound could be heard like the beating out of clothes. And the next instant another hailstorm of abuse was let loose.

"You miserable little puppy, you! Do you think I'll let my own child die of hunger because of a mean little thing like you?—Shut your mouth!" A slight whimper had been audible. "If you don't shut your mouth, I'll give you something that'll keep you going a whole week."

The whimpering did not subside.

The flagman felt his heart pounding in irregular beats. He began to tremble slightly. His glance fastened on the ground as though his mind were wandering, and again and again his coarse, hard hand went up to his freckled forehead to brush back a dank strand of hair. For a second he was about to give way. He stood shaken by a convulsion that swelled his muscles and drew his fingers into a clenched ball. The convulsion subsided. He was left in a state of dull exhaustion.

With unsteady steps he entered the narrow, brick-paved vestibule and slowly, wearily mounted the creaking wooden stairs.

"Pugh, pugh, pugh!" You could hear how with every sign of scorn and fury some one spat out three times in succession. "You horrid, mean, sneaking, cowardly, low-down good-for-nothing!" The epithets followed one another in crescendo, the voice that uttered them breaking several times from strain. "You want to hit my boy, do you? You ugly little brat you, don't you dare to hit the poor helpless child on its mouth. What's that? Huh? If I wanted to soil my hands on you, I'd—"

At that moment the door to the living room was opened, and the rest of the sentence remained unspoken on the frightened woman's tongue. She was livid with passion, her lips twitched evilly. Her right hand raised in the air sank and grasped the saucepan with milk in it. She tried to pour some into the baby's bottle, but desisted as the larger part of the milk flowed down the outside of the bottle on to the table. She clutched at various objects without being able to hold them any length of time. Finally she recovered herself sufficiently to address her husband with violence. What did he mean by coming home at this unusual hour? Was he thinking of spying on her? That would be too much. This last was directly followed by the asseveration that she had a clear conscience and need not lower her eyes before any one.

Thiel scarcely heard what she said. He gave a hasty look at Toby, who was crying aloud, and for a few moments he had to restrain forcibly something dreadful rising within him. Then the old phlegm spread over his taut features, and at the same time a furtive, lustful light came into his eyes. His glance played over his wife's heavy limbs while she with averted face, bustled about still making an effort to be composed. Her full, half-bared breasts swelled with excitement and threatened to burst her corset. Her drawn-up skirts accentuated the width of her broad hips. A force seemed to emanate from the woman, indomitable, inescapable. Thiel felt himself powerless to cope with it. Tightly, like a cobweb, yet firmly as a mesh of steel, it laid itself around him, chaining him down, robbing him of his strength. In this condition he was incapable of saying a word to her, much less a harsh word.

Thus it was that Tobias, bathed in tears, cowering in a corner, saw his father go over to the oven bench without looking round at him, pick up the forgotten sandwich, hold it out to Lena by way of the only explanation, give a short, distraught nod of his head in good-bye, and disappear.

3

Thiel made all possible haste back to his solitary post in the woods. Even so he was a quarter of an hour late. The assistant who relieved him, a consumptive, the victim of the unavoidably rapid changes in temperature to which the work subjected one, was waiting prepared to leave on the sanded little platform of the hut, on which the number, black on white, gleamed from a distance between the tree trunks.

The two men shook hands, exchanged a few brief reports, and parted, the one disappearing within the hut, the other taking the continuation of the road by which Thiel had come. His convulsive cough sounded further and further away among the trees, until finally the one human sound in the solitude fell silent.

Thiel as always, after his fashion, set about preparing the small square room for the night. He worked mechanically, his mind occupied with the impression of the past hour.

First he laid his supper on the narrow, brown-painted table beside one of the windows like slits through which the stretch of track could be conveniently viewed. Next he kindled a fire in the small, rusty stove and placed a pot of cold water on top. After that he straightened out his utensils, a shovel, a spade, a wrench and a few other things, and then cleaned his lantern and filled it with fresh oil.

Scarcely were his arrangements completed when the signal rang shrilly, three times, and three times again, to announce that a train from the direction of Breslau was pulling out of the near station. Thiel showed no hurry, allowing a few minutes to pass before emerging from the hut with flag and cartridge case in his hand. And it was with a lazy, dragging shuffle that he walked along the narrow strip of sand to the crossing, about sixty feet away. Though there was scarcely any traffic along the road at that point, still he conscientiously let down and raised the gates before and after the passage of each train.

This operation now concluded, he leaned idly on one of the black-and-white barred anchor-posts.

The tracks cut in a straight line right and left into the green forest stretching beyond the reach of the eye. On each side the mass of needles stood apart to leave, as it were, an avenue free for the reddish brown graveled embankment. The black tracks running parallel looked like the strands of a huge iron net drawn together to a point on the horizon in the extreme south and north.

The wind had risen, it drove light waves of mist along the edge of the forest into the distance. A humming came from the telegraph poles alongside the tracks. On the wires that stretched from pole to pole like the sustaining cords spun by a huge spider perched swarms of chirping birds. A woodpecker flew with a laugh over Thiel's head. The man did not so much as look up.

The sun hanging from under the edge of vast masses of clouds and about to sink into the dark green sea of treetops poured streams of purple over the forest. The pillared arcades of the pine trunks on the yon side of the embankment took fire as from within and glowed like metal. The tracks, too, began to glow, turning into the semblance of fiery snakes. They were the first to pale. The glow, leaving the ground, slowly ascended upward, resigning first the bodies of the trees, then the lower tops to the cold light of dissolution. For a while a reddish sheen lingered on the extreme crowns.

Silently and solemnly was the exalted drama enacted.

The flagman still stood at the gates motionless. At length he made a step forward. A dark point on the horizon where the tracks joined became more than a point. Increasing from second to second it yet seemed to stand still. Then of a sudden it acquired movement, and drew nearer. A vibrating and humming went through the tracks, a rhythmic clang, a muted thunder. It grew louder and louder until at length it sounded not unlike the hoofbeats of a storming cavalry regiment. From a distance the air pulsated intermittently with a panting and a blustering. Then suddenly the serenity of the forest snapped. A mad uproar filled the welkin, the tracks curved, the earth shook—a blast of air, a cloud of dust and steam and smoke— and the snorting monster had gone by.

The noises waned as they had waxed. The exhalations thinned away. Shrunken to a point again the train vanished in the distance, and the old solemn hush again settled upon this corner of the forest.

"Minna," whispered the flagman, as if coming out of a dream.

He returned to the hut, where he brewed himself some weak coffee, then sat down, sipping from time to time and all the while staring at a dirty piece of newspaper that he had picked up on his round.

Gradually a curious unrest came upon him. Attributing it to the heat from the stove, he tore off his coat and waistcoat. That proving to be of no help, he got up, took a spade from a corner, and went out to the lot that the inspector had presented to him.

It was a narrow strip of soil, overgrown with weeds. The blossoms on the two fruit trees were like snowy white foam. Thiel calmed down, a quiet content possessed him.

To work now.

The spade cut into the earth with a crunch. The wet clods flew and crumbled as they fell.

For a long while he dug uninterruptedly. Then he paused and said to himself audibly, shaking his head gravely:

"No, no, it won't do. No, it won't do."

The thought had suddenly struck him that Lena would be coming there often to look after the lot, and his accustomed life would be seriously disturbed. At one blow pleasure in the possession of the bit of ground turned into distaste. Hastily, as if he had been about to do wrong, he ripped the spade out of the earth and carried it back to the hut.

Again he sank into gloomy reflections. Almost without knowing why, he could not endure the prospect of Lena's presence for whole days at a stretch while he was on duty. Much as he might try he could not reconcile himself to the idea. It seemed to him he had something valuable to defend, against someone who was attempting to violate his holiest sanctuary. Involuntarily his muscles tautened in a slight cramp, and a short, defiant laugh escaped him.

The sound of his own laughter was alarming. He looked about and lost the thread of his thoughts. Finding it again he went back to the same dismal broodings.

Then suddenly a heavy black curtain was torn apart, his eyes so long befogged had now a clear view. He had the sensation of awakening from a deathlike sleep that had lasted two years. With an incredulous shake of the head he contemplated all the awful things he must have been guilty of in that condition. The long-suffering of his child, which the impressions of the earlier afternoon should only have confirmed, now were clearly revealed to his soul. Pity and penitence overcame him, and also great shame, that all this long while he had lived in disgraceful resignation, never taking the dear, helpless child's part, not even finding the strength to admit how much the child suffered.

From the self-tormenting contemplation of his sins of omission a great tiredness came over him. He fell asleep, bent over the table with his forehead resting on his hand.

For a long while he lay like that, and several times uttered the name Minna in a choked voice.

A rushing and roaring filled his ears, as of great masses of water. He tore his eyes open and looked about. Darkness enveloped him. His limbs gave way, the sweat of terror oozed from every pore, his pulse beat irregularly, his face was wet with tears.

He wanted to look toward the door, but in the inky darkness did not know which way to turn. He rose reeling. And still terror possessed him. The woods outside boomed like the ocean, the wind drove rain and sleet against the panes. Thiel groped about helplessly. For a moment he felt himself to be drowning. Then suddenly there was a dazzling bluish flare, as of drops of supernatural light falling down into the earth's atmosphere to be instantly extinguished by it.

The moment sufficed to restore the flagman to reason. He fumbled for his lantern and found it. At the same instant the thunder awoke on the farthest edge of the heavens over Brandenburg. At first a dull, restrained rumble, it rolled nearer in surging metallic waves, until overhead it discharged itself in great peals, menacing roars that shook the earth to its foundations.

The windowpanes clattered. Thiel lighted the lantern, and his first glance after he regained self-control was at the clock. In a bare five minutes the express was due. Thinking he had failed to hear the signal, he made for the crossing as quickly as the dark and the storm permitted. Just as he was letting down the gates the signal rang—the sound was scattered by the wind in all directions.

The pine trees bent over, their branches scraped against each other with uncanny creakings and squeakings. For a few moments the moon was visible, a pale yellow chalice amid the torn clouds. By its light could be seen the wind's mauling of the black treetops. The foliage of the birches along the embankment waved and fluttered like ghostly horses' tails. Beneath them lay the rails gleaming wet, absorbing the pale moonlight in spots here and there.

Thiel tore the cap from his head. The rain soothed him. It ran down his face mingled with tears.

His brain was in a ferment with confused recollections of his dream. Tobias seemed to be undergoing maltreatment, and such horrible maltreatment that the mere thought of it stopped his heart.

Another vision was clearer, of his dead wife. She had come from somewhere along the railroad tracks. She had looked very ill and was wearing rags for clothes. Without looking round she passed the hut, and then—here his memory became vague—she had great difficulty somehow in proceeding, she even collapsed several times.

Thiel pondered. And then he knew that she was in flight. No doubt of it. Else why those anxious backward glances as she dragged herself forward with her legs giving way under her? Oh, those awful looks of hers!

But there was something that she was carrying, wrapped in cloth, something limp, bloody, pale. And the way she looked down on it reminded him of a past scene.

A dying woman who kept her gaze fixed on her newborn babe with an expression of the deepest pain, intolerable torture. It was an expression he could no more forget than that he had a father and a mother.

Where had she gone? He did not know. But one thing was clear in his soul: she had withdrawn from him, disregarded him, dragged herself further and further away into the dark, stormy night. "Minna, Minna," he had cried, and the sound of his own cry awakened him.

Two round red lights like the staring eyes of a huge monster penetrated the dark. A bloody sheen glided in advance, transforming the drops of rain in its course into drops of blood. A veritable rain of blood seemed to descend from heaven.

Horror fell upon Thiel, mounting and mounting as the train drew nearer. Dream and reality fused into one. He still saw the woman wandering down the tracks. His hand wavered toward the cartridge case, as if to stop the speeding train. Fortunately it was too late. Lights flared before his eyes, the train had rushed past.

The remainder of the night there was little peace for Thiel. He felt a great urgency to be at home, a great longing to see little Toby, from whom, it seemed to him, he had been separated for years. Several times, in his growing anxiety over the child's condition he was tempted to quit duty.

To shorten the hours until his release he determined as soon as day dawned to walk his beat. So, with a cane in one hand and a large iron wrench in the other, he went out into the dirty gray twilight and stepped along on the spine of a rail, halting every now and then to tighten a bolt with the wrench or to hammer at one of the fishplates that held the rails together.

The wind and rain had stopped, fragments of a pale blue sky became visible between rifts in the banked clouds. The monotonous tap-tap of his soles on the hard metal and the sleepy drip-drop from the wet trees gradually calmed Thiel.

At six o'clock he was relieved. Without delay he started home.

It was a glorious Sunday morning. The clouds had broken and drifted beyond the horizon. The sun, gleaming like a great bloodred gem, poured veritable masses of light upon the forest. Through the network of the branches the beams shot in sharp straight lines casting a glow upon islets of lacy ferns and here and there turning silvery gray patches on the ground into bits of coral. The tops of the trees, the trunks, the grass shed fire like dew. The world seemed to lie under a deluge of light. And the freshness of the air penetrated to the very core of one's being.

Even in Thiel's brain the fantasies of the night could not but grow pale. And when he entered the room where little Toby was lying in bed with the sun shining on him and more color in his cheeks than usual, they disappeared completely.

To be sure, in the course of the day Lena thought she noticed something odd about him. At church instead of looking in the book he observed her sidewise, and in the middle of the day, when Toby was supposed as usual to carry the baby out on the street, he took it from the boy's arms and laid it in her lap. Otherwise there was nothing conspicuously different about him.

Having no chance to take a nap and as he was to do day duty that week, he went to bed early, at nine o'clock. Exactly as he was about to fall asleep, his wife told him that she intended to accompany him the next morning to dig the lot and plant potatoes.

Thiel winced. He awoke completely, but kept his eyes shut.

Lena went on. If the potatoes were to amount to anything, she said, it was high time to do the planting. And she would have to take the children along because it would probably occupy her the entire day.

Thiel muttered a few unintelligible words, to which she paid no attention. She had turned her back and by the light of a tallow candle was occupied with unfastening her corset and letting down her skirts. Suddenly, without herself knowing why, she turned round and beheld her husband's ashen face distorted by a play of passions. He had raised himself partly, supporting himself by his hands on the edge of the bed, his burning eyes fastened upon her.

"Thiel!" cried the woman, half in anger, half in fear.

Like a somnambulist who hears his name called, Thiel came out of his daze. He stammered something, threw his head back on the pillow, and pulled the quilt over his ears.

Lena was the first to get up the next morning. She went about noiselessly, making the necessary preparations for the excursion. The baby was put into the perambulator, then Tobias was awakened and dressed. He smiled when he was told where he was going.

When everything was ready and even the coffee was made and set on the table, Thiel awoke. His first sensation on seeing the arrangements was of displeasure. He wanted to protest, but the proper opening refused to frame itself. Besides, what arguments could he advance that would weigh with Lena? And there was his child's little face beaming with joy, growing happier and happier each instant, until Thiel, from the sight of his delight in the approaching excursion, could not think of opposing it.

Nevertheless, on the way through the woods, as he pushed the baby carriage with difficulty through the deep soil, Thiel was not free from anxiety.

Tobias gathered flowers and laid them in the carriage. He was happier than almost any time his father had seen him. In his little brown plush cap he hopped about among the ferns and tried, helplessly to be sure, to catch the glassy winged dragonflies that darted above them.

As soon as they reached the spot, Lena made a survey. She threw the sack of seed potatoes on the grassy edge of a small grove of birches, knelt down, and let the darkish soil run between her fingers.

Thiel watched her eagerly.

"Well," he said, "how is it?"

"Every bit as good as the corner on the Spree."

A burden fell from the flagman. He contentedly scratched the stubble on his face. He had feared she would be dissatisfied.

After hastily devouring a thick slice of bread the woman tossed aside head cloth and jacket, and began to spade up the earth with the speed and endurance of a machine. At regular intervals she

straightened up and took several deep breaths. But the pauses were never for long, except when she had to suckle the baby, which she did quickly, with panting, perspiring breasts.

After a while the flagman called to her from the platform in front of the hut:

"I must inspect the beat. I'm taking Tobias with me."

"What!" she screamed back. "Nonsense! Who'll stay with the baby? You'll come here," she shouted still louder.

But the flagman as if not hearing walked off with Toby. For a moment she considered whether she should not run after the two, then desisted because of the loss of time.

Thiel walked down the tracks with his son. The boy was quite excited, everything was so new and strange. Those narrow black rails warmed by the sun—he could not comprehend what they could be meant for. And he kept up an incessant stream of funny questions. What struck him as strangest of all was the resonance of the telegraph poles.

Thiel knew the sound of each pole on his beat so well that with closed eyes he could tell at exactly what spot he stood. And now he stopped several times, holding Tobias by the hand, to listen to the wonderful tones that came from the wood like sonorous chorals from inside a church. The pole at the extreme south end made a particularly full, beautiful sound. It was a mingling of tones that seemed to come without pausing for breath.

Tobias ran round the weathered post to see if he could not through some hole discover the originators of the lovely music. His father listening sank into a devout mood, as in church. He distinguished a voice that reminded him of his dead wife, and fancied it was a choir of blessed spirits, her voice mingling with the others. A deep emotion, a great yearning brought the tears to his eyes.

Tobias asked to be allowed to gather the flowers in the field alongside the tracks. Thiel as always let the child have his way.

Fragments of the blue sky seemed to have dropped on to the meadow, so thickly was it strewn with small, blue blossoms. Like colored pennants the butterflies fluttered and floated among the shining white trunks of the birches. The delicate green foliage gave forth a soft rustle.

Tobias plucked flowers. His father watched him meditatively. Oc-

casionally the flagman raised his eyes and searched between the leaves for a glimpse of the sky, which held the golden sunlight like a huge, spotless bowl.

"Father," said the child, pointing to a brown squirrel which with small scratching sounds was darting up a solitary pine tree, "Father, is that the good Lord?"

"Silly boy," was all that Thiel could find to reply as bits of loosened bark fell from the trunk of the tree to his feet.

Lena was still digging when Thiel and Tobias returned. She had already spaded up half the plot!

The trains passed at intervals. Each time they rushed by Tobias watched with mouth agape. Even his stepmother was amused by the funny faces he made.

The midday meal, consisting of potatoes and a remnant of roast pork, was consumed inside the hut. Lena was in good spirits. Even Thiel seemed ready to resign himself to the inevitable with good grace. While they ate, he entertained his wife by telling her various things connected with his work. Could she, for instance, imagine that there were forty-six screws in one rail, and more like that.

By mealtime the spading had been done, and in the afternoon Lena was going to sow the potatoes. This time, insisting that Tobias must look after the baby, she took him along.

"Watch out!" Thiel called after her, suddenly gripped by concern. "Watch out that he doesn't go too close to the tracks."

A shrug of Lena's shoulders was her only answer.

The signal rang for the Silesian express. Scarcely had Thiel taken his place in readiness at the gates when the approaching rumble became audible. Within a fraction of a minute he could see the train. On it came, the black funnel spitting steam in countless puffs, one chasing upward after the other. There! One-two-three milk white geysers gushing up straight as candles—the engine whistling. Three times in succession, short, shrill, alarming.

"They're putting on the brakes," Thiel said to himself. "I wonder why."

He stepped out beyond the gates to look down the tracks, mechanically pulling the red flag from its case and holding it straight in front of him.

Good heavens! Had he been blind? God, O God, what was that? There—between the rails.

"Stop!" he screamed with every atom of breath in his lungs.

Too late. A dark mass had gone down under the train and was being tossed between the wheels like a rubber ball.

Only a few seconds more and with a grating and squeaking of the brakes, the train came to a standstill.

Instantly the lonely stretch became a scene of animation. The conductor and brakeman ran along the gravel path beside the tracks back to the rear end. From every window curious faces peered. And then the crowd that had gathered in the rear formed into a cluster, and moved forward.

Thiel panted. He had to hold on to something not to sink to the ground like a slaughtered steer.

How's that? Were they actually waving to him?

"No!"

A scream came from the spot where the accident had occurred, followed by a howling as from an animal. Who was that? Lena? It was not her voice, yet—

A man came hurrying down the tracks.

"Flagman!"

"What's the matter?"

"An accident."

The messenger shrank before the strange expression in the flagman's eyes. His cap hung on the side of his head, his red hair stood straight up.

"He's still alive. Maybe something can be done."

A rattle in the flagman's throat was the only answer.

"Come quickly—quickly."

With a tremendous effort Thiel pulled himself together. His slack muscles tautened, he drew himself to his full height, his face was empty and dead.

He followed the man at a run, oblivious of the pale, frightened faces at the windows. A young woman looked out, a traveling salesman with a fez on his head, a young couple apparently on their honeymoon. What were they to him? The contents of those rattling, thumping boxes on wheels had never concerned him. His ears were filled with Lena's lamentations.

Yellow dots swam before his eyes, countless yellow dots like fireflies. He shrank back, he stood still. From out of the dance of fireflies it came toward him, pale, limp, bloody—a forehead beaten black and blue, blue lips with dark blood trickling from them. Tobias!

Thiel said nothing. His face went a dirty white. He grinned as if out of his senses. At length he bent over, he felt the limp, dead limbs heavy in his arms. The red flag went round them.

He started to leave.

Where?

"To the railroad doctor, to the railroad doctor," came from all sides.

"We'll take him," called the baggage-master, and turned to prepare a couch of coats and books in his car. "Well?"

Thiel made no move to let go of the boy. They urged him. In vain. The baggage-master had a stretcher handed out from the car and ordered a man to remain with the father. Time was precious. The conductor's whistle shrilled. Coins rained from the windows.

Lena raved like a madwoman. "The poor woman," they said in the coaches, "the poor, poor mother."

The conductor whistled several times, the engine blew a signal, sent white clouds hissing up from its cylinders, and stretched its sinews of iron. In a few seconds, the mail express, with floating flags of smoke, was dashing with redoubled speed through the forest.

The flagman, whose mood had altered, laid the half-dead child on the stretcher.

There he lay with his racked tiny body. Every now and then a long wheeze raised the bony chest, which was visible under the tattered shirt. The little arms and legs, broken not only at the joints, assumed the most unnatural positions. The heel of one small foot was twisted to the front, the arms hung over the sides of the stretcher.

Lena kept up a continuous whimper. Every trace of her former insolence had disappeared. Over and over again she repeated a story to exonerate herself.

Thiel seemed not to notice her. With an expression of awful anxiety he kept his eyes riveted on the child.

A hush had fallen, a deadly hush. The tracks rested hot and black on the glaring gravel. The noon had stifled the wind, and the forest stood motionless, as if carved in stone.

In muffled voices the two men took counsel. The quickest way to reach Friedrichshagen would be to go back to the neighboring station in the direction of Breslau, because the next train, a fast commutation, did not stop at the station that was nearer to Friedrichshagen.

Thiel seemed to consider if he should go along. At the time there was no one there who understood the duties of the position, so with a mute motion of his head he indicated to his wife that she should take hold of the stretcher. She did not dare to refuse though she was concerned about having to leave the baby behind.

Thiel accompanied the cortege of two to the end of his beat, then stood still and looked after them long. Suddenly he clapped his hand to his forehead with a blow that resounded afar. It might wake him up, he thought. Because this was a dream like the one he had had yesterday. No use. Reeling rather than walking he reached his hut. There he fell face downward on the floor. His cap flew into a corner, his carefully kept watch fell from his pocket, the case sprang open, the glass broke. An iron fist seemed to be clamped on his neck, so tight that he could not move no matter how he moaned and groaned and tried to free himself. His forehead was cold, his throat parched.

The ringing of the signal roused him. Under the influence of those three repeated sounds the attack abated. Thiel could rise and do his duty. To be sure, his feet were heavy as lead, and the stretch of rails circled about him like the spokes of an enormous wheel with his head for its axis. But at least he could stand up a while.

The commutation train approached. Tobias must be in it. The nearer it drew the more the pictures before Thiel's eyes blurred. Finally all he saw was the mutilated boy with the bloody mouth. Then darkness fell.

After a while he awoke from the swoon. He found himself lying in the hot sun close to the gates. He rose, shook the sand from his clothes and spat it from his mouth. His head cleared a bit, he could think more quietly.

In the hut he immediately picked his watch up from the floor and laid it on the table. It was still going. For two hours he counted the seconds, then the minutes, while representing to himself what was happening to Tobias. Now Lena was arriving with him, now she stood in front of the doctor. The doctor observed the boy and felt him all over, and shook his head.

"Bad, very bad—but perhaps—who can tell?"

He made a more thorough examination.

326 • Gerhart Hauptmann

"No," he then said, "no, it's all over."

"All over, all over," groaned the flagman. But then he drew himself up, raised his unconsciously clenched first, rolled his eyes to the ceiling, and shouted as if the narrow little room must burst with the sound of his voice. "He must live, he must. I tell you, he must live."

He flung open the door of the hut—the red glow of evening fell through—and ran rather than walked to the gates. Here he stood still seemingly bewildered. Then suddenly spreading his arms he went to the middle of the roadbed, as if to stop something that was coming from the same direction as the commutation. His wide-open eyes made the impression of blindness. While stepping backward to make way for something, a stream of half-intelligible words came from between his gritted teeth.

"Listen. Don't go. Listen, listen. Don't go. Stay here. Give him back to me. He's beaten black-and-blue. Yes, yes. All right. I'll beat her black-and-blue, too. Do you hear? Stay. Give him back to me."

Something seemed to move past him, because he turned and made as if to follow.

"Minna, Minna,"—his voice was weepy like a small child's—"Minna, listen. Give him back to me. I will—" He groped in the air as if to catch and hold someone fast. "My little wife—yes, yes—and I'll—and I'll beat her—so she's black-and-blue, too—I'll beat her, too—with the hatchet—you see?—with the kitchen hatchet—I'll beat her with the kitchen hatchet. And that'll be the end of her. And then—yes, yes—with the hatchet—yes, with the kitchen hatchet—black blood."

Foam gathered on his lips, his glassy eyeballs rolled incessantly.

A gentle breath of the evening blew steadily over the forest, a rosy cloud mass hung in the western sky.

He had followed the invisible something about a hundred paces when he stood still, apparently having lost courage. With fearful dread in his eyes, he stretched out his arms, pleading, adjuring. He strained his eyes, shaded them with his hand, as if to discern the inessential being in the far distance. Finally his head sank, and the tense expression of his face changed into apathy. He turned and dragged himself the way he had come.

The sunlight laid its final glow over the forest, then was extinguished. The trunks of the pines rose among the tops like pale, decayed bones, and the tops weighed upon them like grayish black layers of mold. The hammering of a woodpecker penetrated the silence. Up above one last dilatory pink cloud traversed the steely blue of the sky. The breath of the wind turned dankly cold as if blowing from a cellar.

The flagman shivered. Everything was new and strange. He did not know what he was walking on, or what was about him. A squirrel hopped along the roadbed. Thiel pondered. He had to think of the Lord. But why? "The Lord is hopping along the tracks, the Lord is hopping along the tracks." He said it several times as if to get at something associated with it. He interrupted himself. A ray of illumination fell upon his brain. "Good heavens! That's madness." He forgot everything else and turned upon this new enemy. He tried to order his thoughts. In vain. They'd come and go and ramble away and shoot off at a tangent. He caught himself in the absurdest fancies, and shuddered at the consciousness of his impotence.

The sound of a child crying came from the birch grove near by. It was the signal for madness. Almost against his will he had to hurry to the spot where the baby, whom everybody had neglected, was crying and kicking on the unblanketed floor of its carriage.

What did he mean to do? What had driven him there? The questions were submerged in a whirling eddy of thoughts and emotions.

"The Lord is hopping along the tracks." Now he knew. Tobias—she had murdered him—Lena—the child had been entrusted to her care. "Stepmother! Beast of a mother!" he hissed between clenched teeth. "And her brat lives."

A red mist enveloped his senses. Two baby eyes penetrated through it. He felt something soft, fleshy between his fingers. He heard gurgling, whistling sounds, mingled with hoarse cries that came from he did not know whom.

Then something fell upon his brain like hot drops of sealing wax, and his spirit was cleared as from a cataleptic trance. Aroused to consciousness, he caught the quiver in the air that was the final reverberation of the signal, and in a trice he realized what he had been about to do. His hand relaxed its grip on the throat, under which the infant had writhed and squirmed. It gasped for breath, then began to cough and bawl.

"It's alive. Thank the Lord, it's alive."

He let it lie and hastened to the crossing. Dark clouds of smoke rolled in the distance, the wind drove them to the ground. He distinguished the panting of an engine that sounded like the intermittent, tortured breathing of a giant.

The stretch was shrouded in a cold twilight. But after a while the clouds of smoke parted, and Thiel recognized the train as being the freight that was returning with open empty cars and bringing home the men who had been working on the roadbed during the day. It had ample running time to stop at each station to drop or pick up the men.

Quite a distance from Thiel's hut the brakes began to be put on, and a loud clanking and clanging and rattling and screeching tore the silence before the train came to a standstill with a single shrill, long-drawn whistle.

About fifty men and women were in the different cars. Nearly all of them stood, some of the men with bared heads. There was a mystifying air of solemnity about them. When they caught sight of the flagman, a whispering began among them, and the old men drew their pipes from between their yellow teeth and held them respectfully in their hands. Here and there a woman would turn to blow her nose.

The conductor descended and advanced toward Thiel. The workmen saw him solemnly shake the flagman's hand, and then saw Thiel with slow steps almost military in their stiffness go back to the rear. None of them dared to address him, though they all knew him.

From the rear wagon they were lifting little Toby.

He was dead.

Lena followed. Her face was a bluish white, brown rings underlined her eyes.

Thiel did not so much as cast a glance at her. She, however, was shocked at the sight of her husband. His cheeks were hollow, his eyelashes and beard were plastered, his hair, it seemed to her, was gone grayer. Traces of dried tears all over his face. And an unsteady light in his eyes that made her shudder.

The stretcher had been brought back for transporting the body home.

For a while there was gruesome silence. Thiel lost himself in black depths of awful thoughts. Darkness deepened. A herd of deer started to cross the embankment. The stag stood still between the rails and turned his agile neck curiously. The engine whistled. He and the rest of the herd disappeared in a flash.

At the moment that the train was about to start Thiel collapsed. The train stood still, and counsel was held as to what had now best be done. Since every effort they made to bring the flagman back to his senses, proved futile, they decided to let the child's body lie in the hut temporarily, and use the stretcher for conveying the flagman instead. Two men carried the stretcher, Lena followed, pushing the baby carriage, sobbing the whole way, the tears running down her cheeks.

The great purplish ball of the moon shone low between the trunks of the pine trees. As it rose it paled and diminished in size until finally it hung high in the heavens like a swinging lamp, and cast a pale sheen over the forest, through every chink and cranny of the foliage, painting the faces of the processionists a livid white.

Cautiously but sturdily they made their way through the close second growth, then past broad nurseries with the larger trees scattered among the younger ones. Here the pale light seemed to have collected itself in great dark bowls.

Occasionally a rattle came from the unconscious man's throat, and occasionally he raved. Several times he clenched his fists and tried to raise himself, his eyes all the time remaining closed. Getting him across the Spree was difficult, and a return trip had to be made to fetch Lena and the baby.

As they ascended the slight eminence on which the hamlet was situated, they met a few of the inhabitants, who forthwith spread the news of the misfortune. The whole colony came running.

Among her gossips Lena broke into fresh lamentations.

Thiel was with difficulty carried up the narrow stairway of his home and put to bed. And the men returned immediately to bring little Toby's body back.

Some of the old, experienced people advised cold compresses. Lena carried out their prescription eagerly, properly, dropping cloths into icy cold springwater and renewing them as soon as the unconscious man's burning forehead had heated them. Anxiously she observed his breathing. It seemed to come more regularly and to continue to improve each minute.

However, the day's excitement had told upon her, and she decided to try to get a little sleep. No use! Whether she held her eyes open or shut, she kept seeing the events of the past hours. The baby slept. Contrary to her wont, she had not paid much attention to it.

Altogether she had turned into a different person. Not a trace of her former arrogance. The sick man with the colorless face shining with sweat dominated her even in sleep.

A cloud passed, obscuring the moon and throwing the room into complete darkness. Lena heard nothing but her husband's heavy though regular breathing. She felt creepy in the dark and considered whether she should not rise and kindle a light. But as she attempted to get up, a leaden weight on her limbs pulled her back, her lids drooped, she fell asleep.

Some time later the men returning with the boy's body found the front door wide open. Surprised at this, they mounted and found the upstairs door also open. They called the woman by her name. No answer. They struck a match. The flare of it revealed awful havoc.

"Murder, murder!"

Lena lay in her blood, her face unrecognizable, her skull broken open.

"He murdered his wife, he murdered his wife!"

They ran about witless. Neighbors came. One bumped against the cradle.

"Good heavens!" He shrank back, ashen pale, his eyes fixed in a horrified stare. The baby lay with its throat cut.

The flagman had disappeared. The search made for him that night proved fruitless. The next morning, however, the man who replaced him found him on the tracks at the spot where little Toby had been run over, holding the shaggy brown cap in his arm and caressing it as if it were a living thing.

The block signaler, apprised of his discovery, telegraphed for help. Several men tried with kindly inducements to lure Thiel from the tracks. He was not to be budged. The express then due had to be stopped, and it was only by the united efforts of the entire crew and the use of force that the man, who had begun to rave fearfully, could be removed from the railroad. They had to bind him hands and feet, and the policeman summoned to the spot guarded his transportation the whole way to Berlin, where he was examined in the jail and the next day was sent to a free psychopathic ward.* He never let go of the shaggy brown cap. He watched over it with jealous tenderness.

Translated by Adele S. Seltzer

*The original has "Charité," a prestigious clinic in Berlin.

ACKNOWLEDGMENTS

Every reasonable effort has been made to locate the owners of rights to previously published translations printed here. We gratefully acknowledge permission to reprint the following material:

The White Horse Rider by Theodor Storm, translated by Stella Humphries, is reprinted by kind permission of Blackie and Son Limited, Glasgow.

From *Great German Short Novels and Stories,* Edited by Victor Lange, Copyright © Victor Lange, *Plautus in the Convent* by Conrad Ferdinand Meyer, translated by William Guild Howard and *Flagman Thiel* by Gerhart Hauptmann, translated by Adele S. Seltzer are reprinted by kind permission of Victor Lange.